THE IRANIAN METAPHYSICALS

THE IRANIAN METAPHYSICALS

EXPLORATIONS IN SCIENCE, ISLAM, AND THE UNCANNY

ALIREZA DOOSTDAR

PRINCETON UNIVERSITY PRESS

PRINCETON AND OXFORD

Copyright © 2018 by Princeton University Press

Published by Princeton University Press,
41 William Street, Princeton, New Jersey 08540

In the United Kingdom: Princeton University Press,
6 Oxford Street, Woodstock, Oxfordshire OX20 1TR

press.princeton.edu

Jacket art: Kamal ol-Mulk, *Exorcist and Clients*, c. 1900. Collection of Dr. Layla S. Diba.
Original painting photographed by Yoav Horesh.

Library of Congress Cataloging-in-Publication Data

Names: Doostdar, Alireza, author.
Title: The Iranian metaphysicals : explorations in science, Islam, and
the uncanny / Alireza Doostdar.
Description: Princeton ; Oxford : Princeton University Press, 2018. | Includes
bibliographical references and index.
Identifiers: LCCN 2017023087| ISBN 9780691163772 (hardcover : alk. paper) |
ISBN 9780691163789 (pbk. : alk. paper)
Subjects: LCSH: Islamic occultism. | Metaphysics. | Uncanny, The (Psychoanalysis) |
Mysticism—Islam. | Islam and science—Iran.
Classification: LCC BF1434.I74 D66 2018 | DDC 130.955—dc23 LC record available
at https://lccn.loc.gov/2017023087

British Library Cataloging-in-Publication Data is available

This book has been composed in Linux Libertine O and Helvetica Neue LT Std

Printed on acid-free paper. ∞

Printed in the United States of America

10 9 8 7 6 5 4 3 2 1

For my parents,
Sue-San Ghahremani and Hossein Doostdar,
And for Elham, Hassan, Ali Sina, and Ava.

CONTENTS

NOTE ON
TRANSLITERATION

I follow the *Iranian Studies* journal in my transliteration of both spoken and written Persian. For Arabic, I use a modified version of the transliteration scheme of the *International Journal of Middle East Studies* (IJMES), with diacritical marks omitted for simplicity. Where an Arabic phrase appears in Persian speech, or a technical term has the same meaning in both Arabic and Persian, I choose one or the other transliteration style depending on the context. For the proper names of public figures, I use the common English-language spelling where available. Unless otherwise noted, all translations are my own.

ACKNOWLEDGMENTS

It has taken me more than ten years to write this book, from its first stirrings as a dissertation research project to the final draft of these acknowledgments. Over these years, the book project has extended its tentacles so deeply into my being and my relationships that I find it difficult any longer to discern who among my friends, family, colleagues, mentors, students, and acquaintances has *not* left an imprint on its formation. The final acknowledgment, I think, must be understood as the very act of completing this book. I could not have done it without the many forms of kindness, generosity, collegiality, questioning, skepticism, critique, patience, forgiveness, laughter, and love that I have been so fortunate to receive. If I did in the end complete the book, it was substantially motivated by the obligation to repay all of this.

First and foremost, I wish to thank my Iranian interlocutors for giving of their time and insight, for sharing what were sometimes very intimate details of their lives, and for putting up with questions that often must have sounded naive or irrelevant. This book would not have been what it is without their openness and generosity, and their many layers of intelligent and articulate commentary. The vast majority of my interlocutors must remain anonymous for their own protection. I would, however, like to thank a few individuals by name: Peyman Eshaghi, Hossein Fattahi, Hossein Ghanbari, Hossein Mirrazi, and Sara Mohammad Kamal provided invaluable research support and introduced me to many of the people whose stories eventually made it into this book. My friend Reza Shahrabi facilitated my access to the National Library. Thanks are also due to Nasser Fakouhi, Mohammad Hadi Gerami, Mohammad Ghandehari, Fezzeh Kashi, Manijeh Maghsudi, Hesam Mazaheri, Nahal Naficy, Mostafa Nik-Eqbali, Jabbar Rahmani, Mahdi Salehi, Mahdi Samimi, and Mahdi Soleimanieh for many fruitful conversations. My friend of twenty-five years, Mojtaba Hosseini, read my entire dissertation and offered extremely helpful suggestions, while Ehsan Noohi, one of the first friends I met as an engineering student at the University of Tehran, gave me insightful feedback on what eventually became chapter 24.

I wrote the first draft of this book as a doctoral dissertation at Harvard University. My dissertation committee, Steve Caton, Afsaneh Najmabadi, Smita

Lahiri, Asad Ali Ahmed, and Engseng Ho, guided me through my earliest attempts to make sense of my materials and to write intelligently about them. The book has gone through many transformations since its incarnation as a dissertation, but I can still discern the profound ways in which their careful readings have molded my arguments. I hope I can follow their example and pay it forward with my own students. While at Harvard, I was also fortunate to learn from Michael Herzfeld, Cemal Kafadar, Arthur Kleinman, Catalina Laserna (without whom I may never have become an anthropologist), J. Lorand Matory, Khaled El-Rouayheb, Steven Shapin, Mary Steedly, Ajantha Subramanian, and Carl Sharif El-Tobgui. Although not members of my committee, Michael M. J. Fischer and Emilio Spadola graciously read the full final draft of my dissertation and offered keen observations and suggestions. I sincerely appreciate all of this help.

One of the most enduring gifts of my years as a graduate student has been the many friendships I developed and that continue to sustain my heart and mind. Among these friends, there are those whose critical engagement and comments have profoundly shaped my work. My thanks especially to Niki Akhavan, Diana Allan, Ata Anzali, Sepideh Bajracharya, Naor Ben-Yehoyada, Will Day, Ujala Dhaka-Kintgen, Aisha Ghani, Maryam Monalisa Gharavi, Vedran Grahovac, Nazli Kamvari, Mana Kia, Satyel Larson, Lital Levy, Darryl Li, Ketaki Pant, Sabrina Peric, Ramyar Rossoukh, Yasmine Al-Saleh, Sima Shakhsari, Anthony Shenoda, Naghmeh Sohrabi, Anand Vaidya, Sarah Waheed, and Emrah Yildiz.

At the University of Chicago, I have been fortunate to count myself a member of a lively and supportive intellectual community. When I arrived at the Divinity School in 2012 and for some years afterward, my dean, Margaret Mitchell, offered vital mentorship and support while acting as one of my most discerning readers. Bruce Lincoln read the entirety of an earlier draft and provided plentiful critical comments with his characteristic incisiveness, wit, and generosity. I have learned more from Hussein Ali Agrama than I can possibly recount here. He read multiple drafts of various chapters and pushed me to sharpen my arguments while keeping my eyes on the bigger picture. If academics were required to reveal the scaffolding behind their intellectual productions, mine would certainly have to include *al-khinzir al-barjuwazi*, mocha, and conversations with Hussein. During the incubation period of this book, the other crucial scaffolding consisted of Regenstein Library, swimming (or jogging, or just chilling out Middle Eastern style), and discoursing with Fadi Bardawil. *Ya akh Fadi*, this book is so much better for your sharp insights and compassionate criticism. Darryl Li has been with this project longer, and has read more drafts, than anyone else. I only hope I can repay him in kind for the care and precision with which he has engaged my work. Angie Heo has been a brilliant interlocutor and critic. Along with my other writing group partners—Elina Hartikainen, Andy Graan, Sarah Fredericks, Leah Feldman, Darryl Li, Kareem Rabie, and Ghenwa Hayek—Angie has read multiple drafts of various sections of this book and offered invaluable suggestions for improvement. I am also indebted to a number of colleagues who have read individual chapters and provided critical feedback. Thanks especially to Dan Arnold, Sarah Hammerschlag, James Robinson, Richard Rosengarten, Michael Sells, and Christian Wedemeyer. None of this work would have been possible without the able support of the staff at the University of Chicago, especially Sandra Peppers, Julia Woods, and Terren Wein at the Divinity School, and Marlis Saleh at the Regenstein Library.

Among the pleasures of teaching at the University of Chicago, I have particularly enjoyed the opportunity to learn from many brilliant students and future colleagues. A number of these students generously read the entirety of my book manuscript and provided suggestions for revision, restructuring, and elaboration. I am thankful especially to Rachel Apone, Rachel Carbonara, Menna Khalil, Harini Kumar, Eléonore Rimbault, Elizabeth Sartell, and my students in a seminar on the occult in the Islamic world that I co-taught with James Robinson in winter 2016.

In the broader universe of the American academy, I am fortunate to have benefited from the insightful comments and suggestions of numerous colleagues and friends. Noah Salomon read a complete draft of the manuscript after having seen earlier versions of several sections. His interventions have been critical in bringing the book to its final form. Lauren Osborne read an earlier draft with her student Tate Jacobson, and both offered extremely useful suggestions. My deepest thanks to Ata Anzali, Torang Asadi, Naor Ben-Yehoyada, Abdellah Hammoudi, Matthew Melvin-Koushki, Daniel Stolz, Ana Vinea, and Jessica Winegar for their astute comments on various parts of the book. For other kinds of help and advice, thanks are due to Abbas Amanat, Kathryn Babayan, Hunter Bandy, Orit Bashkin, Persis Berlekamp, Noah Gardiner, Saeed Ghahremani, Nile Green, Frank Griffel, Christiane Gruber, Juliane Hammer, Angela Jaffray, Arang Keshavarzian, Mana Kia, Franklin Lewis, Tanya Luhrmann, Milad Odabaei, George Saliba, Omnia El Shakry, Kabir Tambar, Yunus Dogan Telliel, and Stefan Wild.

At Princeton University Press, my editor, Fred Appel, his assistant Thalia Leaf, and production editor Natalie Baan have masterfully guided my book through submission, review, and production. I could not have hoped for a smoother process. Three anonymous reviewers provided detailed and nuanced comments on earlier drafts of the manuscript, all of which have improved my work. My deepest thanks to Cathy Slovensky for her copyediting wizardry and to Philip Grant for his virtuoso indexing and proofreading.

Funding for the book project was provided by Harvard University's Center for Middle Eastern Studies and Anthropology Department, the Wenner-Gren

Foundation, and the University of Chicago Divinity School. I gratefully acknowledge all of this generous assistance. Parts of this book have previously appeared in print: sections of chapter 10 were published in an essay for the *New Inquiry* titled "Portrait of an Iranian Witch" (Doostdar 2013) and a significant section of chapters 12 and 13 appeared in an article for *Comparative Studies in Society and History* titled "Empirical Spirits: Islam, Spiritism, and the Virtues of Science in Iran" (Doostdar 2016).

More than anyone else, I owe this book to my parents, my first teachers and closest friends. My mother, Sue-San Ghahremani, has been one of my most incisive and compassionate readers. My father, Hossein Mohammadi Doostdar, has listened to me ramble incessantly about my research and continues to inspire me with his honesty, humor, and wit. My younger brothers Ahmad-Reza and Hamid-Reza have cheerfully and persistently disagreed with many of my interpretations, and I can't thank them enough for this. My uncle Fathali Ghahremani Ghajar has been a sage interlocutor and a trustworthy source on all things historical. My mother-in-law, Faranak Gheisari, kindly tolerated my long bouts of antisocial behavior as I wrote in her home. My father-in-law, Ali Mireshghi, provided perceptive comments on several of my arguments and has remained an enthusiastic interlocutor. My older son, Hassan, who patiently sat (and napped) through my dissertation defense, has kept me accountable for all these years. My younger son, Ali Sina, generously allowed me to write on my computer while *Curious George* and *The Wheels on the Bus* played on the right half of my screen. And just as this book entered production, we welcomed our daughter Ava Layli into the world: the most delightful company for overcoming the boredom of copyediting and proofreading.

Last, I am grateful to Elham Mireshghi, whose ideas and insights I can no longer tell apart from my own. It has been a joy to share life, love, spirit, and intellect with her. If ever there were anything metaphysical or preternatural in this world, Elham's brilliance, patience, and wisdom are ideal candidates for the category.

THE IRANIAN METAPHYSICALS

INTRODUCTION

DEFENSIVE RADIATION

I attended my first exorcism on a chilly Tuesday evening in December 2008. The venue was a condominium on the fourth floor of a newly completed apartment building in a middle-class residential neighborhood in eastern Tehran. There were about thirty people in attendance, roughly two-thirds of them women. Our hosts were a young couple I will call Ahmad and Vida.[1] That night, as well as in the handful of additional sessions I attended at their home, Ahmad busied himself ushering new arrivals into the spacious living room and ensuring that everyone was comfortable. Vida meanwhile oversaw a small group of women in the open-layout kitchen who prepared and served black tea along with Danish pastries at several intervals over the course of around three hours. The atmosphere was welcoming and exuberant, if a bit awkward, like a dinner party where half the guests do not know one another. Most of the participants were students or graduates in a series of underground seminars dubbed "Cosmic Mysticism" (*'erfan-e keyhani*). The exorcism session was part of a weekly "therapy" (*darman*) component that also served as an opportunity for socializing. The lead exorcist, Mr. Sheyda, was an instructor or "master" in Cosmic Mysticism whom I had met only a week earlier when I registered for his seminars. Upon hearing about my research, he immediately invited me to take part in the therapy session, assuring me that I would find it both useful and fascinating. He was right.

Eager to get the therapy process under way, Mr. Sheyda walked over to the opposite end of the living room where most of the women were sitting. He looked at one of the guests whom I could not see. "What's happened?" he asked in a calm but firm tone. There was a moment's silence. Then the "patient" let out a terrifying scream. A series of moans followed, rising and falling in pitch, then another shriek. Mr. Sheyda shot a few quick glances at some of the young women sitting around the patient. He gave them directions to pin her down and begin to "work" on her. Then he addressed the patient directly: "Detach! Get out!"

A man sitting next to me noticed my enthusiasm to see what was happening, and he encouraged me to step up and take a closer look. I eagerly obliged.

The patient—a woman in her early thirties named Zeynab—was now lying on her back, four other women holding down her shoulders and knees. She let out one more scream. Mr. Sheyda ordered her to "calm down" and instructed his students to keep her steady. Zeynab was now weeping and saying, "Oh oh oh, I'm suffocating! Please help me! Please help me! I'm suffocating!" Mr. Sheyda asked someone to open the window to let in some fresh air. He instructed the four women to give Zeynab some room so she could stand on her feet. He took her hand himself and helped her up. She breathed heavily, weeping and moaning.

Again Mr. Sheyda addressed Zeynab: "Who are you? Do you want to speak?" Zeynab let out a few angry snorts interspersed with hisses and a harsh, voiceless "*kh*" sound through the sides of her mouth. "Who are you?" demanded Mr. Sheyda, "Who are you? Huh?" She only hissed back. "Are you a jinn? Who sent you here? Who? *Who?*" Zeynab hissed again. "Move away from her!" Mr. Sheyda ordered, "*Positive Two! Out! Out!*" Zeynab swung her arms violently, stomping her foot and swaying like a drunk. Another scream. Mr. Sheyda looked around for more students. He asked three to step up and transmit "defensive radiation" to Zeynab. He approached her himself and stared her in the eye. Her chest was heaving, hair sweaty and tangled, eyes crossed, lips contorted. "What do you want with Zeynab?" Mr. Sheyda demanded. She growled, then doubled over and made a gagging motion, as if to vomit. But nothing came out. Mr. Sheyda commanded again: "You will leave Zeynab!" She moaned, swaying from side to side. "Positive Two!" he ordered. A student asked for clarification as to what kind of radiation she should be emitting. "Injection," said Mr. Sheyda.

Zeynab's condition seemed to be deteriorating. She was now kicking and hurling punches, attacking anyone within her reach. She howled and screamed. Mr. Sheyda was unfazed. "Defensive Four," he said calmly. Zeynab shrieked as if in pain. Her moaning was now lower-pitched, verging on a male voice. Another woman, pointing both hands at Zeynab, uttered "Positive Two." Zeynab screamed again. Two of the students closed in on her once more, grabbing her arms to subdue her. Zeynab's white shawl flew off her hair. Two more students stepped in and clutched her ankles. The four of them pushed her to the ground as gently as they could. She squirmed and moaned, trying to break free. Another shawl, a black one this time, fell off a student-healer's head.

Mr. Sheyda leaned over her: "She purchased you herself, didn't she?" Zeynab coughed out loud, as if wanting to vomit. "Leave her," Mr. Sheyda demanded. Taking a moment's break, he walked over to me to explain what was going on while his students continued their work. "Zeynab Khanum had consulted a prayer writer and bought a jinn from him to assault her ex-husband. Now the jinn won't let go of her." He said he had been working on Zeynab for three weeks. "You should've seen her the first day," he said. "She was in terrible shape. She was running on the tips of the headrests on these chairs. It was an incredible sight. You wouldn't believe it!"

The master returned to Zeynab once again, leaning over her. "Good," he said, "you must leave Zeynab now." Her breathing was again loud and heavy. "Positive Two," shouted Mr. Sheyda, clapping his hands, "*Out!* Toward the light! Leave her! Detach! It's time to go." Her moaning was louder. "You can't stay!" Mr. Sheyda insisted. "I'll help you. I'll help you. It's time for help. God's mercy has embraced you. Detach. One… Two… It's over! Detach! Out! Out! Out! Out! Out! Out!" He turned to the rest of us. "It's separating." Zeynab gave off a loud orgasmic "aaah," then a burp, followed by a rapidly descending moan. "It's gone," Mr. Sheyda announced. "Thank God," one of the student-healers exhaled. They helped Zeynab up and walked her over to a couch adjacent to the wall. Vida handed her a glass of ice water, which she pressed to her forehead as she relaxed. Another woman fanned her with a shawl.

RATIONALIZING THE UNSEEN

Zeynab's exorcism was one of dozens I observed among participants in Cosmic Mysticism, an Iranian spiritual-therapeutic movement that was at the height of its popularity during my research. These Cosmic Mystics in turn represent only a portion of a much broader landscape of spiritual seeking, therapeutic experimentalism, and occult exploration. The chapters that follow chart this terrain in contemporary Iran. I examine encounters with occult specialists, séances with the souls of the dead, new forms of exorcism and healing, and appeals to marvelous mystical powers. For my interlocutors, a phenomenon like Zeynab's possession by jinn exceeded ordinary experience and expectation, and therefore warranted being labeled "metaphysical" (*mavara'i* or *meta-fiziki*). Even so, there was widespread agreement that such phenomena were best approached by steering clear of superstitions (*khorafat*) and carefully deploying the powers of intellect ('*aql*) and science ('*elm*), with the latter including systematic observation and manipulation. My interlocutors saw their practices as resolutely rational ('*aqlani*). Yet the specters of superstition proved elusive, evading attempts to exorcise them from reasoned inquiries and sneaking back to haunt them at every turn.

Appeals to science and reason notwithstanding, the practices that I study in this book often provoked elite consternation. Religious leaders, intellectuals, journalists, and statesmen criticized engagements with the occult as irrational and downright dangerous. Those elites committed to the more conservative strains of Islamic Republican ideology condemned spiritual experiments like Cosmic Mysticism as so many "deviant" (*monharef*) incarnations of "pseudo-mysticism" (*shebh-e 'erfan*) fomented by foreign enemies in order to corrupt

Iranian society from within. Opposition intellectuals likewise criticized occult practices as superstitious, but they placed the blame at the foot of the Iranian state itself. For some of these elites, the proliferation of irrationality was a result of the state's failure to provide economic and social stability. With rational solutions out of reach, they argued, the desperate had no recourse but to turn to irrational means for assuaging their anxieties. Others saw spiritual experimentalism as a form of resistance, an escape from the state's inflexible imposition of Islamic norms. Still others accused state officials of deliberately propagating superstition as a way of ensuring their own continued domination. The latter position has even found support in English-language scholarship on contemporary Iranian politics.[2]

Their many differences aside, the elite detractors of occult experimentation shared a crucial assumption: that the metaphysical engagements they condemned were fundamentally unlike their own intellectual pursuits; that is, they supposedly lacked commitment to reasoned scientific inquiry and were therefore mired in superstition and unreason. This book argues the exact opposite. I show that the metaphysical inquiries of occult experimentalists and spiritual explorers like the Cosmic Mystics are best understood in terms of attempts to rationalize the "unseen" (*gheyb*)—that is, to grasp phenomena like sorcery and jinn possession in reasoned, scientific, nonsuperstitious terms. Furthermore, the commitments to science and rationality that my interlocutors shared with their elite critics were not mere matters of formal similarity or mimicry. An overarching argument of this book is that metaphysical inquiries have constituted a fundamental aspect of modern Iranian thought since the late nineteenth century. Indeed, they have consistently pushed the boundaries of established norms in ways that have rendered such inquiries edgy and avant-garde. This heritage of inquiry and experimentation has been almost entirely ignored and its epistemic consequences overlooked. In brief, my contention is that we cannot understand contemporary religion in Iran, including its intellectualist and orthodox manifestations, without adequately attending to the metaphysical inquiries of occultists and spiritual explorers.

When I speak of the rationalization of the unseen, I refer primarily to three interrelated processes that have been under way since the late nineteenth century. The first of these is the effort to cleanse metaphysical knowledge of superstition. As I understand it, "superstition," and cognate terms like "nonsense" and "irrationality," are discursive constructs with no independent substance outside of attempts to identify, demarcate, and eradicate them. For groups like the Cosmic Mystics, combating superstition meant staying away from dangerous "prayer writers" (*do'anevis*) or *rammals* and sifting credible knowledge from hearsay. In the exorcism account above, for example, Mr. Sheyda claimed to be counteracting the nefarious work of a prayer writer who had sold a jinn to Zeynab that now took possession of her. In his seminars, he took pains to distinguish the true metaphysical knowledge of Cosmic Mysticism from wrongheaded ideas propagated by prayer writers and their ignorant clients.

The second aspect of rationalization with which I am concerned is the attempt to formulate scientific concepts, methods, and models for grasping metaphysical phenomena. The Cosmic Mystics did so by developing an experimental practice of exorcism that they called "psymentology" or "defensive radiation," which was aimed at expunging "inorganic viruses" like jinn and the souls of the deceased. When an exorcist uttered phrases like "Defensive Four" or "Positive Two," she tapped into an elaborate body of knowledge-practice that was disseminated in Cosmic Mysticism seminars, published in books and articles, and even articulated in the form of scientific conference papers and patent applications.

The third rationalization process I analyze in this book has to do with systematizing and disciplining individual dealings with the metaphysical in the service of attaining pious virtues, achieving health, tranquillity, and joy, or grappling with the problems imagined to be plaguing Iranian society. In Cosmic Mysticism, such attempts amounted, on the one hand, to the development of alternative forms of therapeutic spirituality, which included the practice of exorcism. On the other hand, Mr. Sheyda and his colleagues considered their mission to consist in the dissemination of a totalizing worldview (*binesh*) with its attending prescriptions for everyday behavior that they claimed would eventually solve society's ills. As a sustained project for spiritual and moral reform, Cosmic Mysticism ran up against competing discourses that articulated their own reformist visions through engagements with the metaphysical realm, while deriding the teachings of the Cosmic Mystics as irrational or deviant.

In all three processes, the rationalization of the unseen unfolds with explicit reference to conceptions of reason, intellect, and science, while the substance of these notions is itself up for debate. Even so, rationalization is not merely an intellectual activity but a complex process tightly connected to the emergence and consolidation of the modern state. Superstition is a problem for law enforcement and public order. Science pertains to mass education and the production and policing of legitimate knowledge. And therapeutic and disciplinary reason is entangled with the instrumental logics of bureaucratic classification, evaluation, and decision making. In the past two decades, these reasons of state have found expression in theorizations of "Shi'i rationality" (*'aqlaniyyat-e shi'eh*), a concept favored by state-allied intellectuals and religious leaders who are concerned with critiquing and elaborating the epistemic foundations of an Islamic civilizational alternative to the secular West. Under the rubric of Shi'i rationality, a wide swath of topics have come under critical scrutiny and turned into objects of state planning. These include intellectual disciplines (jurisprudence, theology, mysticism, political theory, social science, and so on), structures of governance (the doctrine of *velayat-e faqih* or "guardianship of the jurist" and its institutional trappings, including those pertaining to education, cultural planning, and policing), normative modes of pious attachment (such as passionate love for the household of the prophet Muhammad and zeal for martyrdom), and ritual behavior (worship, spiritual wayfaring, and mourning for the family of the Prophet).

In focusing on rationalization since the late nineteenth century, and especially under the Islamic Republic, I am not claiming that earlier approaches to the unseen were irrational or indifferent to reason. Muslim thinkers have been concerned with identifying and eradicating superstition for centuries. Theologians have formulated sophisticated theoretical positions toward the unseen for just as long. And premodern philosophers, scientists, occultists, and mystics of various stripes have attempted ambitious syntheses of knowledge to bring human understandings of material and immaterial reality into grand totalities. These efforts have moreover intertwined in complex ways with conceptions of political order, the legitimation of divine kingship, and practices of governance. Modern rationalization, that is, should be understood not as an altogether unprecedented process but rather as a distinctive modality both continuous and discontinuous with the past.[3] Its distinctiveness has to do with the particularities of the modern bureaucratic state, and with the defensive position in which the proponents of metaphysical inquiries found themselves from roughly the turn of the twentieth century onward. Their attempts to cleanse metaphysical knowledge of superstition and to bring it in-line with modern scientific discovery participated in a larger theater in which Iranians encountered Europeans on unequal terms and resolved to catch up, although this meant adopting the latter's criteria for evaluating their own progress. Even the contemporary proponents of Shi'i rationality with their strident civilizational ambitions have been unable to completely break free of this legacy.

My interlocutors in this book could be thought of as model subjects of the modern state's rationalizing projects, even if their commitments to reason do not always match those of state institutions and their allied authority figures. All of the women and men whom I came to know over the course of my research had completed high school. Most had gone on to obtain university degrees. They included graduate students, engineers, doctors, lawyers, teachers, *howzeh* scholars, university professors, businessmen, artists, writers, journalists, and housewives. Reading was an activity in which they engaged as a matter of course, and they were as conversant with books and periodicals as with websites and other digital media (sometimes in English and Arabic as well as Persian). Concepts like "reason," "rationality," and "science" were fundamental in their articulations of their identities. When explaining their orientations toward metaphysical questions, they frequently deployed such concepts and made it plain that they considered it crucial to justify their thoughts, commitments, and activities in rational terms.

Theological reason looms large in the various facets of the rationalization of the unseen that I examine in this book. This is a predominantly Islamic reason that draws on a centuries-old Shi'i tradition of philosophical, theological, and jurisprudential inquiry. It grants a privileged place to the intellect ('aql), whose dominion, capacities, and limitations have been extensively debated and elaborated.[4] The tradition's rationality consists in its systematicity and coherence, as well as its self-conscious attempts to define the limits of respectable inquiry and to exclude "nonsense" or "superstition" (khorafeh). Since the late nineteenth century, its rationality has also consisted in attempts to formulate coherent positions toward newly emerging rival modes of intellection, primarily those of the modern empirical sciences, post-Enlightenment Western philosophy, and new religious and philosophical currents within Iran.

The rationalization of theology pertains to the full range of these endeavors, whether involving accommodation, absorption, rejection, or modification of the positions and approaches of various rivals. But its scope is not restricted to that of orthodox Shi'i Islam. The Cosmic Mystics with whom I opened this introduction have a complicated and ambivalent relationship to Islam, but their outlook is no less theological and their speculations no less rationalist. Their development as an occult-mystico-therapeutic movement is rooted in engagements with and borrowings from Islamic orthodoxy and myriad Iranian heterodox currents, as well as a decades-long history of experimentation with modern European and American esoteric and "metaphysical" traditions, from mesmerism, Spiritism, and Theosophy to New Age–inflected Eastern spirituality, Native American shamanism, and Scientology. The theological projects that characterize these movements are, like their orthodox Shi'i counterparts, centrally concerned with the repudiation of superstition and the elaboration of rational positions, the latter often rooted in some conception of empirical science.

Modern scientific reason also plays a significant role in this book. I focus on its power to adjudicate metaphysical truth, but this power cannot be separated from the broader esteem that Iranians accord the modern empirical disciplines. State officials appeal to science's prestige to justify national projects (the nuclear energy program being one of the more notable examples), experts resort to its authority to support or question government policies, young people compete over its mastery in hopes of securing better jobs and more prosperous futures, and countless others invest it with fantasies—of progress, power, precision, speed, longevity, and other desires.

The power that science wields is a historical achievement, the effect of decades—if not centuries—of human effort. Its history is not one of uniform progress but of convergences and divergences among many different kinds of practice over a long stretch of time and in the face of myriad forms of contestation. These practices have included small-scale acts of discourse—translation and instruction, oral and textual disputation, learned exchange and popular entertainment—but also large-scale biopolitical projects, such as hygiene, eugenics, psychiatry, pedagogy, and so on. They have been implicated in the rise of new classes of professionals—scientists, engineers, technicians, bureaucrats, and educators—and also the building of new institutions and the undermining of old ones. No less important, these practices have been deeply entangled with the state's powers of legislation, disciplining, and coercion.[5]

Just as the history of the rise of modern science cannot be reduced to a tale of unilinear progress, so the actors involved should not be caricatured as secular progressive modernists battling reactionary traditionists. For one thing, commitment to Islamic tradition has translated to a spectrum of attitudes to modern science, including enthusiastic adoption and appropriation.[6] On the other hand, if many "traditionists" over the past century have embraced modern science, many of the Iranian proponents of science typically imagined as "secularists" have been committed to explicitly religious projects. Scientific rationality, that is, has become intertwined with more than one form of theological reason.

Since the establishment of the Islamic Republic in 1979, theological and scientific rationalities have converged in the formation of Iranian state policy.[7] The bureaucracy, meanwhile, has been elaborated in the service of state interests publicly justified in terms of Shiʿi orthodoxy. Two of these interests are significant for the arguments of this book: the inculcation of pious virtues among the citizenry, which includes combating "deviant" spiritualities, and the verification of these virtues in the process of vetting candidates for state employment. In both cases, the disciplinary rationalities that guide individual and communal practices of ethical self-care run up against, or become entangled with, the governmental logics through which the state makes Islamic piety an object of knowledge, cultivation, and evaluation. The metaphysical realm plays a significant role here both as a resource for moral reformers (including those embedded within state institutions) who use stories of divine marvels to bolster specific modes of virtue, and as a refuge for ordinary pious aspirants attempting to come to grips with the moral uncertainties of a society they deem to have fallen into hypocrisy and greed.

FROM OCCULT TO METAPHYSICAL

In speaking of the rationalization of practices that involve spiritual healing, sorcery, jinn possession, dream visions, saintly marvels, and so on, I have thus far used the concepts of "occult," "unseen," and "metaphysical" as though they were interchangeable. Slippages between these concepts do occur, both in ordinary conversation and in some texts. But they are the products of different histories and may be used to refer to very different constellations of phenomena. For this reason, I treat them as distinct concepts both to clarify my analytical arguments and to lay the groundwork for explaining a number of significant religious and intellectual shifts in contemporary Iran. In brief, the metaphysical in this book refers to a modern rationalized form of the unseen and the occult. Even though the unseen and the occult can both become objects of intellectual speculation and rational-ethical conduct, there is a specific sense in which the metaphysical takes on a rationalized character that is lacking in the other two concepts. Just what, then, do the useen and the occult signify, and what does it mean to rationalize them?

The "unseen" or *gheyb* (Arabic *al-ghayb*) is a Qurʾanic term and a key concept in Islamic theology. As such, it is centrally implicated in the human relationship with the divine, as well as with prophecy, theodicy, and eschatology. The unseen brings with it a set of normative associations and prescriptions for ethical attachment. Perhaps this is most clearly demonstrated in the Qurʾanic valorization of those who have "trusting belief" (*iman*) in the unseen—that is, those who invest in a world beyond that which is immediately perceptible through the material senses: God and the hierarchy of angels who do his bidding, divine mechanisms of revelation and inspiration, the final judgment and eternal life in the hereafter.[8]

With the term "occult," I primarily refer to those forms of knowledge and power that Iranians consider within the purview of the centuries-old tradition of *ʿolum-e gharibeh*, which has usually been translated as "occult sciences." *Gharib* has the sense of "occult," which we associate with magic and sorcery, but it also means "strange," "alien," "uncanny," and "exotic."[9] The Islamic occult sciences are sometimes also rendered as *ʿolum-e khafiyyeh* or "hidden sciences," which again returns us to the occult in its evocation of concealment and obscurity. The occult, therefore, usually brings to mind a specific tradition of esoteric sciences, even if Iranians sometimes use it in relation to practices that they associate only loosely with that tradition.

In contrast with the unseen and the occult, "metaphysical" is a concept that has come into popular use more recently and with less technical specificity. The Persian term I am invoking is *mavara*, which is a truncated form of the Arabic phrase *ma waraʾ al-tabiʿa*. The latter means "that which lies beyond the natural" and is the technical philosophical equivalent of "metaphysics." In Aristotelian philosophy, including its Islamic branch, metaphysics treats a range of topics, the most important of which is the study of "being qua being."[10] But mavara as it is used by Iranians today has little to do with this concept, even though their inquiries into metaphysical phenomena do often lead them to metaphysical speculation in the philosophical sense. In their usage, mavara refers to what we typically understand by the word "supernatural" in English. When Iranians deploy the word, however, they are not necessarily positing a neat separation from the world of material nature (which we understand to be graspable through the methods of modern science) but may also refer to extraordinary, paranormal, or uncanny phenomena that are fully natural but lie beyond our ordinary knowledge and experience. It is this *beyondness* that I want to emphasize in the metaphysical, rather than excluding nature or materiality per se.

There is, furthermore, a historical connection between the rise of the concept of mavara and what Catherine Albanese has identified as "metaphysical" forms of religious experimentation in America; that is, those practices and ideas that privilege mental powers, intuition, imagination, clairvoyance, and magic, usually in close concert with commitments to reason and scientific empiricism.[11] This connection is most directly captured in a linguistic equivalence in Persian vernacular between mavara and *metafizik*, such that the latter can at once stand for the "immaterial" (or beyond the physical), the extraordinary and paranormal, as well as the forms of knowledge associated with imported European and American forms of "scientific" spirituality and alternative therapy. It is telling that although esoteric traditions like Spiritism and Theosophy entered Iran from Europe in the early twentieth century, metafizik in the sense I have described did not, as far as I know, become a commonly used term until much later in the twentieth century when translations of American New Age materials became widespread.

Mavara and metafizik can be further distinguished from the occult and the unseen to the extent that the former lack any necessary connection to Islamic ethics and theology. To refer to an entity or phenomenon as metaphysical is only to indicate its quality as uncanny and as lying beyond ordinary knowledge and power. As an example, Iranian film critics often discuss Hollywood fantasies or supernatural thrillers as imaginative renderings of phenomena pertaining to mavara but never to gheyb (or for that matter, the occult). Normative or ethical considerations (Islamic or otherwise) are not essential to the metaphysical as a category, although *specific* metaphysical encounters may become sites for the enactment and development of particular ethical sensibilities.

In sum, the category of the metaphysical as I am using it encompasses those phenomena that might be deemed occult or unseen. In invoking specific Islamic traditions, however (no matter how loosely), the occult and the unseen bring with them certain theological and ethical considerations about which the person using the term "metaphysical" need not be concerned. Practitioners of the occult sciences, and those who engage with them in one way or another, need to reckon with these considerations, even if they ultimately dismiss them. The metaphysical, on the other hand, allows people to think comparatively (even scientifically) about the nature of the uncanny, strange, and extraordinary without being bound to the terms of specific theological or ethical arguments. It also enables conceptualizations of the epistemic and ethical stakes of particular encounters without being restricted to the Islamic occult tradition. It is in these senses that I say the metaphysical is *rationalized*: those who adopt the term usually consider it to be a more general category than either unseen or occult, therefore allowing for comparative statements of the sort that they expect from empirical science and philosophical speculation. Yet the metaphysical represents only one channel along which the unseen and the occult may be rationalized. Both the unseen and the occult are sometimes retained in modern rationalizations, especially where reflection on their ethical entailments or the Islamic theological tradition within which they are grounded is deemed significant.

A SHIFTING LANDSCAPE

The prevalence of the category of the metaphysical and its associated practices in Iran should be understood in relation to specific historical circumstances. I examine these conditions in various parts of this book, with attention to developments from the early twentieth century onward. However, as I collected all of the ethnographic materials for my research after 2005, some general notes are appropriate here for understanding the economic, social, religious, and intellectual shifts that set the stage for the most recent forms of metaphysical experimentation.

At the end of the devastating eight-year war with Iraq in 1988, the Iranian state initiated a number of policies that promoted economic liberalization, reversing some of the key components of a war economy shaped by revolutionary commitments to state centralization, protectionism, and redistribution. The changing economic environment both provided opportunities for increasing prosperity for the middle and upper classes and heightened anxieties about being left out of the promises for a better life. Pyramid schemes, antique treasure hunting, and appeals to occult specialists proliferated alongside seminars by motivational speakers preaching positive thinking as means for acquiring fabulous wealth. Meanwhile, new spiritual entrepreneurs emerged to promote psychological proficiencies like "concentration" and "peace of mind," which would ensure survival and prosperity in increasingly unsettling socioeconomic conditions. Many of these proponents of alternative spirituality drew on scientific models of metaphysics as the ontological ground of their therapeutic teachings.

The end of the war with Iraq in 1988, the death of the Islamic Republic's founder Ayatollah Ruhollah Khomeini the following year, and the ensuing power struggle between various Islamist factions of the revolution also bred an ideological crisis with an important counterpart in the realm of religiosity. This crisis, which remains unresolved to this day, has been focused on the problem of conceptualizing economic reform in relation to other areas of state planning, policy, and control. One crude way to articulate the problem is:

Should the opening of the economy be accompanied by an opening in politics and culture? Put differently, how is the Islamic Republic to continue to foster a certain set of values and ideals while at the same time promoting consumptive practices that—like it or not—lead parts of the citizenry to make lifestyle choices at odds with those values and ideals?[12] One of the more visible symptoms of this ideological crisis has been a nagging anxiety about youthful defiance of dominant norms. State officials and some of their critics have often expressed concern about "flight from religion" (*din-gorizi*) and moral decline among the youth. And while they have disagreed in their diagnoses of the problem, their solutions have shared certain features.

The most influential critical discourse about state-enforced religiosity to have emerged after the late 1980s is that of the "religious intellectuals" (*row-shanfekran-e dini*).[13] Influenced by liberal reformers in Europe and North America, these intellectuals have increasingly emphasized "religious experience" (*tajrobeh-ye dini*) as the most authentic ground for spirituality. What causes youthful flight from religion, in their view, is that the state has monopolized control over Islam and emphasizes outward compliance at the expense of inner faith. Their contention that religious truth is apprehended most authentically at the level of individual experience has lent support—if often indirect—for the bewildering range of spiritual experiments that have accompanied economic prosperity after the late 1980s. The heyday of religious intellectual influence can be traced to the liberalizing administrations of Presidents ʿAli Akbar Hashemi Rafsanjani (1989–97) and Mohammad Khatami (1997–2005).

A very different solution to the youth's perceived turn away from religion has been advocated by some thinkers and activists allied with the state's projects of inculcating Islamic values. This solution has involved the publication of hagiographies of largely apolitical Shiʿi mystics or "friends of God"—figures whose pious lives can be held up as exemplars for the youth without bearing the taint of association with politics. Even though these texts do not, for the most part, adopt the language of "religious experience," they do valorize mystical vision and direct intuition of the divine as the highest forms of communion with God. Hence, these hagiographies should be understood as part of a larger nexus within which the rationalization of metaphysical inquiries has been made both thinkable and practicable.

The year 2005 was a watershed in Iranian politics, but we can look to that year as a signpost for important religious shifts as well. This was the year when the populist Mahmoud Ahmadinejad seized the presidency after defeating former president Rafsanjani and a handful of reformist and conservative rivals. Ahmadinejad was favored by a number of right-wing factions, the powerful Basij militia, and various other critics of economic and cultural liberalization in the preceding sixteen years. His victory signaled a repudiation of politics-as-usual and strengthened voices calling for a return to the values of the Islamic Revolution, including its promises for economic redistribution. But even before Ahmadinejad ran for office, President Khatami's reformist allies were already widely unpopular for failing to deliver on a range of promises: strengthening the rule of law against abuses of power and influence, promoting freedom of speech, and relaxing social restrictions, not to mention their neglect of the more vulnerable segments of society as they pushed for liberalization.

The failure of liberal-style reform overlapped with a sense among some educated Iranians that the religious intellectualist project had reached a dead end. It is this collapse of the reformist synthesis, the attempt to offer a cohesive vision of liberal politics, market-oriented economics, and privatized religiosity that further loosened the centripetal forces restraining a middle-class spiritual free-for-all. Occult experimentation, spiritual seeking, and therapeutic exploration took on a breadth and magnitude unseen since at least the 1970s, if not much earlier, as evidenced in the proliferation of publications, seminars, and critical commentary on these topics. The defenders of state-oriented orthodoxy, meanwhile, found themselves once again resorting to the sorts of polemics that had once occupied their best minds in the 1960s in the intellectual fight against communism. This time, however, they had much more firepower in the way of finances and media infrastructure, as well as a full range of state coercive instruments with which they would attempt to break and intimidate any heterodox movement that grew too popular.

Although the rationalization of metaphysical inquiries in this book unfolds against the backdrop of orthodox anxiety over spiritual deviance and irreligion, we should be cautious about reducing the metaphysical scene to one more instance of the much-vaunted Iranian "underground," those spaces where the subjugated find the freedom to don revealing Western attire, drink alcohol, smoke hashish and pop ecstasy pills, play heavy metal music, and engage in unsanctioned sex. That is, people who participate in metaphysical experimentation are not necessarily trying to escape the dictates of an oppressive state-sanctioned Shi'i Islam. This is not to say that there is always a comfortable relationship between these experiments and Islamic authority. Far from it. But our understanding of metaphysical inquiries will be seriously impoverished if we begin and end with an opposition between state paternalism on one side and popular practice on the other, where the former coerces and dominates and the latter evades and resists.[14] To attend to the centrality of metaphysical inquiries in contemporary Iran is to recognize that such inquiries cannot be reduced to heterodox or counterhegemonic practices. In other words, it compels us to notice the ways in which what we think of as orthodox Shi'i Islam has also been shaped by the modern processes through which the unseen has been rationalized.

ANTHROPOLOGY, RATIONALITY, AND THE UNSEEN

Rationality has long been a central analytic concern for anthropologists, philosophers, and scholars of religion. As ethnographic descriptions of non-Western societies became more complex and nuanced in the twentieth century, a question that began to challenge scholars was how notions of rationality could serve cross-cultural comparison.[15] Were there universal standards by which beliefs held by different groups could be compared? Or was rationality internal to specific phenomenological lifeworlds and the diverse language games that people played? How were scholars to make sense of what Dan Sperber called "apparently irrational beliefs"?[16] Should the phrases spoken in magical rituals, for example, be treated as straightforward propositions about reality, or instead as symbolic, expressive, or performative utterances that could not be judged true or false? For decades such questions pitted universalists against relativists, intellectualists versus symbolists and phenomenologists.[17] While these debates were formative for the discipline of anthropology, however, scholars eventually decided to move on, convinced that the terms of the discussion had been too restricted or that it had missed the point entirely. As far as their various points of departure concerns the study of metaphysical encounters, "moving on" has opened a number of possibilities. I will focus on only three here with the intention of clarifying my own conceptual orientations.

One approach advocated by Bruce Kapferer and others has consisted of treating sorcery and magic as practices apart from or outside of reason, as "imaginative irruptions" with their own distinct "phantasmagoric spaces" that fuse, connect, and transgress different forms of reasoning and diverse registers of meaning.[18] By focusing on phantasmagorias and their "virtuality," Kapferer proposes that we can attend to the fundamental role of the imaginary in constructing reality, a possibility that is impoverished when we put too strong an emphasis on questions of reason and truth or falsity.[19] This approach has echoes among some anthropologists of Islam who have similarly called for attention to the imaginal as a space that transcends the problems thrown up by modern Western reason, although they are not always in direct conversation with scholars like Kapferer who study sorcery and magic outside the Islamic tradition.[20]

A second approach is that of Tanya Luhrmann in her work on ceremonial magic in England.[21] Luhrmann makes the incisive critique that the various sides in the earlier rationality debates took it for granted that "beliefs" were reducible to "propositional commitments held consciously and claimed consistently and in a logical relationship to other such commitments."[22] As a result, when judging apparently irrational beliefs, these scholars were either forced to argue that such beliefs rested on theories about the world (the intellectual-ists), or that they did not involve theories at all but were instead styles of performative poesis (the symbolists). Luhrmann argues that beliefs are much more complex, that they are often formed through "interpretive drift" and post hoc rationalization or justification of experiences that are found compelling or satisfying. The task of the anthropologist is therefore to attend to both experience and the interpretation of experience (including acts of rationaliza-tion) in their full psychological complexity. To the extent that she understands rationalization as the strategic justification of rewarding experience, Luhrmann's approach has resonances with the work of scholars of the New Age who devote attention to the "epistemological strategies" by which prac-titioners attempt to legitimize their practices.[23]

The third theoretical trajectory for circumventing the problems of the ra-tionality debates has been formulated by proponents of what has come to be called the "ontological turn" (OT).[24] If Luhrmann faulted earlier anthropolo-gists for holding too simplistic a notion of belief, some OT scholars argue that belief (and other such "epistemological" concepts) should be altogether aban-doned. This is because they claim that these concepts betray a lingering im-perialistic self-certainty that while we in the West can *know* reality through our superior and universally reliable science, others only *believe* through their culturally contained perspectives. OT scholars therefore call for moving away from epistemological questions so that we can open ourselves up to our in-terlocutors' radically different "ontologies" and be potentially transformed by them as well. In other words, what anthropologists (including Luhrmann) used to call "apparently irrational beliefs" should really be understood as alternative realities with as much legitimacy as the reality that modern Western science purports to describe.

Each of the approaches that I have outlined all too schematically here consists of nuanced contributions to thorny problems, and they have helped significantly clarify the terms of our arguments while opening up productive opportunities for research and analysis. For my purposes, what I see as a com-mon element among all three is a determination to bracket rationality as a concept, a move that Kapferer justifies by asserting that the insistence on continually studying questions of rationality and reason may mire scholars in the "endless repetition of the same insights."[25] But this bracketing relies on an assumption that rationality matters more to the analyst than to her interlocu-tors. What do we make of situations where rationality and affiliated notions like reason, intellect, science, evidence, and so on appear as reflexive emic concepts tied to specific practices? Far from producing endless repetitions of older insights, circumstances like these can provide rich opportunities for comparative anthropologies of epistemology—or, in other words, for under-standing how people know things and how the conditions of their knowing undergo shifts through time. This form of inquiry is central to my book, and it has long been of fundamental importance for anthropologists, historians, and philosophers.[26]

Considered in relation to Luhrmann's arguments, my approach does not discount the crucial insight that people do not always act according to coherent theories, or that they often draw on the intellectual resources provided by their environments to justify activities they have come to value and enjoy. But I also consider it untenable to argue that this is all there is to the relationship between belief and practice. If such were the case, moral philosophy would be rendered a fruitless pursuit, and our very conception of ourselves as agents who do things for reasons would be reduced to nonsense. Of course, this is not what Luhrmann was proposing, and it could be that the manner in which she framed her inquiry—understanding why apparently rational people held apparently irrational beliefs—compelled her to limit the scope of rationality to post hoc rationalization. In doing so, however, she also closed her analysis off to the prospect of discovering genuine intellectual creativity in her interlocutors' accounts, precisely the sorts of possibility that scholars of esotericism and the New Age have identified in earlier periods of European and American history.[27]

What of the call by proponents of the ontological turn to abandon the project of epistemology in favor of recognizing ontological multiplicity? The ontological turn is characterized by an ethical and political imperative to grant radical alterity its due. In this book I am less concerned with alterity (even less of the radical kind) than with historical connection and contingency. The metaphysical experimenters with whom I worked drew on several strands of an intellectual genealogy shared between what we have come to call the "West" and the "Islamic world." This included the Islamic scholastic tradition that has roots in Greek philosophy; the modern empirical sciences whose history similarly comprises centuries of exchange, translation, and dialogue; and new forms of scientized spirituality that have intermingled for more than a century with Iranian and Islamic forms of religious experimentation and speculation. My interlocutors went so far as to view my anthropological project as compatible with their own inquiries into metaphysical phenomena. They would have found it bewildering if I had suggested to them that we somehow inhabited different realities.[28]

In contradistinction to the anthropological approaches I have outlined, then, I view rationality neither as an ahistorical universal metric, nor as a yardstick condemned to relativistic incommensurability between culturally constituted particulars, nor as reducible to discursive strategies for justifying psychologically satisfying forms of experience, and still less as a standard embedded within ontologically distinct realities. Instead, I understand *rationalities*—in the plural—to be modes of reflexivity bound to specific histories of action, argumentation, and change. Some historical forms of rationality (for example, those of contemporary Shi'i jurisprudence and theology) are embedded in particular traditions of inquiry with their distinctive epistemic structures, styles of reasoning, and conceptions of time (that is, ways of relating to the past, present, and future).[29] Others borrow explicitly or unselfconsciously from multiple traditions, constructing eclectic amalgams that may be refined over time (Cosmic Mysticism, for example, draws on Islamic theological reason, as well as post-Enlightenment empiricism and traditions of psychologistic spirituality). As a malleable historical object available for public discussion and contestation, rationality both gives shape to individuals' self-conscious practices and is in turn reshaped by those very practices.

I further define *rationalization* as a reflexive mechanism through which actors recreate their world—bringing new social and cultural forms into being, reinforcing old ones, or charging them with renewed intensities—as they attempt to ensure conformity between their practices and their commitments to reason. This process is fraught and contested: the very definition of reason, the judgment as to who is authorized to evaluate the rationality of a statement or practice, and the criteria by which such evaluations should proceed, are all up for grabs, themselves subject to the rationalization process as I have defined it. In short, rationalization is an engine of transformation, a process through which to understand the emergence of qualitative shifts in the social and material worlds that people inhabit and in the ways in which they orient themselves toward these worlds, where these shifts are in some significant way attached to reflexive understandings of reason.[30]

There is a further fundamental point: Although rationalization is a reflexive process, I do not imply that every change it brings about is the result of intellection and deliberate planning. The shifts that come about through rationalization are sometimes unintended and may go unnoticed. They may at some point enter into people's consciousness and thereby become objects of direct reasoning. But they may also persist in interstitial spaces between various discursive formations, or as immanent aspects of practices that remain invisible to the normative discourses (theological, ethical, scientific, and so on) to which they are nonetheless connected.

This book's approach to rationality as a historically contingent form of reflexivity that is connected to dynamic traditions of inquiry converges with some extant anthropological scholarship on Islam and diverges from others. My emphasis on historical continuities and discontinuities within styles of reasoning resonates with the work of scholars studying Islamic practices of learning, argument, and virtuous striving, and the ways in which these practices have changed under pressure of modernization.[31] In bringing rationality to bear on the metaphysical, however, I move away from scholarship on the unseen that is concerned with resistance, arational excess, or counterhegemonic formations undermining dominant rationalist discourses (whether those of secular modernists, Islamic traditionalists, or Salafi reformers).[32] Janice Boddy, for example, has argued that zar spirit possession ceremonies in

Northern Sudan enabled women to connect with the world outside their limited community and reflect on the circumstances of their gendered subordination.[33] Naveeda Khan has shown how a centuries-old jinn mediated a Pakistani family's access to the prophet Muhammad's pious example while providing a "line of flight" for their young daughter to temporarily escape the confines of her social life.[34] And in a richly nuanced study of Islamic practices of dream interpretation, Amira Mittermaier has argued that dream-visions allow Egyptians access to a space of "in-betweenness" that undermines the illusion of rational, autonomous selfhood and opens dreamers to the ethical possibilities of the imaginary and the emergent.[35] In these scholars' work, the unseen takes on the quality of the different, the other, the indeterminate, the emergent, the excessive, the remainder—in short, that which is recalcitrant in the face of rational ordering.

My book asks, conversely, what do we learn if we view the metaphysical in terms hospitable to rational inquiry? Put differently, I seek to shift away from viewing the unseen as a constitutive externality in order to understand how metaphysical inquiries are *internally* constitutive of modern rationalist subjectivity. This is an approach that has been rarely adopted by anthropologists of Islam but has proved immensely fruitful in scholarship on Western esotericism.[36] Historians of mesmerism, Spiritualism/Spiritism, Theosophy, occultism, modern alchemy, psychical research, parapsychology, ufology, and the New Age have highlighted the avant-garde quality of these movements as forms of experimentation that range from the philosophical and the literary to the scientific, the sexual, and the political.[37] In these studies, encounters with the metaphysical do not serve as zones of exclusion or refuge from rationalist modernity but instead as windows onto the edges of European and North American life, those limit-spaces of respectable inquiry that have become sites for the emergence of new intellectual, social, and cultural forms.

In treating metaphysical inquiries as forms of reasoning with specific styles and distinctive epistemic structures, my approach also differs from recent scholarship on the "magicality" of modernity.[38] A number of anthropologists have made the powerful argument that the stubborn persistence of the occult into the twenty-first century should finally lay to rest the wrongheaded idea that as societies modernize—as market liberalism extends its reach, science and technology become further entrenched, and bureaucratic rationality proliferates—the world becomes increasingly disenchanted, banishing mystical conceptions to the rubbish heap of history. On the contrary, these scholars claim that modern occult discourses and practices can help illuminate the magicality, mystification, and murkiness of modernity itself—especially those dimensions of modern life that we consider most characteristically rational: the market, science and technology, and the state.

My work departs from this scholarship in two ways. First, I am less interested in the enchantment of the putatively rational than the rationality of the supposedly enchanted; that is, my book questions the automatic association of the occult or metaphysical with "enchantment" and all its connotations of mystification and arationality (if not irrationality). This means that I think metaphysical experimentation can be constitutive of rational modernity without necessarily having to take the extra step of arguing for the magicality of the modern. Second, I take metaphysical inquiries seriously in themselves rather than gazing through occult discourse to see how the rest of the world (society, politics, economics, and so on) might be refracted. The latter point is all the more pressing, as so much of the literature on the magic of modernity is premised on reading metaphorical significations into occult practices in analytic moves that bring to mind the hermeneutics of Clifford Geertz or the symbolic analysis of Victor Turner.[39] Attending to metaphysical inquiries as complex practices intertwined with particular forms of reasoning and reflexivity renders such interpretive moves unnecessary.

These critiques notwithstanding, scholars are certainly right to situate the modern occult in relation to transformations in the material realities that shape people's lives. I follow them by examining how economic liberalization, the dominance of modern technoscience, and the increasing bureaucratization of life under the Islamic Republic weigh upon metaphysical experimentation. But I also argue that we cannot understand metaphysical inquiries apart from powerful intellectual discourses that have grappled with the appropriate relationship between the material and the spiritual since the late nineteenth century. Historians and sociologists of modern Iran have studied some of these discourses under the rubric of intellectual encounters with modernity, negotiations of the relationship between modernity and tradition, and conceptualizations of the proper connections between religion and politics.[40] I emphasize the relationship between the material and the spiritual in these discourses both to highlight the intellectual backdrop against which ordinary people engage in metaphysical inquiries and to show how these more elaborate intellectual discourses are themselves contiguous with ordinary metaphysical questioning. That is, this book is at one level a challenge to Iranian intellectual and political historians to take more seriously the landscape of Iranian metaphysical inquiry, not only as an effect but also as a ground for the emergence of some of the most important intellectual movements in the modern period.

UNCANNY REASON

The rationalization processes that I describe in this book are never completely successful in bringing people's understandings of the metaphysical into straightforward conformity with their commitments to reason. Such processes often produce feelings of disorientation and discomfort that in turn become further prompts to rationalization along new pathways. My analysis of this dynamic draws on Katherine Withy's reading of the uncanny affect in the work of Sigmund Freud and the German psychiatrist Ernst Jentsch.[41] Withy describes several situations in which feelings of uncanniness may emerge. Drawing on Jentsch, she argues that the first of these scenarios is characterized by an irresolvable uncertainty about how to categorize a certain phenomenon.[42] Ghosts, for example, are ambiguously alive and dead, past and present, and this may be why they inspire dread. Such anomalous entities reveal to us that the categories by which we come to know things are not always adequate.[43] The second situation is more pervasive and has to do with the fact that the very structure of familiarity that mediates our experience of reality is constituted by a fundamental irresolvable unfamiliarity. This unfamiliarity is ordinarily concealed from us and only occasionally bursts into the open as recalcitrant and perplexing, thereby producing uncanniness.[44]

Freud builds on this understanding of the uncanny by directing his attention to temporality.[45] He argues that uncanniness is not simply—or not even necessarily—about an uncertainty in how to categorize something anomalous. At stake instead is a conflict between our current, seemingly confident way of understanding a phenomenon, and an earlier, seemingly superseded and "repressed" orientation that threatens to reemerge and confound us. For example, lifelike dolls may be uncanny, according to Freud, because we harbor unconscious traces of childish or "primitive" animistic beliefs that have been repressed through socialization and normal psychic development but that may reemerge to disrupt our conviction that dolls, after all, cannot be alive. The encounter with an ambiguously animate doll, then, produces a "conflict of judgment," a disquieting intuition that our old and discarded beliefs may in fact have been truer than our new ideas. In other situations, the repressed that returns may not be a "belief" at all but instead an infantile complex—like fear of castration—that reemerges as an uncanny feeling through association with some seemingly unrelated phenomenon (in Freud's analysis of E.T.A. Hoffmann's *The Sandman*, this phenomenon is the theft or blinding of eyes). In either case, the uncanny encounter is characterized by a play of familiarity and strangeness—what was once familiar and homely has become strange and unhomely or *unheimlich*. The return of the familiar-as-strange renders it uncanny.[46]

How does this conceptualization of the uncanny help us understand metaphysical inquiry and its rationalization? It will certainly not do so by taking us to the world of "primitive beliefs" and infantile complexes invoked by Freud. Considerations of temporality and conflicts of judgment are, however, crucial. Through rationalization, new orientations toward metaphysical phenomena come to replace old ones—as when rationalist discourses disparage those who consult with occult specialists as superstitious. But this substitution seems never to be complete, and there are situations in which traces of older ideas and attachments reassert themselves, producing feelings of uncanniness. A science-minded person who consults an occult specialist "for fun," for example, may encounter inexplicable phenomena that lead to disorientation and the experience of fear and disquiet.

The effects of uncanniness need not be limited to the production of disorientation. In this book, I examine uncanny moments also for the opportunities they open up for new pathways of questioning and rationalized activity, propelling practitioners forward in ways that push against and expand individual and collective horizons. One way to theorize these moments is to probe the uncanny feeling's affinity with wonder and the latter's connection to curiosity. In Persian psychoanalytic literature, unheimlich has been translated as *ashna-gharibi*, or "familiar-strangeness," where "strangeness" is denoted using the same term (*gharib*) that also refers to the occult. Gharib commonly appears in conjunction with a twin concept, '*ajib*, which means "strange" or "wondrous." In the premodern period, the conjunction '*ajib va gharib* often appeared in manuals dedicated to the "wonders of creation," a genre of texts similar to the European mirabilia.[47] Muslim theorists of the wondrous understood the emotion of wonder (*ta'ajjub*) as the starting point of knowledge, a view consistent with the Greek understanding of the same emotion as the origin of philosophy.[48] Some set themselves the task of cultivating wonder in their readers in order to draw attention to the magnificent order of God's cosmos.[49]

Could the uncanny be similarly thought as an incitement to inquiry? Historians of witchcraft, demon-possession, and spiritual manifestations in Europe and North America—all of which have unmistakable uncanny qualities to them—have shown how these phenomena provided occasions for scientific experimentation and questioning.[50] Anthropologists studying similar subjects have also argued that the uncanny can become a prod to knowledge.[51] Even so, when the uncanny feeling enters into anthropological analysis, it is too often collapsed into discussions of witchcraft, usually in the context of suspicion, accusation, and cancellation.[52] I probe instead the ways in which the uncanny arouses curiosity, even (or perhaps especially) as it instills a sense of dread.[53] This approach allows me to examine metaphysical inquiries as avant-garde practices that lie at the forefront of societal shifts and provide useful diagnostics of larger transformations.

The uncanniness of rationalization takes a different form in each of the three parts in this book. In part 1, we read about encounters with *rammals*, occult specialists who led an inconspicuous and relatively unproblematic existence before the twentieth century but whom modern rationalization relegated to the margins of respectable inquiry, disparaging them as charlatans and purveyors of superstitious nonsense. Yet this rationalization has only been partially successful, and those who encounter rammals sometimes face the uncanny feeling that the latter may genuinely possess incredible powers, throwing their grasp of what truly counts as reasonable or superstitious into turmoil.

Part 2 focuses on attempts since the early twentieth century to formulate scientific concepts, models, and methods through which to understand the metaphysical in ways that are hospitable to modern reason. These rationalizing moves have in part responded to accusations by secularist and materialist intellectuals that metaphysical conceptions amount to so much baseless speculation. But again, they have only partially succeeded. Those who subscribe to scientific models of the metaphysical are forced to contend with skeptical discourses that similarly appeal to the authority of science, producing the uncomfortable feeling that metaphysical pursuits may not be so easily justified.

In part 3, I shift attention to attempts after the 1980–88 war with Iraq to formulate new exemplars for pious discipline, just as Iranian society began to undergo widespread social transformations keyed to economic liberalization. These changes produced anxieties among some segments of the pious population about the viability of a form of life that would accord with God's commands, something they imagined had been more or less realized in the immediate aftermath of the 1979 revolution and in the ensuing eight-year war. The new pious models, recently deceased "friends of God" renowned for their feats of asceticism and spectacular marvels, were introduced partially as substitutes for revolutionaries and war martyrs, whose activist example was more suited for social circumstances now relegated to the past. But these models, too, have generated their share of disorientation and alienation, as pious seekers attempt to reconcile the imperative toward moral self-cultivation with the instability they perceive in forms of moral verification that have become increasingly entangled with bureaucratic power. No less an entity than the pious conscience has been rendered uncanny.

In all of these instances, uncanny disruptions have not so much put an end to projects of rationalization as opened up new paths along which such projects may be pursued. What makes metaphysical experiments uncanny, that is, also grants them an edginess or avant-garde quality that pushes the envelopes of existing norms and produces new forms of sociality. These possibilities include allowing oneself to be thrilled and entertained in the indeterminacy of an occult encounter (chapters 8 and 9), the justification of metaphysical inquiries in terms of personal experience or the pursuit of psychological calm (chapters 17 and 18), and the technologization of self-knowledge to overcome the radical unreliability of the pious conscience (chapter 24). The picture that comes into focus as the chapters proceed is therefore not one of unilinear rationalistic progress but of the increasing multiplicity of rationalized possibilities.

APPROACHING THE METAPHYSICAL

I was forced to come to grips with the uncanny very early in my research. In 2007, while still in the initial stages of my dissertation project, a Turkish graduate student warned me to be cautious, as the subject of my research could drive me to madness. This was something I had heard repeatedly in early interviews in Tehran, but I was taken aback when the same warning came to haunt me in Cambridge. Late at night some time later, I was chatting with my younger brother online when he sent me video clips of the newly released Tim Burton horror musical, *Sweeney Todd: The Demon Barber of Fleet Street.* I reminded him that I had a phobia of movie scenes depicting the slitting of throats, especially in the setting of a barbershop, and that I imagined this had something to do with an assassination scene in a historical drama I had viewed on Iranian television as a child. My brother prodded me to watch the scenes and I finally obliged, finding them altogether as horrid as I had expected.

I went to sleep a few minutes afterward and was immediately tormented by nightmares. At one point I found myself in a state between sleep and wakefulness, staring at the curtains as they gently danced in the ghostly moonlight. It then seemed to me that the window behind the curtains was creeping open of its own accord. My home had suddenly become unhomely. Still half-asleep, I surprised myself by asking aloud, "Am I being possessed by jinn?" As if on cue, three ominous figures strode into my bedroom and stood next to my bed. I climbed out to face them and recognized the person in the middle, a Canadian friend with whom I often chatted online. The two large beings flanking her sides were dark and menacing but featureless. Still distressed by my half-dreams, I mumbled to my friend that I thought I might be possessed. She stomped toward me like a giant reptile, clutched my two shoulders with her large hands, and proceeded to lick my nose like a snake. I awoke with a scream.

The next morning, I told myself that my research would prove very difficult if I were to lose my mental composure as a result of uncanny encounters of the sort I had endured overnight. My solution was to actively deny the reality of anything occult or supernatural, to keep my topic of study at arm's length as an anthropological object rather than as something that could trouble the boundaries of my understanding of reality. During fieldwork the following year, my interlocutors would occasionally ask me a version of this question: "Now that you have done all this research, what have you seen that you would consider *really* metaphysical?" My answer was always a standard anthropological one that would inevitably disappoint them. The point of my research, I said, was not to definitively distinguish real from unreal but rather to identify the criteria and procedures by which people made such distinctions. It was only toward the end of my research that I made the realization that my active denial of metaphysical phenomena was preventing me from understanding that I had been engaged in a metaphysical inquiry just like my interlocutors. The chief difference between us was that I deliberately structured my inquiry through a particular affective discipline (of distance and denial) that most of my interlocutors did not share, even if their inquiries were also shot through with both disciplined and undisciplined affects (virtuous caution being one of them).[54]

As a result of deliberate choices that I made early on in my research and sustained for the most part through my fieldwork, the materials I collected for this book are drawn from extensive observations and interviews but are rarely based on anything that could count as direct "experiential" evidence of metaphysical phenomena (my nightmarish experience after viewing Tim Burton's throat-slitting movie scenes being an exception). Even when I actively participated in my interlocutors' practices—among them exorcisms with the Cosmic Mystics and an occasion in which I helped a self-described witch write a spell to make trouble for her ex-boyfriend[55]—I did so with the consciousness that I was just playing along. A proponent of the ontological turn in anthropology could justifiably accuse me of failing to open myself up to my interlocutors' "alternative realities," although I would respond that a stance of cautious distance and even denial and ridicule was not foreign to them. While my interlocutors sometimes argued that denial would close me off to witnessing or understanding some phenomena, they did not consider such a stance to mark the boundaries of a different reality. Some of them practiced very similar distancing moves, as we will see.

Regardless of what one thinks of my choices about how to conduct my research, I can acknowledge that a different researcher more amenable to an experiential style of ethnography would have produced a very different text from the present one. On the other hand, my practiced self-distancing allowed me to explore things that I would not have otherwise been able to observe had I been continually tormented by nightmares, or worse, descended into madness as my interlocutors had warned. My cautious but deliberate "anthropological atheism" was the very condition of possibility for researching this book.[56]

The research that grounds my arguments includes not only ethnographic and interview data but also textual and archival materials. I spent about two years in Tehran—including a continuous fourteen-month stretch in 2008 and 2009—meeting occult practitioners and their clients, attending seminars teaching new forms of spirituality, participating in occultist web forums, visiting gatherings of devotees of friends of God, and tracking news reports, commentaries, and published research on these subjects. Even though the bulk of my material is gleaned from observations and interviews in 2006 and later, I have drawn on older historical sources in two ways. First, I conducted archival and textual research on trends in the century before the 1979 revolution, particularly on the reception of French Spiritism but also the legal mechanisms through which the modern Iranian state attempted to tackle what it saw as a problem of superstition. Second, I have drawn on scholarship on the premodern Islamic world on such matters as the delimitation of nonsense, the development of the occult sciences, the place of wonder in pedagogy and entertainment, and the rise of Shiʿi mysticism. For most of this premodern material, I have relied on the scholarship of others, including some excellent work that began to be published just as I was completing my own research. In some instances I have abandoned caution and overstepped my disciplinary training to engage with the premodern primary sources myself.

Each of the three parts that follows begins with a chapter consisting of a single extended narrative recounted to me by one of my interlocutors. The rest of the chapters progressively unpack the most important issues raised in these inaugurating stories, usually by drawing on additional ethnographic and historical material. I do not attempt a fully exhaustive treatment of the opening chapters, however, preferring to leave the reader with a sense of the messiness of ordinary life and its recalcitrance before any authorial effort to provide an all-encompassing, cogent, intellectual explanation. In the conclusion, I return to the problem of the rationalization of metaphysical inquiries and their relationship with Shi'i Islamic reason.

PART 1 **RAMMAL**

CROSSING THE LINE

I first spoke with Nafiseh on a gusty afternoon in May 2009. She was a twenty-nine-year-old divorcée and an avid enthusiast of the metaphysical. Even though she was not a professional, she had enough financial cushioning to pursue her interests with leisure—perhaps she had inherited family wealth or had received a large *mehriyyeh* payment from her ex-husband; I thought it impolite to ask. Her pursuits included working on the sets of several television serials, taking acting classes, and enrolling for private singing lessons. In the meantime, Nafiseh had honed her skills at lucid dreaming and claimed to pick up nonverbal communications from other people while asleep. She had encountered jinn on many occasions, some terrifying, others amusing. She wrote prayers and made talismans for close friends and kin to solve specific problems, like returning an estranged lover or cleansing negative energies from a home. She had practiced Reiki (a modern Japanese form of alternative medicine) for a time and experimented with hypnotism and telekinesis. She read widely on all matters metaphysical and occult, and participated in a number of Persian-language forums on the Internet where such topics were discussed.

Nafiseh attributed the greater part of her dedication to metaphysical inquiry to an unsettling meeting with a *rammal*. We met at Laleh Park, a sprawling garden just north of the University of Tehran's main campus. The park was full of Friday picnickers relaxing on the grass or playing volleyball and badminton, while children screamed and chased each other in the playgrounds. We sat at a wooden picnic table in a secluded corner of the park, and Nafiseh began to tell me of her metaphysical adventures.

The story with the rammal had started some years earlier when a middle-aged businessman at the office where she worked fell in love with her. Nafiseh had already ended her first marriage by this time, but she had no interest in this coworker. "The problem was," Nafiseh told me, "he had a wife and two grown boys." He claimed that he would be willing to provide enough for his first family to live in extravagance for the rest of their lives, if only Nafiseh would move to the south of Iran to live with him. She wanted to turn him away, but apparently a simple "no" would not do. So she came up with a plan to "create obstacles" for her suitor. "Since when I was sixteen or seventeen," she told me, "I had studied a lot of fortune-telling books. I told Mansur, 'let's go find someone who can determine if we are really suitable for each other.' I believed in energy and I thought that if I were to send negative waves toward our fortune-teller—because this really can happen—then he will tell us that we are not suitable for each other. That's what I hoped." Mansur agreed. He found a rammal, a dervish of the Qaderi Sufi order from Kermanshah who had settled in Karaj, near Tehran, and made an appointment.

Nafiseh frowned and shook her head as she recounted the event: "I didn't know this back then and only realized recently that the Qaderis are Sunnis. I've come to the conclusion that we should completely put them aside and not have anything to do with them. Even if they have any kind of [occult] knowledge, they are terrifying creatures. Charlatans." She paused and pointed to a long, thin crack on the surface of the picnic table: "You see this line? These incidents are precisely like this line. As long as you're on this side, you're on this side, and you don't know what is going on across the line. But if you cross the line, you're on the other side. You've seen, and you can no longer say 'I haven't seen.' The cost might be that you get to a point where your acquaintances tell you that you're mad. But it's not in your hands. Because it's happened to you and you've really seen."

So Nafiseh had accompanied Mansur to the dervish's house in Karaj. Mansur had said, "Shaykh, we are here to ask you something. I love this woman very much and can't let her go. I want to know whether or not we are suited for each other. We are here on her suggestion to find out." No sooner had Mansur finished his question than the dervish responded, "Yes, you are appropriate for each other and your stars match. But she has some problems and you have a problem too." "And this is why I say they are charlatans!" Nafiseh said with a knowing laugh:

> You see, I can do coffee reading. It's true that I see shapes in the cup and can identify certain things, but I mostly use the sources of energy, including the energy that the person transmits to me. It suffices that you know some psychology and have a flowing sense that can capture the waves of your interlocutor. This is enough. As soon as you say two or three things [in your coffee reading] and you see the other person acknowledge it or grow pleased or volunteer more information, you just pick it up and continue from there. You still seek help from your senses; I'm not saying that it's pure charlatanry. But it has its own mechanisms, so to speak, and it's not that people just spontaneously access the unseen [gheyb]. I think that with the dervish, it was the same. And this is something that I realized later on. I wasn't thinking this way back then.

By that point though, matters had already slipped out of Nafiseh's control. She had planned to use a fortune-teller in the service of her own complicated ends, to mentally manipulate him to provide a negative reading so that Mansur would be persuaded to leave her alone. But this "charlatan" had masterfully taken charge of the situation and was pulling both Mansur and Nafiseh along.

The rammal told Nafiseh that she had been bewitched, and he would need to spread out a *sofreh* or dining cloth for her, in her own apartment. "I had heard the word 'sofreh' before but never knew what it meant. I wish I had never seen it." Meanwhile, the dervish instructed Mansur to buy a male goat, but he did not explain the purpose. Mansur obliged. Within an hour or two, the dervish killed the goat, extracted its bile (*zahreh*), and poured it into a vial. Mansur, "being a generous man," donated the meat to the dervish and his family. The three then drove to Tehran for the dining cloth ritual. Along the way, they bought some rope, safety pins, and melamine plates. The dervish made sure that Nafiseh had a pot and blanket at home. "For the entire trip," Nafiseh told me, "I was feeling awful and felt I was going to pass out. But Mansur had fallen in love with the dervish, who was constantly bragging about his magnificent feats."

In the apartment the dervish sat across from Nafiseh and placed a large pot of water between the two of them. Mansur stood near the wall. Across the pot's rim, the dervish placed a dagger engraved with spells, prayers, and indecipherable shapes. He instructed Nafiseh to recite a verse from the Qur'an, but she couldn't recall what it was. He then told her that when the jinn came, she would have to announce their arrival and recite a *zekr* (a short devotional phrase—Arabic *dhikr*) of her own choosing. Meanwhile, he asked Mansur to tie his hands and feet with the rope, ten knots on top of one another. Nafiseh saw him tightly bind the dervish. Mansur then used another piece of rope to form a lasso around his neck and tie it to his wrists so that the man would be completely immobilized. "I don't know if all this was sleight of hand or charlatanry or what. I just don't know what to make of what happened afterward," Nafiseh told me. Finally, the dervish ordered Mansur to use safety pins to affix the four corners of a blanket to the shoulders of the dervish and Nafiseh. These are the events that followed:

> So I'm sitting there cross-legged with my palms facing up. The dervish is sitting across from me, tied up with rope. And the blanket is stretched out between us like a tent, with the pot of water and dagger underneath. He said it needs to be dark underneath the blanket for the jinn. He started his work and I don't know what he did. All of a sudden... And I've wondered later on what courage I had! But it was stupidity, not courage. As I was sitting I felt that there were creatures moving around under the blanket. And he had said that he was going to make them present [*ehzar*] so that they would bring the talismans that had been made for me [to bewitch me]. He said that if the jinn are female they will drop the talismans in my hand, and if they are male they will fling them at me. And what a scene it was! He began to recite some formulas. And the creatures came. They were very soft. It was as though they had long hair, brushing against

me like cats. Later I was able to see them in a state of half-sleep, because he didn't expel them from the apartment and it got to the point where they were bothering the neighbors. So he was saying these formulas and these things were moving around under the blanket and under my arms, and I was trembling, because like it or not, you start to tremble, thinking, "What is going to happen next?"

Their movements were very rapid and they would either brush against my hands or feet. It was very strange. On the one hand I couldn't say they were totally material like us, in a way that you could grab them, and on the other hand it wasn't that they were totally immaterial because I could feel some material touching me. And I was wondering why the man, Mansur, wasn't having a heart attack [watching all of this]. So they came and I announced, "They're here." The dervish told me to say a zekr. I said a zekr. They threw things at me. Two muddy, wet packages. As though they had been taken out of the pot. So he said that as soon as you say, "I got it," Mansur needs to start reciting the Qur'an and put the melamine plates on the blanket over where the pot is. The dervish had scribbled my name, my mother's name, and some spells and prayers around the rim of each of the twelve plates. So Mansur would bring a plate and put it on top of the blanket, and then all of a sudden something would hit it from underneath, as if it were the head of a creature gone wild. They would hit the plates like football players doing headers, and the plates would fly off to the walls or the ceiling like flying saucers. Twelve plates flying around. It was such a scene. So the twelve plates were done and Mansur stood trembling and reciting the Qur'an.

The last scene was terrible. I'm telling you I saw Satan in front of me at that moment. Imagine that the dervish had long but tidy hair at first. Now at the end of it his hair was disheveled, his eyes bulging and terrifying. Then I saw the dagger emerge from underneath the blanket and slide across his throat, inching toward his eye. He kept saying, "Don't do it! Get out of here!" and reciting spells to ward them off and prevent the dagger from poking his eye out.

At last there was calm. Mansur unfastened the blanket and untied the ropes. "But did I have any energy left?" said Nafiseh. "I was dying." On the dervish's instruction, Nafiseh opened the muddy packages to see what was inside. "One of them had a wolf or hyena's tooth. I don't remember which it was. A very long and sharp tooth. He said you need to burn all of these and cast the ashes into flowing water. But he said that there's still much more to be done. I have to recite prayers for you and do this and that. In short he was making up stories and dragging it on. So in the other package, there was a piece of sheepskin with some prayers written on it and a piece of cloth from an old shirt I had. I saw a piece of my own shirt."

Here was something that was more mundane and more shocking than anything else Nafiseh had witnessed that day. "I'm still thinking all of it was charlatanry, but what was that piece of my shirt doing there?" When she was seventeen, Nafiseh had been deeply in love with a boy. "It was adolescent love," she said, "and the boy's family also really liked me. So the boy's mom asked me to bring her a photograph of myself and a shirt, because she said 'we want to spread out a dining cloth for you.' I didn't understand what she meant at the time." The boy's mother, Nafiseh later realized, was worried that her son, who was handsome and popular with girls, might be bewitched by some envious family. So they wanted to check if Nafiseh had been entangled with any sorcery. "See, my shirt had a very distinct color," Nafiseh told me. "It was a mix of green and blue. In the course of what happened [with the rammal], whatever else I consider to be fake, I know that I got back a strip of that same exact shirt. The same color. The same fabric. This was a shirt that I had used to paint and it had paint all over it, so I said to myself that I don't need it anymore and I gave it to the boy's mother with my photograph... And never mind that various things occurred and that that relationship ended. But after some years, I saw a piece of my old shirt with my own eyes."

Still more disturbing events lay ahead. The dervish told Nafiseh that the next stage in his sorcery cancellation had to happen in private, in the bedroom. "And what did I know?" Nafiseh said. "I followed him into the bedroom, and it's bad because sometimes curiosity gets you into trouble." The dervish instructed Nafiseh to lie down and close her eyes. He pressed his fingers on her eyelids and, as Nafiseh put it, he "made his intentions clear." He said he needed to insert the bile he had extracted from the slaughtered goat into her vagina. Nafiseh was alarmed, recognizing the dervish's words as a poor excuse for sexual abuse.[1] She leaped to her feet, faced him sternly, and ordered him to leave her house. Mansur, meanwhile, sat in the living room, oblivious. "He must have been thinking he had brought God into my house, he trusted him so much." The dervish stormed off, but before he left, he turned around and looked at one of Nafiseh's paintings on the wall—an image of an angel. He smirked and said, "Yes, a divine spirit! Nice. You paint too!" Then he took a few steps toward Nafiseh, grabbed and twisted her ear, and said, "Watch yourself." Nafiseh stood her ground: "You should be the one to watch yourself!" The two men departed, leaving Nafiseh dazed and trembling. The dervish took the melamine plates with him. Nafiseh thought she should have prevented him from taking them because he clearly wanted to menace her with more sorcery. With the plates in his possession (inscribed with her name and her mother's name), he would have more to work with.

The encounter with the rammal started Nafiseh on a bumpy ride into the world of the metaphysical. That night, she was too frightened to sleep in her own apartment, so she visited her grandmother's house. Her younger brother was also there and they slept next to each other in the same bed. Throughout the night, she felt kicks and punches from underneath her mattress. Her brother ground his teeth loudly like he had never done before and would not stop no matter how many times Nafiseh tried to shake him awake. She was convinced that both the blows to her mattress and her brother's unusual brux-ism were the work of jinn. "I was not hallucinating [*tavahhom nabud*]," she told me. The next day, she returned to her own apartment, where she faced even more harassment from the jinn. "They would not let me sleep," she said. Whenever she was about to fall asleep she would feel a poke on her leg or a pinch on her thigh, or there would be noises from the kitchen. One night she asked one of her neighbors, an elderly woman, to sleep next to her, but the poor woman was similarly distraught throughout the night and refused to sleep over with her the following day. For two or three months, Nafiseh could not sleep properly. "The apartment had become troublesome," she said.

Eventually the jinn showed themselves to her in full physical form. Once she woke up to see a lazy, dwarfish creature sitting on her chest with two others playing nearby. It was grayish in color, chubby, and covered in hair, with thin, vertical eyes. On another occasion, a Japanese-looking female dwarf sat on her chest. She gently placed a golden crown on Nafiseh's head and told her with a smile, "You're our queen now." Fed up with all this menace, she called a friend, a young dervish, for advice. The man told her not to repeat her jinn stories to anyone. To ward them off, he said, she should recite *la hawla wa la quwwata illa billah* (there is no power or strength except with God) and the *ayat al-kursi* (the Throne verse) ten times before going to bed, and place a Qur'an and a knife next to her pillow.

None of this worked. The encounters grew more dramatic, with out-of-body experiences (*parvaz-e ruh*). One night Nafiseh took sleeping pills before going to bed. Suddenly she awoke to a noise in her kitchen and walked over to in-vestigate (she realized later that it was her soul that had left her body—she had not physically woken up). In her living room she saw a large casino table with twelve identical women sitting around it cross-legged, all facing the center. They were slender and wore shiny knee-high boots, shorts, mini-jackets, and garish makeup, like cabaret dancers in American movies. Nafiseh stood in awe, looking at the women, but was interrupted by another noise from the kitchen. So she walked into the kitchen and saw a man peering inside her refrigerator, his back toward her. He was wearing a long white shirt, like an *ihram* dress.[2] Nafiseh called out to him, asking who he was. The man swung around and faced her. He was short, around Nafiseh's height, with very short copper hair, and "he looked like he was ten thousand years old," with wrinkles cutting deep across his entire face (she said she could paint his image if she wanted to). "But he was beaming." He glanced at Nafiseh with a chuckle, say-ing, "Apparently I came in through this window!" pointing to a small patio window in the kitchen. Nafiseh responded with a simple "yes," but just then, the man grabbed her wrist and said, "I'm never going to leave you again! You and I will be together forever." Before she knew it, the man had shot out of the small window, pulling Nafiseh along with him. The two of them flew over the city at high speed. She could see the buildings underneath her and felt the wind on her face, a sense of exhilaration and fear taking over her body. "I felt that I was metamorphosing as I flew," Nafiseh said. "We then hurtled toward the ground and came to a rapid stop underground. It was exactly like that scene in the first *Matrix* film where Morpheus and Neo suddenly appear in a completely white space with only a monitor in front of them." Nafiseh felt the hard ground under her feet and looked around, only to find herself in an entirely new land, with her companion nowhere in sight. "It was a very cute [*ba mazzeh*] and quaint old market, with old buildings and carts where people sold fruits and other things. At that moment, I remembered the zekr the [young] dervish had taught me, and having practiced intoning full sentences in sleep, I was able to say it. *La hawla wa la quwwata illa billah.* And my soul returned. But how did it return? I could hear my own heavy breathing. I was soaked in sweat. My body ached all over. And I could hear the gurgling of flowing water, even though I knew there was no water nearby."

At some point in our conversation, I had told Nafiseh that I was interested in learning how people distinguished truth from illusion and falsity in their experiences with the metaphysical. She now found the occasion to comment: "It is possible, when you are immersed in a whimsical atmosphere [*faza-ye vahm-angiz*], for some of your illusions to become mixed in with reality. But on the other hand, you can't say that there's nothing but delusion to all of this. If that's the case, I need to go straight to an insane asylum and get institutionalized." Nafiseh paused for a moment. "It is true, though, that the science of psychiatry would reject these things. If you tell a psychiatrist that you see jinn, she'll give you medicine for mental illness, like extreme schizophrenia or something," she laughed.

Nafiseh must have received more than one indication that her friends thought she was slightly crazy, that the extraordinary experiences she described were products of a psychiatric condition, some eccentricity of character, or an overactive imagination. This was what she gestured toward when she told me that there was a line that separated those who had seen the extraordinary and those who had not. "The cost," she had said, "might be that you get to a point where your acquaintances tell you that you're mad. But it's not in your hands. Because it's happened to you and you've really seen."

Nafiseh had even realized that there were physiological indications for her condition. More than once, she had been asked by complete strangers if she used glass (*shisheh*—a street name for methamphetamines). On the third occasion that she was asked this question, by a woman sitting next to her on a flight to Shiraz, she inquired as to what she had in common with meth addicts. The woman explained that glass dilates the pupils, and Nafiseh's pupils were unusually dilated. But this dilation, as Nafiseh explained to me, had been caused by the "stare that fixes the eye" when one perceives otherworldly beings, much like the wide-eyed characters portrayed in horror movies (*zhanr-e vahshat*), although she also commented that in the moment of any particular encounter, she seldom experienced fear. Repeated sightings, she said, condition the muscles of the iris to keep the pupils wide open. It was a symptom she sometimes looked for to identify other people engaged with the metaphysical.

The occasional disparagement aside, a new world was opened up to Nafiseh when she crossed the line. This was a world filled with novel experiences, friendships, and insight. She read everything she could get her hands on about the metaphysical—reincarnation, dreaming, out-of-body experiences, cosmic energies, jinn, karma, chakras, hypnotism, magnetism, telepathy, and the occult sciences. Her erstwhile suitor Mansur eventually dropped out of her life, but she made new and rewarding friendships with spiritual travelers like herself, each trundling along on their unique journeys into the exciting unknown. She joined discussion forums online—including Asrar, where I was also a member—to connect with dozens of other enthusiasts of the metaphysical. To some of her old friends, she became an authority on the occult. They asked her for advice or requested written prayers for solving specific problems—to return an estranged lover, ward off negative energies from a home, and so on. For a time, she aided a friend and colleague from television who had a private Reiki healing practice in her apartment. She experimented with hypnotism and telekinesis with the same friend. Gradually, she grew more and more attuned to the waves and energies pulsating through her environment, learning to intuit unspoken messages from other people, picking up their colors, sensing their intentions. She found herself developing connections with animals, some of whom brought her messages from beyond, like a dove that came to stay with her for a few weeks and left shortly before her father passed away.

Nafiseh's commitments to different forms of metaphysical experience ebbed and flowed. But she told me that her perception of herself and of her world had been permanently altered. "The world as I see it," she said, nodding toward the cypress trees that surrounded us, "is not this world of trees and birds, even though when I look at these trees, I really do love them, more than human beings even, because the tree is at least perfect in what it is, whereas we humans are very imperfect." "How do you see the world then?" I asked. "I see it as devoid of time and space, and yet as being anything I want it to be, depending on my spiritual power [*qodrat-e ruhi*]." She compared this view to the philosophy of the *Matrix* movies, where the universe bends to the spiritual power of the films' protagonists. She explained that she was able to send pulses to whomever she wanted, to make them think of her. At night, she left her channels open to receive messages from others. "I believe that our wakefulness is not now. Our real wakefulness is when we are asleep. That is our real self. Not this self that is present in the world." This view explained her interest in true dreams, of insights and images received during sleep, of which there were many, especially in the year after her father's death. In the course of her spiritual journeys, Nafiseh had learned to accept certain notions and discard others. Yet much of these were provisional judgments, open to reevaluation with the emergence of new encounters or new moods. At the time of our interview, she told me that the only notion she definitively held on to "in this realm [of the metaphysical]" was "energy" and "energy sources." Perhaps this, too, was open to change.

2

POPULAR NONSENSE

Nafiseh was the consummate metaphysical experimentalist. Among my inter-locutors, few embodied the many overlapping and conflicting forces of the metaphysical landscape as thoroughly or intensely as she did. In articulating her spiritual ideas, Nafiseh effortlessly moved from the Qur'an through New Age literature to Hollywood sci-fi. While some of her friends saw her as su-perstitious, she defined her orientation toward the occult in rational empiricist terms. She pursued her inquiries as matters of serious existential import, but she also possessed an appreciation for the aesthetic pleasures of the meta-physical. And yet further still, she had an intimate sense of the terrors of the occult, recognizing that, more than once, she had flirted with madness and grave peril.

My concern in this first part of the book is to untangle some of these in-tertwining threads in the subjectivity of a metaphysical explorer like Nafiseh. To do so, I take the figure of the rammal as a pivot around which a range of competing discourses and sensibilities rotate. As a social type, the rammal is elusive and contradictory, difficult to define and impossible to pin down. Ac-cordingly, while most people show little difficulty in condemning the rammal as a peddler of superstition and charlatanry, their disparagement barely con-ceals a much more complex set of attitudes.

Contemporary discourses of rationality often take the rammal as their quintessential enemy, the negative against which reason can come into focus. By keeping the rammal at bay, the story goes, one can protect one's piety and rationality.[1] But the metaphysical experimenters who encounter the rammal are often forced to reckon with the uncanny realization that he may nonethe-less (for rammals are mostly men) wield awesome powers. The boundaries between true and false, permissible and forbidden, rational and superstitious, thus become blurred. These zones of indistinction invite both intellectual reas-sessment and a rearrangement of one's ethical and affective moorings: ratio-nalities multiply, as do opportunities for uncanny returns.

A chief reason—though by no means the only one—for the rammal's elu-siveness is that the term is used in contemporary Iran to refer to a diverse range of occult specialists. In the most technical sense, the rammal is a prac-titioner of *raml*, the divinatory science known in English-language scholar-ship as "geomancy" (see chapters 5 and 6). But in common usage, a rammal might be any number of things, regardless of whether he practices geomancy: a fortune-teller, a palm reader, a prayer writer, a sorcerer, a "traditional" healer, an Avicennan physician, an exorcist, a shaman, or a talisman maker. As a concept, "rammal" thus possesses a large referential domain and finds near-synonyms in the many labels that are used to identify these diverse practices.

These practices possess multiple, complicated histories. Some are directly connected to the development of the Islamic occult scientific tradition, while others are of more distant or ambiguous lineage. I cannot attempt an exhaustive treatment in this book of the entire range of practices that the term "rammal" may cover. The outlines of some specific practices and knowledge systems will become clearer in subsequent chapters, while others will have to await future research. My concern, then, is not to provide a definitive account of the rammal but to approach him from a number of vantage points in order to unravel the discourses and sensibilities that circulate around his figure, and that are crucial for our understanding of contemporary metaphysical inquiry.

I will begin with the ways in which the rammal is disparaged as charlatan and *rammali* as hocus-pocus. My focus in this chapter and chapter 3 will be directed to the processes of rationalization initiated by intellectuals, religious leaders, and state officials for policing the "line" that Nafiseh crossed. In this chapter I do so by examining the denigration of superstition and nonsense. In chapter 3 I turn my attention to state attempts to circumscribe rammals' activities through legislation and coercion. As we will see, there is more than one rationalist position opposing the rammal, and these are sometimes in conflict with one another. But there are internal cracks within each of the various discourses of rationality too—points of indeterminacy and equivocation through which the rammal has the chance to reemerge and wield his eerie powers. In later chapters I turn my attention to the possibilities that are opened up by these uncanny returns, openings that go beyond the mere denunciation of superstition and the attempt to suppress it by force.

The image of rammal as charlatan pervades rational public discourse as an idiom through which the elite express concern about popular superstition. Ten percent of the population, we are told, visit rammals and other occult specialists and spend hundreds of billions of *tomans* for their services annually.[2] In 2008–9 when I was conducting my fieldwork, newspapers regularly carried reports of criminal activity involving rammals. Critics denounced the *khorafat* (superstitions, sing., *khorafeh*) of the ignorant, naive, or uneducated people who fell victim to these charlatans. Over time, a discursive shift occurred to account for the fact that many of those who consulted rammals were highly educated.[3] Regardless, commentators were consistent in singling out young women—sometimes "gullible women and girls" (*zanan va dokhtaran-e sadeh lowh*)—as those most likely to fall prey to the ruses of rammals.[4] The least harm that threatened these women, the critics argued, was to be defrauded of their money. But in more serious cases they could be robbed, drugged, intimidated, extorted, kidnapped, sexually abused, raped, or even murdered.[5] In reporting on rammal fraud, the media took on the charge of instructing the public to stay away from the dangerous purveyors of superstition. This they did through regular news reports from across the country about incidents of criminal activity, as well as occasional warnings from police and judicial authorities declaring that these charlatans (*shayyad*) or fraudsters (*kolahbardar*) would be arrested and prosecuted. Both the print media and state television produced more in-depth reports as well, ranging from journalistic exposés to commentaries by psychologists and sociologists. The next page provides a sampling of news headlines (in bold) along with my own summaries from a few reports in 2008, all with one exception from *Jam-e Jam*, the official newspaper of the state media organization Islamic Republic of Iran Broadcasting (IRIB).

Concern with charlatanry and popular superstition has been a constitutive element of modernist discourse in Iran since the nineteenth century. Contemporary journalistic preoccupations with the dangers of the rammal are heirs to this modernist discourse. But criticism of unreasonable ideas far predates the nineteenth century and its particular aspirations and anxieties. Philosophers, scientists, and guardians of Islamic orthodoxy have long cast their disapproving gaze at popular gullibility and unreason in the course of attempts to provide rational accounts of the relationship between material and immaterial reality.

The Iranian historian Rasul Ja'farian has briefly but usefully enumerated medieval understandings of nonsense as part of his investigation into the concept of khorafeh, including among those who singled out women as especially prone to absurd conceptions. Womanly nonsense purportedly encompassed ridiculous stories about animals, silly tales passed off as history, and fantastic delusions about astrology and sorcery.[6] What we can deduce from Ja'farian's account is that premodern denunciations of nonsense shared with their modern counterparts an understanding of khorafat as a set of unreasonable ideas that persist due to a deficiency of knowledge or of the capacity to reason. But beyond this, there are some important differences between the way khorafat was understood in the premodern period and how it has been conceptualized in the modern era. First, in premodern discourse it was not uncommon for an author to identify the intellectual positions of an opponent as khorafat. That is, the charge of "nonsensical speech" or "absurd ideas" that the notion of khorafeh was to express was not by any means limited to uneducated commoners and women. For example, the great polymath Abu Rayhan Biruni (d. after 1050) criticized the khorafat of commoners but also of Pythagoras, who espoused a doctrine of reincarnation. Much later, Muhammad Baqir Majlisi (d. 1698), author of the voluminous hadith collection and commentary *Bihar al-Anwar* (Seas of Lights) used the term "khorafat" to denounce specific

February 25, 2008—*Jam-e Jam*: **THE TRICKS OF KIDNAPPING RAMMALS FOR EXTORTING PARENTS OF 13-YEAR-OLD YOUTH**—A criminal gang in an unspecified city in the southern Hormozgan province abducted a child. One of them posed as a rammal and told the boy's parents that he would locate the child in return for a few million tomans (a few thousand dollars) cash. The gang members were arrested and the boy released. A police official warns the public to instruct their children to stay away from strangers.

April 27, 2008—*Jam-e Jam*: **RAMMAL WOMAN'S PRESCRIPTIONS FOR GOOD FORTUNE BLACKENED WOMEN'S FORTUNE**—A woman in Karaj, a city near Tehran, was arrested for fraud after police received complaints from several women who had received love prescriptions from her. Police searched the rammal's house and confiscated business cards, talismans, locks, and prescriptions for good fortune (*noskheh-ye khoshbakhti*). A police official warns the public not to trust charlatan rammals with their life problems, since often these criminals acquire personal information which they use for extortion and blackmail.

May 14, 2008—*Jam-e Jam*: **CUNNING RAMMAL**—A rammal man was arrested for fraud and theft in an unspecified city in the northern Golestan province. A young woman complained to police after she went to the man to receive a love prescription but was instead drugged unconscious from a water bowl fed to her as part of a magic ritual. She later woke up to find her jewelry stolen. The rammal's wife was his accomplice and helped him recruit "gullible young women" to rob.

May 26, 2008—*Jam-e Jam*: **CALLING HERSELF A DOCTOR, RAMMAL WOMAN DEFRAUDED PEOPLE**—A rammal woman in an unspecified city in the northern Gilan province claimed to solve family problems, transform people's appearance (beautifying them with magic), and help women lose weight. She was arrested after police received multiple complaints of fraud from her customers.

July 26, 2008—*Iran*: **DECEIVED WOMEN AND GIRLS IN THE TRAP OF SATAN**—A man was arrested in the central city of Qom on charges of illicit sexual relations with several women. The man deceived "lonely, helpless" women into thinking he would solve their life problems by voiding the sorcery that afflicted them. He would then trick or intimidate his victims into having sexual intercourse with him. Police discovered dozens of "immoral" photographs of his victims on the man's cell phone. The prosecutor general of Qom requested that newspapers publish the suspect's full photograph so that other victims could come forward and file complaints.

August 10, 2008—*Jam-e Jam*: **CUNNING RAMMALS MADE GOLD DISAPPEAR**—A criminal team comprised of three women and four men defrauded families seeking to increase their wealth through magical means. The team, which operated in the southern provinces of Fars, Khuzestan, and Hormozgan, claimed to be able to double their customers' gold. But when victims presented their jewelry to the rammals for doubling, they would secretly swap them for fakes, wrap them in cloth and instruct their owners not to open them for forty days, the time required for the magic to work. A police official warned the public to stay away from rammals, since "if [these individuals] could solve anyone's problems, they would first solve their own."

absurdities spoken by commoners, Jews, Zoroastrians, and Sufis, but also philosophers and theologians, including the great Fakhr al-Din Razi (d. 1209). Second, premodern khorafat was not limited to the sphere of what we might today call supernatural conceptions. Scholars would denounce false hadiths, erroneous historical accounts, and wrongheaded ideas about the natural world all as khorafat. Whatever they found to be wildly unreasonable was fit for the term.

The most detailed premodern Shiʿi criticism of women's beliefs and practices is the ʿAqaʾid al-Nisaʾ (Creed of Women), a social satire by the seventeenth-century Shiʿi scholar Aqa Jamal Khʷansari (d. 1710) mocking the practices of well-to-do women in Isfahan, the seat of the Safavid empire. Khʷansari ridiculed the norms of sociability and religiosity among Isfahani women, particularly their passionate bonds of sisterhood (khʷahar-khʷandegi); their disregard of ritual obligations; their recourse to heterodox supplications, magical invocations, and amulets; and their liberties in mixing with unrelated men.[7] In one chapter he mockingly suggested that women would rather avoid their husbands and other male relatives, as well as any seeker of knowledge or man wearing a turban,[8] preferring to associate instead with the Jewish lace maker, the vegetable seller, the cloth merchant, the doctor, the rammal, the prayer writer, the sorcerer, and the minstrel.[9] His criticism continues to find echoes in the concerns of modern authors who see a direct connection between women's association with occult specialists and a dangerous flouting of sexual boundaries and norms of modesty.

The premodern Islamic world also had its debunkers—those who exposed the tricks and ruses of false prophets, fraudulent Sufis, illusionists, sorcerers, jugglers, quack doctors, and beggars.[10] One such debunker was the thirteenth-century author ʿAbd al-Rahim ibn ʿUmar al-Jawbari, whose book Kitab al-Mukhtar fi Kashf al-Asrar wa Hatk al-Astar (The Book of Selection in the Revelation of the Secrets and the Tearing of the Veils) is a treasure trove of the medieval arts of deception.[11] Al-Jawbari's book had a wide readership across the Islamic lands from the Maghrib to India. He described it as a warning to his audience to beware of being duped by any of thirty categories of deceivers, to each of whom he devoted a separate chapter. Al-Jawbari was clear, however, that he distinguished between the righteous saint's true marvel and the impostor's trick. He himself practiced astrology and geomancy but was suspicious of most claims about extraordinary powers and cautioned his contemporaries to be likewise on guard.

Beginning in the second half of the nineteenth century and continuing well into the twentieth, superstition gained renewed salience in the eyes of Iranian modernist intellectuals who laid siege to the "delusions" (mowhumat) of commoners (ʿavam) and especially "traditional women" as obstacles to progress and nationalist renewal (tajaddod).[12] This criticism was part of a much broader attack on the political, social, and religious foundations of the Qajar dynasty.[13]

Some intellectuals identified superstitions as spurious folk accruements to a true Islam. Others equated Islam itself with superstition. The Shi'i clergy usually bore the brunt of the modernist attacks as those held most directly responsible for disseminating superstition among the masses.[14] What added urgency to the modernist project was the conviction that superstition undermined the destiny of an entire people as it resolved to catch up with a more advanced and rational European civilization. In their view, ridding society of superstition required reform on a massive scale, a complete restructuring of educational, legal, and religious institutions. It would thus become harnessed to the political projects of constitutionalism, republicanism, and eventually revolutionary Islam.[15]

When discussing sorcery, fortune-telling, divination, geomancy, and jinn exorcism, modernist critics saw women as most susceptible to false belief and most in danger of being duped by charlatans.[16] But they went much further than many of their premodern forebears and diagnosed the problem as one of oppression by a self-interested clergy and other ignorant and corrupt men.[17] To eliminate superstition, they held, women needed to be educated and set free from the shackles of traditional society. By the mid-twentieth century, some of the most prominent modernists had grappled with the problem of superstition and its affliction of women. Mirza Fath 'Ali Akhundzadeh (1812–78) wrote plays about it.[18] 'Ali Akbar Dehkhoda (1879–1956) incorporated it into his biting social satire. Ahmad Kasravi (1890–1946) dedicated an entire treatise against it to "ladies of pure religion [*banovan-e pakdin*]."[19] And Sadeq Hedayat (1903–51) attacked it in his dark and scornful short stories.[20]

The modern adversaries of superstition included thinkers committed to Islam. In the late nineteenth century, the reformer Jamal al-Din Afghani (1838–97) argued that Islam, by virtue of its absolute monotheism, "purifies and cleans off the rust of superstition, the turbidity of fantasies, and the contamination of imaginings."[21] He further argued that nations needed to clear their minds of the "muddiness of superstition" in order to achieve perfection. For Afghani, true Islam was identical with universal reason and favorable to modern science. He therefore called on the ulama to drop their opposition to the new sciences so that the Muslim world would be able to regain its past glory.[22]

Although Afghani was born and raised in Iran, his thought left a stronger mark on Muslim modernism in Egypt, India, and the Ottoman Empire than in Iran itself.[23] However, his influence may have been partly responsible for shaping the views of a handful of outspoken Shi'i scholars some decades later who attacked their own colleagues for propagating superstitions among the masses. Shari'at Sangalaji (1890–1944) was the most well known of these thinkers, and his critical project very likely drew inspiration from Salafi reformers like Rashid Rida, who were themselves influenced by Afghani.[24] In the 1930s and early '40s, Sangalaji launched a series of scathing assaults on a range of beliefs and practices he found common among his contemporaries, from intercessory prayer to the imams and their descendants to praying on tombs, wearing rings and precious stones for warding off misfortunes, practicing astrology, watching for portents, and dedicating vows to trees and public water dispensers. He also disparaged certain widely accepted Shi'i doctrines, especially belief in the *raj'at* or avenging return of the imams before the final resurrection.[25]

The mainstream Shi'i ulama were not silent before these assaults. They defended Shi'i doctrines from charges of superstition and went to great lengths to show that Islam was not antagonistic to reason or science. Sometimes this required them to distinguish correct belief and practice from unreason and superstition. Of course, the ulama had been demarcating true doctrine from unreason for centuries, but now they found themselves in the position of doing so defensively and against a new adversary, who not only attacked their ideas but made every effort to curtail their social and institutional power.

One of the most vigorous of these defensive battles was waged by Ruhollah Khomeini (1902–89) in the mid-1940s, soon after the new shah, Mohammad Reza Pahlavi, assumed power in the chaotic aftermath of an Allied occupation that deposed his father, Reza Shah. Around 1944, Khomeini wrote a lengthy and ferocious polemic responding to a series of venomous attacks by Sangalaji and the anticlerical intellectuals 'Ali Akbar Hakamizadeh and Ahmad Kasravi.[26] Titled *Kashf-e Asrar* (Unveiling of Secrets), Khomeini's book deployed theological, philosophical, and jurisprudential reasoning and marshaled a wide range of evidence—from the Qur'an and hadith to the claims of European scientists—to defend, inter alia, Shi'i doctrines on intercession, the veneration of entombed imams and their descendants, sanctioned forms of divination (*estekhareh*), the healing power of soil from an imam's grave, and other miracles and marvels attributed to the prophet Muhammad and his progeny.

While advancing rational explanations for these doctrines, Khomeini also took pains to distance the ulama from certain beliefs and practices that he acknowledged as superstitious. For example, he argued that those who consulted rammals, exorcists, seers, and the like were not the pious people who had close contact with the ulama, because the latter considered these practices to be forbidden.[27] "What are the poor mullas to do when they have always been opposed to these sorts of nonsense?" he wrote.[28] The same went for people venerating a stone in Mashhad or enthralled by fantastic tales told by vagrant storytellers. The ulama and those who interact with them, argued Khomeini, are the last to believe these kinds of things.[29] Even in the case of marvels attributed to the imams and their descendants, Khomeini stressed that the pious do not accept everything. "The knowledgeable among them," he wrote, "are those who believe later than anyone else. Yes, if [the marvels] are proven on the basis of standards [*mavazin*], they believe because they have faith in the powerful God. They do not reject anything without reason, just as they do not accept without reason... One who rejects or accepts something without clear reason cannot be counted among the rational and the pious."[30]

By vigorously claiming a position that was at once rationalist and remained faithful to central Shi'i doctrines, Khomeini thus argued that his anticlerical opponents were not only heretics but manifestly unreasonable as well.

Khomeini's interventions were important early formulations of a rationalist discourse that was to become dominant in the Islamic Republic that he founded more than three decades later. In this discourse, it is admissible to simultaneously uphold the possibility of miracles and marvels in the here and now while rejecting certain unreasonable ideas about the marvelous and the magical as ignorant and superstitious. As we will see in later chapters, the ambiguity in the "standards" that Khomeini gestured toward makes it difficult for those who strive to live according to Shi'i Islamic precepts to do so while presenting a coherent account to themselves and others. Nor is such ambiguity restricted to the ulama. While secularists have attacked rammals and exorcists as purveyors of superstition, they have rarely done so without equivocation. Kasravi, for example, held out that some people may experience true dream-visions.[31] Hedayat argued that sorcery should be seen as an evolutionary precursor for the legitimate sciences of magnetism and hypnotism.[32] The communist intellectual and politician Ehsan Tabari (1917–89) endorsed parapsychological laboratory research.[33] Other modernists, as we shall see in part 2, participated in Spiritist séances with the souls of the dead.

In spite of such equivocations, or perhaps because of them, anticlerical intellectuals and Muslim reformers have been united in their denunciations of appeals to occult specialists as superstitious and ignorant. This orientation has found direct expression in the continuity of state attempts over the past century to stamp out the practices of rammals as threats to public order, a topic to which I now turn.

3

LEGAL CENSURE

On May 17, 2009, state television aired a report on the arrest of a rammal in Tehran. The story was produced by the Channel Two news show *Bist o Si* (Twenty and Thirty), an investigative program known for its fast pace, aggressive tone, and strident partisan politics. It opened dramatically with a young male journalist and his film crew marching into an apartment. At the outset, the police officers who would arrest the rammal lurked somewhere in the background invisible, announced only by a caption that read, "Agents enter charlatan's home." Snippets of an interview followed:

Caption: Rammal taking advantage of people's beliefs.

> REPORTER: Do you have contact with jinn?
> RAMMAL: (*nods vigorously*) Definitely.
> REPORTER: So why didn't these jinn tell you that the [police] agents would be coming here just now?
> RAMMAL: (*repeats the question, as if surprised*) The jinn didn't tell me that the agents would be coming here?

Scene cuts to a shot of the rammal leafing through a prayer book.

> REPORTER: Is this one of your prayers, sir? Can I touch it?
> RAMMAL: (*hands him the prayer*): Look, you need to watch out. I'm telling you seriously. Don't mock these things. (*raises voice*) I'm telling you seriously.

Video cuts again. Reporter reading from the prayer prescription, midsentence.

> REPORTER: "[P]ut with the jinn and obtain response." (*turns to rammal*) You mean the jinn respond to this?
> RAMMAL: To me, yes.
> REPORTER: They make a mark on the page?
> RAMMAL: They respond to *me*.

Video cuts again. Now we see the rammal showing the reporter a small photo album. He points to what appears to be a picture of a cat.

> RAMMAL: One of my *movakkels* [jinn agents] who had gone into [the cat] passed away, God bless him.

REPORTER: A cat?

RAMMAL: (*leans forward to speak loudly into the microphone*) Yeah!

Scene cuts again. Rammal is now standing and speaking with panache. The news crew has gathered around and watches with amusement.

RAMMAL: A jinn can enter into the skin of a cat! A jinn can enter… a goat. A jinn can enter you!

Cut to another scene. Rammal reads from his appointment book while seated at his desk.

RAMMAL: On Sundays I have [appointments for] opening fortunes [*bakht gosha'i*]. I even have [appointments for] talismans and exorcisms.

REPORTER: What does that mean, talismans and exorcisms?

RAMMAL: It means we cancel their talismans. We exorcise their jinn.

Scene cuts.

REPORTER: I've heard that you also do telepathy.

RAMMAL: I don't do telepathy. I *fly*. I fly to wherever I like.

Scene cuts. Now the rammal is standing.

REPORTER: Where is your vase?

RAMMAL: (*points at a vase near the wall*) It's right there. Turn off the lights and take out [the jinn] if you can.

REPORTER: (*now standing above a vase decorated with blinking, multicolored lights*) What is this vase?

RAMMAL: There are jinn in that vase. Touch it if you can.

REPORTER: (*interrupts him*) There are jinn in this vase?

RAMMAL: Touch it and take it out if you can.

The reporter now addresses the camera.

REPORTER: He is telling us that this vase is a vase of jinn. "Pick it up if you can," he says, "and see what consequences will befall you."

The reporter is shown touching the lights on the vase, now turned off. He takes out a pouch and some sticks. Video skips ahead to show the vase lying on the ground. The reporter overturns it to empty its contents. Something resembling sand pours out onto the rug.

REPORTER: See, this thing was full of nails and…

Video cuts again. Rammal explains his fee structure.

RAMMAL: It starts with five thousand tomans. If the talisman is really heavy and affects the entire family, it could go up to a million one hundred.

REPORTER: You suggested to our friend that it could cost up to twenty or
twenty-five million.

RAMMAL: (*raises voice*) No! I said that's what it is in the market. He's lying!

In what remains of the report, we see the rammal again showing a picture
of a cat, this time on his cell phone, and claiming that the cat was inhabited
by a jinn. The reporter is unmoved and mocks the rammal. In another brief
scene, he tells the reporter that "God willing," he will spread a "dining cloth
of talismans" (*sofreh-ye telesmat*) for him so that "his faith will be strengthened." Immediately the report cuts to a scene of the reporter holding a plastic
bag in his hand. He asks the rammal if it contains opium. The rammal is defiant, accusing the reporters of planting the drugs. In the final scene, a police
officer appears on camera. He explains that there have been twenty complaints
against the rammal for fraud. The police will hold the man for some time to
allow other victims to come forward and lodge their complaints. He instructs
viewers to "take care so that they are not duped by such individuals and do
not give their money away to them."

The investigative journalist in this report performs a rationalist debunking
of the rammal. He mocks and teases him, exposes his ludicrous claims, and
shows everyone that his "vase of jinn" is full of sand and nails. He accuses him
of charging people millions of tomans for his antics. He charges him with drug
possession. The rammal is presented as a boastful charlatan or madman. He
speaks with drama and force. But through quick editing and multiple cuts, the
reporters have reduced his speech to half-witted ramblings. He never speaks
more than a sentence or two without being cut off, either by the reporter who
interrupts him or the editor who cuts to the next scene. If he is allowed to
speak, it is to let him make a fool of himself. In the conclusion, the police officer who will arrest the rammal speaks in a calm, measured tone. He does not
engage with any of the rammal's claims. He only explains the facts of the case
and instructs the public to avoid such characters. Women do not appear in the
report, except one or two customers standing in the background. But printed
newspaper reports that followed the television broadcast mentioned that the
majority of the rammal's customers were "women and girls." A few news
websites, beginning with the television-owned *Jam-e Jam*, uploaded the video
and introduced it with a mocking caption: "We must now wait and see if the
rammal's jinn friends can unlock the prison cell so that he can fly out."

Like the newspaper examples I cited in chapter 2, this report of a rammal's
arrest dramatizes state authority and surveillance over its subjects. Rammals
are among a class of professionals whose practice is unregulated by any bureaucracy and who continually attempt to evade the gaze of the state's disciplinary apparatuses. This resistance to state regulation can be glimpsed in the
spatial location of their practices. There are no shops or businesses where
occult professionals may legitimately sell their services. Their profession is

almost always based in their private residence. Some of my interlocutors told me that the rammals they consulted changed their addresses frequently to avoid state surveillance. Reports about rammal crime, then, allow the state to perform its triumphant image of a total power that extends its arms of justice and care to every corner of society, weeding out even the most slippery of its adversaries.

Official concern with the activities of rammals has been a feature of modern governance since the latter's inception more than a century ago. As we will see, this concern has not always been as pressing as it has become in the early twenty-first century. It has taken different shapes over time and has elicited responses of varying intensity. Before the twentieth century, occult professionals in the Islamic world could be found practicing their crafts in the open—in the marketplace, on thoroughfares and public squares—as well as at some royal courts and elite homes.[1] Although there is evidence of attempts here and there to circumscribe their activities in public, their practices seem to have been seen as innocuous enough to be tolerated.[2] A census conducted among residents of Tehran in 1852–53 found such professionals as rammals, prayer writers, and astrologers (*monajjem-bashi*) openly practicing their crafts. Half a century later, between 1899 and 1903, another census included rammals and prayer writers on an inventory that also listed dervishes, pharmacists (*'attar*), preachers (*va'ez*), lute players (*tar-zan*), clerics (*akhund*), eulogy singers (*rowzeh khʷan*), and wrestlers (*pahlavan*) among the city's professions.[3] An 1879 police code drafted by the Italian officer and Tehran police chief Count Antonio di Monteforte listed various offenses to public order, like drunken disturbance, gambling on the streets, and yelling "as madmen," but there was no mention of those who offered occult services.[4] Police reports submitted to Count di Monteforte some years later (between 1885 and 1888) likewise showed little preoccupation with occult specialists as criminals. The activities of rammals did begin to draw attention as a disturbance to public order, however, just as the capital was undergoing Paris-style reforms. In June 1880, Kamran Mirza, the governor of Tehran, issued detailed instructions outlining the duties of the Ministry of Inspection and Public Hygiene (*vezarat-e ehtesabiyyeh va tanzifiyyeh*), which included prohibiting itinerant tradesmen, cobblers, rammals, and fortune-tellers from providing their services on the streets to prevent congestion and obstruction of movement.[5]

In the late nineteenth century, then, occult specialists seem to have been a concern to the state only to the extent that their practices disturbed city traffic. The one exception I have found is instructive. A police report submitted to Count di Monteforte on 24 Dhu'l-Qa'da 1303 (August 24, 1886) writes of a Jewish itinerant who visited the house of the former prime minister's chief butler (*abdar bashi*), advertising that he could prescribe prayers and read fortunes. The women of the household paid him nine thousand dinars in cash and two black hens in return for the promise of love prayers and a talisman to enhance intimacy. The next day, the prayer writer brought them a "nonsensical talisman" (*telesm-e mohmal*). The report continues: "Haji Shir, the late Prime Minister's eunuch, discovered the Jew's fraud and dragged him to the chief butler, who sent the Jew to the Foreign Ministry where he would be punished and made to return the money and hens."[6] What we can surmise is that for elites in the royal establishment (such as the chief butler and the eunuch in this report), itinerant prayer writing was likely a form of charlatanry. But it would only be prosecuted on the basis of individual complaint. The state had no interest in eradicating such practices when they were based on the mutual consent of the professionals and their customers.

Matters changed significantly with legal and institutional reform after the 1905–11 Constitutional Revolution.[7] Three developments conspired to criminalize the occult professions. First, postrevolutionary modernists redoubled attention to issues of public order, civility, and hygiene as part of efforts to remake urban space along modern European lines. Second, these reforms were coupled with calls for enlightened education and assaults on superstition and irrationality under the ancien régime, as I described in chapter 2. Third, legal reform became the locus of heightened activity, particularly as modernists understood the establishment of a particular kind of public order to depend on the codification and enforcement of a set of laws. The criminalization of occult professions was hence bound up simultaneously with an evolving vision of rational social order and a decades-long struggle over legal change.[8]

At first, and for a long time, occult professions were treated as petty offenses, lesser violations than felonies and misdemeanors. Their first appearance on the legal scene came in the 1917 Customary Penal Code (*qanun-e jaza-ye 'orfi*), which was ratified by ministerial decree and remained in effect until 1922. The code was adapted from the 1810 French Code Pénal,[9] and like it, viewed rammali and similar practices as "contraventions" (*khalaf*) or police offenses.[10] It set a penalty of three days' imprisonment substitutable with a fine for "individuals who, in the name of spell casting, sorcery, exorcism, rammali and the like, perform public demonstrations [*ma'rekeh-giri*] or open up shop to deceive people and make these activities their profession and source of livelihood." In terms of punishment, the violation was equivalent to the performance of "offensive" demonstrations in the streets and public squares, "letting loose idiots and the insane who have been entrusted to one's care, or savage animals or attack dogs, and provoking them to [assault] passersby," disturbing people's peace and quiet by creating a ruckus, and damaging public streets and alleyways. It was, however, marginally less serious than certain other petty offenses, such as ignoring traffic guidelines, selling spoiled food and drink, deliberately dumping trash on others, and gambling in public.

These penalties remained in place with minor modifications for the following few decades under the Pahlavi monarchy, but they finally became obsolete in the course of legal reforms initiated after the birth of the Islamic Republic

in the 1979 revolution. In recent years, prosecutors and lawyers have sometimes spoken of punishments for occult professions as "panhandling" (*takaddi*)
or "extortion" (*kallashi*), which is punishable by one to three months of imprisonment. A more dramatic transformation, however, has occurred since the
mid-2000s: these professions are now sometimes treated as fraud, a much more
severe classification than the old category of contravention. But even the fraud
designation has not satisfied every opponent of the occult. The judiciary bill
for a revised Islamic Penal Code presented to parliament in 2007 stipulated
the death penalty for "Muslims who are involved with witchcraft and sorcery
and propagate it in society as a profession or cult." But parliament struck all
references to sorcery from the revised law, and the final ratified version
avoided such specific language. As we will see later, the category of sorcery
(*sihr*) in Islamic jurisprudence cannot easily be identified with rammali,
fortune-telling, and the like. Moreover, it is possible that legislators were re-
luctant to endorse the reality of sorcery by encoding it into penal law.[11] The
compromise solution for now has been to continue to use the existing category
of fraud to curtail occult activities.

The intensification of punishments for occult professions in recent years,
when coupled with the dramatic projections of state power through the media,
highlights an anxiety beyond one about civility, rationality, and social order
of the kind that animated early modernist opposition to superstition. In the
Islamic Republic, the occult professional does not merely represent an exception to rational order but presents a challenge to the authority of clerical
leadership. Therefore, the art of government as it pertains to subduing the
rammal is not only concerned with establishing civil order but with maintaining the monopoly of the ulama on matters of moral guidance and the health
of the soul. Or it would be better to say that the conception of rational civil
order under the Islamic Republic is closely intertwined with the moral leadership of the ulama. In the following chapters we will see that there are deep
ambiguities in this moral guidance that are rooted in ambivalence toward the
credibility and desirability of the occult sciences. These spaces of hesitation
have allowed the rammal to survive the discursive and legal assaults I have
outlined so far, while enabling the emergence of alternative pathways for
rationalization. Metaphysical experimentation is deeply impacted by these
rational attitudes toward rammals, as well as the indeterminacies at their core.

DO JINN EXIST?

Given the prevailing intellectual and legal suspicions toward rammals, we might ask if these are rooted in Islamic doctrinal skepticism toward jinn and sorcery, that is, those invisible forces with which the rammal claims to traffic. As we will see in this chapter, the predominant position among Muslim theologians—some exceptions notwithstanding—is to accept the existence of both, even if their purported everyday manifestations are viewed with doubt or denial.

Islamic cosmology, as rooted in the Qur'an and hadith, and elaborated through centuries of exegesis and theological speculation, incorporates a number of invisible entities and realms beyond the sensible material world. These include most obviously God, but also angels, jinn, heaven and hell, the interstitial imaginal realm of the *barzakh*, the throne (*'arsh*), news of the unseen in the form of prophecy and inspiration, and so on.[1] Muslims, to the extent that they give credence to doctrine or accept the Qur'an as divine speech, have a relationship, a position, toward these entities. This relationship can take on very different forms. It may be contextually specific and shift from one form to another within the same person in response to different situations. Firm and trusting belief (*iman*) is one of these relationships and the one most privileged in doctrine. The Qur'an endorses firm belief in the unseen (*al-ghayb*) at the very beginning of the second chapter, "The Cow" (Al-Baqara):

> This is the book; in it is guidance sure, without doubt, to those who fear God. Those who believe firmly in the unseen, are steadfast in prayer, and spend out of what we have provided for them. (2:2–3)

But just what is this unseen toward which God invites firm belief? The word *al-ghayb* is used dozens of times in the Qur'an in different contexts and with obviously different meanings. Exegetes differ on the specific referents of the word in some verses, including the one above. According to the influential twentieth-century philosopher and exegete Allameh Sayyed Mohammad Hoseyn Tabatabai, al-ghayb in this verse refers to "that which is not subject to sense perception [*hiss*]," meaning "God exalted and his greatest signs which are absent from our senses."[2] *Iman* is the "firming of belief in the heart, acquired from trust and security [*amn*]," and guarded from "doubt and uncertainty," which Tabatabai says are a "pestilence" (*afa*) afflicting belief.[3] This firm belief in an unseen God is, he adds, in the first instance the result of a sound creation (*fitra*) and the product of an inborn reason.[4]

Other commentators have argued that the unseen in which one must firmly believe includes revelation, heaven and hell, resurrection, the Day of Judgment, angels, prophets, divine recompense, and the coming of the promised Mahdi.[5] But certain difficulties emerge once we try to include jinn and sorcery in this list. The jinn are primarily thought to be invisible beings, and sorcery depends on invisible forces. Both are mentioned in the Qur'an. Must Muslims therefore firmly believe in them? I have not encountered any Qur'an exegeses that include jinn and sorcery alongside the other items above. It is possible that this is because iman in the unseen has to do with attachment and commitment to the divine, where revelation, recompense, angels, heaven and hell, the prophets, and the Mahdi are all part of a divine apparatus and plan. Sorcery and the jinn are not. If anything, the Qur'an disparages belief in jinn in the sense of putting one's trust in them or taking them as associates with God.[6] Furthermore, the Qur'an strips the jinn of some of their purportedly extraordinary powers, including the ability to eavesdrop on the secrets of the heavens.[7] In more than one way then, the jinn are actually excluded from the divine unseen by the Qur'an itself.

A similar difficulty attends interpretations of the Qur'anic attitude to sorcery.[8] The Qom-based scholar Reza Ramezan Nargesi has argued that historically the Shi'a have conceptualized sorcery in two diametrically opposed ways on the basis of their reading of two different Qur'anic verses.[9] First there are scholars who believe that sorcery does not exist. As proof they rely on the story of Moses's contest with Pharaoh's sorcerers, particularly verse 116 of Al-A'raf (The Heights):

> Said Moses: "Throw ye [your ropes]." So when they threw, they bewitched the eyes of the people, and struck terror into them: for they showed a great (feat of) sorcery.

According to the interpreters, "in reality, nothing was created [in the sorcerers' feat]. Rather, they had used special tricks and sleight of hand so that the spectators imagined that the strings and ropes [of the sorcerers] had turned into real serpents."[10] On the other hand, there are interpreters who argue for the reality of sorcery on the basis of verse 102 of Al-Baqara (The Cow), which discusses sorcery among the followers of the prophet Solomon:

> They followed what the evil ones gave out against the power of Solomon: the blasphemers were not Solomon, but the evil ones, teaching men sorcery and such things as came down at Babylon to the angels Harut and Marut. But neither of them taught anyone without saying: "We're only for trial; so do not blas-

pheme." They learned from [the two angels] the means to sow discord between man and wife. But they could not thus harm anyone except by God's permission. And they learned what harmed them, not what profited them. And they knew that the buyers of (sorcery) would have no share in the happiness of the hereafter. And vile was the price for which they did sell their souls, if they but knew!

Here, the interpreters point out that the Israelites used the methods of sorcery they had learned from the angels Harut and Marut to hurt each other and separate husbands and wives. Still, as Ramezan Nargesi shows, the scholars arguing that all sorcery is illusion would partially explain this verse through a psychological account. On this point he quotes the seventeenth-century jurist and compiler of hadith Muhammad Baqir Majlisi (d. 1699):

> Majlisi says: Most scholars are of the belief that sorcery is superstition. As for why it is efficacious, no one denies the effect of sorcery. But to explain it they say: If the bewitched knows that someone has bewitched him, the illusion of being bewitched will lead to the appearance of the results of sorcery in him; like suggestion [*talqin*] to the sick. But if he doesn't know at all that he has been bewitched, although none of the scholars have denied this kind of effect, they have no explanation for it other than saying that these actions are the result of employing jinn and devils against the bewitched person.

Note here that some of the scholars who argued that sorcery was illusory explained purported cases of sorcery's efficacy through recourse to jinn. That is, they held that sorcery was either illusion *or* it was the result of the activity of jinn. But it could not be anything else, say, for example, some separate, invisible force.

Not every Muslim scholar admitted the existence of jinn. Some medieval theologians and philosophers were known to have doubted or denied their existence, Avicenna being the most notable among them.[11] Among theological schools of thought, the Mu'tazilis, who were early adopters of Hellenistic philosophical methods and categories, were particularly notorious for harboring skeptical attitudes toward jinn, sorcery, and the marvels of saints.[12] Still, for most commentators, it simply would not do to deny the existence of jinn. This is not because jinn are somehow worthy of firm and trusting belief but because their existence has been attested by divine revelation. To deny them, these commentators argue, would be to deny revelation. Trusting belief in one unseen (revelation) leads to attestation of the existence of another (jinn).

The medieval contest between revelation and speculative theological reason over the existence of jinn is illustrated nicely in a twelfth-century CE story from Muhammad ibn Mahmud Hamadani Tusi's "The Wonders of Creation" (*'Aja'ib al-Makhluqat*), a compendium of marvelous creatures and phenomena. The story, which is probably apocryphal, recounts a dispute between two ninth-century Mu'tazili theologians:

[Abu Ishaq] al-Nazzam the theologian was in debate with Abu al-Hudhayl [Muhammad ibn 'Abdullah—known as al-'Allaf the Mu'tazili, the former's uncle] over jinn. Nazzam says that jinn exist. Abu al-Hudhayl says jinn do not exist.

Their enmity ran long. The caliph of the time made peace between them and said: "Demons cannot be shown by proof, but must be firmly believed in by virtue of the Qur'an."

And Abu al-Hudhayl had a well from which he drew water. Nazzam concealed himself in that well. When Abu al-Hudhayl threw a pail into the well, Nazzam held it with his hand. Abu al-Hudhayl pulled. Nazzam made a horrible cry and said: "Why do you insult demons and spirits [pari]?"

Abu al-Hudhayl sealed the well with a stone and informed the caliph that "Nazzam has hidden in the well and pretends to be a demon and threatens me."

The caliph sent someone to bring him out, and, slapping him, took him to the caliph.

The caliph says: "What is unseen, if someone wants to make visible and treat with proofs, he will fail. Thus it is with the punishments of the grave and the munkar and nakir [the angels that interrogate the dead during the first night after death]. One must have firm belief in these all. They are of the ear [one must hear and listen], not of reason. And he who seeks to prove them will become humiliated like you did."

By this we mean that since the Creator said that jinn exist we must have firm belief.[13]

As we see in this account, firm, trusting belief in revelation is made to triumph, not only over rational theological speculation but over attempts at empirical verification as well. An analogous position is evident among many contemporary Iranians who look dismissively upon reports of jinn sighting, possession, and exorcism, and yet claim that they believe in jinn because they are mentioned in the Qur'an. One person who articulated such a position to me was Dr. Mahluji, a psychiatrist at a large teaching hospital in Tehran. I was speaking to him about exorcisms among the Cosmic Mystics (an example of which I described in the introduction). Dr. Mahluji quickly responded that "if they aren't charlatans, what is happening is what we call dissociation."[14] That is, the issue is psychopathological and has nothing to do with invisible spirits. He added that he believed in jinn because God mentions them in the Qur'an, but he did not believe that jinn interacted with humans.

Another skeptical approach to jinn and sorcery consists in understanding them as cultural artifacts of the pre-Islamic Arab society that became the recipient of God's revelation. Baha'oddin Khorramshahi, an author, poet, translator, and Qur'an scholar, has defended this position, arguing that this "cultural reflection" is part of a divine plan rather than the spontaneous influence of a milieu on a text (which would be more damaging to the divine origin of the Qur'an). God has purposely taken advantage of "slices of the culture of that era" in order to express "the infinite in terms of the finite" and to "reflect the sea in the pond."[15] Among his examples of cultural reflection, Khorramshahi refers to the jinn: "In the Qur'an there are references to the existence of jinn and there is a chapter named 'The Jinn' and verses describing how some of them became believers and listened, captivated, to Qur'anic verses... but it is unlikely that today's science or scientist would attest to the existence of jinn."[16]

Most Qur'an scholars, however, find such reasoning unpersuasive. Reza Haq Panah, for example, has countered in this way:

> That the Qur'an has spoken of jinn and today's science might not accept it can-not be the basis for [arguing] that the Qur'an has been influenced by the culture of the *jahiliyya* [the era of pre-Islamic Arabs, labeled by Muslims as the "age of ignorance"]. The Noble Qur'an has spoken of many other things that today's science is unable to comprehend, like angels, the soul, revelation, the unseen world, and unseen forces. The Qur'an explicitly accepts the existence of jinn without reflecting the degenerate culture of [pre-Islamic] Arabs... If the exis-tence of jinn were fictitious, why would there be a chapter in the Qur'an named after the jinn that would—we seek refuge in God—falsely describe their belief and unbelief? Today's science cannot say anything in the way of proving or disproving the existence of jinn, and one cannot deny the existence of jinn, which has been explicitly cited in the Qur'an, based on the silence of science, just as one cannot deny the existence of angels, the soul, revelation, the realm of barzakh, heaven and hell, to which the empirical sciences have no access.[17]

To sum up, some Muslim scholars have doubted the existence of jinn and sorcery since the medieval period. Even so, the fact that both of these have been mentioned in the Qur'an has precluded most from denying them out-right. An intermediary rationalist position with regard to jinn has been to accept their existence but to deny their reported empirical manifestations. With sorcery, an intermediary rationalist position between acceptance and rejection has been to explain its reported harms as the product of illusion and suggestion. Both of these positions in effect disqualify everyday reports of encounters with jinn and sorcery while affirming the absolute truth of the Qur'anic revelation.

These formulations share discursive space with those of scholars who admit the reality of occult phenomena like jinn and sorcery, as well as their mani-festations in everyday life, while still attempting to isolate and condemn non-sensical ideas and superstitious practices. In pragmatic terms, scholars advo-cating for this position recognize manifold dangers in the realm of the occult and yet refuse to reduce every occult practice to sorcery. Rather than forbid-ding occult engagements altogether, they therefore call for caution as the most reasonable course of action. As we shall see in chapter 5, caution is a mode of virtuous comportment rooted in the disquieting realization that the occult can neither be simply denied nor straightforwardly embraced. Faced with the impossibility of certain knowledge and harmless engagement, rational, prudent Muslims must either keep away, the reasoning goes, or proceed with utmost care. Virtuous caution, then, emerges as one rational modality by which experimenters can approach the metaphysical.

VIRTUOUS CAUTION

Since the establishment of the Islamic Republic in 1979, the formulation and implementation of state laws and policies have been brought under Islamic jurisprudential oversight. As far as state authorities and their allies are concerned, the attacks on rammals waged through the apparatuses of lawmaking, the police, and the media are consonant with Islam. But considered in itself and apart from the exigencies of governance, the dominant Shi'i ethicolegal tradition can enable a very different orientation toward the occult. For those metaphysical experimenters who are committed to Shi'i orthodoxy, this orientation opens up a number of possibilities for engagement.

Shi'i jurists have not set unequivocal rules for the occult sciences the way one finds with many other areas of practice that may be more straightforwardly permitted or forbidden. Recognizing the murkiness of their boundaries, these jurists call for caution or *ihtiyat*. This is a virtuous sensibility that is rooted, on the one hand, in appreciation of the many risks of engaging with the occult. On the other hand, it is based on an understanding that the boundaries between licit and illicit modes of occult practice and the criteria by which virtuous practitioners of the occult are to be distinguished from charlatans are far from certain. Virtuous caution allows one to wade into the occult's murky realm and to extract certain benefits without succumbing to its perils.

The most obvious dangers associated with the occult and those most commonly discussed by jurists have to do with committing forbidden actions, either as prerequisites for sorcery—like defiling the Qur'an or ingesting forbidden substances—or as ends in themselves, like harming others or causing hatred between husband and wife. Other dangers are less obvious. I became acquainted with some of them in the summer of 2006 as I was conducting preliminary fieldwork. I had begun then to hear stories of occult encounters from friends and relatives and decided to investigate further. As part of this early research, I sought out and purchased grimoires (occult manuals) for divination, writing prayers and incantations, constructing talismans and amulets, and summoning and controlling jinn. Most of the grimoires in circulation in Iran at the time were lithograph prints. They did not have official Culture Ministry permits and could not be found in most bookstores—in fact, when I asked about one grimoire at a well-known bookstore on Enqelab (Revolution) Street, the bookseller sneered that "we don't sell such trash here." That is not to say the grimoires were difficult to find. Plenty of itinerant booksellers sold them on the streets (including Enqelab), along with other out-of-print or permitless books. Some bookstores carried them too, including long-established and respected ones; you had to know where to look. Most grimoires I sought were also available as PDFs on compact discs and online, some of them in bundles of dozens of electronic books and manuscripts.

Some of the most serious occult dangers, I learned, were also dangers of working with grimoires. The least occult of these was the risk of getting caught by police selling a permitless book on the street. I became aware of this risk when an itinerant bookseller refused to allow me to photograph the pile of books he had set up on a sidewalk along Enqelab Street. He then asked me if I was a journalist. When I explained that I was not, he relented and allowed me to snap a picture of his books, but without him in the frame. We can think of this first risk as one of running afoul of the state's policies for stamping out superstition and charlatanry.

Other dangers are more specific to the nature of the grimoire as a manual of the occult. My friend ʿAbbas, a thirty-year-old Arabic instructor who gave me directions to a bookshop in the old Tehran bazaar where I could find a wide selection of grimoires, offered a stern warning about their use: "Do not copy down the incantations. Do not read them out loud. Do not even copy or read out partial phrases. If you do, you might call forth jinn who will attack and fuck you." I understood ʿAbbas to be saying that the jinn would severely hurt me or drive me mad (one of the words for insane—*majnun*—literally means "jinn-possessed"), but I later learned that he also meant "fuck" in a quite literal sense, as we will see in chapter 6. To the extent that the occult involved dealings with jinn, they could bring about serious harm.

Grimoires also pose hazards if improperly handled. A bookseller from whom I bought a half dozen grimoires told me of a man in his neighborhood who for some time dedicated all of his energies to writing spells for the purpose of increasing his wealth. Not only did his efforts fail to bear fruit but his obsession with the occult left his financial affairs and his relationship with his family in shambles. Finally, pressured by his wife, he decided to rid himself of his grimoires by burning them. This was a terrible mistake, the bookseller said: the proper way to dispose of these books was to bury them or soak them in water until their ink dissolved. The jinn associated with the spells in the grimoires visited vengeance on the wretched man by torching him. "He is still in the hospital after some weeks," the bookseller said. The moral of the story was that one who engages in occult practices needs to be well informed about the risks and take appropriate safety measures, including the proper forms of ritual preparation, correct modes of comportment, and awareness of the salience of particular times, spaces, and materials.

Yet another danger has to do with the sociality of sorcery and rumor. I learned of this risk one afternoon as I was gleefully showing off my recently acquired grimoires to a group of friends visiting my parents' home in Tehran. A friend of my mother, a middle-aged woman who had obtained a master's degree in theology and was married to a surgeon, pulled me aside to quietly impart a word of caution. "You shouldn't show these books to just anyone," she said, "because not everyone knows and trusts you as we do. If some acquaintance of one of your friends should suffer serious misfortune, you never know, they may remember your books and think that you worked sorcery on them."

Given these assorted hazards, how do Shi'i scholars approach the occult? It is commonplace to hear that Islam forbids sorcery (*sihr*). A famous hadith attributed to the prophet Muhammad has him saying that "the fixed punishment [*hadd*] for the sorcerer [*sahir*] is a blow of the sword."[1] While this hadith is widely accepted as authentic, jurists disagree over the precise circumstances that would warrant such a punishment. Some say it should be reserved for when a sorcerer kills another with his sorcery or when he claims prophethood, both of which seem to empty sihr of its transgressive qualities and bring it under the sign of other offenses like murder and false prophesy.[2] In any case, in contemporary Iran there are few open discussions about the punishment of sihr qua sihr. When punishments are discussed at all, it is usually for the crime of fraud, not sorcery, as we have already seen.

Our confusions multiply when we consider comparative jurisprudential scholarship on sihr that attempts to get to the bottom of things. One such work of scholarship is an article by Reza Ramezan Nargesi, whom I cited in chapter 4.[3] The upshot of his discussion is that sihr is forbidden in three instances: when harm is done to someone, when some form of deception is involved, and when there is some disrespect to the sacred (presumably through defiling the Qur'an, cursing the Prophet, and so on, although the author does not make this explicit).[4] But not all sihr has been ruled forbidden, says Ramezan Nargesi. Some scholars sanction sihr deployed to counter the ill effects of other sihr. Others have permitted sihr put to use for "correct objectives," like "locating [something or someone] missing," or "conquering the lands of infidels."[5]

So at least for some scholars, sihr seems to be forbidden only when it is deployed for forbidden purposes or when it involves forbidden actions. In practical situations, however, it is seldom easy to ascertain whether a particular instance of sihr meets these criteria. For example, one of my interlocutors, a man in his forties, obtained a prescription from a prayer writer to bring his wife home after she left him and moved in with her parents. Was the prayer writer doing the man good and the woman harm? Was he doing them both good? Or harming both by prolonging an unhealthy marriage? Mersedeh, a prayer writer I will introduce in chapter 10, told me that she regularly wrote prescriptions for women who were worried about the infidelity of their husbands. To do this, she had to bind (*bastan*) each man to render him unattractive to other women. Clearly this is an instance of harm. But

Mersedeh was also preserving a marriage. Forbidden or not? We are in the realm of equivocation.

So much for sihr. What complicates matters further is that few scholars reduce the occult sciences to whatever they consider the category of sihr to contain. Among the Shiʿa, certain occult sciences have long found acceptance and even prestige. Geomancy—*raml*—in particular has been understood as a legitimate, even noble (*sharif*) divinatory science founded by the prophet Daniel, who learned it from the archangel Gabriel.[6] Other Muslim sources trace the genealogy of geomancy to the prophet Idris.[7] For centuries, geomancy has been privately studied, taught, and practiced in scholarly circles alongside *jafr*, *awfaq*, and other occult sciences.[8] There is, moreover, a rich corpus of "prophetic medicine" (*al-tibb al-nabawi*), augmented among the Shiʿa by "medicine of the imams" (*tibb al-aʾimma*), that incorporates Qurʾanic verses and prayers for prophylactic, apotropaic, and curative uses, as well as amuletic and talismanic inscription.[9] Despite this avowed permissibility and even nobility of certain occult sciences, however, Shiʿi jurists warn that most of the occult specialists known and consulted by ordinary people for the purpose of solving everyday problems are charlatans or delusional. That is, validation of the occult sciences is coupled with suspicion of its practitioners to produce juristic ambivalence.

To develop a deeper understanding of jurists' views about the occult, I sent an *estefta* (request for a legal opinion) to the offices of all the major Shiʿi *marajeʿ-e taqlid* (sources of emulation; sing., *marjaʿ-e taqlid*) in June 2009, asking them to clarify whether learning and practicing these sciences was permissible according to Islamic law. I have reproduced a translation of my question below:

> Salam alaykom,
>
> Is the study and learning of occult sciences such as jafr, geomancy, awfaq, and the sciences of talismans and amulets permissible according to the shariʿat? If the study of these sciences is permissible, what is the status [of permissibility] of their practice according to the shariʿat? Thank you and with best wishes for your health and a long life.

Over the course of a few weeks, I received responses from most of the jurists' offices. Only one, the office of Grand Ayatollah Sayyed ʿAli Sistani (the most widely followed jurist in Iraq, who maintains a large following among other Shiʿi communities, including in Iran), replied in what would seem to be an unambiguous negative: "It is not credible" (*eʿtebar nadarad*). Even so, the opinion made no comment as to whether engaging with these sciences was permissible, as I had asked. The other replies were more equivocal:

The Office of Grand Ayatollah Sayyed ʿAli Khamenei (currently supreme leader of the Islamic Republic of Iran): What currently exists of these sciences among the people is mostly not reliable to the point that it would lead to certainty and assurance about the discovery of unseen [*gheybi*] affairs and news about them; however, learning sciences like jafr and geomancy correctly is acceptable with the condition that there is no corruption attendant on them.

The Office of Grand Ayatollah Yusef Sane'i (a jurist close to reformist and opposition politicians): One must not spend one's life on these kinds of sciences, and if they entail *haram* actions, they are *haram*. One must not pursue these activities and make them a source of obtaining livelihood, and one must abandon these activities. Some of these activities are also certainly *haram*.

The Office of Grand Ayatollah Naser Makarem Shirazi (a jurist with close connections to conservative politicians): Given that the science of jafr is not known in its complete form by people other than the infallibles [e.g., the prophets and imams], and that its incomplete form does not have much effect, it is not approved and you should not pursue it. [The response made no direct comment on geomancy or other occult sciences.]

The Office of Grand Ayatollah Lotfollah Safi Golpayegani: Learning these kinds of sciences is unnecessary for most persons, and some of them are even forbidden. What is necessary is to learn [what is] halal and haram in religion and to perfect religious knowledge.

The Office of Grand Ayatollah Sayyed 'Abdolkarim Musavi Ardebili (a jurist close to reformist and opposition politicians; he died in November 2016): Learning the occult sciences, including jafr and geomancy, with methods that are not forbidden in the shari'at, is acceptable in itself. Practicing it, too, as long as it is not through haram actions and does not entail harassing or harming others, is acceptable in itself. However, one must note that the vast majority of those who claim to possess these sciences are either lying or delusional.

The Office of Grand Ayatollah Hoseyn 'Ali Montazeri (a widely respected dissident jurist; he died in December 2009): Studying and learning the mentioned occult sciences is acceptable in itself as long as they are not used to commit actions that are against the shari'at.

The overall impression that emerges from these responses is that it is not forbidden to learn and practice geomancy, jafr, and some other occult sciences; and yet, it is not a good idea to do so. Still, if one is adamant, one should proceed with caution, maintaining distance from actions that are unambiguously forbidden (harming others, engaging in illicit sexual conduct, defiling the Qur'an, and so on), recognizing that most of the knowledge and practice that exists on the subject is unreliable, and keeping in mind that the majority of those who claim to possess occult knowledge are charlatans or mentally ill.

We might read the hesitation in these fatwas as a reflection of doctrinal ambiguity: On the one hand, certain occult sciences cannot easily be forbidden in themselves, and on the other hand, the jurist recognizes that there are major pitfalls in pursuing such sciences. But to limit oneself to an analysis of doctrinal ambiguity would be to misunderstand the fatwa as merely a statement on correct doctrine—a purely legalistic pronouncement on halal and haram. As Hussein Ali Agrama has shown in his work on the Al-Azhar Fatwa Council in Cairo, it would be much more productive to examine the fatwa as an element in a collaborative process of ethical self-care, one in which the fatwa-seeker and the fatwa-giver work together to develop a virtuous solution to a difficult life question.[10] I may have asked the *maraje'* their opinions in order to discern points of doctrine for the purpose of an academic project. But they responded to me as guides trying to help me live life as a good Muslim. They were not just instructing me about whether a certain practice was forbidden or not but also commenting on whether or not I *should* be engaged in such practices as someone who wants to live a virtuous life. Even when they saw no reason to discourage me from proceeding, they advised caution.

The virtuous caution I am elaborating here is different from the procedure of the same name (*ihtiyat*) in Shiʿi legal theory. Jurists have developed the latter procedure as a tool for determining the proper course of action when faced with a situation where textual indicators in the Qurʾan and hadith do not unambiguously spell out an obligation. For example, relying on the Qurʾan and hadith, a jurist determines that if a dog has eaten out of a bowl, the bowl is polluted (*najis*). But the texts are unclear about how many times the bowl needs to be rinsed before it returns to a state of purity. There are some traditions that report that the Prophet rinsed such a bowl once, others that indicate he rinsed the bowl three times, and still others that say he rinsed it seven times. To overcome this uncertainty, a jurist may seek recourse in the procedure of caution and rule that one should rinse a dog-polluted bowl seven times—that is, err on the side of the more difficult obligation—to ensure its purity.[11]

In the case of the occult sciences, some of the jurists I cited above were unambiguous that certain sciences—geomancy, jafr, amulets, and so on—were permissible. That is, the problem to which caution was a solution did not lie in the ambiguity of the authoritative texts of the Qurʾan and hadith but in the real-life situations where the occult sciences were practiced. In such situations, halal and haram may sometimes be mixed and the distinction difficult to discern (see my example above about binding a wayward husband). Or a permissible action may be proximate to a forbidden action such that engaging in the former may raise the risk of falling into the latter. For example, by learning the techniques for counteracting sorcery, one also acquires knowledge of sorcery. One who lacks the requisite, pious self-control may succumb to the temptation to deploy sorcery for blameworthy ends, even though she has learned it for ostensibly praiseworthy reasons.[12]

Advising caution in these situations is an ethical imperative irreducible to the act of delineating boundaries between permissible and forbidden. Those who invite such virtuous caution are fond of citing a section of verse 187 of Al-Baqara (The Cow): "Those are God's bounds. Do not go near them." The verse, they explain, does not merely warn against crossing the boundaries God has set between the permitted and the forbidden but commands the virtuous to keep well within those limits. The closer one gets to the boundary, they reason, the stronger becomes the temptation to transgress it. So the best course of action is to protect oneself by staying a safe distance away.

In chapters 6 and 7, I introduce two figures who will help me further flesh out the ambiguity of the occult sciences and the cautious sensibility that some of my interlocutors adopted in relation to them. As we shall see, virtuous caution provides a rational pathway for metaphysical experimenters to come to grips with the uncanny realization that the rammal cannot be summarily dismissed. But this is a delicate path that can rapidly descend into peril.

A SCHOLAR-RAMMAL

Sayyed Ahmad Yazdi the rammal received us on a carpeted patio adjoining his modest house in Chizar, once a village in the northern suburbs of Tehran but now a neighborhood in the expanding megalopolis that has swallowed the village and erased most vestiges of rural life. It was a hot day in late June 2009. The patio overlooked a small orchard with a handful of fruit trees and a family of rooster, hens, and chicks chirping and clucking about. The rammal was speaking into a wireless handset as my research assistant Mehdi and I took our seats on the carpet and leaned against two large, firm cushions: "In the house where you live, try to recite the azan once every day. Yes. And recite the Kawthar chapter eleven times a day and blow on the cell phone that he/she uses to communicate. Yes, yes. The chapter that begins with 'inna a'taynaka-l-kawthar.' Do it with the intention of separation between the two of them. It will be fixed, don't worry. I'll call you next week when I return and you can come visit me." I deduced that the petitioner on the other end of the line was a woman and she was asking for Shaykh Yazdi's help in breaking off a resented amorous relationship in her family. Perhaps she suspected her husband of an affair. Or perhaps her son or daughter had fallen in love with someone whom the family did not approve.

There were two others in our presence, older pious-looking men who may have been shopkeepers or bazaar merchants. When he ended his conversation on the phone, Shaykh Yazdi turned to them and gave them a few prayer prescriptions for a woman named Zahra who I guessed was the wife of one of the two men. He instructed them to recite the azan in her home and to place a pencil-written copy of the Abu Dajjaneh prayer—known for its efficacy in warding off the menace of jinn—underneath her sleeping pillow. He also told them to try to convince her to wear a *haft jalaleh*, a ring set with a hematite stone engraved with prayers invoking God's glorious name for protection. Before the men left, Shaykh Yazdi gave them a small printed book of prayers that he had compiled, with the specific prescriptions for Zahra identified in pen. As they departed, the rammal turned to us while gently shaking his head: "In Iran there are many people who are afflicted with *vasvas*.[1] This lady is one of them and she is driving her husband crazy."

Two young men entered soon thereafter and took the elder merchants' place. The older among the two complained of being unemployed for three weeks and of failing to hold down any job for very long. The rammal asked him a few details about his family and his professional skills, then called to his wife (whom we could not see) to bring him his geomantic dice—two small brass rods each transecting four rotating cubes. The four visible faces of each die were engraved with a number of dots—two sets of three dots arranged like a triangle, one with two dots, and one with four dots arranged like a square. He asked the young man's name and his mother's name, whispered a prayer, and let the dice roll off his right hand and onto the carpet. Examining the formation of dots on the dice, he proceeded to divine the man's fortune. "First, this young man's star is Jupiter," he began. "Second, Jupiter is absolute auspiciousness (sa'd-e motlaq). Third and fourth, his nature is sweet, hot, and wet. Fifth and sixth, he is dear to everyone around him and dearer to his family. Seventh and eighth, my dear son's status and position will exceed that of his father and his father's father. Ninth and tenth, yes, his financial situation will improve. This family has good economic instincts." The rammal paused to inspect his dice a bit more closely. "You do have some sorcery afflicting you. That's what I see in the sixth station. The seventh station tells me it's someone in your family. Someone has performed sorcery and taken away your power of decision. You are anxious and perturbed in everything you do. You begin something and abandon it before completion. There are five things I will prescribe for you. Don't worry; I will write it all down." A few minutes later, the two men left with faces beaming. Shaykh Yazdi brought Mehdi and me a tray of tea and sat with us for the next two hours to speak about the occult sciences.

Shaykh Yazdi was a very different sort of rammal from those we have met in previous chapters. For one, he was less invested in shamanistic theatrics and more interested in fashioning himself as a Shi'i scholar. Having grown up in Yazd and studied in the howzeh in Qom, he had apprenticed himself to a number of luminaries to learn the "noble science of geomancy," as well as astrology and other occult sciences, and to engage in ascetic exercises on the mystical path. He talked of books he had authored and sciences he had mastered. And he spoke with the quiet, measured tone of a mulla, peppering his speech with classical Arabic utterances and quotations. While Shaykh Yazdi had clearly succeeded in gaining the respect and devotion of his clients, such attempts by occult specialists to present themselves as men of learning have to contend with a range of skeptical discourses. For example, Mehdi told me that the occult sciences were one of three leisure activities available to howzeh students, the other two being smoking and temporary marriage.[2] I also heard from more than one of my interlocutors that those howzeh graduates who made a career of the occult did so after failing to distinguish themselves in more respectable pursuits, such as in jurisprudence, philosophy, theology, exegesis, hadith scholarship, or even in preaching, not to mention any of the range of professions that have become available to those with howzeh learning since the 1979 revolution—from researchers and consultants to administrators.

Shaykh Yazdi differed from most rammals I met in another way: he was surprisingly forward in describing his own adventures with the occult—either the kinds of forces he had unleashed on others or those to which he had fallen victim himself. I found this forthrightness perplexing given that some of the stories he told could be interpreted in deeply unflattering ways, such that they would tarnish the persona of scholar and healer that he tried to fashion. I will retell two of these stories to provide a deeper glimpse of some of the dangers against which the jurists I cited in chapter 5 advised caution.

The first story had to do with Shaykh Yazdi's recent past when he lived in Qom. He recounted it as he explained the suspicion with which the occult sciences were greeted, a suspicion that, he said, had historically compelled the greatest practitioners of the occult to conceal their knowledge. "When I revealed my knowledge of only one of these sciences," he declared, "they harassed me so much that I had to leave the city of Qom, for if I hadn't, they would have certainly slapped me with three to five death sentences." Shaykh Yazdi then told us that in the spring of 2004 (five years before our interview), he had an office in Qom where he received hundreds of people seeking his assistance every day. Given that increasingly large numbers of people were turning to him, he decided to build a *hoseyniyyeh*—traditionally a neighborhood center where mourning ceremonies were held for the prophet Muhammad's martyred grandson Imam Husayn, but increasingly also a venue for lectures and other religious and cultural activities. Shaykh Yazdi intended his hoseyniyyeh not only as a place for welcoming his patients but also as a major research library, which he claimed would rival the best in the Middle East. He continued:

> I told the mayor of Qom, "Give me a license; I want to build a hoseyniyyeh." He said, "Mr. Yazdi, you want to turn all of Qom into a center for sorcery and rammali. The howzeh is fed up with you." I said, "I am sorry that you have been misled by impostors who claim to be scholars, but I am ordering you, give me a license or else I will bind you." He said, "Go do whatever you want." I bound him so that when he drank water, he could not relieve himself in the bathroom. When he found out what had happened, he sent a delegation to me to apologize. I said, "By the Qur'an, I will not unbind you until you issue my license." They issued the license and handed it to me at 6:00 p.m. I unbound him and heard from some friends that he entered the bathroom at 6:00 p.m. and did not leave until 9:00 or 10:00 p.m.

The mayor had not retaliated immediately, but Shaykh Yazdi said that these events precipitated a hefty court case against him that was inaugurated with a raid on his office and home and the confiscation of 108,000 books and antiques, as well as equipment he had used for alchemical experiments.

Shaykh Yazdi did not provide many details of the trial against him, but a partial picture later appeared in a special issue of a state-owned newspaper focusing on "newly emerging deviant cults." The newspaper devoted three pages to Shaykh Yazdi but referred to him only by his initials. Titled "Rammali in the Garb of People of Knowledge," the report accused him of "taking advantage of people's religious emotions," extorting them, and engaging in various forms of fraudulent activity. The article mocked his religious education and even his penmanship, saying that he had not learned much in his years at the howzeh in Qom but had instead wasted thirty years on "research into matters pertaining to jinn," as he had claimed in an interview in 2004. The report concluded by describing the 2006 indictment against Shaykh Yazdi and the eventual court verdict. According to the paper, the charges against him included defrauding the plaintiffs in the case, possession of sexually explicit CDs, publishing books without permit, and violating the dignity of the clergy.

After deliberation, the judge convicted him on a number of charges, including the acquisition of illegitimate wealth, spreading lies, and committing haram actions. Shaykh Yazdi was reportedly fined a sum of 73.8 million tomans and sentenced to a six-month prison term, suspended for five years, and fifty lashes, suspended for three years. Reprints of his books were banned and existing copies were ordered confiscated from publishers.

In telling us the story of his showdown with the mayor of Qom, Shaykh Yazdi was attempting a few things. On the one hand, he wanted to show the suspicion with which the occult sciences were greeted by Iranian officials and the tyranny with which someone as learned and popular as he had been treated. On the other hand, he wanted to give us a sense of his extraordinary learning, his God-given capacity to aid people in need, and his power to deploy occult forces to vanquish his oppressors. But in making the claim that he could—and would if necessary—bind someone, such that his victim could no longer urinate, he also risked being taken as a malicious sorcerer, a liar, or one susceptible to boasting and delusion. At the very least, his words betrayed little of the cautious sensibility I have described.

The rammal's second story was about his youth in Yazd, and he recounted it by way of explaining how he became an apprentice to a well-known mystic and healer. Shaykh Yazdi told us that as a young man he was "afflicted" (*mobtala*) with early puberty. On the one hand, he intensely desired sexual union with a woman. On the other hand, he recognized that he would not have the opportunity to marry for another few years. He also hated engaging in haram actions, by which he presumably meant fornication and masturbation. Hope for a solution presented itself in the form of a slim manuscript that he found in his father's library. Titled *Nikah al-Jinn* (Marriage or Sexual Intercourse with Jinn), the manuscript provided instructions for how to summon a female jinn and tame her for coitus. Shaykh Yazdi explained with a soft and deliberate voice:

I saw instructions in that book for writing a talisman on the palm of the hands, the inside of the thighs, and a word—with my apologies—in the space between the penis and the testicles. Incidentally, I did this on the night of a Monday. A beautiful girl appeared resembling Turkish girls, with the same beauty and the same attire as girls from Turkey. And yes, coitus ensued. If you will excuse me, during orgasm she transformed into an ass. *Jinn take on different forms even of dogs* [he phrased this in Arabic]. Fear overcame me at that moment that she would kick or bite me. The following week, the night of a Wednesday, I repeated the procedure. Again she came to me and the same things happened exactly. All of a sudden she transformed into a terrifying dog. If you will excuse me, I was locked in that position such that I could not ejaculate. I suffered immensely [*zajri keshidam*]. The following nights I no longer repeated this, but they [the jinn] would not leave me alone. Every Monday and Wednesday night they would come after me.

Shaykh Yazdi consulted several mystics for solutions to his plight without success. Finally, he was saved by the prescription of Shaykh Ja'far Mojtahedi, a giant of mysticism and occult sciences to whom he apprenticed himself for the next twenty years (I will have more to say about Shaykh Mojtahedi in part 3).

In telling this second story, Shaykh Yazdi intended to assert his intimate connection with a well-known mystic and friend of God from whom he could claim to have received knowledge, legitimacy, and perhaps even sanctity. The problem was that in so doing, he could also be seen to have revealed his youthful recklessness or, again, his susceptibility to delusion. Both of these could be interpreted as deficiencies that the rammal had failed to outgrow as a mature adult. When we left Shaykh Yazdi's presence that afternoon, I noticed that his stories had made a particularly unflattering impression on my research assistant. No sooner had we shut the outer door of his house behind us than Mehdi burst out laughing and continued to chuckle until tears streamed down his face.

While Shaykh Yazdi's anecdotes undercut the persona of pious scholar that he attempted to construct for us, they were consonant with the contradictory figure of the rammal as represented in the popular imagination and official discourse. Mehdi took him to be a buffoon, but others may have interpreted the same stories as indications of Shaykh Yazdi's closeness to mighty powers. His eccentricity, that is, may have been an asset to the extent that his clients relied on his expertise in manipulating jinn and the powers of sorcery. We will meet one such client, a retired officer of the police force, in chapter 7.

THE HESITANT OFFICER

Shaykh Yazdi's run-ins with the law might have us assuming that security officials would prefer to keep their distance from him. In fact, just the opposite was the case. I first learned about the rammal in an interview in the late spring of 2009 with Brigadier General ʿAli Shirazi, a recently retired officer in the police force of the Islamic Republic of Iran. At the height of his career in the mid-2000s, he had been appointed deputy chief for criminal investigations in one of Iran's most populous and urbanized provinces. I spoke with Mr. Shirazi about the "criminological dimensions" of the occult sciences. As it turned out, he had overseen arrests of occult specialists like rammals and fortune-tellers on multiple occasions during his career. These individuals, he explained, duped their gullible victims, robbed them of their wealth, instigated familial strife, and spread corruption and prostitution. But there had also been instances when Mr. Shirazi had sought the assistance of occult specialists to solve seemingly intractable problems, including one criminal case that he had cracked with the help of an accused charlatan whose arrest he had ordered himself.

That a functionary of the state should flout the very standards the state has instituted should not occasion surprise. Nor is there anything remarkable in the explanation that the state's agents may consider the smooth functioning of society to require the occasional infringement of its norms. Mr. Shirazi's story is valuable not merely as evidence of the incoherence and fragmentation of state practices, but his example teaches us that there are important tensions between the two modalities for understanding the challenges raised by the occult sciences, which I have outlined in previous chapters: state governmental rationality on the one hand, and Islamic ethicolegal reasoning on the other.

Mr. Shirazi was a deeply pious man and keenly sensitive about the dangers of involving oneself with the occult. Few of my interlocutors demonstrated their commitment to virtuous caution as clearly as he did. Yet as a former police commander, he also enjoyed considerable power. When he exercised caution, that is, he did so from a position of strength. As I understood it, there were four ingredients to his cautious sensibility. First, he steadfastly avoided engaging in any occult practices himself. Second, he was dubious of most claims to occult power and argued that he only accepted those things he had seen with his own eyes—although he acknowledged, on the strength of his faith in Islamic doctrine, that certain extraordinary powers did exist in principle. Third, he conducted research to increase his knowledge of those individuals who claimed to possess occult powers and reflected analytically on the phenomena he had witnessed. Fourth, he exercised discretion in his experiments and only revealed them to those he held in intimate trust. On this last point, the only reason he shared his stories with me was that I was introduced to him by a close friend and former comrade from the front lines of the 1980–88 war with Iraq.

I opened our conversation by asking Mr. Shirazi to explain when a rammal normally turned into a problem for law enforcement and how the police specifically viewed such individuals. Mr. Shirazi began by arguing that a distinction needed to be made between specialist (*takhassosi*) and popular (*ʿavamaneh*) approaches to the occult:

> I don't know if you know this or not, but the sciences of geomancy and jafr are in our shariʿat. Some people trace them back to Imam ʿAli. Geomancy and jafr and the like are real and they are acceptable. The results... how do I put this, the results that can be achieved with numbers are real. Part of this is in the science of geomancy, and part of it is in jafr. As far as prayer writing is concerned, there are certain beliefs in our shariʿat. The Qurʾan itself is said to be a cure. We are told to recite various chapters in order to achieve certain results. Or people who believe in the Nur verse obtain important results from reciting it. We have to make a distinction between the specialized dimension and the popular dimension of these things. The specialist dimension pertains to people who are knowledgeable about the Qurʾan, who know the science of jafr and have studied it as a science. The criminal and judicial cases that have been opened into these matters all deal with a domain that is outside the specialized dimension. There are some people who take advantage of the pure beliefs that people have in order to make a living. They know a few things about the science of geomancy, they know part of it, and they use that to make money.

So far, as Mr. Shirazi explained, the distinction between specialized and popular hinged on three things: knowledge of the Qurʾan, the correctness of occult knowledge, and the attitude toward money. The specialist (*motekhasses*) knows the Qurʾan intimately (including its healing effects), has learned the occult sciences methodically and properly, and will not ask for financial compensation. The popular rammal who is arrested by the police does not know the Qurʾan, has not properly studied the occult sciences (even though he or she may know a few things about them), and yet takes payment for his or her services.

In Mr. Shirazi's various examples, the figure that came closest to an unambiguous image of the popular charlatan was the gypsy fortune-teller. After telling me in some detail about sociological research he had conducted for Iran's National Security Council on the criminal activities of Iranian gypsies, he recounted the following story about his meeting with a palm-reading gypsy woman in Neyshabur, near the northeastern shrine city of Mashhad:

> My family and I were visiting the tomb of Kamal al-Molk in Neyshabur. There was a gypsy palm reader there who insisted on reading my fortune. Just for fun, I said, "Fine, read my palm." She took a look at me and said, "Velvet-mustache [*sibil makhmali*]! I see something written on the forehead of one of your children [that is, she had seen something in the child's fate]." My wife and children were there with me. I had done this only for laughs. But then I saw that my wife was starting to believe it! I told her, "Look, they understand some things based on our appearance. They may say four things that are correct and a lot of things that are incorrect. Why do you see only the things that are correct and ignore the ones that are incorrect? Sometimes the fortune-tellers are able to discern things based on their prior knowledge. For example, they might say, 'I see a sadness in your face.' Well, if the person is sad, it's possible that there will be some visible trace of it in his face."

As Mr. Shirazi explained, the gypsy woman had no knowledge of geomancy or jafr but was able to read people's fortunes by recourse to her social intelligence and by interpreting cues from her customers. On the other hand, even partial knowledge of geomancy and jafr could go a long way. "With just a little bit of knowledge of geomancy," he continued, a person who has no prior knowledge of one's background can discover the number of one's siblings, one's marital status, the number of one's children, and their genders. But the rammal of imperfect knowledge goes on to use this partial information to dupe his customers and cause major family problems, for example, by telling a woman that "'your husband's eyes are seeking after another woman,' when really all the man has been doing is to visit his mother's house without telling his wife about it." In addition to this, Mr. Shirazi told me that rammals have encouraged the spread of corruption and prostitution (*fesad va fahsha*). "In Qom, for example," he said, "a lot of women have been duped, robbed, and humiliated by getting dragged into shameful things." To summarize, he told me:

> People use numerous tricks, immoral methods, sleights, and ruses in order to deceive. The boundary is that the person who really knows the sciences of geomancy and jafr is not up to the business of rammali and taking money. The person who really knows sorcery is not up to the business of destroying people's lives. The person who is really immersed in mysticism does not play these kinds of games. The person who has attained these matters keeps them to himself so that it is not known about him until after he dies.

So how is one to distinguish between the specialized and the popular? According to Mr. Shirazi, it has not been possible to properly delineate the two in society, because "it's not such an easy task to make a distinction." Sure, one can point out the rapist rammal as the ideal charlatan and the spiritually elevated mystic as the ideal possessor of occult knowledge. But between these two lies a vast chasm of ambiguity, where, as Mr. Shirazi put it, "it has all become mixed up, so that it's difficult for people to distinguish one from another. They see one thing that works, and they start believing in the person."

Perhaps it is in navigating this very ambiguity, this difficulty in distinguishing the specialist from the charlatan, that the prudent, rational man can set himself apart from the ostensibly gullible superstitious women who are the objects of so much anxiety. In Mr. Shirazi's own account of his encounter with the gypsy palm reader, we see him emerge as the wise and incredulous one, who, even while having fun with the gypsy, has to upbraid his impressionable wife for believing her lies. And yet, Mr. Shirazi admitted with exasperation, "I am like that too." That is, he, too, found it difficult to distinguish. He, too, had "believed" when he had seen things that "worked."

As it turned out, his stories about such problematic cases outnumbered both the definitively true and the unambiguously fraudulent. One of his encounters involved Shaykh Yazdi, the rammal we met in chapter 6. Mr. Shirazi introduced him as an "undisputed master of geomancy and jafr." He said he "believed partly in his knowledge" because "I've seen that he can give you information using geomancy; he can read information about your life circumstances, and even give you information about the future." He thought that it was the specialist knowledge of genuine rammals like Shaykh Yazdi that had made it possible for charlatans to take advantage of people for their own greed.

Mr. Shirazi had much respect for Shaykh Yazdi. He called his cell phone to introduce us to him and to ask if the three of us could visit him later on. When we met for the first time, I saw Mr. Shirazi extend the kind of humble courtesy to Shaykh Yazdi—who was more than a decade his junior—that many pious Iranians show the clergy. Yet as we saw, Shaykh Yazdi was a rammal who was both denigrated in the press and ridiculed in private. Mr. Shirazi knew of the legal actions against him. He did not elaborate on the specifics in our conversation, but he did mention that he thought the primary cause of his prosecution had been the steady growth of his following, so that at one point he had had more than a hundred visitors in a single day. "The Intelligence Ministry," he explained, "is against *morid va morad-bazi* [that is, the establishment of publicly visible Sufi-type relations of master and disciple] and they will try to stop it at every stage." He likely also knew that Shaykh Yazdi bragged about deploying sorcery against his enemies, as in his account of binding the mayor of Qom so that he could no longer urinate (the rammal told Mehdi and me this story in a later meeting when Mr. Shirazi was not present). In either case, he could not have easily fit the figure of the specialist Mr. Shirazi had in mind. Perhaps this is why he told me that he only "partly" believed in Shaykh Yazdi's knowledge of the occult.

The difficulty that even a man of such power and prestige as Mr. Shirazi would face in distinguishing true geomancy from charlatanry, legitimate from illegitimate practice, most likely informs the overarching government policy of confronting occult specialists when they become publicly visible. As clear-cut distinctions cannot be made, it is thought best to eliminate situations in which people are called to make such distinctions. When people themselves cannot be trusted to be cautious, the state proceeds to create a safe environment for them. "These are realities of our society," Mr. Shirazi told me, "and when one of these people acts openly [*'alani*], the police confront it."

As Shaykh Yazdi's prosecution shows, police occasionally confront people whom they themselves may consider to be knowledgeable in the occult sciences. Mr. Shirazi had other experiences to indicate that such tensions are common. About a decade earlier, while he was chief of police of a small town near Tehran, Mr. Shirazi's forces had raided the house of a certain elderly Sayyed Hasan, an occult specialist who "possessed jinn." "He had books dealing with jinn possession," Mr. Shirazi told me, "and the police confiscated them after holding him for a few hours." Some weeks later, one of Mr. Shirazi's friends had sought police assistance in finding his stolen car:

> Police couldn't locate the thieves. My friend insisted that "now that the police can't do anything, let's ask Sayyed Hasan for help." People had gotten results with Sayyed Hasan, and my friend knew it. I finally said, "Okay, fine, let's go." There was a time when I didn't believe in any of these things. I rejected all of them absolutely. But today I don't think this way, because of certain things that I've come across. So we went to Sayyed Hasan. And he said, "Salam. You've taken my knowledge away. If you teach at a university, you use a book. My knowledge is in my book. If I don't have it, I can't do anything." So I said, "Well, Sayyed, why don't you try and help out this friend of mine." He gave us an address and the car was found two days later.

In a different time and place, Mr. Shirazi had himself sought the assistance of an occult specialist to solve a difficult criminal case. It was 1993 and he was chief of police of Damavand, a small city in the Alborz mountain range. One evening, an elderly goldsmith was walking home from his shop carrying a loaf of sangak bread when three men on motorbikes ambushed him. They struck him with the blunt side of an ax, took a few hundred grams of gold he had been carrying on his person, and rode off. As it happened, the goldsmith's son was Damavand's representative to the Majlis (the parliament), a certain Mr. Sa'idi, and so there was pressure from high places to solve the case as soon as possible. Mr. Shirazi described it to me like this:

> I went through hell with this case. We interrogated more than two hundred suspects in the span of a month: criminals recently released from jail, criminals from other towns and neighboring provinces. Anyone who had a criminal record, we interrogated. A month passed. Mr. Sa'idi was invited to speak at a popular mosque for the twenty-first of Ramadan. I had gone to see him imme-

diately after the robbery and had assured him that I would find the culprits. But he went to this mosque a month later and publicly announced a rumor claiming that it was his political rival from the opposing faction who was responsible. He said that his father's gold had not been worth the theft. The thieves wanted to intimidate the goldsmith's son. The issue became political and the governor of the province ordered that I couldn't leave town until I solved the case. The MP, Mr. Sa'idi, had a lot of friends in the Rafsanjani government, and it reached a point where all kinds of politicians and security officials would be calling me asking for updates on the case. So I was under all this stress and didn't know what to do.

When the suspects failed to turn up through ordinary investigative procedures, Mr. Shirazi decided that he would try to enlist the help of someone with occult skills:

I called my three deputies for intelligence, criminal investigations, and traffic into my office. I placed a Qur'an in the center of the table, and I asked them to swear by the book that no matter what I did, they would not say anything to anyone. No information would ever leave that room. Then I asked my deputy for criminal investigations, "Do you know of a rammal or a sayyed who can help us?" And you won't believe me when I tell you that I did not believe in this stuff at all back then. I rejected it all. He said, "Let me see what I can do." There was an old mystic he knew who had given him good information in the past. He went to see him, but the mystic insisted that "You can't tell Mr. Shirazi who I am or where I live." My deputy then told me that the mystic had said that one of the thieves was in Tonekabon, one in Qazvin, and one in Shahriyar. He gave physical descriptions, three first names, and a few more details. He also said that the thief in Shahriyar had a criminal record. We would've required a judicial warrant to arrest him since he was in a different city. But I was under so much pressure that I dispatched my men to arrest him without a warrant. So they brought him in. We threatened that if he refused to cooperate, we would hand him over to the Tehran investigations bureau. He was deathly afraid of Tehran, so he told us the name and whereabouts of one of his accomplices. We arrested the second person, and he gave us information on the third. The file was complete exactly on a Thursday. I had postponed my deadline for solving the case to Friday, saying that I would resign if I had not found the thieves by then. By Friday morning I had a taped confession from the thieves.

The case continued to puzzle Mr. Shirazi, not only because it was a strange story in itself, but because it disturbed his sense of the boundary between true and false, legitimate and illegitimate appeals to the occult:

I did not believe in these things. I never thought we would be able to solve the case so easily. But he gave us the addresses and the information we needed to make arrests. People like this mystic and others have attained certain realities through ascetic practice. They have the ability to help people. But at the same time, their existence is cause for some people going astray. How do they go astray? Because everyone thinks that whoever has a long white beard and says certain things can help them out. There are things that we believe in, as Shiʿa. We appeal to the imams for help and we have all these prayers. But then, alongside the great mystics, other people emerge who take advantage of people. And how can one explain the boundaries to people? I don't know.

Mr. Shirazi did not know how distinctions between the true mystic and the charlatan could be explained to ordinary people. But that did not mean that he himself could not make appropriate distinctions in practical situations. As his examples show, he proceeded with skepticism and discretion, ready to explain away the ruses of charlatans but remaining open to the possibility that he was in the presence of true occult knowledge and power.

Looking back on my interview with Mr. Shirazi, I suspect there was another element in his virtuous caution having to do with his granting the benefit of the doubt to Shaykh Yazdi the rammal. Given all the controversy around the rammal—much of which he himself seemed to invite—Mr. Shirazi had to actively look the other way to continue respecting him as a pious, selfless man with reliable knowledge of geomancy. Perhaps something in his personal experience warranted a righteous blind eye—he made an offhand remark about Shaykh Yazdi saving his daughter-in-law's life, but the situation did not allow me to probe further. Maybe his assessment of Shaykh Yazdi was not so much based on the latter's current moral condition as one he hoped he would achieve over time. In any case, the virtue of caution in assessing another person's piety (that is, granting them the benefit of the doubt and turning a blind eye to their errors) is at cross-purposes with the necessary prudence with which the pious are called to evaluate their trust in another's occult knowledge. In the end, Mr. Shirazi may have been duped in spite of himself.

What gives caution its stamp of pious virtue? For Mr. Shirazi, the cautious sensibility was shot through with utterances and practices organized by a larger concern with responsibility and commitment to God. For some of my interlocutors, caution was mostly reactive, an attempt to conserve what they already had in security, health, and sanity. Mr. Shirazi's caution was proactive, attempting to develop an orientation to the occult sciences that was not merely harmless but sound when measured against the metrics of Islamic tradition. Hence, his virtuous caution required him not only to suspect that most claimants to the occult were charlatans but also that some of them may be authentic. In this we could see him as a follower of Ayatollah Khomeini, who, as I mentioned in chapter 2, declared that "[o]ne who rejects or accepts something without clear reason cannot be counted among the rational and the pious." Similarly, his caution was not only expressed through disdain for the impieties of most rammals encountered by ordinary people but also the blind eye he turned to the extravagant and blatantly impious utterances of Sayyed Yazdi.

Suspicion and openness, revulsion and forgiveness: These are, at face value, contradictory orientations. Caution is one modality through which they may be reconciled and sustained while navigating a complex terrain like that of the occult. Perhaps Mr. Shirazi was in the end an unsuccessful navigator. But his failure—if it was that—only reinforces the importance of caution from within a pious orientation to the world, highlighting as it does the many pitfalls that threaten even those most committed to maintaining a cautious disposition while experimenting with the metaphysical.

For those metaphysical experimenters who do not find themselves similarly compelled by the call to live life as virtuous Muslims, caution may play a much less significant role. There are other ways, however, to develop an appropriately rational orientation toward the metaphysical, one that takes stock of the uncanny disorientations provoked by the rammal. Playful nonseriousness is one such orientation. Rather than representing a retreat from or suspension of reason, playfulness is based on a reflexive recognition of the limits of one's understanding and a compartmentalization of the putatively metaphysical as something thrilling, wondrous, or aesthetically pleasing. Chapters 8 and 9 examine this sensibility and the pleasures that it enables in metaphysical encounters.

METAPHYSICAL PLEASURES

The orientations toward the metaphysical I have discussed thus far have been partly constituted by judgments of truth or falsity: Do such metaphysical entities as jinn and forces like sorcery exist? Is this specific person who claims to wield occult power a charlatan? As we have seen, simple answers to these questions were mostly the stuff of public ideological discourse, such as what appeared in media denunciations of rammals. Those who had direct encounters with the ostensible metaphysical were rarely so certain. And yet their uncertainty in no way diminished the urgency of their questions.

That these questions were characterized by such urgency largely had to do with the seriousness of the problems for which those we have encountered thus far sought metaphysical solutions. Nafiseh was trying to rid herself of an obstinate suitor. Shaykh Yazdi's petitioners were grappling with complicated family problems. General Shirazi needed to solve a sensitive criminal case. But not everyone appeals to occult professionals with such seriousness, and some of those who begin seriously do not necessarily sustain their seriousness throughout the length of their encounter. As Mehdi remarked to me when commenting on Shaykh Yazdi the rammal, for some howzeh students, the occult sciences are a form of entertainment akin to smoking and sex. Mehdi told me this by way of ridiculing Shaykh Yazdi's self-seriousness and the weight he attached to his knowledge and spiritual stature. But Mehdi's words also drew attention to the pleasures of metaphysical experimentation. To study occult practices in terms of the pleasures they offer would be to move beyond the confinement of judgments of truth or falsity and into the domain of leisure and play. As we will see in chapter 9, judgments of truth or falsity may indeed have something to do with pleasure, but this pleasure often depends precisely on these questions' irresolution.

I begin by examining metaphysical pleasure arising from wonder and astonishment, drawing on the way these emotions, typically known through the concepts of *'ajab* and *ta'ajjub*, have been understood in the premodern Islamic tradition. I do not want to suggest that contemporary expressions of wonder are exactly the same as their expressions before modernity. Premodern formulations do, however, provide a useful model to think with analogically. This is because, first, premodern wonder has been richly elaborated in a fashion that is nonexistent in the contemporary period. Second, the relationship between truth and the fictive, knowledge and entertainment, vexed medieval thinkers in productive ways that can help us ask more nuanced questions of modern metaphysical experimentation, even if the answers we provide are not the same as those given by premodern thinkers.

After discussing wonder, I move on to explore the pleasures of contemporary aesthetic and literary consumption. As we will see, these pleasures are enabled by a trend toward subordinating the metaphysical to a set of secular sensibilities governing the appreciation of literature, cinema, graphic arts, and fashion. Wonder in the premodern sense is no longer operative here. But as the example of the reception of Hollywood fantasy and science fiction will show, even this apparent disenchantment is not without ambivalence.

Those who denounce appeals to rammals as superstitious generally presuppose that such appeals issue from ignorant and credulous minds. *Khorafeh*, the contemporary word for superstition in Persian and Arabic (*khurafa*), shares the root kh-r-f with the Arabic words for senility (*kharaf*) and a young sheep (*kharuf*). But a different sense of the word *khorafeh*, largely forgotten among Persian speakers today, allows us to think of the encounter with the rammal as something more than the action of a feeble imbecile. This is khorafeh as legend, fable, or delightful tale.[1] If the purportedly unreasonable and fantastic may be deployed for entertainment, then the sentiments and dispositions proper to it cannot be adequately captured by judgments of reason and unreason. One does not have to be credulous to be entertained.[2]

In the premodern world, khurafa could refer to any false but pleasing story meant for entertainment, but it usually described tales with outrageous, fantastical elements. A fascinating origin myth for this concept exists in the form of a hadith about the prophet Muhammad. Widely considered a weak hadith, it has been variously cited in classical Arabic and Persian dictionaries under the definition of khurafa. In it, the Prophet identifies Khurafa as a righteous man he knew personally who was abducted by the jinn but survived to tell marvelous stories about them. His people were astonished at his stories and called him a liar, giving birth to the construction *hadith khurafa* or "khurafa story," which was later applied (or so the account goes) to other similarly incredible tales. In some versions, as, for example, in the *Lisan al-ʿArab* dictionary of Arabic, the Prophet confirms that what Khurafa had recounted of the jinn was true (*haqq*). ʿAli Akbar Dehkhoda's encyclopedic dictionary of Persian presents the story as follows:

> [Khurafa is] the name of a jinn-possessed man from the tribe of ʿUdhra who recounted what he had seen of the jinn. People disbelieved him and considered [his words to be] false. They would say: This is khurafa speech, which is false but pleasant speech… His name is not listed among the Prophet's companions; it has only been said that [the Prophet's wife] ʿAyisha recounted his story from the Prophet, who one day said: "He was a righteous man who left me one night

only to be attacked and taken captive by three jinn. One of them wanted to kill him. The other wanted to imprison him. The third said it would be best to release him. Then a man came upon the jinn," and the story goes on. Others have told the story of Khurafa differently, saying that once the Prophet was relating a story to his wives and family. One of them said: "This is khurafa speech." The Prophet responded: "You do not know Khurafa. He was a man from the ʿUdhra who spent some time in the captivity of jinn and told many stories about them."

A much more detailed account of Khurafa's adventure appears in the *al-Fakhir* of al-Mufaddal ibn Salama (d. 903) and other later sources.[3] In this story, as the three jinn contemplate their captive's fate, three men chance upon them one after another. Upon learning of Khurafa's plight, each of the three men asks the jinn if they would make him a partner in deciding what to do with the captive if he (each of the three visitors) were to tell them a strange and astonishing story. The jinn agree, and each man recounts a story more astonishing than the one before. With all three men thus made partners, the jinn agree to release Khurafa and allow him to return to his people.

The themes of wonder and the lifesaving value of storytelling in this anthropomorphized origin tale of Khurafa are also common to the *One Thousand and One Nights*. Almost a century ago, D. B. MacDonald showed that the Khurafa story was extremely similar to the first tale recounted by Shahrazad in the *Nights*—"The Merchant and the Jinn"—so much so that there is speculation that the hadith was either directly influenced by the *Nights* or they both drew on a shared source.[4] But how are we to understand wonder, and what does it have to do with the appreciation of a fabulous story, let alone the encounter with a rammal?

In the Islamic scholastic tradition, ʿajab and taʿajjub were understood as states of a person's soul—what we might today call a psychological state or emotion—when he or she could not understand the cause (*sabab*) of something.[5] In his well-known book of definitions, ʿAli ibn Muhammad Jurjani (d. 1413) defined ʿajab as "the change of the *nafs* [spirit or soul] through something the cause of which is unknown and goes out of the ordinary."[6] Premodern literature is replete with descriptions of extraordinary things that inspire wonder: delicacies like the dates of Basra, the intricate anatomy of a bee, manmade instruments and monuments, celestial phenomena, angels, strange faraway climes, monstrous races, talismans, jinn, and so on.[7] As these examples show, the "extraordinary" as conceived in this literature was by no means limited to what we might today deem supernatural or fantastic but also dealt with everyday objects, phenomena, and events that authors considered remarkable in some way.

Wonder and astonishment were sometimes understood as ethical states to be cultivated for the purpose of appreciating the oneness and transcendence of God.[8] In the Qur'an, words with the root ʿ-j-b often indicate wonder-inspiring signs of God, whether in the form of divine actions or marvelous creations.[9] In the genre of texts known as "wonders of creation" (ʿajaʾib al-makhluqat), authors drew their readers' attention to beings both familiar and strange to instill an intellectual understanding of created order and induce awe in the magnificent and intricate design of God's cosmos.[10] The path to experiencing awe in divine majesty, however, did not exclude aesthetic appreciation and delight—the latter was often conceived as a necessary step for attaining the former. Illustrated manuscripts emphasized this aesthetic dimension with their use of rich imagery.[11] But even in their prose, authors were very much conscious of the pleasures of reading about wondrous reality and appealed to these pleasures to full effect.[12]

The authors of wonders of creation texts were aware that some of the things they wrote about stretched credulity. That they still included such accounts—of dog-headed men and plant-animal hybrids, for example—suggests that they viewed literary entertainment as more than just a means to the end of instilling awe in divine grandeur. While veracity was certainly a concern, they could find various ways to justify the inclusion of even the most dubious-sounding reports.[13] That is, they viewed perplexity and wonder as legitimate sources of delight even when concerning things that they admitted were perhaps no more than imaginary.

The pleasures of wonder in the obviously fictive are much more pronounced in the case of stories like those of the One Thousand and One Nights, which were never understood as true in the sense of representing real historical events. Roy Mottahedeh has argued that in the world of the Nights, these pleasures arise from a nexus of astonishment and patience, which together generate what might be understood as literary suspense:

> The encounter with things and events, the sabab or reason for which is unknown, creates suspense; and it is the promise that things more astonishing and strange, aʿjab and aghrab, lie ahead that sustains suspense... [Patience] to control oneself emerges as partly cognate in meaning with suspense itself. [It] is the quality that should sustain us between the appearance of astonishing things and their explanation.[14]

The moral injunction to wait in patience for an explanation of an astonishing event or for a story yet stranger than the one just told is central to the frame story of the Nights, in which the king holds off on having Shahrazad killed so that she can finish her stories. It also appears in many of the tales within the frame story, including that of "The Merchant and the Jinn," which is paralleled, as we saw above, in the prophetic hadith about Khurafa. At the end of that particular tale, the jinn who is holding the merchant hostage hears the third and last shaykh's story and is so astonished that he falls into ecstasy: "So the [jinn] was astonished to the utmost limit of astonishment, and shook with ecstasy [*ihtazza min al-tarab*]."[15] His patience thus rewarded, he agrees to free the merchant whose life hung in the balance.

Pleasure in literary accounts of the strange and fantastical had its counterpart in the delights of medieval street performances. Historians of Islamicate civilization have long acknowledged the existence of a host of colorful figures in the Middle Ages who lived on the lower rungs of Muslim society and scrounged a living by storytelling, begging, conning, stealing, or by entertaining the public and selling them their services as quack doctors, mountebanks, astrologers, exorcists, and amulet makers.[16] Stefan Wild has shown that the same men who sold amulets, remedies, and prognostications in public also performed entertainments and demonstrated extraordinary feats to convince their would-be customers of their supernatural powers.[17] He quotes al-Jawbari, the debunker of frauds, for example, explaining the trick of a juggler who would blindfold himself and guess the secrets of his audience through a code communicated by his assistant, a routine that still exists in magic shows around the world.

From what we know of the Islamic occult tradition, entertainments like jugglery, illusions, and sleight-of-hand tricks were often classified as occult sciences alongside astrology, alchemy, and talismanic magic. This is illustrated nicely in the popular occult manual *Asrar-e Qasemi* (Secrets of Qasem) authored by the prolific fifteenth-century moralist and exegete Hoseyn Va'ez Kashefi (d. 1504/1505), a book that continues to circulate among occult enthusiasts to this day. One of Kashefi's five categories of occult science, *simiya*, is "the science of illusions" (*'elm-e khiyalat*) with which imaginations are manipulated "to create imaginary appearances that have no external existence."[18] Its procedures include manipulations of bones, ashes, and inks; the control of jinn; the deployment of talismans and magic formulas; and invocations addressed to the stars.[19] A master of simiya can change his appearance, make himself invisible, appear to be engulfed in flames, or seem to levitate, fly, or walk on water. He can, moreover, make the sun disappear during the day and make it appear during the night, or create the appearance of leaves on a dried-up tree, or lightning, rain, and snow in the sky.

Another category of occult science in Kashefi's book is *rimiya*, the science of jugglery or prestidigitation (*sha'badat*), which consists of "knowing the forces of earthly essences and combining them to produce strange effects."[20] As with simiya, we are dealing here with appearances and psychological manipulations, although the forces harnessed in rimiya are earthly and natural, as opposed to the subtle and spiritual forces of the more powerful simiya.[21] The practitioner of rimiya is able to induce artificial laughter or weeping, put people to sleep, or make women dance. He can transform the appearances of people in a room to look like angels, donkeys, or camels, and to perform other feats that amuse and impress.

Some street entertainments directly trafficked with literary wonder. Al-Jawbari provides an example that he says he personally witnessed in Harran—now in southern Turkey—in the year 613 AH (1217 CE).[22] There he says he saw a performer who had trained an ape to behave like a refined human and had clothed him in princely attire. A group of Indian slaves escorted the ape to the central mosque where he greeted the people and proceeded to brush his teeth, pray, and thumb a rosary. A slave then explained that his master, the ape, was the son of a king in India and had been married to the daughter of another king. They had lived together for a while until rumors reached the princess that her husband was involved in an affair with a slave boy. The couple quarreled until the princess departed to stay with her family and bewitched her husband, transforming him into the ape he was now. The prince's father banished him from his land for fear of humiliation. Meanwhile, his wife agreed to lift the spell in return for an enormous ransom. The ape was thus reduced to touring the earth in hopes that kings and commoners would pity him and help him raise the funds he needed to return to his human form. Al-Jawbari then tells us that the ape began to weep, melting people's hearts and moving them to donate large sums to the fraudsters.

The story of the prince who became an ape is mirrored in its outline by the "Second Dervish's Tale," which is part of the "Story of the Porter and the Three Ladies" in the *One Thousand and One Nights*.[23] There also, a prince is punished for an amorous affair by being transformed into an ape. His punisher is not his wife, however, but a murderous jinn meting out revenge on the prince for sleeping with his mistress. In this story, too, the ape-prince is described as humanlike in his behavior (he wins the protection of a ship captain with his weeping) and immensely cultivated and learned (he impresses a king with his knowledge of poetry and chess). While we cannot know for certain, it is likely that the street performers al-Jawbari met were appealing to sensibilities for appreciating wonder that were similar to those involved in reading or listening to stories from the *Nights*.

Let me turn now to a brief discussion of modern metaphysical pleasure. The literary heirs of the *One Thousand and One Nights* in contemporary Iran include European and American fantasy and science fiction texts, from J.R.R. Tolkien to J. K. Rowling, Jules Verne to Isaac Asimov. Magical realism also has a following, with representatives like Italo Calvino, Gabriel García Márquez, Paulo Coelho, and a number of prominent Iranian novelists: Gholam Hoseyn Sa'edi, Reza Baraheni, Moniru Ravanipur, and Shahrnush Parsipur, among others. My anecdotal sense from speaking with readers and consulting book reviews is that these authors' works are read much the same way that people commonly read novels in the United States. That is, fabulous and fantastical elements are either taken as symbolic or read in a mode of suspension of disbelief. Not all literature has been treated this way, however. In the mid-twentieth century, for example, some magazines translated and serialized ghost stories just as urban Iranians were experimenting with séances with the souls of the dead.[24] The magazine stories were read for entertainment, and many people participated in séances for fun. But this did not require them to disbelieve in ghosts, which meant that "suspending" disbelief may have been superfluous. Some séance participants entertained the possibility that a form of spiritual presence may be involved. Others became committed Spiritists.

In terms of popular reach, the more rightful heirs for the *Nights* would have to be Hollywood fantasy, science fiction, and supernatural horror. My interlocutors regularly spoke of *The Matrix*, *The Lord of the Rings*, *Harry Potter*, *Constantine*, *The Exorcist*, and many other films. They had seen some of these dubbed into Persian on national television or in movie theaters, and others in English on bootleg VHS, VCDs, and DVDs. Most viewers took these films as fictional products of the imagination. But among occult enthusiasts, I commonly heard filmic references as more than just objects of entertainment, although they were that too. Some viewed Hollywood depictions of supernatural creatures like demons and orcs as accurate representations of jinn, which they argued could only have been inspired by real-world encounters with these beings. To others, supernatural cinema provided imaginative resources with which to conceptualize aspects of their own spiritual experiments—something that we saw in Nafiseh's invocation of *The Matrix* in the opening of part 1.[25] This latter orientation is paralleled in efforts by some Iranian filmmakers and critics to develop a globally attuned "spiritual cinema" (*sinama-ye ma'nagara*) with which to not only depict but also promote particular spiritual values and experiences.[26]

I will conclude with a few words about graphic arts and fashion. One of the most prominent Iranian artistic movements to emerge in the past half century is what has come to be known as the Saqqakhaneh movement. Named after public water reservoirs dedicated to saints and martyrs, Saqqakhaneh art is distinguished by its appropriation and abstraction of popular religious imagery and objects of daily ritual use—calligraphy, zodiac signs, astrolabes, locks, amulets, talismans, and so on. The artists associated with this movement have been widely praised as the first successful modernists for understanding Western art history and engaging with its stylistic innovations, while employing a recognizably local visual language.[27] But as Anna Hazard points out, there is a class-based distancing involved in Saqqakhaneh appropriations of local imagery, where objects and images produced and used by a lower social class are relegated to a "primitive" or superseded past that can be discovered or excavated for modern aesthetic and folkloric appreciation.[28]

This orientation is clearly evident in a book titled *Talisman: Iran's Traditional Graphic Art* (*Telesm: Gerafik-e Sonnati-ye Iran*), first published in 2006 by Parviz Tanavoli, a sculptor, collector, and Saqqakhaneh pioneer. *Talisman* inaugurates a series on "Forgotten Arts" that now includes a book on locks, one on kohl vessels, and another on scales and weights. Featuring 170 full-color and black-and-white images, the book provides an excellent overview of the occult sciences in Iran, its lettrist and numerological foundations, the astrological calendar, various techniques for making amulets and talismans, and the myriad objects (rings, pendants, shirts, bowls, mirrors, locks, prints, and so on) constructed to bring good fortune, avert evil, and cure illness.

Tanavoli's discussion of these objects is shot through with nostalgia. He begins by describing his childhood recollections of curative magical practices by his mother and her neighborhood friends, as well as their consultations with itinerant rammals who performed divinations and sold them amulets, talismans, and magical recipes. These early encounters, he says, instilled a sense of wonder in him at the materiality and aesthetic qualities of magical implements, which he later amplified and honed with the cultivated sensibilities of an artist and collector. He writes that "These rammals' metallic tools and the writings and shapes that they drew in purple ink on paper bewitched me so much that I was willing to give half of my life to own those tools, writings, and shapes."[29] Further on, Tanavoli makes this surprising assertion:

> Nothing remains anymore of that rich culture. Those prayer writers and rammals are long [gone] without any heirs or replacements, but there are relics of these people left as mementos. These relics are not only an important part of Iran's visual arts, they also conceal wishes and dreams. Many mothers attached their hearts to these relics in hopes of curing their children, and many wives resorted to these objects for fear of losing their husbands. Many lovers found their way to their beloveds through these hand-made implements, and many men relied on them to carry out profitable transactions.[30]

The task of Tanavoli's book, then, is twofold. On the one hand, he wants to draw attention to talismanic arts as the "fountainhead of Iran's graphic arts."[31] On the other hand, he aims to record a history and culture threatened by obscurity, as "indifference to a superstitious past and attempts to conceal it will not change anything other than to consign a part of our past culture and the mentalities of our ancestors to oblivion."[32] Tanavoli even finds things to salvage in Iranians' supposedly archaic occult practices beyond their aesthetic accomplishments, including "teaching primary mathematical operations to novices," enabling leisure and calm through repetition, stimulating the brain, encouraging cleanliness and discipline, and strengthening self-confidence.[33]

The Saqqakhaneh artists' fascination with the aesthetics of talismanic imagery and its evocation of an archaic and mysterious past has recently expanded beyond avant-garde art circles and made a mark on women's fashion. Shirts, scarves, shawls, and robes with talismanic motifs and elements of Qajar-era paintings came into vogue not long before the time of this writing.[34] Jewelry incorporating amuletic and talismanic forms also became fashionable. I first noticed such jewelry marketed by Iranian diasporic designers on peer-to-peer e-commerce websites like alangoo.com, but later found out that similar designs were popular within Iran as well (something that is unsurprising given the speed by which images, objects, and their associated tastes and sensibilities circulate between Iran and other locales).

What is particularly significant about talismanic jewelry is its repurposing of mostly concealed implements worn for protection and good fortune into mostly visible ornaments worn for aesthetic delight and as signifiers of good taste. The few women among my interlocutors who had adopted such jewelry as ornamental objects indicated that they were unconcerned about any potential metaphysical quality to them. But just as Hollywood films and published ghost stories may be approached with more than one sensibility, it is possible that such jewelry will also provoke complex or ambivalent feelings (even though I have no evidence that this is the case). We already have a precedent in traditional men's jewelry, such as agate and turquoise rings that are thought to bring spiritual benefits but are also pleasing to the eyes and form an important part of pious men's sartorial self-fashioning.[35]

I have shown that metaphysical pleasures are rooted in multiple sensibilities, which include literary and aesthetic delight as well as wonder and astonishment in the face of the inexplicable. Each of these sensibilities provides rationalized pathways for approaching the metaphysical that do not require one to answer questions of truth or falsity. In chapter 9, I examine a detailed account of a dramatic meeting with a rammal to ask how such sensibilities may combine with skeptical empirical inquiry to produce a thrilling experience.

9

THE FANTASTIC

"So what was the story of the dining cloth?" I asked Shokufeh, as we drove to the house of Haj Aqa Yusefi the rammal. I was referring to the procedure called *sofreh andakhtan* (spreading out a dining cloth), through which an occult specialist calls forth the jinn he controls in order to ascertain whether a particular customer has been bewitched. Shokufeh had gone to one such specialist about a year earlier to consult him about suspicious Hebrew-like markings she had discovered on the ceiling of her living room, which she was told may have been sorcery.

I first met Shokufeh through a mutual acquaintance at the University of Tehran. She was around thirty-four, had recently divorced, and lived on her own. She had a master's degree in English literature and was applying for doctoral programs abroad, while teaching half-time at a large English-language instruction institute and occasionally working as a private tutor for advanced high school students studying for university entry exams. She was successful at her work and supported herself financially. She owned a small apartment and an Iranian-manufactured Peugeot 206, which, as I learned that day, she drove with reckless speed in Tehran's congested streets.

Shokufeh had noticed the strange markings on her ceiling soon after her divorce. "They looked as though they had been etched with a matchstick into the plaster around the chandelier," she told me. Mildly concerned and curious to get to the bottom of the issue, she invited a few friends over to take a look. One friend suggested it was just the trace of an ant crawling across the plaster before it had fully dried. "This was not likely," she said, "unless the ant had danced its way coquettishly all around the chandelier." The owner of the apartment complex, who lived upstairs, said that he hadn't seen anything like these markings in any of the other apartments. Her mother weighed in with the idea that it was some kind of sorcery. Another female friend agreed and suggested that Shokufeh visit Haj Aqa Yusefi, a rammal who could figure out whether she had been bewitched and void the sorcery if necessary.

Shokufeh had resisted at first. "I don't believe in sorcery," she told her friend. "And when there is God, what can anyone else do for me?" But her friend insisted and she finally gave in. As it turned out, the rammal was not keen on meeting Shokufeh either. The first time she called Yusefi, he told her that he would be away for a forty-day spiritual retreat and she should contact him after that. In later phone calls he shrugged her off with other excuses, giving the impression that he wanted to avoid her—or perhaps he wanted to make sure she was serious before making time for her in his busy schedule. Frustrated, Shokufeh told him that she didn't believe in jinn or sorcery but she wanted to give him a try. In any case, she would only see him if God wanted it and this was the last time she would call. Yusefi told her to come to his house on the northeastern fringe of Tehran the next day.

"When we met, he asked me my name and my mother's name," Shokufeh told me. "When I told him, he said that someone had bewitched me. I said that I had found those markings on the ceiling and I had only been slightly preoccupied by them. So he said he could spread out a dining cloth to check things out if I wanted. I agreed." "What did he do exactly?" I asked. "He spread out one of these brown bedsheets on the ground, and then he took a really big *tasbih* [rosary], one of those with the giant beads, and he put it around me. Then he brought a copper pot filled with water and placed it in front of me." "On top of the sheet?" I asked. "Yes, on the sheet in front of me. He was sitting on the other end. Then there was a lid, kind of like a copper skillet, that he overturned and put on top of the pot, to cover it. And he also brought a knife with an antique-looking handle, and a small traditional-looking salt container. He put both of them there." Shokufeh was beaming as she continued: "He recited some abracadabra [*ajji majji*] and then he told me to take some salt, to repeat everything he said after him, and to deposit the salt into the pot without looking inside. Then he said something like, 'By Moses and Jesus, by Noah and—something like—the Psalms of Abraham...'" "You mean the Psalms of David," I offered. "Yes, 'by the Psalms of David, and by the Qur'an of Muhammad: Find her sorcery; Make it appear; Void it' [*peyda kon, zaher kon, batel kon*]. As I poured the salt, he murmured some other things and then he told me to recite the *salavat* ten times.[1] I was then to lift the lid only enough to slide the blade of the knife inside and stir the pot. But I wasn't supposed to look inside. He told me to look straight at him and nowhere else as I stirred. So I stirred." Shokufeh's voice now changed to a deliberate lower-pitched quiver while she continued to speak with a wide smile, as though she were reenacting the fright and excitement of the experience: "I was stirring, and then I felt the water get heavy. I felt that something was clanging against the knife in the pot. I told him that it was getting heavy. But he told me to keep stirring. I stirred some more until he told me it was enough. He asked me to remove the lid and to put it to one side with the knife. I looked inside the pot and saw that the water had become muddied. And there was some colored woven string and some Kleenex sticking out. I thought that was all that was there. I thought probably the salt had somehow turned to mud. But when I saw the colored string I became frightened. So he told me: 'Now take out whatever you see.' 'But I'm frightened, Haj Aqa,' I said, 'I can't!' He told me not to be afraid: 'Take out whatever you see, shake off the water, and put it to one side.' So I dipped my hand inside and took out the crumpled, wet Kleenex. I squeezed the water out and put it to one side. I dipped my hand inside again and this time took out two locks, an open lock and a closed lock. I thought that was the end of it, but he told me there was more. So I dipped in again and took out five metallic plates, one of them white and in the shape of a pear, the rest of them dark gray squares. They were all covered with lines, shapes, and other markings. I asked him if I could take the plates home with me to show my dad. He said no. So I asked if I could at least take a picture of the plates to show my dad so he'd know I had really seen these things. But he wouldn't let me. That was it. It was really scary though."

I asked Shokufeh if the sorcery had been voided through this operation. She said Yusefi told her that he would have to void it later. "But he said if you want I can give you an amulet [*ta'viz*], an agate stone, to protect you from sorcery. He said he had different kinds, with one movakkel, two movakkels, or three movakkels, at different prices.[2] I said, 'Haj Aqa, I really absolutely don't believe in any of this stuff. But maybe this is really just a kind of consolation [*delgarmi*].' He said, 'If you want to feel assured, I can give you one of these amulets. All you have to do is read the *am man yujib* prayer over it ten times and it'll do whatever you want it to do.'[3] So I thought to myself, 'I've already doled out the cash, I might as well get this too. It sounds interesting.' So he took out an old-style pouch that was full of these agate stones. He picked one out and gave it to me. He asked my name and my mother's name and recited some prayer over it and told me that a movakkel would always be with me from now on." Shokufeh was close to laughter again. "But you know what, Alireza? The only benefit I've derived from this Mr. or Mrs. Movakkel [the jinn] is that it's a fantastic park-guard [*parkban*]. Whenever I've needed parking and haven't been able to find a spot, I've recited ten *am man yujibs* over the stone. And I swear by the Qur'an, it finds me parking spots that I couldn't even imagine! This has happened at least ten times, I can swear by my mother's life!" "How much did he charge you?" I asked. "He charged me two hundred and fifty thousand tomans [about two hundred and fifty dollars at the time]. A hundred and fifty for the dining cloth spread, and a hundred for the agate [amulet]. But when my friend visited him from Isfahan, the scoundrel charged her four hundred thousand tomans." I whistled my surprise. "That's why I'm saying," she continued, "he'll skin you alive if he gets the impression that you'll pay. I told him you're from Harvard, but tell him you're not going anymore. Or tell him you're unemployed so he won't think he can charge you too much. When I complained to him for charging my friend so much when I had paid much less for the same procedure, he said, 'That's because I have to do something different for her.' And how could we ever tell if what he did really was any different?"

We have seen that both men and women who visit rammals regularly express skepticism about the truth of their occult encounters. We have also seen that these expressions of skepticism and of denigrating superstition have a long pedigree both in a scholarly Islamic tradition and in a modernist discourse drawing inspiration from the European Enlightenment. Furthermore, as the discussion in chapter 8 showed, the metaphysical may become an object of wonder, aesthetic delight, and literary appreciation quite apart from any judgments of truth or falsity. This chapter argues that skepticism can be a condition of possibility for occult experimentation, as was the case in Shokufeh's encounter with the rammal Haj Aqa Yusefi. By expressing skepticism, Shokufeh not only laid claim to rationality but also opened up experiential possibilities that may have been closed off had she been more credulous. Most importantly, her skeptical inquiry made it possible for Shokufeh to be thrilled and entertained by an encounter that she could not decisively judge as either truly metaphysical or a series of well-crafted tricks.[4]

In asserting a primary commitment to rational, scientific explanations, Shokufeh was affirming the primacy of a world that does not admit sorcery.[5] This heightened and dramatized the wonder and puzzlement she felt when she experienced something that seemed to rupture the consistency of her world. To understand this puzzlement, I find it fruitful to draw on Tzvetan Todorov's notion of "the fantastic." I want to argue that the fantastic quality of the encounter with rammals is precisely what renders the experience a site of possibility.[6]

Todorov is concerned with defining fantastic literature as a genre positioned between two other literary genres, the uncanny and the marvelous. "The fantastic," he writes, "is that hesitation experienced by a person who knows only the laws of nature, confronting an apparently metaphysical event":

> The person who experiences the event must opt for one of two possible solutions: either he is the victim of an illusion of the senses, of a product of the imagination—and laws of the world then remain what they are; or else the event has indeed taken place, it is an integral part of reality—but then this reality is controlled by laws unknown to us... The fantastic occupies the duration of this uncertainty. Once we choose one answer or the other, we leave the fantastic for a neighboring genre, the uncanny or the marvelous.[7]

As with fantastic literature, a person hesitating over the nature of an apparently metaphysical encounter is implicitly affirming a distinction between that which is real and ordinary, and things that are imaginary, extraordinary, or miraculous.[8] For most of my interlocutors, everyday experience in Tehran did not admit sorcery, except in the form of a nagging hesitation.[9] Shokufeh, for example, would tell her mother and friend, "I don't believe in sorcery," even though she could not produce a rational explanation for the strange markings on her ceiling. Later, as her hesitations grew, she would tell Haj Aqa

Yusefi, "I don't believe in jinn or sorcery, but I want to give your [method] a try." Even after she had witnessed the dining cloth ritual and watched in fright as talismans, locks, and colored string mysteriously appeared in her pot, she told the rammal that "I really absolutely don't believe in any of this stuff." And yet she was willing to buy an amulet from him at an exorbitant price, because she thought it was "interesting" and it might work for her as a kind of "consolation."

When Shokufeh insisted to her friends, the rammal, and me that she did not believe in sorcery, she was both affirming, performatively, a commitment to modern scientific reason and loosely allying herself with orthodox rationality ("When there is God, what can anyone else do for me?"), at the expense of the superstitious, the gullible, and the ignorant, but also the heterodox and the polytheist. But Shokufeh also hesitated, and her hesitation was thrown into relief precisely in opposition to that rational universe toward which she had so vociferously performed her commitment. Regarding the dining cloth ritual, I asked her if the talismans might have been lodged in some secret compartment in the pot, or taped to the skillet she used to cover it. She answered "No" in both instances, and said she had seen with her own eyes that the pot was only filled with clear water, and that the skillet had nothing inside it. Yusefi was sitting too far from her to be slipping things into the pot as she stirred it. "I thought maybe the salt [which she had stirred into the pot] was some chemical that turned into mud," she said, "but what about the talismans and the locks?" Her brother Amir had also told her that there must have been something in the pot. "But I saw with my own eyes that it only had clear water in it," she protested, "and the bottom was copper, like the rest of the pot. Otherwise, I still can't believe it myself. Was it the salt? But how could salt turn into locks?"

For Shokufeh, these hesitations did not finally carry any serious consequences. It was all just "interesting." She had been frightened, but she had also clearly had fun—enough that she would be willing to meet the rammal again and take me along. The talismans that appeared in the pot did not provoke the kind of dread that would make her want to get rid of them as soon as possible. They were objects of curiosity that she wanted to take home with her or photograph and show her family (this was, for the rammal, an inappropriate attitude toward them, and he would not allow her to indulge her curiosity; from the perspective of folk talismanic theory, it would have been outright dangerous for her to do so). Similarly, the agate amulet and its jinn provided amusement and laughs: it was a parking spot locator, certainly an asset in Tehran gridlock, but little more. All in all, the sensibility she brought to her encounter was not just one of empirical detective work but also of delight in the fantastical.

Here is one possibility, then, that emerges from the strangeness, indeterminacy, and hesitation of a metaphysical encounter hedged in by expressions of rationality and skepticism: a thrilling experience. It is an encounter with the metaphysical that makes very little demand on one's cosmological attitudes and commitments (at least as long as one is prepared to repeatedly declare that "I don't believe in sorcery"), but that, by forcing one to momentarily entertain the incredible, enables rich kinds of imaginative engagement.[10]

As with readers of the *One Thousand and One Nights*, Shokufeh found herself encountering one astonishing event after another. In each case she was bewildered as to the cause of the phenomenon she was witnessing, her wonder sustained through a trucking back and forth between the sense data of an empirical observation and the rational judgment that it could not have been the case: Where did the strange markings on her ceiling come from? Ants, sorcery, or something else? How did the water in the pot all of a sudden produce solid objects? Jinn, sleight of hand, chemical reactions, or secret compartments? How could an agate stone help her find parking? Coincidence or real magic?

At each stage, Shokufeh's wonder piqued her curiosity and moved her to try to find a causal explanation. But instead of answers, she only found more surprises. Her curiosity allowed her to experience a thrilling succession of astonishing events as not only perplexing but pleasurable. She would afterward be able to narrate the experience to herself and others as a suspenseful mystery—a source of entertaining perplexity for her family and friends and a doubled source of thrill for herself as something experienced once and dramatically retold multiple times afterward.

So far we have seen two pathways for metaphysical experimenters to come to terms with the uncanniness of the rammal (imagined as a charlatan who may yet possess awesome powers) while staying true to their rational commitments: practicing virtuous caution to avoid occult danger and inhabiting a skeptical position that is open to wonder. In the final chapter of part 1 (chapter 10), we will catch a glimpse of yet another path for confronting the rammal's uncanniness, one that strives to sublimate it under the sign of science. This scientized orientation toward the metaphysical will be more fully elaborated in part 2. For now I will examine some of its contours and show how it may be combined with the playfulness that the indeterminacy of the occult enables.

RAMMALI REFASHIONED

One can be a rammal while maintaining a complex metaphysical sensibility that incorporates aspects of seriousness as well as play, commitment as well as aloofness or even disavowal. This chapter is about one such rammal, a young woman named Mersedeh who taught me a few lessons on the theory of sorcery and shared insights into her own practice. I will show how Mersedeh fashioned a professional persona as a rammal—or a prayer writer (*do'anevis*), as she preferred to call herself—by appropriating the knowledge and power of those she deemed "traditional" rammals and at the same time distancing herself from them. I will pay particular attention to five aspects of Mersedeh's self-fashioning: her aesthetics of self-presentation, her view of the scientific basis of sorcery, her relationship to Islam, the therapeutic ecology within which she placed her practice, and her avowed skepticism about sorcery's usefulness.

Mersedeh was a twenty-four-year-old master's student in psychology at Azad University. She rented an apartment in Ariyashahr, a young and populous district in western Tehran settled mostly by middle-class immigrants from other towns (her own parents lived in Karaj). She also rented a small suite in the lower level of an apartment complex not too far from where she lived. This was her work space where customers came to seek her expert assistance. Sometimes she received clients at a hole-in-the-wall café nearby where she interpreted their coffee grounds, performed tarot readings, and made appointments for more in-depth sessions at her suite.

Most of the rammals I had met before Mersedeh were middle-aged and elderly men who operated out of ramshackle quarters on the city's fringes. Haj Aqa Yusefi, the rammal we met in chapter 9, looked every bit a worn-out opium addict—or, I preferred to imagine, a defeated Saruman after the fall of Isengard: hair disheveled, cheeks hollowed, jaws missing a few rotted teeth. The old man's house was run-down and sparsely furnished, its only memorable feature a larger-than-life portrait of himself that he kept in his small audience chamber, as if to double his menacing presence. By contrast, Mersedeh was neat if eccentrically dressed, with loud pink and orange makeup to accentuate her eyes and cheekbones. She worked out of a gleaming suite decorated in bright and garish pinks and yellows: a heart-shaped pillow here, a lip-shaped telephone there. ("I have a strange taste, don't I?" she asked me playfully.) Her state-of-the-art stereo system pulsated with the soulful nostalgia of Lady Hayedeh, a prerevolutionary diva. She kept a bamboo plant and a bowlful of miniature Singapore turtles on a bed of yellow pebbles. She cleaned the tiny reptiles every day, she assured me, with water and antifungal medicine applied with an eyedropper.

Mersedeh told me that her decorative choices were deliberately "strange": She wanted to emphasize a chic modern style but was not afraid to express a sense of youthful mischief. This "strangeness," as Mersedeh explained, was crucial in creating an air of charisma around her persona as a prayer writer, much in the same way that Haj Aqa Yusefi's harrowing features and dilapidated quarters would have helped convince clients that he knew what he was doing. As she put it:

> Someone goes and sees a prayer writer at the far end of south Tehran, a dervish with a long beard and bizarre dress and a felt hat, okay, and he's got bull horns and bells hanging on the walls and there are swords and such around him. She enters and sees him and says, "Wow, he is a total dervish! My job will get done." And she no longer wavers afterward with wonder and doubt over whether or not it will work. Right? The more strongly your client believes in you, the better the result.

Where her competitors resorted to the antique and exotic, Mersedeh fashioned her charisma out of modern kitsch. To me, it seemed that her carefully crafted aesthetic sensibility was also intended to signal a propensity for sexual-cum-metaphysical mischief, which had the power to unleash terrible forces. My research assistant Mehdi told me after our first meeting (and the only meeting at which he was present) that he felt the sting of Mersedeh's "Satanic" eyes and that I should avoid seeing her alone, lest she create problems for me later on. He was ambiguous as to whether these problems would be caused by sorcery or something like a sexual scandal, although his tone hinted at both.

Mersedeh told me that her interest in the occult had grown out of a dramatic encounter with a rammal. "Ten years ago," she said, "I did not believe in any of this." But things changed when she became afflicted with a severe case of eczema, and she found no relief after multiple visits to dermatologists. A friend suggested that she might have been bewitched. "So I went and saw an Arab man," she said.

> He gave me an empty bucket and told me to fill it with water. He also asked me to check the bucket and make sure that there was nothing inside. Then he began to recite incantations. I was sitting there cursing myself over what I had gotten myself into, thinking that it was all fake. He gave me a knife to stir the water and some dirt to pour into the bucket while I recited *hamd o qol hova-llah* [the

first and 112th chapters of the Qur'an]. I also added one or two spoonfuls of sugar, rosewater, and salt. He recited an oath [*qasam*] over the bucket. Then all of a sudden I saw a stream of smoke enter the room. It rippled and approached me slowly, then plunged into the bucket. I heard the sound of an explosion as the smoke entered the water. I kept stirring the bucket with the knife that he had given me. After a while the knife stopped moving. It would not budge. The water had hardened into something like cement. He did something that loosened the knife, then told me that there were things in the bucket that I could take out. He said that most women would not dare put their hands into it, but I could if I wanted to. So I dipped my hands into the water and took out, one by one, a lost earring from a pair I had owned, a button from a manteau, a fake gold ring that I had lost, a bunch of rusted locks attached to a chain, and a piece of fabric from a shroud. I began to stutter, "These things are mine!"

The implements through which Mersedeh had been bewitched were thus discovered and neutralized. Mersedeh said she left the rammal feeling a lightness and a "genuine feeling of drunkenness that no wine in the world can give you." She felt as if she were suspended in a different dimension apart from space and time. The treatment she had undergone with some of the best doctors had finally worked, she said, and her eczema was gone. "I am still friends with this man."

After this first encounter, Mersedeh became interested in learning prayer writing and sorcery. The Arab man, now her teacher, was "stingy" with information. Others she consulted asked ridiculous sums to teach her the art. So she conducted much of the research on her own as specific practical needs arose, like winning the love of a man she desired. At one point she stole some of the Arab master's grimoires, photocopied them, then asked someone else to return them for fear that she would face the rammal's wrath and, she laughed, "be turned into a cockroach." "These men," Mersedeh told me, "have a certain snobbishness ['*ojb*] about them that is similar to the arrogance of the dervish who is constantly praised by his devotees. This leads them to be stingy with their knowledge." In her view, this, along with state-led persecutions of sorcerers throughout history (including witch burnings in early modern Europe and North America), had been an important cause for the inaccurate and incomplete form in which occult science had been passed down.

Here Mersedeh asserted a strong contrast between her knowledge of sorcery, which she said was scientific, and that of the rammals, which was superstitious. "Superstition has mixed in with a large part of [our knowledge of] prayers and talismans," she said. "Some of the information that is out there is purely commercial, and most prayer writers are a bunch of drug addicts." Still, she insisted that "every single one of these things has a scientific aspect. It is a science that has reached us in an incomplete form." Later, as she taught me theoretical sorcery, she elaborated:

See, you shouldn't look at prayer as a complicated thing, okay? Our dervishes and our prayer writers have always been used to confusing people. Because they thought that they had a very special and exclusive form of knowledge (*'elm*) that has power, they would act in a bit of an exaggerated way and would attempt to refrain from completely conveying their knowledge to their apprentices so that power would always remain in their own hands. And because they were, in the end, ignorant plebeians (*'ammi*), they thought they had a special kind of knowledge and science. In reality, prayer consists of a series of very general and ordinary and simple topics. Prayer and talismans are not superstitions. A series of issues have gotten mixed in with this, which have turned into superstition. But otherwise it is made up of the general laws of physics, chemistry, psychology, and, in fact, metaphysics, which is the science of the cosmos (*ka'enat*). There is a very general and basic framework for everything, and that is *frequency*.

Mersedeh's theory of scientific sorcery was a creative synthesis of her practical knowledge with her interpretation of Persian grimoires, material she had garnered from a Persian translation of the 1948 book *The Mirror of Magic* by the Swiss American surrealist painter Kurt Seligmann, and, most importantly, Rhonda Byrne's 2006 film *The Secret*. A dubbed version of the latter was broadcast on Iranian state television and spawned a series of books, CDs, calendars, stationery, and other merchandise. It captured the spirit of the "success" (*movaffaqiyyat*) industry of self-help and prosperity literature and seminars that emerged amid economic liberalization and progressive commercialization after the end of the 1980–88 war with Iraq. Byrne's ideas were received with the same enthusiasm as American speakers like Wayne Dyer, who inspired dozens of authors and motivational speakers to blend business and financial advice with a spiritual-cum-mystical ethos.

In Mersedeh's apt if idiosyncratic formulation, *The Secret* was the scientific foundation of prayer and sorcery: "To explain it in very simple terms," she said, "all the world around us is energy. Sorcery and prayer writing and talismans are all energy. Even the body consists of compressed energy." The energies that humans emit can be either positive or negative. And they remain in the world forever. "Say you want a Mercedes Elegance car. There is a wavelength to your desire that wells up from within you. This is what the cosmos hears." These are frequencies that already exist in the cosmos. Yet by making a wish, expressing a desire, feeling a certain way, we make the relevant frequencies resonate. When a certain prayer has resonated frequently enough through a specific channel—a word, a written sign, or a talismanic symbol—it becomes all the more likely for that particular channel to materialize the specific prayer or wish. Sometimes this is a matter of what Byrne calls "creative visualization." Mersedeh offered, "If you stare at a picture of a Mercedes Elegance car long enough and imagine that it belongs to you, you emit the proper kinds of frequencies to the cosmos, and the cosmos will eventually give you the car." Repetition is crucial for the efficacy of such images and symbols:

> Whenever something is repeated, its power increases in the cosmos. It's like if, from afar, I keep saying "Alireza, I love you, I do, I do, I do." This eventually affects your heart. Now, the more I say this, the more it infiltrates your unconscious. With the cosmos, there's no difference whatsoever. Everything in the cosmos is like an unconscious self. It's as if it's a storehouse where frequencies accumulate.

She took my notebook and drew a few short parallel lines on a blank page:

> Now a prayer writer has at one point drawn four lines like this with the intention that this is meant to bring love. Okay? He's drawn this for ten years and his teacher has drawn this for ten years and the teachers before them for another hundred years, so this now exists in the cosmos. It is recorded that these four lines mean love. Okay? When the prayer writer draws this for you now, this frequency is already there in the cosmos, so it immediately connects up to it and you see the result quickly.

I looked at my notebook and wondered whether Mersedeh had just written me a love spell. She continued:

> Now as a prayer writer, I either have this knowledge that these lines are all my creative visualization, or I don't, in which case, like the ignorant prayer writer who doesn't have this knowledge, I accept that because my grandfather drew this, this shape will take Alireza to this woman.

Finally, as if to reemphasize her distance from the traditional rammal, she offered:

> You've seen a lot of these prayer writers and you know what they're like. They're a bunch of ignorant illiterates who write something that they've been writing for generations. Some of them do good work that is effective. But not the rest. They're opium-addicted lowlifes who write prescriptions out of a bunch of offset-printed manuals and give them to wretched women.

Mersedeh's relationship to Islam was as complicated as her debt to the traditional rammal. The rammals that I met underlined their commitments to Islam in various ways. Haj Aqa Yusefi told me that doing anything that would make a halal into haram—as in inducing hatred between husband and wife— was off-limits for him and would incur the wrath of God. Shaykh Yazdi styled himself a learned, pious Shi'i scholar and mystic. For both, the occult sciences were distinctively Islamic. This meant not only that they drew on Qur'anic verses and Islamic supplications in their occult operations but also that they considered it important to subordinate their practice to an Islamic ethical regime. Mersedeh cared little for Islamic ethics or doctrine. I asked her if there was any limit to what she was willing to do through sorcery—murder, for example. She responded in the negative and gave me the example of having once written a spell to kill a troublesome ex-boyfriend. She changed her mind later, but it was almost too late and the man was seriously injured in a car accident.

Mersedeh was no less dismissive of Islamic theology. She believed in god as a higher universal energy that encompassed everyone and everything, but thought the Qur'an and other holy books were man-made. She told me that she could open up the Qur'an on any page and point at a verse and tell me the specific problem with that verse. One of her problems with Islam and religions in general was their patriarchal foundations. "Have you ever heard of a female prophet?" she asked me. "All societies are patriarchal because in every religious book, the prophets have always been men. They would enslave women or say that the women were to obey their husbands and other men."

Even so, Mersedeh attested to the efficacy of the Qur'an for prayer writing and sorcery. In fact, she told me that she had learned to recite and understand the Qur'an not in public school, where she horsed around during Qur'an class, but through her education in sorcery. Within her theoretical scheme, there was no contradiction in this. To the extent that Qur'anic verses had been used in prayer writing for generations, they had been ingrained in the cosmos and would be effective if called upon with the requisite creative imagination and confidence.

Another aspect of Mersedeh's reconfiguring of rammali was the therapeutic ecology within which she situated her practice. The other rammals I knew supplemented their occult prescriptions with folk healing techniques that drew in part on the corpus of Avicennan medicine. Mersedeh, by contrast, compared her prayer writing with Reiki on the one hand and clinical psychology on the other, both of which she practiced. With her degree in psychology, she had secured a part-time counseling job at a local community center, where she worked primarily with families and young people. As she put it, her counseling work and her prayer writing shared a concern with helping people succeed and heal but also emphasized generating confidence to serve their efficacy—except that prayer writing was more successful. She illustrated her argument with an example:

> On any given day a girl might come to counseling and say: "I want to slash my wrist, I feel awful." This person's mind is a collection of negative frequencies and thoughts. Now I tell her, "Look, don't think negatively, your life will be fixed up, go do this or that." I offer her some strategies. But these words won't change her beliefs. She'll try to think as I tell her, but it won't work. Now for the same person, I do counseling and I also do prayer writing. But my prayer writing is much more successful than my counseling. Because even though the girl comes in and

gets counseling, she doesn't come to believe. From her point of view, I've shown her a strategy. But sometimes I'll say, "I know how to do prayers, and I'm telling you: Go off, and take this prayer with you, and do this or that to it for forty days, and this issue of yours will be sorted out." The person leaves, and holding fast to the belief that it will work, she discards all those negative thoughts, and all those negative frequencies go away and her soul is purified. And during this time, either her lover returns to her, or her issue is sorted out, or she gets some money, or some new opportunity presents itself to her and her life changes for the better.

Mersedeh clearly understood sorcery as a means to power. She herself had used it for years to advance her interests, whether it was to threaten her sister's irritating suitor, to win the heart of a desirable man, to prevent that man from falling for other women, or to strike at enemies. But she also recognized sorcery as an archaic tool of the weak, better suited for her clients than herself. She preferred it when she was able to exert power through other means:

It's true that sorcery and prayer have effects. They're not ineffectual. But for every person there's a weak spot that you can exploit. Maybe sorcery belonged to a time when, if someone wouldn't come to me, I would have had to resort to it to bring him toward me somehow. But right now there are telephones. For every person there's a point, a word, a need, or a weak spot that you can use to tame them, calm them. If you put your finger on that and use it to get to them, it's the best sorcery.

Later she told me that she thought it was "illogical [*bimanteq*] people" who went after sorcery to solve their problems. Logical people pursue logical means. Sometimes a friend would tell her that she had learned a new style of fortune-telling and wanted to try it out on her, and she would agree to it just so that she wouldn't disappoint the friend. But she didn't really like it, because she thought the need for fortune-telling, spells, and prayer is rooted in weakness. "When I know that everything is only one step away from my grasp and that we ourselves are the greatest power, why do I need to waste my time with this sort of thing?" Mersedeh may have been performing this skepticism for my benefit, the researcher from America who had taken a scientific interest in sorcery. But given the prevailing atmosphere of suspicion toward the rammal, her declared skepticism could just as well have long preceded our meeting. By performing skepticism, she could engage in sorcery while trying to evade its negative social entailments. She may also have justified the practice to herself from this skeptical standpoint.

Mersedeh's answer to the disorienting picture of the rammal as a purveyor of superstition seemingly in possession of awesome powers was thus to offer an equally paradoxical counterimage: in contrast to the "ignorant" rammals, she claimed a firm scientific grasp of the metaphysics and psychology of sorcery while being prepared to dismiss the whole enterprise as a waste of time. She doubly distanced herself from the rammals even as she made a lucrative business out of rammali. If this seemed contradictory, she was ready to wave off the inconsistency with a mischievous laugh. The question was whether her customers were able to laugh along with her, or if they were disturbed by the rapid and seamless shifts she was capable of effecting in her positions. Perhaps it was both, and therein lay her uncanny power.

SUPPRESS, ACCOMMODATE, SUBLIMATE

As a figure of many imagined transgressions—of piety, civility, rationality, and good taste—the rammal inspires near-universal revulsion and condemnation. Since the late nineteenth century, rationalizing the unseen has in part meant suppressing the rammal through the combined forces of intellect, propaganda, and coercion. But as the preceding chapters have shown, this suppression has only partially succeeded. Shi'i hesitations over the legitimacy of the occult and secularist uncertainties over superstition have combined to weaken the thrust of the discursive assaults against the rammal. In everyday encounters, moreover, some Iranians have been impelled to reconcile their rational disdain for the rammal-as-charlatan with the sense-data apparently pointing toward the presence of extraordinary powers. A meeting with a rammal can thus become the site for an uncanny return of a repressed "irrational," wreaking havoc on the boundaries between true and false, reasonable and superstitious, genuine power and imposture.

We have seen that there is more than one way to deal with the rammal's uncanniness while experimenting with the metaphysical. Some maintain cautious distance to protect their virtue from peril and sin. Others adopt a skeptical stance while remaining open to the wonder and thrill of the inexplicable. Both pathways forego attempts to suppress the uncanny in favor of finding a suitable modus vivendi while maintaining a commitment to reason. There is a third way, as well, leading neither to suppression nor to accommodation but to sublimation: scientific discourse provides an opportunity for abandoning the vicious binary between rational disavowal and superstitious acceptance in favor of a new differentiation between scientific understanding and superstitious ignorance. Science holds out the promise, that is, that the rammal—or at least the knowledge and power with which he traffics—can be saved from irrationality.

Part 2 of this book examines the scientific path to metaphysical inquiry. I will elaborate the range of ways—epistemic, moral, imaginative, and rhetorical—through which new kinds of rational certainty about the metaphysical have been made possible over the past century. We will also see that these certainties are fragile and prone to producing further uncanny disorientations.

PART 2 **SCIENTIST**

QUANTUM UNDERSTANDING

Arezu Khanum welcomed me into her home one early afternoon in December 2008. She served me delivery pizza for lunch and spent three hours explaining the trajectory by which she had arrived at the teachings of Cosmic Mysticism. She was in her late forties and lived with her husband, a successful businessman, and three teenage sons in Shahrak-e Gharb, an upscale residential and commercial neighborhood in western Tehran. Hers was a large, modern apartment with four bedrooms, an open kitchen, and spacious living and dining rooms. The furniture gave off the golden glitter of wealth: French-style seats, a display case showing off chinaware and various decorative objects, a Chinese figurine on a small table, an analogue clock, and more. In a corner of the living room there were several gold and brass-colored Buddha statues, a large sword, and expensive-looking vases. Various photographs and framed hand-woven cloths adorned the walls. She had been working out on her treadmill immediately before I rang the bell, expecting that I would arrive later. Her bleached hair was uncovered. "No need to take off your shoes!" she exhorted as I walked in.

Arezu Khanum was an eager storyteller, the ideal anthropological informant. She shared with me some of the most intimate details of her life, couched within a narrative of spiritual journeying, of ultimately having attained balance, power, and peace. At the time of our meeting, she was eight months into her study of Cosmic Mysticism, having continuously taken classes with Mr. Sheyda—the exorcist we met in the introduction—who himself was one of the first students of the group's founder, Mohammad 'Ali Taheri. She described these eight months as a period of healing and spiritual uplift, following upon years of crisis, illness, and depression. To Arezu Khanum, they had been the culmination of various struggles in her life that she had waged with a loving faith in God, a voracious appetite for reading and acquiring "consciousness" (*agahi*), and a trust in the intuitions of her heart.

This journey was punctuated at two critical points by dramatic visions. These, as well as multiple lesser visions, had been crucial in forming Arezu Khanum's mystical sensibility, including her orientation toward Cosmic Mysticism. I will structure her narrative around these two visions and the significance she accorded them.

The first vision, of two glowing angels, had come to her five years earlier. It was this vision that had launched Arezu Khanum on her path of mystical discovery. Before this, she told me, she had always been afraid of getting too close to religion. "At a young age," she said, "a book by [Ayatollah Naser] Makarem Shirazi fell into my hands, and honestly, I thought it was idiotic. I thought to myself, 'Is God a tyrant or a savage to turn someone away or burn a woman in the fires of hell because her hair is uncovered?' "[1] She was attracted by certain aspects of Islam but was repelled by others. Most of all she was concerned that if she were to accept certain things—for example, if she were to begin to pray regularly—she would have to commit to other things, like the hijab, for which she was not prepared. "To tell you the truth," she said, "I just became defensive about religion. Not about Islam per se, but the people who represented it. I thought they were scammers. They were making money off of religion and they frightened us to keep us around them. This is not religion and this isn't God."

Arezu Khanum attributed her eventual interest in spirituality to her experience of hardship and its role in "building up" her soul. For example, her husband had been a wealthy businessman from the time they had married, but he also had a penchant for disappointing Arezu Khanum's material desires. "He would buy me jewelry, which I would pick out myself," she said, "but then if he needed money, he would sell it without asking my permission." After repeated disappointments, she said she acquired a "spiritual satiety," a lack of desire for material possessions. At first this was accompanied by bitterness, but eventually, with "intellectual development," it aided her spiritual growth. Years later, after bearing three children, she was forced to contend with a different kind of difficulty, this time in her love life. She fell head over heels for a married man with whom her family had friendly relations. The man was pious and upright, "a gentleman, noble, with character, not a cheap, dirty man." They never attempted an affair, nor did they even announce their love to each other. But Arezu Khanum knew that the emotion had been there. Once, the two families traveled as part of a larger group to the forests of Sisangan in northern Iran. While hiking in the forest, the secret lovers' eyes connected for a moment. "Suddenly there was something like a spark," Arezu Khanum said, "And God is my witness, I saw the spark in the air, like a brilliant star. And my heart sank. I'm sure he also felt the same thing. After that we never spoke again, nor even came face-to-face, even when we were at the same gathering." Arezu Khanum attributed this deliberate separation to her own restraint. She had recognized what disaster might have struck both families if they had so much as attempted to act on their love. It took her two or three years to overcome her attachment. But the restraint bore spiritual fruit. The "earthly love" for the married man, she told me, led to divine love. Her refusal to satisfy that love helped her overcome her lower self (*nafs*) and strengthen her soul.

It was after this that Arezu Khanum saw the glowing angels. She was vacationing with her husband and children at an orchard they owned in the north. At night, with everyone in bed, she stayed up to read in the light of a bedside lamp. At around 3:00 a.m., she began to hear the song of a reed flute in the distance. "God is my witness," she said, "I thought to myself, 'there's no one around us. Who's playing the reed flute in the middle of the forest, in the middle of the night?'" After about a half hour, she fell asleep. Then she woke up startled. Arezu Khanum lit a cigarette as she described to me what she saw in front of her:

> I can tell you that at certain times of the day, the frequencies of the body change. It could be that when I woke up, my frequencies had changed and so I was able to see what I saw. Or perhaps they had a message for me. I don't know. I woke up startled. I wasn't asleep, nor was I half asleep. I suddenly saw two angels in front of my eyes. God is my witness. It wasn't a hallucination. It wasn't my imagination. I had never even imagined what an angel might look like; that it might be total and pure light. I just hadn't thought about it. Sure, when I was a child I had seen little figurines of angels that looked like children, but that was it. I saw two angels with wings made only of light. They had no bodies or volume. And they were small. They had no faces, but I could see their laughter. They were looking at me and laughing. One of them was positioned higher. It flapped its wings and flew away. The second one was sitting on something like a prayer mat of light, looking at me. I was afraid. I wanted to utter *ya abol fazl, ya hazrat-e 'ali*, the kind of reaction that I had been accustomed to since childhood.[2] But I was mute. Mute. It laughed and looked at me. And I was mute. A few minutes passed. I can't say if it was five minutes, two minutes, or three minutes. Then suddenly my tongue unlocked and I voiced *ya abol fazl*. So I saw this scene. And my reaction was initially one of fear. I thought, "What is this? What if I'm supposed to die and that's why I'm seeing these things?"

The vision of the two angels stoked Arezu Khanum's interest in books about religion and metaphysics. She began with books on Buddhism and practiced meditation to complement her readings. She was enamored particularly with Baird T. Spalding's *Life and Teaching of the Masters of the Far East*, published first in 1924 and translated into Persian as *The Temple of Silence* (*Ma'bad-e Sokut*) in 1997. It is an "awe-inspiring book," Arezu Khanum told me. "It's like the Qur'an for me. Whatever page you open the book to, you learn something." Later on, she read about Christianity and even considered conversion after repeated viewings of a Persian Christian satellite channel. She read other spiritual literature as well. Paul Twitchell's *The Tiger's Fang* was her introduction to Eckankar (ECK). She realized the power of ECK after receiving several visions while reading the book. Even so, she decided that it would not be the path for her. "These books don't make my heart happy, with their talk of all kinds of different gods, and levels and levels of gods," she said. "It's not that I'm a particularly rigid religious person. I can't even read the Qur'an properly. But I feel like it's not my path. I still felt that I needed to understand it though, to study and understand." Intellectual understanding aside, her heart would ultimately be her guide: "I really believe in listening to the call of my heart," she said. "There have been times when my heart has told me not to do something, and I've done it and regretted it later."

These studies would gradually set the stage for Arezu Khanum's embrace of Cosmic Mysticism. In particular, she would be primed by her familiarity with various formulations of ideas about a "cosmic mind" or "cosmic intelligence" that ostensibly ruled the entire universe, as well as notions of ubiquitous "cosmic radiation" or "power" understood in terms of physics, especially quantum physics. She insisted to me that she would not have "just picked a path with my eyes closed." She listened to her heart, yes, but she also conducted research and eventually settled with a mystical system whose claims most closely matched those she already found compelling.

Science was to play a crucial role in this. When describing Spalding's book, Arezu Khanum made much of the fact that the book had been based on research conducted 130 years earlier by American scientists who had set out to collect the wisdom of other nations. It was ventures like theirs, she said, that contributed to America's contemporary might. For example, American scientists were conducting research on stem cells now, but Spalding's book already spoke of stem cells more than a century ago, which suggested that the discovery had been inspired by, or even taken from, the knowledge of Himalayan sages. More important was Spalding's discussion of cosmic rays, attributed to the soul of Jesus Christ, with whom the American researchers had spoken at length. Arezu Khanum read a passage to me from the translated book, which I quote here from the English original:

> It will soon be known that these cosmic rays have such tremendous penetrating power that they penetrate through all mass, shattering as it were, the very heart or nucleus of a so-called atom, transmuting it into atoms of other substance and thereby creating other elements of higher order; and in this way, creation advances into a higher emanation of pure light or life itself.[3]

Arezu Khanum saw here intimations of nuclear energy and atomic weapons. But more important was the prediction that "cosmic rays" would soon be discovered. Mohammad 'Ali Taheri was the one who made this discovery, or at least formulated it in the compelling form of Cosmic Mysticism and its therapeutic systems. She found confirmation of other elements of her newfound mystical path in books like *The Holographic Universe* by Michael Talbot (which she read in translation), and *The Quantum Thoughts of Mowlana* (Rumi) (*Andisheh-ha-ye Kwantomi-ye Mowlana*) by Mohsen Farshad, both of which she read prior to discovering Taheri's teachings.

Between the vision of the two angels and her enrollment in Mr. Sheyda's Cosmic Mysticism seminars, she spent five years studying on her own. But this was also a period of intense physical and emotional anguish. For much of this time, Arezu Khanum suffered from bloated intestines, sluggishness, and oversleeping. The easiest tasks seemed to her like enormous burdens. She visited various doctors to find a cure but obtained few results. One doctor diagnosed her with irritable bowel syndrome triggered by stress. A psychiatrist diagnosed her with depression. She took American-made antidepressants for several months to no avail. "The pills made me fat," she said. "I gained fifteen kilos, but they didn't have the slightest effect." Meanwhile, she visited two or three rammals who told her she was bewitched. There was an array of suspects to consider, from her mother-in-law, who she knew had been engaged in sorcery for many years, to a brother-in-law who had divorced and then reconciled with her sister, to the wretched wife of her aforementioned unconsummated love interest. Whether or not sorcery was involved, the rammals' prescriptions did not help, partly because she was unable to muster the will to properly follow them.

Toward the end of this period, a second dramatic vision came to Arezu Khanum. Her many troubles at this point included a rocky relationship with her older son, who was in his early twenties. "I was worried that he was taking drugs," she said, "so I pleaded with him not to do it. I was also very depressed and weary. Maybe it was my own anxiety that was causing him to fall into error by sending him powerful negative energy." Her son admitted that he had been smoking hashish, but argued that there was nothing wrong with that. He even suggested that Arezu Khanum try it for herself. She responded by admonishing him further, telling him that nothing was more precious than his health, that he was young, and that grass and hashish destroyed brain cells. "But just so that he would listen to me," she said, "and because he had already promised that he wouldn't do it anymore, I said, 'Okay, I'll try it once.'"

Arezu Khanum sat down with her son and smoked two joints with him. She was already familiar with the mystical uses of narcotics, from Shams Tabrizi's criticism of the hashish-smoking dervishes of his time to Carlos Castaneda's hallucinogenic adventures with Don Juan Matus. But she had never experienced it for herself:

> So I smoked the hashish. And sir, what a visionary journey I went on [*aqa 'ajab sayr-o soluki kardim*]! I don't know if it was hallucination or what. I know all these consciousnesses [*agahi-ha*] already exist in our minds. But they're locked, and we have no permission to access them. That's why we have control over only 5 percent of our brain, and even that was only the case with Einstein. But I think this consciousness is inside us already. By smoking the grass, because I had no experience and my brain had contracted somewhat with age, the grass opened up my brain and those consciousnesses started coming back. That's how I explain it to myself.

Arezu Khanum proceeded to describe her visions to me:

> You have no idea the kinds of things I saw. I realized that in this world, the beginning is the same as the end and the end is the same as the beginning. Maybe it was the case that the kind of thing that Mowlana realized through his *sama'* dance, I realized by smoking grass. I had become a philosopher. Any question I asked, I received an answer. My brain would go out and fetch the response and return, as though it was sailing across the sky. If you were to ask, for instance, what part of the body sugar is bad for [she pointed at sugar cubes on the table], I would be able to demonstrate the answer for you with proof and argument and philosophy and logic. I had become a genius physician, a genius philosopher. Now I regret it and wish there had been someone next to me who had written down what I was saying, all these consciousnesses streaming out.

She lit another cigarette and inhaled deeply as she continued to describe what she had seen:

> So anyway, I smoked the grass, and I saw a steep hill dotted with cedar trees, each about one meter tall. At the top of the hill was paradise. It was as though my soul was flying overhead and I could see these things, and someone was telling me, or the consciousness was inside me [describing what I was seeing]. There were many cedar trees at the foot of the hill and they got fewer the more you ascended the slope. It was a simile for humans, that humans are like these cedars growing toward paradise. This was a time when I had been considering becoming a Christian. So in that state, the question crossed my mind: Which of the prophets is the true and legitimate [*bar haq*] one? Then it was shown to me that among these one-meter cedar trees, there were a few three-meter trees scattered on different parts of the hill. These were the prophets, all of them messengers of God in their own time and place. It was shown to me that Christ, Muhammad, Buddha, Moses, all of them, are messengers for their own time and place. The bloodthirsty savage Arabs who would not abide by any law needed to be set straight with force and fear. And it's true that Muhammad was chosen, but he took the first step himself. Jesus took the first step himself. And we too can become a Muhammad or a Christ, if we take a step.

Arezu Khanum's visions also opened her mind to scientific truths, particularly in the realm of quantum physics. "I didn't even know what physics was before this," she said, "but now I can understand if two physicists sit here and talk to each other. Not that I've become a know-it-all [*'aql-e kol*]. But I've understood what quantum physics is, for instance, without anyone explaining it to me. What it talks about, what it relates to. I've felt it without having studied it, that everything, every cell, every moment, is different from the one before it. Every state is different from the one before it and after it." She realized, moreover, that there was an outward, apparent aspect (*zaher*) to quantum physics having to do with materials and bodies, as well as an internal spiritual aspect (*baten*).

The sum of these consciousnesses transformed Arezu Khanum into a new person. It was as though her long-desired path was suddenly revealed to her. For many years she had prayed to God to illuminate her heart, to show her the path. Now her prayer had been answered and the love of God was on her side. Her path was Cosmic Mysticism. All of her physical and psychological ailments were miraculously cured through metatherapy treatments. Her emotional relationships, particularly with her sons and other family members, were significantly improved. She found Taheri's books and CDs to be works of tremendous mystical insight. The man himself, she said, was no less than a prophet.

These teachings did not detract from the importance of her personal visions or understandings. If anything, they magnified them. At times Arezu Khanum detected a tension between her own knowledge and the knowledge imparted by Mr. Sheyda. She attributed the difference to experience:

> Mr. Sheyda is very knowledgeable in metatherapy. But he's traveled on a closed path. He's very informed. But in practice, his knowledge and experience and his reading [*motale'eh*], I don't want to suggest... He's young, too, in any case... even though he's been among the first circle of Taheri's students. But the questions that I ask him, the kinds of analysis that I do myself based on my own experience and reading, he maybe hasn't reached that level yet. When you ask him a few questions, he will twist the answers to get out of giving a proper response. Or he'll say things that are wrong.

The most significant of Mr. Sheyda's errors had to do with his interpretation of Arezu Khanum's vision of the two angels. Following a standard line argued by Mr. Taheri, Mr. Sheyda had said that angels are neither anthropomorphic nor do they take visible form. In fact, Arezu Khanum may have seen inorganic viruses—demons—a suggestion she found unacceptable:

> When my heart says they were light, and light only comes from God... how could it have been a demon? He was seeing this from his own perspective.

Arezu Khanum granted the possibility that Mr. Sheyda's perspective may also be correct insofar as it was based on his own experience. She mentioned having read in a book that no two mystics shared the same visionary journey. And yet there was something superior in her visions that Mr. Sheyda had not been able to grasp. Arezu Khanum's sense of the superiority of her knowledge emerged in equal measure from her mystical experience and her individual studies. Although she did not suggest that her knowledge was superior even to that of the founder of Cosmic Mysticism, she seemed to me confident enough to have argued precisely that, if necessary.

EMPIRICAL SPIRITS

Arezu Khanum's account of her metaphysical adventures opens up a window onto multiple trends within the landscape of contemporary Iranian spirituality. My primary concern is to explore the range of ways in which modern science has been recruited to serve metaphysical experimentation, allowing seekers to reconcile their spiritual commitments with the demands of reason. This chapter and chapter 13 begin by examining some of the earliest attempts at synthesizing theological speculation with the methods of the empirical sciences. I will attend particularly to the epistemic and moral consequences of such syntheses. In later chapters I probe some looser, more self-consciously imaginative deployments of science, as well as the interweaving of modern scientific imaginaries with emerging conceptions of mystical experience and therapeutic spirituality. As we will see near the end of part 2, therapeutic justifications for metaphysical exploration have become more commonplace, partly in response to the disorienting realization that the scientific road to metaphysical inquiry may lead to a dead end.

The rise of the modern sciences in Iran was intimately connected with state centralization and with efforts to reform society on the model of powerful European nations.[1] The twentieth century saw the expansion of modern educational institutions, mass literacy, and the emergence of a middle class for whom science was an important aspect of both cultural and economic capital—bureaucrats, doctors, lawyers, teachers, engineers, and other professionals.[2] Science gained ever-wider currency in articulating problems, furnishing solutions, and defining the horizon of progress for a rapidly modernizing nation-state. In the first half of the twentieth century, the biomedical disciplines were dominant, with the health and vigor of the national body taking center stage in modernist discourse.[3] With increasing industrialization, however, the engineering fields, their allied natural scientific disciplines, and eventually the social sciences also entered the scene and made their mark.[4]

These transformations had major repercussions for religious thought and practice, particularly as pertaining to projects for moral reform. Scholars have noted the myriad ways in which Muslim activists and intellectuals in Iran and elsewhere have drawn on modern scientific knowledge and notions of rationality and progress in order to accomplish a variety of objectives: countering charges of reaction and superstition; attacking materialist, secularist, and heterodox religious doctrines; and criticizing the conditions of Muslim communities with the aim of advancing alternative reformist agendas.[5] Researchers' emphasis on Islamic reform, however, has tended to obscure the overtly religious projects of some of the most influential—but seemingly "secularist"— champions of science, including Spiritists, Theosophists, and others. Scholarship on these individuals is scant, usually limited to less than a handful of intellectuals whose religious commitments are by and large described as solitary and eccentric.[6]

In this chapter, I will draw attention to the neglected influence of Spiritism and psychical research among Iranian intellectuals in the first half of the twentieth century. Spiritism enabled these intellectuals, as it did many of their fellow travelers in Europe and elsewhere, to ground their religious cosmologies in what they took to be universal modern science and to tether their moral teachings to what they defended as objective empirical research. Their aspirations may now seem quixotic and their practices bizarre, but their claims once circulated in respectable modernist circles and were taken seriously by intellectual, religious, and political elites.

In the early decades of the twentieth century, Spiritism attracted Iranian elites seeking to reconcile their commitments to modern science with their religious longings and dedication to moral reform. The most active of these elites were francophone intellectuals devoted to education and scientific popularization. Their visions were global in scope. Europe set their intellectual compass, even when they were deeply critical of the increasingly calamitous events there. And although they focused their activities primarily in Iran, they saw themselves as participants in an international ecumene committed to achieving global peace and unity through moral reform. In their universalist visions, commitments to science and education, reliance on global networks of elite sociality, and harnessing of the new infrastructures of steam, print, post, and telegraph, the Iranian Spiritists joined Freemasons, Baha'is, reformist Sufis, Theosophists, and other innovators while also establishing a new grammar and practice of scientized spirituality that would endure far beyond their own immediate horizons.[7]

Spiritism's arrival in Iran can largely be credited to one man. Mirza Khalil Khan Saqafi (1863–1944) was a physician, educator, bureaucrat, diplomat, essayist, and translator. He studied modern medicine at the Dar al-Fonun polytechnic college before securing a series of government assignments. Around 1895, he won the blessings of the Qajar monarch Naser al-Din Shah (1831–96) to travel to Paris for further medical training. Four years later, he returned to Tehran and joined the physicians in the employ of the Qajar court. He became a personal physician and close confidant to the new monarch Mozaffar al-Din Shah (1853–1907) and received the title of A'lam al-Dowleh (the Most Learned of the State).

During the second half of his life, Khalil Khan augmented his medical practice with public intellectual engagements and state administrative positions, including a three-year stint as Tehran's first postrevolutionary mayor. He translated textbooks on medicine, agriculture, and industry, a book on space and time, Jules Lermina's 1881 novel *Le Fils de Monte-Cristo*, and selections of Persian classical literature that he cotranslated and published as *Le Jardin des Délices*. He also compiled a Persian-French dictionary, authored original works on chemistry, literature, and moral refinement, and penned essays on culture, politics, and society.

Khalil Khan considered his greatest accomplishment to have been the introduction and propagation of *ma'refat al-ruh-e tajrobati* or "experimental spirit science."[8] By this he principally meant Spiritism—the movement founded in France by Allan Kardec (1804–69) in 1857 that was devoted to communication with the spirits of the dead through turning tables, planchettes, and human mediums.[9] Like Kardec, Khalil Khan considered Spiritism to be a scientific doctrine. At the time, *ma'refat al-ruh*—the science of spirits/soul/psyche— was a concept that could refer to a range of knowledge systems and practices that in Europe had gradually clustered into Spiritism, psychical research, and experimental psychology. The boundaries between these were still contested at the turn of the century when Khalil Khan was in Paris for medical training. The eventual victory of experimental psychology and the waning of the other two were only decided later.[10] In Iran, too, experimental psychology was established as an academic discipline only after 1925 when 'Ali Akbar Siyasi (1895–1990) coined the neologism *ravan-shenasi* to translate *psychologie* and replace the older *'elm al-nafs*, which had primarily been understood to refer to the scholastic philosophical psychology based on introspection.[11] Siyasi used the Persian word *ravan* for *psyché* and equated that with both the Arabic *nafs* and *ruh*.[12] But all three terms—*ravan*, *ruh*, and *nafs*—were interchangeable in scientific discourse beyond the 1920s and to some extent even today. Khalil Khan the Spiritist's *ma'refat al-ruh* and Siyasi the psychologist's *ravan-shenasi* were easily exchangeable terms, even if their authors used them toward clearly differentiated—even opposing—ends.

To understand Khalil Khan's fascination with Spiritism, we need to return to his years of graduate training in Paris. It was there that he says he met Dr. Jules Bernard Luys (1828–97), a neurologist who had made important contributions to the understanding of human brain anatomy and neurological diseases.[13] Luys had long been fascinated with hysteria and hypnosis, conducting experiments on the effects of medication at a distance, storing cerebral activities in magnetic crowns, and visualizing brain and body emanations.[14] Many of Luys's experiments were performed in public, either at the Hôpital de la Charité or at his own residence, and they attracted crowds of Parisians curious to see his strange demonstrations firsthand.

By the time Khalil Khan arrived in Paris in the mid-1890s, Luys was near the end of his life in the public spotlight. He died in 1897, but his brief acquaintance must have been enough to launch Khalil Khan into the world of Spiritism and psychical research. It was probably at La Charité or Luys's residence that he was introduced to the vibrant Parisian Spiritist scene. In time, he would translate and popularize many works of Spiritism and psychical research, including by Allan Kardec, Camille Flammarion, Charles Richet, and Gabriel Delanne. He was joined in his efforts by a coterie of fellow travelers, all from among the Iranian bureaucratic and military elite, which included 'Ali-Reza Bahrami Mohazzeb al-Saltaneh, an ophthalmologist and Khalil Khan's colleague at the mayor's office; Reza Qoli Rafi' al-Molk, an employee of the antiques office in the Ministry of Education; Dust-Mohammad Khan E'tesam al-Dowleh, a grandson of Naser al-Din Shah and colonel in the army; and Mahmud Vahid Sa'd (Vahid al-Dowleh), a member of the fifth parliament, director of an educational society promoting adult literacy, and son of Javad Sa'd al-Dowleh (himself a famous politician and briefly prime minister).

In the mid-1920s Khalil Khan founded the Society of Experimental Spirit Science (*Anjoman-e Ma'refat al-Ruh-e Tajrobati*) in Tehran as a venue for regular communication with spirits. The society met weekly, first at the personal residence of Colonel Mohammad Baqer Khan Nakhjavan, and later at the house of Colonel Mohammad Khan Razmara.[15] Both men had served in the powerful Cossack Brigade and were the fathers of prominent military men who also took part in the Spirit Society's meetings.[16] Within a year or two, the meetings were moved to the house of Vahid al-Dowleh, who would eventually succeed Khalil Khan as director of the society.

The staple event each week was a séance. If a suitable medium—often a young, frail woman—was available, she would be hypnotized by Khalil Khan in order to enter a trance state and communicate with the spirits of deceased individuals awaiting reincarnation. Once contact was established, the medium would write down the spirits' messages or speak them out loud. In the absence of mediums, members would sit around a wooden table and communicate with the spirit world telegraphically using a wooden cigar box that glided on a sheet inscribed with the letters of the Persian and French alphabets.[17]

The Society of Experimental Spirit Science hosted séances with some of the most renowned souls in history. They included statesmen (Mirza Taqi Khan Amir Kabir, Karim Khan Zand, Yazid ibn Mu'awiya, Józef Piłsudski), scientists (Avicenna, Camille Flammarion), and poets (Hafiz, Sa'di, Khayyam). The souls reported on their circumstances in the "fourth dimension," on the good and evil deeds they had committed during their many lifetimes, and on the workings of the cosmos and reincarnation. The loftier the souls, the richer their insights. For example, Mirza Taqi Khan Amir Kabir (1807–52), Naser al-Din Shah's famous prime minister and the founder of Khalil Khan's alma mater, the Dar al-Fonun, told the Spirit Society that he was on the "first level" of the spirit world. His first earthly life had been as a "jungle savage," but he had gradually ascended the ranks such that by his five thousandth return when he lived as Amir Kabir, he was so elevated that he did not require any additional returns to Earth. The reason, as he explained it, was that "On Earth, I did nothing but good. I always tried to do good for people. I was never selfish, and I never wanted anyone to be harmed. I never desired to do anything out of ostentation. And this is why I am very comfortable."[18]

Other souls were not as fortunate. Yazid ibn Muʿawiya, the seventh-century Umayyad caliph who ordered the murder of Muhammad's grandson Imam Husayn, confessed that he had been wicked in all 2,059 of his lives, most recently as a depraved menial worker in Africa. ʿOmar Khayyam pled guilty to having been a "materialist" who had composed much nonsense in his poetry. Hafiz lamented that he had wasted his life away in debauchery and drinking. And Avicenna had been a selfish opportunist who had read all he could of the Khwarazmshahi library before torching the building to prevent others from benefiting from the knowledge within.[19]

These revelations were not mere fodder for casual conversation and amusement. They provided firsthand testimonies with which Spiritists could debate and evaluate the various legacies they had inherited from Iranian, Islamic, and European history. As a mode of critical historical inquiry, their séances were very much of a piece with broader modernist concerns. But for the Spiritists, this historical inquiry was explicitly positioned within a framework of moral reflection and self-scrutiny. Khalil Khan wrote that experimental spirit science was in the first instance "an instrument for moral exercise [varzesh-e akhlaqi] for traversing the stages of spiritual progress." He argued that nothing was more effective in awakening people, prodding them to reflect on their actions, and encouraging them to improve themselves than listening to the confessions of those spirits who had committed ugly deeds on Earth and learning about their current condition.[20]

Spiritists considered their method of communication with disembodied souls to be the fruit of modern scientific discovery. They believed that their séances would lead to "a revolution in both science and religion; that they would bring about a dawn of spiritual science and a faith supported by concrete evidence."[21] Like the movement's founder, Allan Kardec, Khalil Khan viewed Spiritism in positivist terms.[22] Playing on the two meanings of the word ʿelm as both science and knowledge, he wrote:

> Science/knowledge [ʿelm] means knowing realities [haqayeq], which means knowing things that are true and are not false or uncertain [mashkuk]. For example, the science of constructing automobiles means knowing realities or true things that, should one act according to them, an automobile will be made and will run and reach a determined destination. The same goes for the science of chemistry, the science of physics, the science of arithmetic, the science of geography, experimental spirit science, and other positive sciences.[23]

Before long, experimental spirit science attracted interest from outside the network of committed Spiritists. This may have been what Khalil Khan had hoped when he began to popularize Spiritism in his essays and in his society's meetings. But as séances propagated, adherence to the doctrine of reincarnation and the progression of souls became dispensable. Other authors wrote about hypnotism, telepathy, communication with spirits, and other "spiritual sciences" independently of Kardec's dogmas. For example, Heshmat Allah Dowlatshahi (1904–80), who founded a religious movement he dubbed "The New Universal Unity" (Vahdat-e Novin-e Jahani), incorporated hypnotism, telepathy, and communication with souls into his group's spiritual practice without accepting Spiritist reincarnation.[24] Mohammad 'Anqa (1887–1962), a bureaucrat and Sufi whose son Sadeq would establish the universalist Oveysi Shah Maqsudi order, also dabbled in hypnotism and communicated with spirits following years of association with Khalil Khan's Spiritist society.[25] And in what was perhaps the most mainstream of Sufi appropriations of hypnotism, Soltan Hoseyn Tabandeh Gonabadi Reza-'Ali Shah (1914–92), the future pole (*qotb*) of the Ne'matollahi Soltan 'Ali Shahi order, wrote an essay in 1939 on "magnetic sleep" (hypnotism) to be appended to his great-grandfather's treatise on sleep and dreaming.[26] In the essay, he suggested that Western research into hypnotism may have been informed by the works of Indian ascetics, Muslim mystics, and "spiritual occult science."[27] As with natural sleep, Tabandeh wrote, the "artificial sleep" induced by hypnotism proved the immateriality of the soul (*tajarrod-e ruh*) and the existence of a realm beyond the material.

The Shi'i ulama soon took notice too, although their exposure to Spiritism and psychical research largely occurred independently of the mediation of Khalil Khan and his circle. An influential alternative source was an Arabic-language encyclopedia published in the 1910s by the Egyptian scholar Muhammad Farid Wajdi (1878–1954). Wajdi spent a considerable part of his career attacking materialism and defending the truth of Islamic doctrine.[28] In the fourth volume of his encyclopedia, a full thirty-six pages of the section on *ruh* (the spirit) was devoted to sensory evidence of the existence of spirits as reported by European scientists, among whom he included chemist and physicist William Crookes, astronomer Camille Flammarion, neurologist Jules Bernard Luys, electrical engineer Cromwell Varley, and naturalist Alfred Russel Wallace. These pages would prove extremely valuable to Shi'i ulama in their own polemics from the 1940s onward.[29]

Ayatollah Ruhollah Khomeini (1902–89) was an early adopter of Wajdi's arguments in his well-known 1944 treatise, *Kashf-e Asrar* (Unveiling of Secrets). The book was a ferocious counterattack against anticlerical intellectuals who had accused the clergy of disseminating superstitious doctrines among a gullible populace.[30] One of these was belief in the power of the deceased imams to intercede with God to forgive petitioners' sins and cure their diseases. Ahmad Kasravi (1890–1946) had asked, for example, if there was any belief more misguided than considering the helpless dead to be God's colleagues.[31] For Khomeini, the dispute turned in part on whether spirits survived their mortal bodies and could continue to be efficacious in the world of the living. The permanence of the spirit beyond death, he wrote, was attested by philosophical reason.[32] In support of his argument, he cited evidence from the Qurʾan as well as enumerating the views of a range of philosophers—Thales of Miletus, Anaximenes, Empedocles, Pythagoras, Socrates, Plato, Aristotle, Avicenna, Suhrawardi, Mulla Sadra, and Descartes—finally arriving at modern European and American Spiritualists, mesmerists, hypnotists, and psychical researchers. Of the latter, he wrote:

> Magnetism or magnetic sleep [*nowm-e meqnatisi*] has strongly shaken the world, and the materialists are breathing their last breaths. In the near future, science will completely lift the veil from this topic and will make manifest the world of spirits and their eternal life and their strange phenomena, such as the insensitivity [to pain] of those in magnetic sleep, and their reports of the unseen [*gheyb-guʾi*] and hundreds of other astonishing secrets. [This science] will forever remove the foundations of materialism from the world.[33]

While discussing hypnotism and séances with disembodied spirits, Khomeini made several references to Wajdi's encyclopedia. As an example of astonishing spiritual manifestations, he translated Wajdi's account of an incident that allegedly involved Jules Luys, whom, it might be recalled, Khalil Khan had cited as his inspiration for studying experimental spirit science:

> One of the things that [Wajdi] cites in the encyclopedia is that Luys, who is a famous hypnotist [*khʷab-konandeh*], put a woman to sleep in the presence of a group and told her to go home and see what people were doing there. The sleeping woman said, "I went there. Two people are doing the house chores." Luys told her to put her hand on the body of one of them. At this point the sleeping woman laughed and said, "I put my hand on one of them as you ordered me to do, and they were very scared." Luys asked those present if anyone knew the woman's house. One said that they did. He asked them to go to her house and see if the story was correct or not. They went and saw that the residents of the house were in fear and panic. They asked the reason and were told that they had seen a figure [*heykal*] in the kitchen that moved and put a hand on someone there.[34]

Like Wajdi, Khomeini saw the significance of reports like this to lie in their verification by sense-data of what had already been confirmed by revelation and philosophical reason. Moreover, they were attested by "recurring scientific testimonies" (*tavator-e naql-ha-ye ʿelmi*), reports so numerous that they left no space for doubt about error or conspiracy to fabricate.[35]

The Spiritist reimagining of religious truth in terms of positive scientific knowledge was a novel contribution on the Iranian religious scene. As we will see, Wajdi and Khomeini's repurposing of Spiritist evidence for Islamic theological polemics also introduced something new, if more tentative and circumscribed. Their arguments that European experiments provided confirmation of the existence of souls by sense-data and recurring testimony drew on classical Islamic epistemological categories. But in order to accommodate the peculiar nature of their data, they also stretched these categories beyond the bounds of their classical formulations.

According to the philosopher Avicenna (d. 1037), propositions based on sense perception and recurrent testimonies were among those claims that the intellect gave assent to *by necessity*—or in other words, they furnished certain knowledge as opposed to supposition, beliefs taken on authority, and so on.[36] *Mahsusat*, sense-data, are those things we know to be true through the observation of the external senses as filtered through the faculty of common sense. For example: We know that snow is white because we can clearly see that it is white. *Mutawatirat*, on the other hand, are those sensibly observable things that we have heard about through recurring testimony, so much so that certainty is impressed on our minds and we consider it impossible that these testimonies have all been the products of error or of collusion on a lie.[37] For Avicenna, recurring testimonies included propositions about faraway cities: for example, even though I have never seen the city of Lahore, I know that it exists due to the recurring testimony of people who have been there and told others about it, and these testimonies have reached me from many different directions. The same goes for historic individuals like Galen and Euclid.[38]

We begin to run into difficulties once we apply these categories of certain knowledge to the empirical observation of disembodied souls. On the matter of sense perception, Wajdi left open the possibility that souls may leave material traces identifiable by the external senses. Muslim scholarly views are divided over whether the human spirit (*ruh*) is immaterial or a corporeal substance separate from but penetrating the body. With notable exceptions like the great theologian Ghazali, the corporeal doctrine has historically dominated Sunni views. The theistic philosophers, some Mu'tazili theologians, and the Shi'a on the other hand have held the opposite.[39] As a Sunni, Wajdi may have accepted the materiality of the spirit. Khomeini certainly did not. The latter's acceptance of sensory evidence for the existence of disembodied human spirits would therefore represent a radical departure from accepted doctrine. In fact, Wajdi seemed to have been more cautious on this issue than his Iranian readers: at one point, he writes that he attests to the existence of spiritual manifestations such as those reported by European scientists but suspends judgment as to whether these are manifestations of the spirits of the dead or of beings from some other world.[40] By the latter he probably meant the jinn, beings whose materiality is more widely accepted.[41] Khomeini did not repeat this statement of caution.

Spiritists and Shi'i scholars alike might respond to this objection by arguing that what the senses perceive is never the immaterial spirit but the subtle body that envelops it after death. Following Allan Kardec, Spiritists called this envelope the *perispirit*, a "fluidic," vapor-like substance that may take on forms resembling the spirit's corporeal incarnations. On the other hand, some Shi'i theologians—especially those influenced by the philosophy of Mulla Sadra, among whom Khomeini would have counted himself—subscribe to a notion of a *barzakhi* or "isthmus" body that is immaterial and yet perceptible through an imaginal (*mithali*) vision.[42] It is this imaginal isthmus body that some people perceive in dreams or waking states when encountering a deceased individual—usually a prophet or saint. Although the perispirit and the barzakhi body may seem like compatible concepts, however, they are, in fact, very different. Most important for our purposes, a barzakhi body is decidedly immaterial (the perispirit is subtle but material) and is unavailable to everyday sensory perception. To attain imaginal vision, the perceiver must normally undergo a regime of moral self-purification resulting in detachment from material wants. In the wakeful state, it is a vision restricted to prophets, certain elect friends of God, and other people of extraordinary self-control and spiritual power. If the perispirit became visible, on the other hand, it was visible to everyone at the séance. That is, it could become the object of repeatable empirical observation. The barzakhi body, by definition, could not.

On the second point—the transmission of sensory observations of spirits by *al-tawatur al-'ilmi* or recurring scientific testimony—it is important to note two things. First, *tawatur* was not classically restricted to reports narrated by a specific class of people such as scientists. That which was attested by recurring testimony was understood as having been reported by many ordinary people with no special qualifications. The sheer number of reports was such that it would overcome any doubts about isolated, unreliable narrators. Second, before the modern period the *mutawatirat* were not applied to what we would think of as empirical scientific observations. Even today this application is idiosyncratic. Their classical usage had to do with attestation of events or entities available to sense perception but beyond our reach due to their geographical or temporal distance: the existence of faraway cities, historic figures in the distant past, the burial locations of saints' bodies, the words and deeds of the prophet Muhammad, and the Qur'anic revelation.[43] Empirical observations had their own category in Avicenna's list of propositions that were attested by necessity: the *mujarrabat*, or things that have been tried repeatedly and proven through methodical experience. The philosophers' and theologians' favorite example of this was that "scammony purges bile."[44] But the mujarrabat were not private or one-off experiences: the purgative effect of scammony, for example, could be observed firsthand by anyone with access to the plant. Thus, it made no sense to think of such empirically observable phenomena in terms of recurring testimony.[45]

Wajdi's concept of recurring scientific testimony (*tawatur 'ilmi*), then, fused the older notion of recurring testimony of many people observing single events or entities (*tawatur*) with repeated empirical observations of a recurring phenomenon (*tajriba*), adding the twist that the reporters were now men of science and their empirical observations occurred under tight experimental conditions. By repeating this same epistemological move, Khomeini was doing more than adducing yet another kind of evidence for preexisting theological claims. His theological epistemology expanded and contorted in the process of citing empirical evidence. Even so, this transformation has not had far-reaching consequences for Shi'i theology. In fact, I have only seen analogous moves employed in very similar contexts where proof of the existence of im-material souls is concerned, and only in situations where theologians address a public, rather than in specialized scholarship. What these episodes illustrate, that is, is not so much an example of epistemic shift within Islamic theology but tentative and experimental attempts to push at the boundaries of classical thought within narrow and instrumentally specific contexts.

The Spiritists may have succeeded in promoting empirical observation as a reliable means for verifying the existence of souls. But they did not convince everyone, and some of their opponents also relied on empirical testing to debunk their claims. The strident anticlerical intellectual Ahmad Kasravi (1890–1946) was one such adversary. Kasravi lumped "communication with the dead" together with other "superstitions" (*pendar-ha*) like fortune-telling, astrology, sorcery, and belief in luck.[46] This particular superstition, he wrote, was new and originated in Europe:

> There was an era when priests boasted of speaking with gods. Then the time came for exorcists to speak to jinn and fairies. Now, in the era of the sciences, the worshippers of superstition have opened another door and converse with the spirits of the dead.[47]

While Kasravi mostly formulated his arguments through appeals to his readers' common sense to realize the absurdity of Spiritist claims, he also drew on his own dramatic experience at a séance to demonstrate that communica-tion with the dead could not be anything but baseless. The séance occurred in Tehran at the house of Sa'd al-Dowleh, a well-known politician whose son Vahid Sa'd inherited the leadership of the Spiritist society from Khalil Khan. Kasravi noticed that a few guests were sitting around a turning table, each engrossed in their activity. Every so often, the tabletop would turn and some words would be exchanged. He asked what the guests were doing and heard that they were communicating with a spirit:

> It was the first time I had encountered such a device. I had seen many articles about it in the Egyptian *al-Hilal* and *al-Muqtataf* monthlies, but had not read any of them. I only knew that many famous scientists supported it and wrote about it in their books, and so I did not have any negative thoughts about it and never suspected that it could be this baseless.[48]

As the men prepared for a new séance, Kasravi accepted their invitation to join. They sat around the table and rested their palms on top, concentrating. After a few moments the table began to turn. They were in the presence of a spirit, and it turned out to be a woman Kasravi knew, the mother of a friend who had died in a battle in the northwest several years earlier. Kasravi spoke to her and then to the spirit of her son, whom she fetched. He was deeply moved by the exchange:

> When we left the table, the veins in my body were trembling. It was as though I had been with that young man, in the same room, and was about to part from him. When I went home, I could not sleep until near dawn. I tossed and turned, struggling with different emotions and thoughts. Sometimes I would say: "What a pity! All this time there has been such an easy path for companionship with the dead; why haven't I known about it and taken to it?" Again I would think: "I only asked questions to which I already knew the answers. I should have asked of things I did not know." I passed the night with such anxieties.[49]

The next day Kasravi wrote to his brother in Tabriz to ask why he had not been informed of the death of his friend's mother. He heard back after a week that the old lady was alive and well. Kasravi was shocked. He realized that his conversations with his dead friend and his friend's ostensibly dead mother had all originated from within himself:

> It was here that the curtain was raised from baseless superstitions and I understood the mechanism of that device. I went to Saʿd al-Dowleh's house two or three times afterward and performed more experiments. The result from all of them was that there is no spirit involved. All that happens comes from those sitting around the table. And I thank God that I discovered the truth so easily.[50]

Kasravi concludes by asking how it was possible for such an unfounded issue to receive so much support from "thousands of professors and scientists." "I realized," he writes, "how deceivable humankind is. I realized that the sciences by themselves cannot prevent the worship of superstition, and that if some superstitions are eliminated, other superstitions can appear."[51]

Few of Kasravi's contemporaries, or, indeed, the inheritors of the debates in which he participated, would disagree with the claim that scientific knowledge by itself could not prevent superstitious folly. Even the Spiritists recognized this. For them, what was important in science was not merely a modality for acquiring true knowledge but a moral system that secured the epistemic enterprise. It is to a discussion of the morality of science that I now turn.

SCIENTIFIC VIRTUES

The Spiritists promoted a vision of empirical science—as a resource for moral leadership and reform—that they shared with some of their most vociferous critics. This meant not only that they thought scientific knowledge could be deployed in refining the moral character of their followers but that they also drew on their understandings of the virtues of scientific practice in fashioning their moral subjectivities. It was a vision of moral reform rooted in a tradition for which the refinement of character was essential to political practice.[1]

Nineteenth- and twentieth-century Iranian modernists called for sweeping reforms, with even political demands often couched in moral terms.[2] A unifying feature of modernist moral discourse prior to the 1905–11 Constitutional Revolution and for some decades afterward was to identify the political, economic, and military weaknesses of Iran with the moral deficiency of the Qajar monarchy (1794–1921/26), and sometimes with Islam and Arabs. This corruption was articulated as part of a larger package of ills, which also included the superstition and torpor of the masses, apathy and lack of manly zeal among the elites, and reactionary leadership among the ulama. Modernists offered a variety of prescriptions for overcoming these ills, including the adoption of modern scientific knowledge.[3]

Modernist attempts at reform have been primarily understood in terms of a break with the recent past and an aspiration toward a future imagined on the model of European progress (itself sometimes imagined in terms of a glorious ancient Iranian past). This has led to a scholarly neglect of certain important continuities, including the enduring relevance of the Perso-Islamic tradition of moral refinement and virtuous conduct.[4] Mana Kia has shown that modernists up to and through the constitutionalist period drew on a Persian tradition of moral cultivation and refinement of character in shaping their reformist discourse.[5] Even the acquisition of knowledge—including modern science—was articulated in terms of virtue: "In the context of older Persianate ideas, knowledge had long been the cornerstone of moral perfection, and was linked to ideas about the virtuous conduct of individuals and communities. This was because learning was thought to bestow the discernment necessary for the practice of moderation, the highest virtue."[6]

Studies of the reception of the modern sciences in Iran have neglected its connection to the development of the virtues. Hence, Cyrus Schayegh, in his excellent study of the rise of the sciences between 1900 and 1950, amply documents how modern psychology and pedagogy were deployed for moral reform—especially for the development of "willpower" necessary for producing "self-reliant personalities"—but he does not attempt to connect these projects of moral reform to the older tradition of the virtues.[7]

The Perso-Islamic tradition of moral refinement was centrally concerned with *self*-cultivation.[8] If moral reformers saw themselves as participants in this tradition, they must also have considered it necessary to cultivate certain virtues in themselves (or to appear to have done so) as proper to their role as reformers. Such specialized virtues were elaborated for a wide range of practices in the Islamic tradition. For example, Mehmet Kadri Karabela has discussed postclassical theories about the virtues proper to the practice of argumentation, including thoughtfulness, fairness, avoiding wheeling-dealing, and abstaining from pretension.[9] Muftis, those scholars called on by their followers to provide fatwas, have long had their own dedicated literary genre—known as *adab al-mufti*—for defining their qualifications and virtues. These have included self-reliance, generosity, pleasant manners, a quick wit, and professional competence in Arabic.[10]

As we will see in this chapter, modern science provided the imaginative resources with which some moral reformers could define their own qualifications on the model of professional scientists—that is, in terms of the virtues proper to scientific practice. Historians of science have long recognized the centrality of certain virtues and their attendant sensibilities and modes of comportment for disciplined scientific activity. These scholars have shown how practitioners of science are trained to develop distinctive modes of feeling, perceiving, and understanding; particular embodied relationships to their objects of inquiry through observation, experiment, and manipulation; and specific norms of relating to their peers and others whom they view as their audience.[11] These affect-charged constellations of understanding, perceiving, and behaving are at the very heart of science—determining, for example, what it means to quantify or maintain objectivity.[12]

Scientific virtues may be elaborated out of sensibilities prevalent in a broader social milieu. For example, Steven Shapin has shown that in seventeenth-century England, scientists negotiated the problem of the credibility of observations, experiments, and testimony by recourse to the codes of gentlemanly honor and trust.[13] More recently, Matthew Stanley has argued that the astronomer A. S. Eddington drew on a Quaker concept of "seeking" to develop an approach to scientific exploration on the basis of "physical intuition and observation."[14]

The borrowing of virtues also occurs in the opposite direction. While to my knowledge there have been no systematic explorations of the ways in which the virtues thought to constitute scientific practice have been adopted outside the community of scientists, we do have a rich literature on how certain religious movements have modeled their epistemologies on those of empirical science.[15] Scholars have also described religious practitioners who imagine their own work in terms of testing, experience, and experimentation.[16] I build on the insights of this research but place more explicit emphasis on the normative valences attached to the virtues of professional scientific activity as something to be emulated by religious leaders and moral reformers.

According to Khalil Khan and other Spiritists, not only were séances based in sound principles derived from positive science, but the very moral lessons garnered from these séances amounted to positive knowledge as good as any other scientific fact. These moral facts were counterpoised to a cacophony of conflicting moral systems based not on reason but on blind faith:

> Up till now the foundations of morality have been laid upon various blindly followed beliefs ['aqayed-e gunagun-e ta'abbodi] and these beliefs are different in each nation and are at odds with one another. On the other hand, scientific beliefs which have led to the progress of natural civilization are the same in the whole world and there is no variation among them... There is only one truth and there is no difference in that which is real. An internal [moral] police which would pertain to all nations would be founded upon scientific beliefs; that is, it should be based on the new discoveries of experimental spirit science.[17]

Just as the sciences of nature were everywhere the same, Khalil Khan argued, so should be the sciences of morality. The former had given rise to an advanced "natural civilization," but until moral truths were established through the discoveries of experimental spirit science, this civilization would be morally backward. The outward policing of morality needed to be bolstered by an inner police or conscience fully convinced of the truth of positive moral facts as discovered by Spiritism.

According to Khalil Khan and his associates, Spiritism taught the virtues of forgiveness, sacrifice, charity, patience, duty, respect for the Golden Rule, controlling one's lowly passions and desires, equity, avoidance of idleness and sloth, education, and putting one's knowledge to practice.[18] Some of these virtues were characteristic of a broader modernist orientation—these included discipline and avoidance of laziness, pursuing knowledge, and fulfilling one's duties.[19] Others were clearly adopted from Kardec's teachings. The Golden Rule, as Monroe points out, was the basis for Spiritism's social conception of morality, in which the locus of good and evil was found in one's conduct in relation to others. Spiritists therefore placed a high premium on charity and denigrated selfishness.[20] But these virtues were also fully consonant with the Persian tradition of moral refinement, in which, as Kia has noted, moral substance was manifest in proper conduct in relation to others.[21]

Despite his contention that, prior to the emergence of Spiritism, moralities were everywhere based on blind and conflicting faiths, Khalil Khan's own biography shows a more complicated picture. What changed in his approach to the virtues when he converted to Spiritism was not that he abandoned his prior commitments wholesale but that he jettisoned only certain aspects, namely, those requiring absolute respect for the commands received through authoritative Islamic sources. In 1891/92, only a few years before departing for France, Khalil Khan authored a treatise on moral refinement for children and youth. He began the text in the name of God, then proceeded to offer moral advice in fifty-odd pages on every aspect of daily conduct. On the first page, he wrote:

> The best virtue and the highest moral refinement for a human is to act according to the command of God and the Prophet, to obey whatever the great men of religion [*bozorgan-e din*] have ordered, and to not violate them by even as much as a hair's tip, so that he will enjoy life in the world and count among the good in the afterlife.[22]

He proceeded to offer that:

> Whatever a human being does and whatever he says should be on the basis of thinking and contemplation and in agreement with reason. For example, thought and reason say that compassion is good and harming is bad. So humans should act according to this same issue that reason tells them, that is, they should help others and show compassion whenever possible and not harm or abuse anyone.[23]

Both of these positions were received from the moral tradition that Khalil Khan inhabited as a Qajar aristocrat. Spiritism would lead him to abandon all references to prophets, imams, and "great men of religion." He even stopped opening his texts in the name of God. But he would preserve his inherited commitment to reason. The virtues he had espoused—all with the exception of fealty to Islamic authority—seem to have remained unscathed as well. Only now he bolstered them with empirical verification. Finally, his works hewed close to the Persian tradition of virtue in his use of short didactic aphorisms, his deployment of the format of *hekayat* (stories or anecdotes meant to impart moral lessons), and in his reliance on the vocabulary of *nasihat* (moral advice).[24]

This continuity notwithstanding, the role of moral scientist required additional capacities and dispositions, and these Khalil Khan adapted from his understanding of the virtues of professional scientific practice. As a positive science, he considered Spiritism to share certain features with physics and chemistry in terms of the sensibilities it demanded from seekers of knowledge. First, empirical science required a freedom of thought unbridled by the arbitrary dictates of blindly followed religion. If anything, Khalil Khan argued that only empirical scientific knowledge should set limits on freedom of thought (*azadi-ye khiyal*).[25] Sometimes he went as far as defining freethinking in terms of receptivity to scientific truth. For example, he wrote that there were two kinds of people—those who followed reason and humanity (*'aql va ensaniyyat*) and those who obeyed false beliefs and delusions (*'aqayed-e bateleh va mowhumat*):

> The first group makes progress day by day with the advance of positive sciences, including experimental spirit science. The second [group], who are bound by false, blindly followed beliefs, can never attain correct knowledge and awareness of truths and realities as they are, unless those beliefs are first taken out of their heads and the slate is wiped clean and they are, so to speak, made free-thinkers [*azad khiyal*].[26]

Khalil Khan wrote that as an adolescent, he himself had long been ensnared by superstitions like belief in evil omens, which disrupted his disciplined pursuit of knowledge. Over time he had worked on himself and succeeded in discarding many of these illusions, but his thought was not fully freed until he attained complete awareness of "the realities of contemporary spirit science."[27]

Second, empirical scientific research required ascetic discipline, strong will, and patient struggle. Quoting Voltaire—one of his heroes—Khalil Khan wrote that science or knowledge of the truth was a reward achieved only through hard work. It would not just fall to a person "from the sky" as if by divine grace. Sloth and lack of discipline would deprive one of the reward of knowledge.[28] In the context of the séance, disciplined effort took concrete form in the calibration of the experiment, the management of participants' conduct, and the guidance of communication with the spirits. According to Khalil Khan, the séance leader needed to carefully select the participants to ensure success, as the spiritual states of the members and their "fluidic reserves" could promote or hinder the manifestation of spirit phenomena. The correct choice of participants would be verified either by a guardian spirit (*ruh-e hami*) or through practice, and the séance leader would make modifications as necessary. Positive results could sometimes take months or even years to achieve, so participants needed to be serious, diligent, and patient. The leader also had to be decisive in his management of participants' behavior, forbidding unreasonable requests and preventing personal opinions and jealousies from intruding into the experiment. Once contact was established with a spirit, the leader needed to exercise his skill to discern the true identity of the interlocutor and unmask any impostors. He had to endeavor to "purify the morals of inferior spirits" and thwart the disruptions of "vulgar and riotous spirits" who often wreaked havoc on séances.[29] This spirit-sifting was, in effect, a method of distinguishing admissible experimental evidence from errors and deceptions. Moral facts could speak for themselves only when extraneous noise and interference was silenced.[30]

Khalil Khan considered his moral ideas and his scientific interest in spirit communication to have evolved in tandem. These moral ideas had something in them of the virtues of positive science as Khalil Khan had come to understand the latter through his education at the Dar al-Fonun and in Paris. Like the facts of physics and mathematics, he thought of moral facts as universally valid and transcending the fruitless squabbling of theologians. These facts could only be grasped by a freethinker dedicated to a disciplined study of the empirical facts of the spirit world, not through theological speculation or blind imitation of religious authority. And although this study was ostensibly open to anyone with the right instruments, it required a virtuoso ability to manage experiments to sift admissible evidence from the wiles of mischievous spirits and the jealousies of participants.

The Spiritists were not alone in emphasizing the scientific virtues. We can see analogous attempts some decades later among Muslim theologians who took it upon themselves to combat the influence of a newly resurgent and popularizing Spiritism. One of these theologians was Naser Makarem Shirazi (b. 1924). In the late 1950s, Makarem was among a rising generation of media-savvy scholars in Qom who founded *Dars-ha-yi az Maktab-e Eslam* (*Lessons from the School of Islam*), a monthly magazine that addressed the urban, educated classes with a clear and unapologetic Shi'i Islamic revivalist voice and quickly established itself as an articulate public-outreach arm for the Qom howzeh.[31] The magazine set a new standard for Islamic discourse that was shorn of complicated scholarly prose, openly engaged contemporary national and global events (while attempting to steer clear of direct criticism of the Pahlavi regime), embraced scientific discoveries and technological progress, and did all of this with philosophical sophistication. Its editors and contributors performed much of the groundwork in shifting educated public opinion toward an activist, progressive, universalist, scientifically minded Islam, which would form the discursive bedrock for the eventual founding of the Islamic Republic in 1979.[32]

A decade after its founding, the magazine had the occasion to flex its intellectual muscles against Iranian Spiritism. The latter had found a new and energetic advocate in Abol-Qasem Farzaneh, an essayist for the popular modernist weekly *Ettela'at-e Haftegi* (Weekly Information). Farzaneh wrote stories about communication with the spirits of the dead, explicated the doctrine of reincarnation and the progression of souls that was once promulgated by Khalil Khan and his circle, and instructed his readers on simple methods for holding séances. Soon thereafter, "summoning spirits" (*ehzar-e arvah*) became a common household pastime. Critics called it an "epidemic" (*epidemi*) and a "fad" (*mod*). In January 1969, Makarem tackled the subject by authoring a series of critical essays published in *Lessons from the School of Islam* over the span of a year. He began by arguing at length against the doctrine of reincarnation, and later examined the séance as a site of alleged communication with the spirits of the dead. Makarem did not reject the possibility of contact with spirits outright. Rather, he investigated the specific circumstances in which Iranian Spiritists operated to show that they could not withstand scrutiny:

> No one can deny the existence of the soul… because the philosophical, sensory, and empirical reasons that have been provided for proving the existence of the soul are too numerous to be ignored. Moreover, given the ample evidence that exists, one cannot deny the possibility of contact with souls through appropriate scientific means for those experienced individuals who have truly worked and struggled toward this end… But no logic or reason can accept a condition in which such an important matter is belittled to the point that anyone can construct a turning table for fun and entertainment… one night to summon the soul of Avicenna and another night to bother Razi, and a third night to menace Einstein… and to make anything and everything into a topic of discussion— from the due date of Mrs. X to the truth or falsity of religions and sects and philosophical schools.[33]

Even so, the monthly invited readers to submit evidence from "sense-data and observation" (*hess va moshahedeh*) to "practically demonstrate the possibility of contact [with spirits]," saying it would be open to publishing the results, no matter what, to complement the discussion.[34]

Rather than waiting for such evidence to be presented by his readers, Makarem decided to conduct his own experiment in the city of Sabzevar to evaluate the claims of the Iranian Spiritists. In the span of three short essays, Makarem provides a wonderfully detailed ethnographic description of a séance, along with a discussion of the technology of the table, the procedures for establishing contact with spirits and interpreting their messages, the beliefs and opinions of different practitioners and participants about the process, and the social and historical context of the recent "fad."[35]

The particular séance that Makarem attended was led by a young man who also doubled as a medium. A private meeting of only a few men was convened at around 11:00 p.m. The young man used a small but heavy square-shaped table for contact. Seated on a chair and with both palms on the table's surface, he recited a *hamd va sureh* and asked the participants to do the same, then stared at the table and asked the spirits in a quiet but deliberate tone to establish contact.[36] After a few moments, the wooden planks in the table made a slight noise. The young medium again entreated the spirits to enter into communication with him: "Please, I ask you to establish stronger contact." All of a sudden, the front side of the table rose about ten or twenty centimeters from the ground. Makarem notes that one of the participants thought the table had risen as a result of the medium's manual pressure, "and it was indeed something to suspect!," but the idea was that the movement was caused by the spirits, and Makarem decided to follow along.

Having established contact, the medium asked the spirit to introduce itself. He recited the alphabet from the beginning and whenever the table rose, two participants would jot down the letter at which the movement had taken place. The table would then fall back to the ground and the medium would start the alphabet from the beginning. "Soon it became apparent," Makarem writes, "that the spirit ... was 'B-O-R-U-J-E-R-D-I,' that is, the late Ayatollah [Hoseyn] Borujerdi," who—it so happened—had been Makarem's teacher and his magazine's most powerful advocate from its founding till his death.[37]

Borujerdi had a message in Arabic for the gathering, which the men recorded as follows: "qala-llah ta'ala qulu la ilaha illa-llah tuflihu" (God Almighty said: Say there is no god but God, [so that] you will succeed). But when the participants examined the disjointed letters that they had connected to form the sentence, they realized first that there were several discrepancies (an extra letter here, a missing letter there). Second, there were spelling errors that were "improbable to have been committed by the late Ayatollah Borujerdi," as he had been a master of Arabic literature. But if these were negligible issues, there was an even more important matter—the famous saying the spirit had quoted came from the prophet Muhammad, not God: "This error by the spirit of Ayatollah Borujerdi could not be ignored! And it gave us the right to doubt the veracity of the contact."

Makarem was asked if he wanted to put any questions to the spirit of Ayatollah Borujerdi. He said he wanted to know what would become of the howzeh in Qom, since this was an issue that had worried many howzeh scholars since the death of their doyen. The spirit gave a "general response, which we all knew." Unsatisfied, Makarem asked the medium to request that the spirit provide a "sign" pertaining to the relationship between Ayatollah Borujerdi and Makarem and others among the former's students who lived in Qom during his lifetime. This needed to be a private sign, something of which others had not been aware. Alternatively, Makarem suggested that he could ask the spirit a question and request that he respond in Arabic. Or he could think of something and ask the spirit to read his mind, since the medium and others had claimed that spirits could read minds. At least one of these items would be required to convince Makarem that they had in fact been communicating with the spirit of his teacher.

At this point, contact broke off for "unknown reasons," and the spirit left the gathering. The medium attempted to reestablish communication, but other spirits made themselves available in Ayatollah Borujerdi's stead. Each offered some rather uninteresting statements. But Makarem wanted to speak only to Borujerdi and insisted on receiving his private sign. "The point in all of this was," he writes, "that we should not accept something without examination. Reason would not allow us to yield with our eyes and ears closed, and God would not be satisfied either." Such a sign was not forthcoming. One spirit launched into a tirade against Makarem for his skepticism. Another said that he would make himself manifest but then appeared only to the medium. Makarem concluded that "the issue of the round and long tables" is more of a game than reality, and the messages that were communicated were the products of the medium's unconscious working through the nerves in his hands rather than the intervention of any spirits.[38]

Although Makarem thus publicly discredited a single séance, he did not generalize his finding to all séances. Not only did he accept the testimony of European scientists about their communications with spirits, he also left open the possibility that he could be persuaded of such contacts in Iran. This opening, however, was presented as a challenge that proved his victory over the Iranian Spiritists by default. "In two issues of the magazine printed in tens of thousands of copies," he wrote:

> [W]e invited those who claim to establish contact with spirits… to do so in practice at a gathering of people of virtue and knowledge [*majma'i az ahl-e fazl va danesh*]. We promised to print what we observe exactly in the magazine… We once again renew this invitation and we add that the magazine will pay the expenses of such a person's travel to Qom and five days' stay at one of Qom's first-rate hotels on the condition that this person obtain convincing signs from the spirit that are acceptable to the knowledgeable [*ahl-e ettela'*].[39]

In sum, as far as Makarem was concerned, trustworthy evidence of communication with spirits was of two kinds: either it had to come by way of recurring testimony of respected "people of virtue and knowledge," such as European scientists and Muslim jurists, or it had to be the product of sensory perception verified by a rational, skeptical mind. With the first kind of evidence, Makarem established an equivalence between modern scientists and howzeh scholars. With the second kind, he acknowledged that the spirit could be the object of sensory perception while adding the qualifier that the kind of evidence that could point to the existence of spirits could also point to trickery or the movements of the unconscious mind. Only a select few had the ability to discern the difference, and they did so under strictly controlled experimental conditions.

The Egyptian scholar Muhammad Farid Wajdi (whose work I discussed in chapter 12) had provided the details of the strict experiments under which European scientists had ostensibly observed genuine spiritual phenomena. Makarem cited Wajdi's claim that these scientists would "tightly bind the medium to a chair, and sometimes even confine him or her to an iron cage, lock the door of the room in which the experiment was taking place, and attach electric wires to the medium's hands to detect any movement, no matter how slight or quick… in order to ascertain that these [extraordinary] actions were related to spirits, not the person of the medium."[40] Makarem concluded that "one can accept that Spiritism… has passed the threshold of theoretical interest to become an empirical science based on sense-data," but this scientific endeavor had been misappropriated by charlatans and the naive, who thought that they could "establish contact with spirits great and small without any scientific information and merely using a turning table or a cup on a page full of letters."[41]

In his yearlong polemic against Iranian Spiritism, Makarem did more than refute a set of doctrinal statements and empirical claims about spirits. He also modeled what he thought theological reasoning in a mass-circulating magazine should look like. The norms to which Makarem self-consciously adhered had to do both with the conventions of public reasoning his readers took for granted and a set of virtues that he and his colleagues at the magazine wanted to promote. Although Makarem's polemics against reincarnation merit attention in their own right, I will focus my remarks only on his empirical arguments, as it is here that we can find the enactment of certain virtues associated with professional scientific practice.

Like Khalil Khan, Makarem believed that scientific practice required dedication and hard work. The former would have agreed with Makarem's assessment that contact with spirits was possible only "for those experienced individuals who have truly worked and struggled toward this end."[42] For Makarem this dedicated struggle involved, as I already indicated, an unflinching attention to controlling the setting of the experiment to weed out any possibility of error or deception. Khalil Khan believed this was necessary too, but since he was convinced that it was indeed spirits who were responsible for the turning of tables and the automatic writing of mediums at his séances, he was less concerned with human trickery and observational error than with the disruptions of inferior spirits.

If Makarem's European Spiritists confined mediums to iron cages and attached galvanometers to their limbs to detect the slightest movements, Makarem himself would scrupulously note every detail of the experiment he observed—the time at which it occurred, the features of the table used for contact, the behavior of the medium, the details of the messages that were conveyed, and so on. It was through this scrupulous attention that he was able to detect signs of conscious or unconscious human intervention—did the table rise as a result of the medium's manual pressure? Were the Arabic spelling mistakes committed by the spirit of Ayatollah Borujerdi?—that invalidated the claim that the experimental evidence the medium produced had an otherworldly provenance.

This brings us to another virtue Makarem emphasized as proper to scientific discovery: skepticism. Given the range of possible causes for alleged spiritual phenomena, Makarem believed that a scientific approach to these phenomena required that the experimenter maintain a skeptical posture in order to rule out the alternatives. The scientific testimonies he read in Wajdi's encyclopedia were all the more compelling because the European scientists cited there had embarked on their studies with a spirit of suspicion and even of contempt. Khalil Khan, in his attention to the control of experimental conditions, would have recognized the importance of skepticism as well. But for the latter, as for the French Spiritists and psychical researchers who inspired him, the skepticism of the majority of the representatives of organized science amounted to a dogmatism that undermined the spirit of scientific exploration that depended on open-mindedness and curiosity.[43] Rather than emphasizing skepticism, he called for suspending judgment until scientific confirmation could be secured, even though by suspension of judgment, he really meant suspending the urge to deny.[44] Makarem too, as we saw, demonstrated his scientific open-mindedness— both by accepting the testimony of European scientists and by claiming that he was willing to entertain any evidence provided by the Iranian Spiritists as long as it met his conditions. The balance of skepticism and open-mindedness, however, produced very different results in the two men's work.

Dedication, scrupulousness, and skepticism were the ingredients that went into the making of "people of virtue and knowledge"; that is, those whom Makarem considered trustworthy sources of scientific testimony. In the course of his polemical engagement with Spiritism, he performatively modeled these virtues while hinting that "virtue and knowledge" may not be restricted to jurists and theologians in Qom but characterize European scientists as well. In the context of a mass-circulating Islamic magazine of the 1960s, this was a masterful move. In one fell swoop, he showed his audience that Muslim theologians were men of reason and science rather than of superstition and backwardness, he undercut the Iranian Spiritists' claims to association with European science, and he modeled for his pious readership what a synthesis of Islamic rationality with a commitment to science and progress should look like. In this context, his insistence that "[r]eason would not allow us to yield with our eyes and ears closed" merely reinforced a commitment central to the mission of his magazine (and one in which he participated repeatedly himself) to demonstrate the firm, rational grounding of Shi'i doctrine.[45] Of course, this also meant that Makarem was making theological reason— *'aql*—commensurable with scientific rationality.[46]

While Makarem's theologico-scientific exploration was characterized by certain scientific virtues, its object too was ultimately moral. In this, again, we see an affinity between Makarem's project and that of Khalil Khan and his Spiritist colleagues, and, again, there are important divergences. Makarem was worried about a condition of moral and epistemological anarchy in which anyone with a talent for the "game" of table-turning could not only make claims about religion, philosophy, and the order of the universe but attract a following as well.[47] His concern was particularly acute in an era of uncertainty about the future of Shi'i religious leadership and the role of the howzeh after Ayatollah Borujerdi. It was only fitting that his one experience with a séance should turn into a showdown over who had the right to inherit the authority of—indeed speak for—the great marjaᶜ: his qualified student or a young provincial medium.

If Khalil Khan had discovered positive moral facts through his séances with the spirits of the dead, Makarem undercut such claims to moral truth—which he saw as anarchic—by discrediting the séance. Moral truth, for Makarem, was not to be found in a turning table or the automatic writing of a medium. Even though he did not explicitly state this, there is little doubt that he saw the "people of virtue and knowledge" not only as good empirical observers but as trustworthy exponents of virtue as well. On the latter, he would have restricted the people of virtue and knowledge to the jurists and theologians in Qom. None of the European scientists Wajdi had cited said anything about morality beyond affirming the truth of immaterial existence and disparaging materialism. For Makarem, this was as it should have been.

How might the virtues proper to scientific experiment be related to those virtues discovered, sustained, or defended *through* such experimentation? For Khalil Khan and his Spiritist colleagues, the two were inseparable. Scientific virtues like freethinking, discipline, and patient struggle were valuable in themselves, but they were also indispensable as enabling virtues—that is, as those dispositions through which positive, infallible moral facts could be discovered and secured. Without the first set of virtues, séance participants risked falling prey to their passions or to the deceptions of inferior spirits.

For Makarem, scientific virtues like skepticism, diligence, open-mindedness, and scrupulousness belonged more squarely with the scholarly elite. The task of investigating the séance was not one that he would recommend for everyone. "I confess," Makarem wrote, "that participation in these meetings might not be appropriate for ordinary people. But for those who have a duty to conduct research or provide guidance to others, it sometimes gains an aspect of necessity."[48] Ordinary people did not need to equip themselves with the tools of scholarly investigation as long as such scholars as Makarem were around to guide them. The point of this series of public engagements, that is, was not so much to instruct his readership in the inculcation of the virtues of scientific or theological scholarship as to persuade them that their guides had the scholarly competence and virtuous sensibilities that qualified them for their job.

As we have seen, the gift of modern science to Iranian religious thinking has not been purely epistemological but moral as well. The virtues of professional scientific practice imagined by moral reformers—values like open-mindedness, skepticism, diligence, and scrupulousness—were sometimes treated as fully consistent with an existing tradition, as by Shiᶜi scholars like Makarem, and at other times as affecting a break with the past, as by Khalil Khan and his Spiritist circle. I have shown that it was both: the scientific virtues were new to the extent that their formulations depended on representations of modern European scientific activity, but they were absorbed into a long-standing tradition of moral refinement and therefore rendered continuous with a cherished past.

Viewed in this way, the religious appeal to science may constitute a mode of serious inquiry directed toward securing a virtuous future.[49] But it need not always do so with the kind of commitment to empirical method we have seen in the Spiritists and their opponents. Looser, more self-consciously creative deployments are also possible, and our picture of science's epistemic significance for religious thought and practice will be incomplete unless we consider them. I turn to these imaginative uses of science next.

WINGS OF IMAGINATION

The Iranian Spiritists' claims to knowledge were based on a positivist conception of empirical science that left very little room for gaps between what could
be known and what could be entertained as plausible, if not demonstrable,
truth. Not every religious appeal to science is as strident. In this chapter I will
present a number of examples that show a looser, more tentative, and more
experimental deployment of science, one that is concerned primarily with
imaginative constructions of the plausible and worries less about ascertaining
the accuracy of such constructions. These examples will give us a richer grasp
of the myriad ways in which *scientific imaginaries* permeate understandings
of religious phenomena, even such central theological concepts as the Day of
Judgment and divine rewards and punishments.

In my usage, a scientific imaginary consists of two things: first is an experimental template for transposing ways of knowing (concepts, models, methods,
evidential considerations, styles of reasoning, interpretive schemas, subjective
orientations, and so on) from one or more well-established contexts of scientific knowledge-practice to less-explored terrain. The "scientific" in the scientific imaginary thus locates the origin point of diffusion in some kind of practice conventionally understood or imagined as scientific. The "imaginary," on
the other hand, indexes imaginativeness and a quality of emergence. It indi-
cates that scientific diffusions may be more or less flexible, more or less playful,
and more or less faithful to the original—with the exact degree of flexibility
and playfulness varying, depending on the specific imaginary under consid-
eration. Understood in this way, the transposition of structuralism from the
study of language to analyses of mythology involves a specific scientific imaginary, as does the adoption of empirical methods in communicating with the
dead, or the deployment of mathematical modeling in Qur'anic exegesis.[1]

Second, a scientific imaginary comprises images and representations that
capture a range of aspirations, hopes, fears, anxieties, and moral judgments
attached to scientific knowledge and practice.[2] These might include, for example, idealized images of objectivity, precision, progress, rationality, and
technological mastery, or conversely of alienation, victimization, and ecologi-
cal destruction. Given the wide currency of some of these images and their
power to shape people's understandings of their own social existence, their
relationship to others, and the normative conceptions that undergird their

collective practices, a scientific imaginary may also become entangled with one or more *social imaginaries*.[3] I examined just such a situation in chapter 13 by showing how understandings of scientific virtues informed ideas of moral reform geared toward national progress and renewal. By analytically linking the two kinds of imaginary (the scientific and the social), it becomes possible to notice that the impetus for acts of scientific transposition—what makes these translations desirable, plausible, or persuasive—may have to do with concerns that go beyond the mere efficacy or prestige of a certain branch of scientific knowledge-practice.

Let me turn now to three examples of self-consciously playful and tentative deployments of scientific imaginaries.

One—In June 2008, I had a conversation with Hadi, a senior undergraduate student in mechanical engineering who had taken an interest in my research and introduced me to various people for interviews. Hadi told me that he was fascinated with extraordinary phenomena, particularly divinations and premonitions. But he had never found the time to seriously pursue such matters, and furthermore, he feared they might cause misfortunes (*nahsi*). Still, what little experience he had acquired had given him invaluable insights.

His examples were simple and undramatic. In his grandparents' village in the northwestern province of Ardabil, a custodian for an orchard owned by his grandmother possessed a large, flat, circular stone, about thirty centimeters in diameter, that showed signs of divinatory properties. Hadi explained the divination process as follows: One person would lower the stone onto two others' hands, each of whom were to use only their thumbs and index fingers to balance the stone. When the stone was still, they could ask it a question. The stone would then make a very slight circular motion in response, indicating "yes" or "no" depending on the direction of its spin. It was possible, he said, that the stone's slight movement could be caused by the motion of fingers adjusting to its weight. But he had tested it enough times to conclude that there were other forces at work than mere gravity and the twitching of muscles.

Hadi's other experiences had to do with premonitions. He had paid the most attention to intuitions he felt while watching football matches, but also in relation to car accidents and the death of loved ones. Had he the requisite time, he said, he would experiment with his premonitions to come up with a "theory for predicting reality" (*te'ori-ye pishbini-ye vaqe'iyyat*). To do so, he said, he needed to focus on the feelings and carefully analyze them as they occurred: "You try to find out where it has come from and how it might be amplified. You check off your mental factors one by one. You put your different feelings together. If you have a spiritual connection with God, you try to amplify that connection through prayer, abstaining from lying, and so on.

The point is to be able, in the end, to differentiate between different kinds of intuitions."

Hadi spoke with precision and took care to weigh his arguments with logic. He distinguished those things that he had personally witnessed from those he heard from others, like his grandmother. If he was uncertain about something recounted to him, he would say so. Even when describing something uncanny that he had seen with his own eyes, he was careful to mention alternative explanations, to rule them out if necessary, and to provide logical arguments as to why the metaphysical explanation should be more favorable or probable.

Hadi also recognized the limits of his speculations. After elaborating at greater length about the process whereby he thought premonitions about football incidents occurred, he admitted that his "academic" perspective might be completely off the mark:

> Maybe because my mind is an engineering mind, it messes things up. People who study medicine have a totally different approach compared to engineers. Maybe it's better to use their methods. Maybe if you arrange these matters through a different arithmetic (*hesab ketab*), you will achieve better results. It's like with different coordinate systems. Among the polar, Cartesian, cylindrical, and spherical coordinate systems, the easiest and best seems to be the Cartesian system. But sometimes you realize that, wow, if you adopt the spherical or cylindrical system, your problem becomes so much easier to solve. There are things that might make sense in the Cartesian system but are completely wrong in the spherical system, for example, in the representation of vectors. In the same way, it could be that what we see through an academic lens and think, "oh, this doesn't work" or "it's a counterexample" would not be a counterexample at all if viewed in a different coordinate system. It could be that the two are really equivalent points.

Hadi understood that there were different frameworks through which one could theorize metaphysical phenomena, and that these were possibly incommensurable. His distinction between Cartesian, cylindrical, polar, and spherical coordinate systems pointed toward the different possibilities for modeling and problem-solving that exist in alternative representational orders. Furthermore, by comparing medicine and engineering, he suggested that his own analytic apparatus might be too limited to conceptualize the full range of possibilities required for tackling the difficult problems he had been thinking about. In other words, Hadi recognized that successful metaphysical inquiry required a capacious and flexible scientific imagination.

Two—In the summer of 2010, Dr. Amir Movahhed, an electrical engineer and university professor, told me about a set of simple calculations he had performed to show that it would be possible for a human being's good and evil deeds to be recorded within a miniscule portion of his or her bodily substance, in order to be retrieved in the afterlife for the final judgment. The idea came to him in a gathering at a friend's house some years earlier, when one of the guests, a staunch materialist, ridiculed the Islamic idea that there were two angels (known as the *keram al-katebin* or "noble scribes") appointed for every human being to record every one of his or her deeds in minute detail. Performing a few quick calculations in his head, Dr. Movahhed responded to the guest that it was completely unnecessary to imagine anthropomorphic scribes sitting on people's shoulders and writing down their actions. All such deeds could be encoded in numbers and recorded in a tiny fragment of the human body, in its very electrons. Later, he performed the calculations in greater detail on his computer. He e-mailed me a Microsoft Excel sheet and explained the numbers to me like this:

> Let's take the typical human life span to be eighty years. In microseconds, that would be about 2.5×10^{15}. Now, let's say that we were to score the person's behavior or even thought process every microsecond (that is, every millionth of a second), assigning at each moment a numerical value between, let's say, 0 and 1,000. We would need 10 bits of information to represent each such value. So for a total lifetime, we would need about 2.5×10^{16} bits. To store such data, we could use electrons, with the assumption that the spin direction of each electron can store one bit of information. That is, we would determine that a spin up would equal a 1, and a spin down would be a 0. To record all the information, we would therefore require 2.5×10^{16} electrons. Using the Avogadro Constant, we know that each microgram of hydrogen has 6.02×10^{17} electrons. So to store a lifetime's worth of information as we've defined it, we would need approximately 0.04 micrograms of hydrogen from the person's body. If we imagine that after death, even only less than a tenth of a microgram of the hydrogen in the individual's body were to survive, we would still have enough to contain information on a lifetime of actions and thoughts.

Dr. Movahhed went further. To be able to match each personal record to an individual identity, we would require a unique number for each person—a kind of identity number. To calculate the number of bits required to store such information, we would first have to know how many humans will have lived on Earth before Judgment Day. Estimates for the total number of humans up to the present time range from 100 to 115 billion people. Dr. Movahhed suggested that we could take the final number to be as large as we want. "Let's assume that it were 100 billion times 100 billion, or about 1×10^{22}." He left it to me to calculate how many bits would be required to represent a unique identity number for one person among so many, but he said that whatever the number, it would only be a negligible addition to the amount of bits we had already set aside for the lifetime's worth of data (he was right: no more than seventy-four bits would be required for each identity number).

Despite the intricacy of his formulation, Dr. Movahhed emphatically denied that the model represented reality in any way. "All I am saying," he told me, "is that it is possible to conceive of this aspect of the hereafter in a way that makes sense given our current scientific knowledge."

Three—Mehdi Bazargan (1908–95) was a French-trained thermodynamics engineer, Iran's first prime minister after the 1979 revolution, and a lifelong activist for democratic reform. He was also a leading representative of what has come to be known as "religious modernism," an intellectual movement that emerged after the 1940s in response to the concern that communism and Baha'ism were corrupting the minds of Iranian youth.[4] Aside from Bazargan, the key figures within this movement were Mahmud Taleqani (1911–79), a cleric, and Yadollah Sahabi (1905–2002), a geologist, also trained in France. In 1961, they founded the Liberation Movement of Iran (*Nehzat-e Azadi-ye Iran*), which went on to become one of the central forces of the revolution and formed the interim government before falling from favor and becoming an opposition group.

Religious modernists were concerned with reconciling Islam with modern science and liberal politics. Their intellectual orientations were shaped both by their training in modern science and engineering and their pious upbringing. Situating themselves within the circles of urban intelligentsia, their approach to the relationship between science and religion was rather loose, undisciplined, and unbound by the strictures of the Islamic exegetical and theological tradition as practiced in the howzeh and represented by a journal like *Lessons from the School of Islam* (see chapter 13). As they found themselves battling a powerful materialist current that was armed with logical and scientific arguments, they decided to harness science to fashion an alternative ideology. In the process, they created an Islamic worldview shot through with a scientific imagination that proved appealing to their educated audience.

One of Bazargan's approaches was to use contemporary scientific knowledge to rethink classical Islamic teachings. Thermodynamics, the subject of his university training, furnished him with his favorite models.[5] The idea for a book on the topic came to him while he was incarcerated by the Pahlavi regime in a military prison in the spring of 1955:

> Thankfully, reading and writing was not forbidden. So my main preoccupation... was leafing through books. A few novels and books of legends, that is, love stories, and a few religious books including prayers and biographies and discussions of matters of belief, that is, books whose end is worship of the Eternal Essence... In addition, I had asked [my family] to bring me my industrial

thermodynamics book from home, so that I could use the available opportunity to think through a topic about the similarity between [industrial thermodynamics] and chemical reactions.[6]

He called the resulting book *Love and Worship, or Human Thermodynamics* (*'Eshq va Parastesh, ya Termodinamik-e Ensan*). It was, he admitted in good humor, "a difficult-to-digest confection," which, "good or bad," should be credited to those who were responsible for his idleness in captivity.[7]

In his book, Bazargan brought the first and second laws of thermodynamics to bear on a full range of human phenomena: the individual life cycle with its biological, emotional, intellectual, spiritual, and social dimensions; the dynamics of societies and economic structures; the development and functioning of moral systems; life after death; and worship of the divine. He believed that any system in which some kind of energy was produced and transformed could be analyzed through the laws of thermodynamics. "In life," he wrote, "there is heat, and there is activity. Therefore there are thermodynamics as well":

> This is not the first time that thermodynamics has intruded upon the terrain of other sciences so that, by sniffing that which exudes [from its objects], it would be able to figure out their workings, take the theorems and laws that they have deduced after years of experience and explained in complex and involved language, and return them as simple mathematical formulas that can be used for further inference. It has done this in thermoelectrics, in the melting and extraction of metals, in thermal radiation, and in chemical reactions. What should keep it from experimenting with biology, and even with human economic, moral, and religious activities? Thermodynamics is a young science. There is no blame upon the youth for entertaining wishes [*arezu bar javanan 'eyb nist*]![8]

And so Bazargan produced mathematical equations and curves for various human systems and processes, treating them as so many thermodynamic systems and "Carnot heat engines," defining in each case variables like heat, pressure, volume, energy, and entropy. In footnotes, he supplemented his scientific analyses with Qur'anic verses and hadith from the Prophet and imams. Like a good scientist, he saw his work as a form of modeling: it could very well be flawed, but it should invite critique, fine-tuning, and improvement.

Bazargan was most self-conscious about his method when writing about the hereafter. Here he was treading completely speculative ground, writing of things that could not be empirically tested or verified. But there was still a scientific logic to his imaginative enterprise. He said that if one were to begin with the assumption that another world and another life existed after death, thermodynamics would help explain the processes and the conditions under which such life would come to be. This would only be "extremely approximate and incomplete, in the form of specters and speculation."[9] But perhaps more importantly, such a model would help us judge the signs provided to us by the prophets:

> This [method] is a means by which we can judge the acceptability of those signs that the prophets have given us about the other world, assuming they will occur. If the collection of reports that have been given about resurrection and heaven and hell turn out to be reasonable and coherent, and if contemporary science also to some extent bears witness to its logicality, it will become apparent that the basis [of these reports] has not been delusive and imaginary. The issue of the hereafter is so far from fantasy and reason and so inaccessible to humankind that, should someone tell a story about it, it will inevitably have to be either one hundred percent meaningless and irrelevant, or, if there is some evidence for some parts of it, it should be taken seriously in its entirety.[10]

Thus, thermodynamics cannot prove the existence of the hereafter, but it can help us judge whether a hereafter is scientifically plausible, and, if so, whether its attributes—as determined by thermodynamics—match those descriptions that have been handed down to us by the prophets. It is clear where Bazargan himself stood on this issue. He wrote his book partially as a refutation of materialism, after all. But he saw his effort as an imaginative exercise, albeit one fortified by the rigors of science. He wanted to "fly in a hypothetical world on the wings of scientific imagination."[11]

Like many other Islamic appropriations of modern science, Bazargan's construction of plausible fictions about the hereafter was a fundamentally defensive project. It was because a traditional Islamic cosmology had been attacked as illogical and superstitious that a scientific model of that cosmology needed to be attempted in the first place. If some science fiction literature makes it possible for us to imagine space-times radically different from our own by building and populating compelling, internally coherent technological worlds, Bazargan's plausible fictions likewise rendered the eternal hereafter thinkable for an audience that had an easier time conceptualizing thermodynamic laws than the order of angels and jinn.

Hadi, Dr. Movahhed, and Mehdi Bazargan were engineers with sophisticated understandings of scientific theory and practice. Their attempts to grasp metaphysical phenomena in scientific terms cannot be reduced to rhetorical strategies for legitimating a worldview by appealing to a hegemonic discourse. Instead of thinking of these efforts as strategic, the notion of a scientific imaginary allows us to grasp some of the features of the modes of reasoning—and the imaginative leaps associated with them—involved in carrying a style of inquiry from one context to a very different one.

In Hadi's imagination, the precision, objectivity, and accuracy of empirical scientific practice prompted him to experiment with the idea that a puzzling phenomenon like a stone with apparent divinatory properties could be understood in ways that avoided what he considered to be the ossified and unproductive thinking of simple people like his grandmother. Dr. Movahhed and Mehdi Bazargan, on the other hand, were inspired by the elegance of mathematical formulations in physics (particle physics for the former and thermodynamics for the latter), their fit with observable phenomena, and their ability to provide solutions to a range of scientific problems, to try to extend the application of these formulations to metaphysical questions. In each instance, the act of transposition involved restatements of a problem-at-hand in the language of scientific inquiry, including conceptual redefinitions of metaphysical ideas (like the recording of virtue and sin) in terms of variables relevant to specific branches of physics.

As tentative attempts to reimagine a conceptual problem by applying and tweaking instruments from an existing theoretical tool kit, these engineers' formulations had the quality of scientific bricolage.[12] The tentativeness was evident in their insistence that their efforts to model intangible matters had serious limitations, including epistemological ones. But rather than seeing these admissions as expressions of pious modesty about the powers of science, it may make more sense to understand them as elements of a pervasive imaginary in which the scientific enterprise is valorized as a ceaseless search for improved models for coming to grips with reality. The recognition of limits, that is, may itself be an admission of faith in scientific progress.

For the numerous Iranians who have been trained in modern scientific disciplines and the even larger group of people who are exposed to scientific models and terminology without understanding their technical nuances, the overwhelming success of science in explaining the material world and making it available to technological manipulation has granted scientific imaginaries a kind of a priori plausibility. What this means is that to articulate an explanation of any unknown phenomenon in scientific terms—whether those of thermodynamics, quantum mechanics, biology, statistics, and so on—is to ensure at the very least that it receives a serious hearing. Professional scientists and others with strong disciplines of scholarly inquiry—and here I particularly mean the ulama—understand the limits of such explanatory frameworks where laypeople may be oblivious to them. But the anecdotes above show that even among some professionals, the allure of scientific imaginaries is difficult to resist. This attraction gestures beyond the imagined efficacy of science to its symbolic currency as a vehicle of rationality, progress, intellectual rigor, and even virtue, all values that are fundamental to the social imaginaries Iranians have inhabited since the rise of nationalism in the nineteenth century.

The syntheses of science and metaphysics I have examined thus far have served influential intellectual and moral projects. For the past three decades or so, science has also been recruited in the construction of powerful movements of therapeutic spirituality. The stakes of these syntheses are different, pertaining not only to the securing of virtues or the persuasiveness of religious cosmologies but to the health and well-being of individuals as worldly beings subject to a variety of ills. I turn now to a discussion of these projects and the challenges they face.

COSMIC MYSTICS

In February 2008, the *Jam-e Jam* daily owned by the state radio and television organization published a sixty-four-page special issue titled *Kazhraheh* (Crooked Path) devoted entirely to attacking newly emerging "deviant" and "false" "mysticisms" (*'erfan-ha-ye enherafi* or *'erfan-ha-ye kazeb*). A column on page eleven focused on Cosmic Mysticism or "Interuniversalism," which I partially translate below:

> COSMIC CONSCIOUSNESS, MR. ENGINEER'S PRESCRIPTION
> FOR BRINGING THE DEAD BACK TO LIFE!!
>
> There is no end to strange and outlandish claims, and some claimants [*modda'iyan*], in order to influence their audience, attempt to insinuate seemingly scientific thoughts and worldviews that mostly have no basis or foundation.
>
> Energy therapy, metatherapy, cosmic therapy, word therapy, etc., have seen increasing growth in the past few years, and it suffices to visit the book market to witness books with other strange and outlandish content as well.
>
> Another topic having to do with the claimants, but of an intellectual [*rowshanfekri*] variety, is related to cosmic consciousness. In one of the meetings in which a group has gathered to use cosmic consciousness to do what they call metatherapy, an individual who considers himself… an undisputed master of the discovery of cosmic consciousness claims that by learning the methods of metatherapy and by relying on cosmic consciousness, one can even bring the dead back to life. He then refers to Jesus Christ (peace be upon him) and says, "He, too, brought the dead to life by employing cosmic consciousness!"
>
> In a general view, one can conclude that the presence of a large gathering of enthusiasts in the classes of this claimant who pay fifty thousand tomans in tuition will have at least added a few zeros to the bank accounts of Mr. Engineer, even if it has not brought any benefits to the enthusiasts themselves.

The claimant "Mr. Engineer" the author refers to is Mohammad 'Ali Taheri (b. 1956), the founder of Cosmic Mysticism, who, at the peak of his career in 2008, oversaw an impressive network of seminars and informal therapy clinics spread across urban centers in Iran and beyond. Taheri was arrested in early May 2011 and prosecuted on a range of charges. Around the same time, reports emerged that several maraje' had declared that his teachings were tantamount to apostasy (*ertedad*) after reviewing his published materials and recorded lectures. In 2012 a court sentenced Taheri to imprisonment and fines for blasphemy (*towhin beh moqaddasat*), illegal meddling in medical treatments, unlawful contact with female patients without a medical permit, and acquiring illegitimate wealth. Later, judicial officials announced that Taheri was on trial once more for the capital crime of "corruption on earth" (*efsad fel-arz*), a charge usually reserved for armed opposition groups and other enemies of national security. In July 2015 it was reported that he had been sentenced to death with the opportunity to appeal, and in December the Supreme Court overturned the death penalty, sending his case back to a lower court. In the meantime, a number of Taheri's associates were arrested and convicted in court, including sixteen "masters" who were handed a total of thirty-seven years of imprisonment. These convictions and the threat of death hanging over Taheri's head threw his vast organization into disarray. Increasingly, the group was also plagued by internal discord as some masters focused their energies on campaigns for his release while others—in particular, an influential faction based in Los Angeles—argued that the movement needed to move on under new leadership.

The severity of action against Taheri mirrors the strength of his appeal. Accurate numbers of his followers are impossible to determine. But there are various hints of the group's widespread popularity. For example, *Ensan az Manzari Digar* (The Human Being from a Different Perspective), one of the founding texts of Cosmic Mysticism, went into eight reprints between 2007 and 2009, for a total of 90,000 prints—a best seller by Iranian standards.[1] At one point, an official fan website listed contact information for representatives in Karaj, Hamadan, Kerman, and Tabriz, as well as Ankara, Chicago, Dubai, Frankfurt, Istanbul, Kuala Lumpur, La Jolla, Melbourne, Nottingham, Sydney, Toronto, Vancouver, Vienna, and Zurich.[2] In November 2013, the Immigration and Refugee Board of Canada published a report on the "situation and treatment of practitioners of Interuniversalism" in response to increasing requests for asylum from Iran on grounds of religious persecution.[3] A simple experiment I conducted during my fieldwork can also provide a general idea of the group's appeal. I had many occasions to speak about my fieldwork to various gatherings of friends and relatives. Often I would be asked to recount strange and interesting things I had witnessed firsthand. Stories of exorcism sessions dubbed "defensive radiation" would never fail to arouse fascination and glee, and so I was always prepared to relate a few anecdotes about them. Almost without fail, there would be someone present who had either attended classes or treatment sessions in person, or was intimately familiar with someone who had done so.

The popularity of Cosmic Mysticism should be understood within the context of a widespread proliferation of spiritual-therapeutic movements since the early 1990s, a development that is in turn connected to significant economic and social shifts in the years following the end of the 1980–88 war with

Iraq. A dual process of economic and cultural liberalization enabled the rise of alternative spiritual models, on the one hand encouraging entrepreneurship, material ambition, and self-realization, and on the other hand lessening restrictions on publishing, such that a wide variety of mostly translated texts on spirituality (*ma'naviyyat*) and mysticism (*'erfan*) could be printed and find a wide readership.

As part of efforts at postwar reconstruction, the government of President 'Ali Akhbar Hashemi Rafsanjani (1989–97) initiated what would lead to sixteen years of haphazard economic liberalization and progressive commercialization of various aspects of urban life.[4] With liberalization came increased opportunities for the middle and upper classes to accumulate wealth, particularly in a reemerging private sector weakened in the years of Islamic populism during the revolution and war. While the fortunes of these segments of society improved as a whole, their success was uneven and plagued by uncertainty: the vagaries of the market, fluctuating oil prices, and corruption and rent-seeking ensured that some made spectacular gains while many others struggled.

In the same period, competition increasingly became a part of everyday life and a social obsession, not just business rivalry but competition in sports, admission to good schools and universities, and all manner of contests (religious, literary, cultural, artisanal, professional, and so on) sponsored by state or private entities and covered by the mass media. Fariba Adelkhah has analyzed the rise of the culture of competition in postwar Iran in relation to growing social differentiation and individualization.[5] The prevailing forms of competition were almost always keyed into processes of commercialization and bureaucratization, and the prize almost always included a material aspect—money, consumer commodities, or the promise of future success, wealth, and prestige.

These transformations were accompanied by a rising interest in professional psychiatry and psychology as Iranians came to grips with deepening social problems at the war's end. Psychiatrists were increasingly called upon to provide expert advice to families on state radio and television, and publish accessible essays for a nonspecialist audience. It thus became more common for ordinary people to articulate their lives and their difficulties in terms made legible by professional psychiatric and psychological discourse.[6] The circulation of this discourse also encouraged (and was reinforced by) the proliferation of texts of popular psychology and self-help, which met the rising demand for simple, practical guides for dealing with everyday personal challenges.

Religious leaders were slow to adapt to these changes. During the upheavals of revolution and war, they had grown accustomed to promoting the virtues of courage, self-sacrifice, contentment, communal solidarity, and loyalty to the authority of the supreme leader. They could not turn around overnight and promote materialist ambition and competition—values on which economic liberalization relied. Nor were they equipped to provide solutions for the myriad problems that emerged alongside privatization and economic growth.

While these leaders threw up their hands in frustration, new spiritual entre-preneurs entered the scene in droves to fill the void. The desire for success and the opportunities opened up in the private sector enabled the emergence of a lucrative "success" (*movaffaqiyyat*) industry marketing mostly translated self-help and prosperity literature and seminars. Some of the most popular authors and motivational speakers were those who blended business and financial advice with a spiritual-cum-mystical ethos inspired by American power speak-ers like Wayne Dyer, whose translated works are still widely available.

Increasing attention to the needs and desires of individual selves also en-couraged the emergence of literature and seminars promoting self-care through healthy living, emotional well-being, physical beauty, and harmoni-ous relationships. Strong spiritual currents ran through many of the ideas and practices on offer, but this was not the spirituality of the Shi'i jurists. Facili-tated by the relaxation of state cultural oversight, particularly under the presi-dency of Mohammad Khatami from 1997–2005, alternative spiritual ideas and practices (some of which had already circulated prior to the 1979 revolution but were curtailed by the revolutionaries) proliferated—from novels and short stories by Paulo Coelho and Gibran Khalil Gibran to books on Theosophy, New Thought, Eckankar, Buddhism, Hinduism, Gurdjieff, Krishnamurti, Carlos Castaneda, Osho, Scientology, and all manner of New Age titles translated from English or blended into eclectic local systems.[7] By the time religious authorities and conservative politicians took notice of the rapid spread of what they dubbed "deviant" or "false" mysticisms, hundreds of such titles had been published, each with thousands of prints, and dozens of seminars had spread in the cities, promulgating their teachings.

Those of my interlocutors who attended seminars that promoted alternative spirituality frequently told me that they sought *aramesh* (tranquillity or peace of mind) or ways to enhance their *tamarkoz* (concentration or focus) and other capacities needed for success.[8] Others were concerned to reconcile the realities of their material existence with their understandings of cosmological order, ethics, and theodicy. The two usually went together: often some kind of per-sonal crisis precipitated their decision to attend the seminars, and they sought healing as well as a restoration of the intellectual and ethical consistency of their world. When one set of seminars did not satisfy their needs, they moved on to another.[9]

Cosmic Mysticism entered this field of spiritual-therapeutic alternatives with a highly elaborate cosmological doctrine and two integrated healing systems. Its cosmology rests on a tripartite differentiation of existence: There is matter and energy; but above all, there is consciousness (*sho'ur* or *agahi*).[10] Consciousness creates matter and energy in the following way: Matter and energy are "waves" with various degrees of density. Since waves are made of "movement" (*harekat*), matter and energy are also made of movement. To the extent that everything consists of movement, it is only apparent and virtual (*majazi*)—that is, there is no existential "truth" (*haqiqat*) to it, even though it has existential "reality" (*vaqe'iyyat*). Now, any movement requires a mover. The universal mover is consciousness. Therefore consciousness creates movement, which creates matter and energy.[11]

The smallest fragment in the world of existence consists of the three elements of matter, energy, and consciousness. But there is also a network-like Universal Consciousness (*sho'ur-e kol*) or Universal Intelligence (*hushmandi-ye kol*) that contains the information of all the tiny consciousnesses while also being contained by them (this is a derivation of the classic Neoplatonic equivalence between macrocosm and microcosm).[12] This Universal Consciousness is created by God, but it is not God himself. It is the system that organizes and rules over all of existence, mediating their connection with God, who lies at a deistic remove. According to Taheri, Muslims call this Universal Consciousness Jebra'il (Gabriel), and Christians call it the Holy Spirit.

The practical recognition of Universal Consciousness, this "wondrous divine phenomenon" as Taheri puts it, leads to an appreciation of the unity (*vahdat*) of existence and elevates human thought to the level of "the world of existence," a prerequisite for global unity and peace.[13] Taheri defines this as becoming "interuniversal." The concept implies three things: first, universalism—that is, thinking beyond ethnic, national, racial, religious, and "even international" boundaries; second, holistic thinking and avoiding getting trapped in useless discussion of particulars, especially when they do not help to further understanding of existential unity; and third, avoiding religious eclecticism and contradiction. For Taheri and his followers, Interuniversalism is first and foremost a reformist project aiming to change the world through transforming individuals' worldviews (*binesh*).

Most of the practitioners with whom I spoke had found their way to Cosmic Mysticism through its two therapeutic systems: metatherapy and defensive radiation (also called "psymentology"). Both therapies operate through what Taheri calls "cosmic rings," circuits that string followers together and plug them into the Universal Consciousness. In the case of metatherapy (*faradarmani*), Taheri explains its mechanism in terms of an analogy with the Internet. As a "cosmic Internet," Universal Consciousness makes it possible for human beings to access information about their existence by connecting directly to their "manufacturer's website." Just as the users' manuals of various consumer products are available on their manufacturers' websites, human "existential manuals" are also available through the cosmic Internet. By studying these manuals, human beings can better manage themselves, activate their dormant potentials, and avoid the problems that sometimes bring them into conflict with their Creator.[14]

By connecting to this same manufacturer's website, people can cure their own or others' illnesses. Everything is done automatically, from the execution of "troubleshooting software" to the repair of cells and organs. This treatment method can even be extended to animals, plants, and microorganisms.[15] All that is required is for the therapist to will a connection between herself, the patient, and Universal Consciousness. Contact is established immediately and the healing process gets under way.

Psymentology is a much more elaborate science-practice. Taheri explains that the main objective of psymentology is to "understand the human and his existential software programs, and diagnose and treat unknown problems and mental-psychic disorders."[16] Therapy occurs by means of "software" and without any "hardware intervention," by which Taheri means any kind of treatment that includes a physical component (drugs, surgery, physical therapy, massage, and so on). Furthermore, psymentology does not employ any of the common "software-oriented techniques," such as psychoanalysis and psychotherapy. As in metatherapy, Universal Consciousness does the scanning, diagnosis, and treatment.

In Taheri's system, humans are made up of an infinite number of existential components. The influence of modern Western esoteric thought in this aspect of Cosmic Mysticism is clear: humans are composed of various bodies (the physical body, the mental body, the psychic body, the astral body, and so on), chakras and energy channels, energy fields, different software sections, molecular frequency, and cell consciousness. For our purposes, we need only focus on the mental body and the psychic body, or, more simply, the mind and psyche. The mind (*zehn*) is in charge of "software management" of all of the human being's existence.[17] This includes everything from the operations of individual cells to memory, recall, learning, and, most important, cognition. The mind is not localized in the brain but exceeds its confines and manages its operations. It is, moreover, the only part of the human that survives bodily death. The psyche (*ravan*), on the other hand, is the seat of emotions. Its job is to translate cognitive information that it receives from the mind into emotional reactions.

Illnesses come about as a result of any kind of imbalance in the totality of human existence and her connections with the cosmic ecosystem. The illnesses that psymentology attends to most directly are those that are caused by what Taheri calls "inorganic viruses" (*virus-ha-ye gheyr-e organik*) or "inorganic beings" (*mowjudat-e gheyr-e organik*).[18] These are living, sentient creatures that are devoid of any organic or even material substance. "Given their unknown composition," Taheri writes, "the world of science is not able to identify and track [these beings]; rather, one can recognize their existence with the help of certain empirical signs, and cleanse them to alleviate disorder."[19]

Inorganic beings come in two varieties: jinn and mental bodies.[20] Taheri defines jinn as "divine agents" that are assigned missions in the order of existence but have free will and may refuse to carry out their responsibilities. Some jinn are appointed as security guards of the material world, attacking humans who disrespect the sanctity of nature or other humans. Others are available to be possessed by humans through the methods of occult science. As a whole, the jinn aid human evolution and maturity by creating obstacles, doling out punishment, and spreading disorder. The second group of inorganic beings, "mental bodies" (*kalbod-e zehni*), are the surviving elements of dead humans. When a human individual dies, his mental body is invited to proceed to the next stage in his life. But worldly dependencies sometimes weigh the mental body down, in which case it seeks a living human to whom it can attach itself.

Some kinds of illness arise when inorganic viruses occupy an individual's mental body or attach themselves to some other part of the person. They disrupt their host's thought processes, insinuate their own thoughts and inclinations, and implant sounds, images, and other sense-data in the form of hallucinations. They can thus induce phobias, obsessions, sleep disorders, somnambulism, multiple personality disorder, schizophrenia, and bipolar disorder, as well as "abnormal" inclinations like suicidal thoughts, sadomasochism, unnatural passions and hatreds, and homosexuality.[21] Taheri acknowledges that these problems are ordinarily considered to fall within the province of psychiatry. But psychiatrists have been misdiagnosing the source of the problem. Their medications only numb the senses or inhibit the transfer of information between neurons. The inorganic viruses that cause illness, however, remain undisturbed.

According to Taheri, the only solution to mental-psychic disorders is defensive radiation. Like metatherapy, defensive radiation involves direct connection to the Universal Consciousness. But whereas the former includes only one connecting ring, defensive radiation involves multiple rings, each serving a unique purpose in the therapeutic process. In the course of therapy, the psymentologist or exorcist unleashes a carefully regimented barrage of radiations on the patient. There is usually some verbal communication between the therapist and the inorganic being, but this is primarily aimed at helping the creature leave. Sometimes, especially in the earlier stages of therapy, there may be no discernible change at the end of a session. It may take days, weeks, or even months to expunge just one virus. When the virus does finally leave, its departure may be experienced as a sneeze, a cough, or a slight buzz in the ear. The master with whom I studied, Mr. Sheyda, told me that there were severe "breakouts" (*birunrizi*) in about 10 to 15 percent of patients. These high-drama exorcisms were the highlight of therapy sessions.

I observed dozens of exorcisms during my fieldwork and actively participated in a few when I was certified by Mr. Sheyda to transmit level-one radiation (this certification was granted to anyone who completed a monthlong course on psymentology). Most of these took place in the sitting area of a two-bedroom apartment owned by a young couple who were students of Mr. Sheyda. There were between thirty and forty attendees each time, about two-thirds of them women. Therapies were considered a part of the Cosmic

Mystics' "charity work" and no money was exchanged. A soft spatial division of genders usually occurred in the apartment, with the men mostly sitting on the carpet across from the kitchen and near the front entrance and the women gathered at the opposite end of the living room, some sitting on the couches and others on the floor. All of the women wore headscarves, in different styles that indicated a spectrum of pious observance. Below is my account, from my field-notes, of a few minutes from a three-hour session in early January 2009, in which Mr. Sheyda and his students concurrently exorcised a handful of participants.

Mr. Sheyda turns to Milad, a tall, athletic volleyball player in his midtwenties. "Will you establish contact?" he asks him. Milad obliges, walking across the living room to sit on one of the couches. "Okay," Mr. Sheyda addresses his students, "come and do defensive on Milad." Someone jokes with Milad and tells him to move the couch farther back so as to avoid hurting the other guests. "It's okay," Milad laughs, "I'm used to it."

Vida Khanum, our young hostess, is in another corner receiving radiation. She is breathing out loud, groaning and squealing. One of the women utters a lackluster "Negative Three" at her. Mr. Sheyda steps up and says, much more energetically, "Negative Three for Vida!" At this point Vida squeals much louder, hurls herself upward, and lands on the couch with a stomp of her right foot. She jumps again, and again, and again. Now she returns to stillness, exhaling angrily. Applying Mr. Sheyda's example, Vida's female exorcist repeats, "Negative Three for Vida!" but not as energetically as her teacher. Vida groans but remains still.

Milad is meanwhile starting to get into it. I am standing to his immediate left, next to the fireplace. I notice Samaneh, a young college student and regular participant, standing across the room with arms crossed, staring pensively at Milad. She kicks both of her feet nervously, now the right foot, now the left. It is clear that she will soon enter full possession mode. I am told by other participants that the two are "synchronized," such that when one enters possession, the other soon follows.

Milad begins breathing deeply, exhaling with animal-like groans. Each breath produces an angrier groan. The third breath becomes a snort. Mr. Sheyda swings into action: "Defensive! Come up!" Milad snorts and groans. Samaneh is now on all fours, her face covered with her black shawl. She lets out a long, ghostly gasp. Milad responds by stretching out both arms above his head, muscles bulging, fingers in a snarl. His lower back ripples like a snake, producing convulsions in his chest and head as he emits smaller grunts. His eyes are almost completely turned upward, his mouth shaped into an O. Samaneh reciprocates with another grunt, then a gasp, then a menacing scowl. It is a beautiful, macabre duet.

Mr. Sheyda tells his students to announce the radiations. Samaneh coughs. One woman announces a Negative Three. Another repeats the same. Milad gasps again. Samaneh's voice has grown raspy. She extends her hand toward Milad, her fingers like claws, taunting him.

Mr. Sheyda announces a "Negative Three for Vida," and a "disconnection from the negative network." Vida scowls and squeals. "Negative Three for the office of Mr. Peyvandi. Negative Two for Mr. Peyvandi!" Mr. Sheyda tells me that Vida Khanum's condition may be caused by talismans planted at her father's business, a realtor's office. He is cleansing them from a distance at the same time as radiating Vida.

At this point three people are possessed: Milad sitting on the couch near the fireplace; Samaneh in front of him on all fours, about two meters away; Vida on the seat in front of me to Milad's left. Each has a handful of student-exorcists attending to them, with Mr. Sheyda circulating and giving orders.

Milad is standing up now, thumping his chest with his right fist. He swings his arm violently, bringing it down with a thud. He repeats again and again. Mr. Sheyda gives him a Defensive Four. "Milad is ours!" he shouts. The air is stuffy and Milad is sweating profusely. I can smell his body odor from where I stand, barely a meter behind him. As he swings his arms, people back off from him somewhat. But he hasn't left the couch. He still stands with his legs almost resting against it.

Mr. Sheyda claps his hands in front of Milad's face. "Out! It's time to go!" Milad thumps his chest again, slowly, then more rapidly. When he is done thumping, he moans and groans. Samaneh, not to be outdone, responds with loud gasps and demonic screams.

I turn to a student standing next to me: "It's a good thing he won't hit us!" I say. "Yeah," he responds, "he only beats himself. Though I'm always afraid that one of his punches will catch someone." He could beat any one of us to a pulp if he were so inclined.

Two women are still giving Negative Threes to Vida, more energetically now. They have placed a white pillow above her head on the couch's headrest so that she doesn't bang her head on the wall in one of her upward thrusts.

Milad seems to want to say something. His raspy moans are louder and he is saying something like "Manamanamana." Samaneh responds with violent screams. They are now giving each other devil's horn gestures. Earlier in class we had learned a typology of these signs and their associations with Satanism. One woman and one man are restraining Samaneh to prevent her from attacking Milad. I circle around to look at Milad from a different angle. He is totally beside himself, shrieking and beating his chest, his screams punctuated by Samaneh's hoarse gasps. Suddenly, Milad throws himself into the group of seven or eight people in front of him. He lurches around violently, swinging his arms, trying to grab onto something. At one point his hand catches the collar of my sweater and pulls. I hear a cracking sound and worry that my brand-new sweater has been torn (thankfully, it hasn't). "Let him go!" shouts Mr. Sheyda, "Calm! Calm!" There is a moment of confusion as people try to retreat from his line of attack. Mr. Sheyda wants the women to control Samaneh and hold her back. He himself hugs Milad tightly, his head to his chest, and gives him radiation. "I will kill you!" growls Milad with his raspy demon voice.

Samaneh screams again. Milad is desperate, wriggling, convulsing, as if in a wild fever. "It's time to go!" shouts Mr. Sheyda. "I won't go! I won't go!" responds Milad. A bloodcurdling scream rises from Samaneh's throat. Mr. Sheyda now gives Milad a Defensive Four. He gasps desperately, then starts to snort again. "Out!" says Mr. Sheyda. Milad shakes his head and clicks his tongue. "I don't know. I don't know. I don't know," he says, which doesn't seem to make any sense. "I'll lay him down. Calm!" says Mr. Sheyda.

Mr. Sheyda asks someone to turn on the air conditioner. They say it is broken, so they open a window. It is very hot. There are too many of us here; our excited movements and our nervous energy only increase the temperature.

A few more minutes pass this way. The women, louder now, are giving Negative Threes to Vida, trying to help her out of possession. Mr. Sheyda, for the third or fourth time, hugs Milad tightly, injecting radiation into his chest with all ten fingers. Finally, Milad coughs and the jinn is out.

Mr. Sheyda turns his attention once again to Vida with the usual radiations and cleansings. Now that Milad is released, Samaneh wanders around, howling, screaming, scoffing, barking. She grabs the loose ends of her shawl and pulls, strangling herself until she coughs. Every time she does this, someone, usually a woman, grabs her hands and tries to wrest her shawl free. There is the sound of cups and saucers being washed in the kitchen. Someone is preparing tea.

The Cosmic Mystics with whom I spoke found defensive radiation to be one of the more attractive aspects of their seminars. Some regularly underwent radiation, with about a dozen experiencing intense forms of possession like the ones I described above. They explained their treatments in scientific terms they had learned from Mr. Sheyda or read in Mr. Taheri's books. Despite their enthusiastic commitment, however, doubt often lurked only slightly beneath the surface of conviction. How might we understand such doubts in relation to the predominance of scientific discourse? I turn to this question next by more closely examining the Cosmic Mystics' relationship to science and the skeptical attacks against their claims.

SPECTERS OF DOUBT

Taheri's claims to scientific legitimacy have been persistent and forceful. Even so, his relationship to science is ambivalent. A hesitation lies at the very heart of Cosmic Mysticism's epistemology, where science is claimed as a privileged path to truth but empirical methods are circumvented at crucial points in favor of intuition and mystical unveiling. Taheri maintains that by connecting to the Cosmic Intelligence, one can receive "consciousness" (*agahi*) comprising knowledge of both self and world, microcosm and macrocosm. This, he explains, is how he received the knowledge that constitutes the doctrines and practices of Cosmic Mysticism:

> This discipline was created due to my encounter... with the realities and truths of existence, which attracted my intense attention since childhood; contemplation about "Where have we come from? Why have we come? Where are we going? Who is the Creator? Why has he created [us]? What is the result of this creation? Who is the human? What are the ways for approaching and knowing him? How is his potential power activated? What are life and death? And so on..." That is, I had an intense enthusiasm to understand the world of existence and discover the secret of creation, such that these thoughts would not leave me for a moment. Finally, on November 1, 1978, all at once I encountered inspirations and mental receptions after which certain aspects of existence and the human became clear to me.[1]

In other words, scientific knowledge about the world may be received in the form of revelation or mystical unveiling. The idea is not particularly novel, of course. Some Muslim thinkers have argued that modern scientific findings were anticipated by the Qur'an, a perspective that remains popular to this day.[2] Others have extended the argument to the mystics, comparing Albert Einstein and other European scientists to Sufi visionaries.[3] Western esotericists, the Theosophists among them, had earlier made similar claims about the sages of the East.[4] Among Iranians, their views were furthered by intellectuals like the Theosophist journalist and mystical leader Hoseyn Kazemzadeh Iranshahr (1884–1962), the literary scholar and politician Mohammad Parvin Gonabadi (1903–78), and the lawyer and author Mohsen Farshad (b. 1945). Iranshahr defended mysticism and occult science, whose roots, he argued, were established in the East, and whose profound insights would eventually be confirmed by modern science just as "those things that people considered to be sorcery or occult secrets and mysteries several centuries ago are now taught to schoolchildren in their introductory science classes."[5] Parvin wrote that the spirit of scientific enlightenment, discovery, and inventiveness in the West was similar to "the prodigious spirit that existed, in the name of vision [*kashf*] and marvel [*karamat*], among many of our country's great Sufis and authentic holy men."[6] Farshad, whose inspirations include Allan Kardec (the founder of Spiritism) and Fritjof Capra (a physicist whose influential *The Tao of Physics* claimed to identify parallels between modern physics and Eastern mysticism) argued that the discoveries of quantum physicists were presaged by the thirteenth-century Sufi poet Jalal al-Din Rumi.[7] Taheri's claims to cosmic inspiration thus build on an already well-developed discourse.

While Taheri has credited cosmic "receptions" as the origin of his scientific knowledge, he has also attempted to validate this knowledge in terms more readily recognizable to the mainstream scientific community. His supporters' websites cite various awards and honors received abroad, including an honorary doctorate from the University of Traditional Medicine in Yerevan, Armenia. He recruited medical doctors and psychiatrists from among his followers to help formulate metatherapy and psymentology in biomedical language, even encouraging them to publish the results of empirical research in scientific journals. One example is a special issue of *Danesh-e Pezeshki* (Medical Knowledge) printed in 2011 and devoted entirely to psymentology. The issue includes an introduction by Taheri, an interview with a psychiatrist and practicing psymentologist, and several case reports about patients suffering from psychiatric disorders who showed marked improvement after undergoing defensive radiation.[8] Taheri and his colleagues have also presented at conferences abroad and published in the English-language journal *Procedia: Social and Behavioral Sciences*, a non-peer-reviewed journal printed by Elsevier that publishes conference proceedings for a fee. Article titles include "Classification of Disorders as Approached by Psymentology," "The Effect of Faradarmani [Metatherapy] on General Health," and "Study of Faradarmani Therapy on Schizophrenia (A Case Study)."[9] In November 2012, Taheri (or someone acting on his behalf) also filed an application with the US Patent and Trademark Office to patent a "method for applying a consciousness field to industrial processes." The request remains open at the time of this writing.

These efforts notwithstanding, Taheri understood early on that the mainstream scientific community would not be keen on granting him recognition. Where acknowledgment was lacking, he argued that science had yet to catch up with his discoveries but would do so soon. For example, he compared his identification of inorganic viruses to the achievements of Robert Koch and Louis Pasteur: "The subject [of inorganic viruses] might seem strange and unbelievable at first, just as it seemed ridiculous when Koch and Pasteur first spoke of the existence of 'microbes,' but their existence was gradually proven."[10] Scientists, he argued, should remain open-minded and subject his claims to testing rather than dismiss them outright.

As one might expect, these appeals did not generate much enthusiasm among Taheri's critics. One author and howzeh-trained scholar, 'Ali Naseri Rad, published a book in 2011 debunking the central tenets of Cosmic Mysticism. The thrust of Naseri Rad's contentions were philosophical and doctrinal: he argued that Taheri's claims were either unfounded, were logically inconsistent, or contradicted Islamic precepts. Of the concept of Cosmic Intelligence, for example, he wrote that the notion found support neither in Qur'anic revelation and prophetic tradition, nor in the experience of the senses, nor in rational proofs (since, he argued, none had been offered).[11] The only support Taheri provided, the author continued, was from his own mystical unveiling, but this had no value for rational argument unless backed by some external criterion.[12] Naseri Rad similarly critiqued Taheri's anthropological conceptions—the system of bodies, chakras, energy channels, cellular intelligences, and molecular frequencies that shaped the human person—by arguing that they were derived from yoga but had no evidence to sustain them from empirical observation, deductive reason, or Islamic sources of revelation. We therefore have no cause to accept them, he concluded.[13]

Other critics targeted Taheri's scientific credentials. The most sustained attacks were waged by Gomaneh—known also as Setad-e Mobarezeh ba Charandiyyat (Headquarters for Combating Nonsense)—a website modeled after Snopes.com and dedicated to debunking urban legends. In one essay, Gomaneh wrote that none of the awards or honorary degrees claimed by Taheri had any academic value. The "pseudoscientific" papers authored by Taheri and his colleagues were "worthless" too, as they appeared in noncredible journals that published anything with the formal appearance of an academic article. In short, Gomaneh wrote, Cosmic Mysticism "elegantly mixed some scientific realities with pseudoscience and lies" to create an "irrelevant amalgam."[14]

The participants in Cosmic Mysticism were not foreign to such skeptical arguments. When I began attending seminars with Mr. Sheyda, I met a master's student in women's studies who argued at length with the teacher about psymentology, dismissing his descriptions of jinn as myth, legend, and folklore (she continued to participate in the classes, however, and even took part in exorcisms, although when I contacted her a year afterward, I learned that she had left the group). The master anticipated resistance and taught his students that the appropriate disposition in Cosmic Mysticism was one of "becoming witness" (shahed shodan), by which he meant that they should suspend their preconceptions and avoid passing judgment until they had allowed their empirical observations to mature and guide them in accepting or denying his teachings.

Nor were living humans the only skeptics. In one therapy session, I watched as the "mental body" of a deceased nine-year-old girl who had possessed a young woman launched into a tearful tirade against the exorcists. Pointing at the other people undergoing defensive radiation in the room, the young-woman-as-ghost wept and moaned, "What is this nonsense? Why are you doing this? You're frightening Banafsheh [the woman she had possessed]. Stop it. I have to protect Banafsheh. You are frightening her with this nonsense." The pleading and ridicule went on for more than an hour as the ghost stubbornly refused the exorcism script that Mr. Sheyda and his students tried to impose on her, reversing the roles of exorcist-as-protector and ghost-as-menace. Eventually, Mr. Sheyda abandoned the patient in frustration, giving his students a few perfunctory commands on how to proceed.

Such skeptical stirrings could take a toll on the resolve of even the most committed enthusiasts. By rendering scientific accounts of the metaphysical suspect, the arguments of the incredulous caused disorientations that could throw the therapeutic project into crisis. Chapter 17 studies one such situation. I examine the reasoning of a participant in Cosmic Mysticism as she grappled with her doubts, probing the pathways that open up when scientific rationalization appears to be futile.

BECOMING WITNESS

Normally, before students were allowed to participate in defensive radiation treatment sessions, they were required to enroll in the defensive radiation seminar, where they learned the theoretical basis of psymentology and received the cosmic "rings" through which they could perform exorcisms. In part, Mr. Sheyda used these classes to describe and classify inorganic viruses. He was sensitive to the possibility of skepticism and often asked newcomers who had witnessed the exorcisms whether they thought the afflicted had been acting. He asked me this question several times, and each time I gave an evasive response, conceding that the possessions were genuine but suggesting that the explanation did not have to involve metaphysical beings. In expressing such veiled skepticism, I was, in fact, more circumspect than certain other participants, including the women's studies student I mentioned in chapter 16 who accused Mr. Sheyda of passing off legends as science.

At one of the defensive radiation sessions, I met Lili Bayati, a twenty-four-year-old master's student in child psychology who had been attending Cosmic Mysticism classes along with her mother. She had taken classes with both Mr. Sheyda and another master, and had recently registered for a "theory" course with Mr. Taheri himself. At first she had approached the exorcisms with skepticism, but was gradually converted when she saw its effects on herself. Before I had a chance to speak with her, I saw her sitting cross-legged in a corner of the apartment with her eyes closed and her right arm extended, pointing to the empty space in front of her. She wept uncontrollably as three or four other students transmitted radiation at her. The virus usually left her without too much struggle. Her headscarf never came off and she never roamed about or screamed the way some of the other possessed participants did. The treatments seemed to be as effective in her case as in the most dramatic exorcisms.

Later that evening, Mr. Sheyda introduced me to Lili and we spoke for around an hour about my research and her experience with Cosmic Mysticism. She was curious what I thought about the exorcisms. I explained that I could not dismiss their efficacy, but I nonetheless found a neuropsychological notion of dissociation more convincing in understanding what had been going on.[1] She argued with me, saying that she herself had initially dismissed the idea of inorganic viruses, but eventually accepted them after experiencing things that seemed to confirm their reality. We made an appointment to meet again over lunch.

Before meeting Lili, I had largely concealed my skepticism. Lili was clearly interested in learning what I thought and whether or not I believed in the inorganic beings that were supposedly being exorcised a few meters away from us. I began by explaining that my research was not about discovering the existence or nonexistence of these beings, and that I was rather more interested in how people decided what was or was not real, and how they sifted truth from untruth. But as I offered this response, I could not avoid voicing my own opinion: that inorganic beings probably did not exist, that possession was a dissociative phenomenon, and that exorcisms were effica-cious as social curing practices involving a "meaning response"—communal mechanisms for constructing meaning and prescribing moral action to deal with experiences of illness and suffering.[2] As a master's student in psychol-ogy, Lili was familiar with the placebo effect, if not with the medical anthro-pological critique of the concept.[3] My other arguments were not foreign to her either. She had entertained a version of some and could critically engage with others. That is, she did not view my skepticism as a strange or offensive attitude. It was, more than anything, a challenge not unlike others she had faced in coming to grips with Cosmic Mysticism, and she rose to the occasion by engaging me in argument.

Lili began by explaining that she was "extremely logical" and had never pursued metaphysics. Nor had such topics ever been brought up within her family. When she first saw Mr. Sheyda's exorcisms, she explained them away in terms of the suggestibility of the afflicted. But she had also been open to the possibility that there may be truths beyond that which she found accept-able. This was an approach that she said was in-line with the notion of "be-coming witness" in Mr. Taheri's system. To be a witness, she said, meant being "impartial" (*bitaraf*). "It means neither denying nor acknowledging that some-thing exists," she continued, "because you haven't experienced anything yet."

Her mother was the first in her family to take part in Cosmic Mysticism. When she described her experience to Lili and her older brother, they ex-pressed disbelief. Even when their mother practiced metatherapy on them, they would not believe her. But then something strange happened. For some years, Lili had suffered chronic wrist pain from a handball injury. The pain was sometimes so severe that it woke her in the middle of the night. She visited multiple doctors, underwent X-rays and MRIs, and took painkillers on a regu-lar basis. But doctors assured her that her wrist was fine and the pain was stress-related. Then her mother decided to try metatherapy:

> My mom worked on me while I was asleep and she was in her own room. I felt
> as though a liquid had been injected into my hand. So for a while my wrist pain
> flared up and became very intense. I walked around the living room crying from

pain. I took painkillers too, but they wouldn't work. Now I don't have that problem anymore. I don't take painkillers at all, and the pain is 80 percent better. I don't have the sleeping problems anymore either, even if I sleep on my hand.

Contrary to what I had argued about the meaning response, Lili claimed that metatherapy cured her wrist without requiring her belief, nor even depending on her awareness that treatment was under way. It was something in which she had not believed, and yet she had seen its effects. As she put it, "It's like they say, even if you don't believe in it, [Universal] Consciousness does its own work. All that matters is that you don't constantly say 'I deny it.'" That is, the only requirement is that you be impartial, a witness.

It was the same with defensive radiation. The first time she witnessed an exorcism, she had been unable to sleep all night. She was not afraid but puzzled, as she had never seen or seriously thought about anything like it. Over time, certain signs convinced her that there was some truth to those events. The earlier among these signs were indirect. For example, her mother tried to take Mostafa, her youngest son, to defensive radiation to treat his epilepsy, which Mr. Sheyda claimed was caused by inorganic viruses. Mostafa was disturbed by the sessions and refused to go again after one or two visits. But he continued to exhibit anxious behavior whenever Lili and her mother returned from radiation sessions on Tuesday evenings. "There would always be some conflict with Mostafa when we returned," Lili explained. "He would either ignore us and go to bed as soon as we got home, or he would leave the house. If he stayed, there would be some sort of conflict. It was like he was looking for trouble." For Lili, this was a sign that a connection existed between Mostafa's condition and the defensive radiation sessions. If, as Mr. Sheyda claimed, he was afflicted with inorganic beings, those beings would be disturbed by the possibility that they would be hauled before an exorcist.

Decisive evidence for the existence of inorganic beings arrived when Lili herself was exorcised of the "mental body" of her best friend. It began in a completely involuntary fashion. She was aiding several others in transmitting defensive radiation to Milad, the young volleyball player whose exorcism I described in chapter 15. Suddenly Lili felt the intense urge to cry. Her eyes welled up with tears; she sat down on the edge of a couch and wept out loud. She felt her face and body twitching, and her arm, of its own accord, rose up to point in front of her. It was like a force had lifted her arm and kept it suspended for ten or fifteen minutes. "They say that when a mental body wants to leave you, your arm might be raised, or there might be some other upward movement," she explained.

She later determined that the mental body belonged to her best friend Setareh, who had died a year earlier. The two used to be college friends. "We shared many things and were very similar. We did things and enjoyed things together," Lili said. "Then she got breast cancer and died. I grieved for a very long time. But I also felt her presence sometimes." Once, around six months after Setareh had died, Lili was at home studying for the master's-level university entrance exam. At around 2:00 a.m., she and her older brother Mehran were the only people awake in her house:

Something happened and I started recounting something about Setareh to my brother. My eyes welled up with tears. Mehran asked me what had happened, and I said, "I just miss her very much, and I can't visit her grave because I have to study." A minute or two afterward, I went into my own bedroom and there was a really fantastic scent that had spread in my room. What I'm telling you are logical things. I'm not a person who believes many of these things. What I'm describing was a very strange thing for me. This was before I had started coming to these seminars.

There was a very powerful perfume. These [inorganic] beings can reduce their frequencies so that you sense their scent or notice other things, like moving a curtain, or shutting a door, and so on, so that we can feel them. I did not have any perfume on. My closet was open, so I thought maybe the scent was coming from my clothes. I stuck my head in my closet but I didn't notice any scent. I asked Mehran if he had put on perfume. He said, "Are you crazy? Why would I put on women's perfume?" So for a few moments, I could sense this scent. And I very distinctly remember thinking, "This is Setareh." You know? I had a very strong realization that she had come.

Some months later, Lili felt Setareh's presence once more, this time through touch. She had been thinking intensely about her on her way home from the university. In the subway station, her eyes inadvertently fell on a spot where she and Setareh used to wait for the train. "I thought of the things we used to say to each other," Lili said, "and I became very sad, thinking what good times we had had together, and how happy we had been." By the time she arrived home she was so dejected and exhausted that she took to bed for a nap:

While I was sleeping, it was very interesting… only my brother and I were home. While sleeping, I felt her, physically. I couldn't see her, but I felt her. I felt that someone was kissing my cheek. And it was like I knew, I felt, that this was Setareh. And then I wept. I wept and my cheek was kissed once more. When I woke up, I noticed that my face was wet with tears. I asked my brother if he had tried to wake me up. He said he hadn't come near me at all. I asked him, "You didn't come into my room? You didn't kiss me?" He said, "No."

By this time Lili was attending the Cosmic Mysticism seminars. The master told her that she had felt these things because Setareh's mental body was with her, inside her. It would not leave her because Lili was intensely dependent on her. She had not even been able to bring herself to erase Setareh's number from her cell phone's memory. She had kept her text messages. Her photographs were still stored on her phone. As a result, Setareh's mental body had comfortably settled in, leaving Lili in constant anguish.

Two or three days later, Lili participated in the exorcism that made her weep uncontrollably. Her arm rose up, and as other participants stepped in to transmit radiation to her, she experienced an "exit" (*khoruj*). That night she finally felt at ease. "It was as though my dependence was cut," Lili explained. "You know what I'm saying? I deleted her text messages and her phone number, things I had not been able to do over the past year. I'm a lot more at ease now. I'm not as dependent. When I think about her, my heart no longer burns so much. I don't miss her as much as I used to."

Lili insisted that she had been a witness throughout this process. She had seen and felt things, and only then had believed. She suggested that if I likewise were to witness and start experiencing, I might accept some of these things. The explanations I had been giving, dismissing inorganic beings and other such phenomena, were those of "the language of science." I found this criticism interesting given the amount of emphasis that Taheri and his followers placed on scientific explanations. But as we have already seen, their reliance on science was an ambivalent one, paralleling modern esotericist and New Age criticisms of materialistic science, which nonetheless posit a holistic, spiritual science that is to eventually replace it. Lili herself understood this ambivalent relationship in temporal terms: There are claims that Taheri makes that are "metaphysical" now, because they have yet to be grasped by science. In a few years when scientific discovery is able to catch up with the receptions of mystics, these same claims will become scientific, or physical. In Lili's classes with Taheri, the latter had cited the example of "auras" (*haleh*). Years ago, auras were the subject of parapsychology and metaphysics, as no one had been able to see or prove them. But now there were imaging devices, such as the Kirlian camera, that could photograph auras, thus bringing them into the realm of science.

I challenged Lili on this and other assertions. I argued that Kirlian cameras and auras were not accepted by mainstream scientists, or at least they were not accorded the significance that esotericists and New Agers granted them. On the exorcisms in which we had both participated, I suggested the hypothesis that the possessed were learning from one another and from Hollywood movies like *The Exorcist* and *Constantine* (which they shared among themselves and spoke about regularly), and were being disciplined through a kind of collective ritual. How else could we explain the similarity between Hollywood exorcisms and those that we had seen in the defensive radiation seminars, when possessions in other parts of the world, including in rural regions of Iran itself, looked very different?

Lili was not prepared to concede the argument, although she did admit that there were "unanswered questions," which she had also discussed with her older brother. Here she showed signs of wavering from the position of witness. That is, she acknowledged that certain claims Taheri and others made were difficult to sustain, but she decided to consciously believe in them despite her doubts because they brought her calm:

> Let's say, as you do, that we don't care whether or not this is true, whether what they're doing is really correct or not. But at least what they're giving us is very easy, and they give us something that requires no effort, no struggle, and there is a peace and calm [*aramesh*] that results from it.

Later, reminiscing about her doubts, she recounted a conversation with her brother Mehran:

> I asked Mehran, "What are we supposed to believe among the things they tell us?" And he said, "Lili, at least believing it is a lot better than not believing it." I'm talking about the totality of the issue, not just the matter of the inorganic beings. He was saying that when you accept and believe it, at least you have tranquillity [*aramesh*] in your life that you wouldn't have without the system. You are always in conflict with yourself. Why have I come here [into this world]? So what? We are in conflict with God, asking what the point was in bringing us into this world so that we would suffer. Because we always thought [based on the teachings of Islamic theodicy] that sickness and calamity are tests. Everything is a trial and a test. And we would ask, "So what? God brought us into this world to run some tests on us and then send us off? And then we would go to hell and burn." That's what it was supposed to be, after all. It was meaningless, wasn't it? But now I see that it's not like that at all. They've given us some new viewpoints with which we can easily derive pleasure from life and being in our own Tehran and our own Iran. Before this, we would maybe say there is nothing, and we should get up and leave this place.

Cosmic Mysticism brought Lili tranquillity after anguish. It helped her come to terms with her best friend's death. It cured her wrist injury. And it furnished accounts of cosmology and theodicy that she found more logical than the ideas she had been taught in religious textbooks in school. More than anything, it brought her calm, a "spiritual and internal tranquillity" that she thought was perhaps the element that drew most people to the mystical system.

A week after our lunch conversation, Lili called me to give me the name of a book on Spiritism that she had read more than a decade earlier. Before hanging up, she told me that after having spoken to me last time, she had returned home with "a head full of questions." For the first time in a long while, she had felt anxious and sad for no apparent reason, to the point that she felt she was once again being exposed to the "negative network." She repeated, as she had done over lunch, that she found tranquillity in Cosmic Mysticism, and her worldview changed as a result of the seminars. The doubts and criticisms that

I had raised had destabilized her progress. She had wept, again for no apparent reason. She told me that she believed the differences of interpretation between various knowledge systems, as, for example, between psychiatry and Cosmic Mysticism, were akin to those between different theories in psychology, where behaviorist, cognitive, and psychoanalytic theories provide competing explanations for similar phenomena. But this uncertainty between different systems and the questions that they raised brought her more turmoil than calm. In the end, Lili decided that "even if what I'm doing is false, I am happy with it because it brings me peace."

Lili's predicament lays bare a tension between the authority of science and that of personal experience. In chapter 18 we will see that reformist religious thinkers have sometimes valorized experience at the expense of theological dogma and legal prescription. What this chapter has shown is that such experience may also overrule scientific judgments. As a scientifically minded practitioner of Cosmic Mysticism, it mattered to Lili that Mr. Taheri's claims should prove resilient against skeptical attack. But at bottom, the substance of his scientific edifice mattered less than the fact that his therapies and the worldview that upheld them "worked." As long as Cosmic Mysticism brought her tranquillity, Lili preferred to ignore questions over the merits of its claims to scientific legitimacy. Experiential efficacy provided a rational way out when the scientific path to authentication seemed obstructed.

AUTHORITY IN EXPERIENCE

At the beginning of part 2, we met Arezu Khanum, an enthusiast of Cosmic Mysticism, who told me that her spiritual adventures had enabled her to grasp complicated scientific ideas like quantum theory, and indicated that her highest guide was not any external teacher (a mystical master, a text, or whatever) but her heart. In chapter 16, I briefly mentioned that some Muslim thinkers (Mr. Taheri among them) have argued that a seeker can receive scientific knowledge through mystical unveiling. In chapter 17 we saw that Lili Bayati ultimately justified her attachment to Cosmic Mysticism in terms of its experiential efficacy, its ability to bring her tranquillity in place of anguish. It is time to bring these threads together to better understand the place of personal experience in contemporary Iranian spirituality.

What we call "experience" is usually captured in Persian with the word *tajrobeh* (Arabic *tajriba*), a notion that bears many of the same subtleties as the English concept. We have already encountered the sense of tajriba as scientific experiment or methodical empirical observation in the discussion of Spiritism (chapters 12 and 13). A sense of tajrobeh as a kind of experience that we associate with cumulative learning and mastery over time was sometimes also implicated, as in Ayatollah Makarem's contention that "one cannot deny the possibility of contact with souls through appropriate scientific means for those experienced individuals who have truly worked and struggled toward this end." These two meanings of tajrobeh share a conception of experience as pertaining to a subject's relationship with things out there in the world, where this relationship is publicly available (that is, others can, in principle, perceive and participate in the experience) and communicable.

In modern European theorizations, the German concept of *Erfahrung* comes close to both of these senses of experience as methodical experiment and accumulated learning. The kind of tajrobeh that concerns me in this chapter, however, is better grasped in terms of *Erlebnis*, experience that is more personal, immediate, intense, and perhaps ineffable than what *Erfahrung* implies.[1] The association between tajrobeh and Erlebnis is not accidental. In the twentieth century, as we will see, the two terms converged in Iranian reformist formulations of "religious experience" inspired by modern European thinkers.

Before religious experience gained currency in Iranian intellectual discourse, there was the "heart," a concept whose significance far precedes the developments of the twentieth century. In everyday Persian language use, the heart (*del*) is invoked as the seat of emotions and desires, but also as a center of personality, character, and mood. The heart's functions—at least as far as linguistic conceptualization is concerned—may further encompass cognitive operations that we associate in English with the mind. These include the capacity to safeguard secrets and receive inspiration—especially in the form of intuitions or premonitions. Farzad Sharifian has suggested that this wide range of conceptualizations has been influenced by Sufi understandings of human material and spiritual anatomy.[2] How then have Sufis understood the heart?

In the Sufi tradition, the heart is conceived as both a fleshy and a spiritual organ, functioning as a seat of conscience, understanding, awareness of God, and one's innermost secrets.[3] It is the organ within which God makes his presence manifest when he wants to strengthen a person's faith. It is the same organ that God "seals" shut when he intends to punish the ignorant and the rebellious. Corresponding to this dual potentiality of manifesting God or being empty of his presence, the heart is the locus of opposing impulses. These include carnal desires insinuated by Satan, as well as the desire to overcome the lower self to achieve union with God. To prepare their hearts as dwellings for the divine, Sufis thus instruct themselves and one another in a speculative and practical "science of hearts" through which they become conscious of their various desires, learn to conquer impulses that arise from their lower selves, and amplify those that arrive as inspirations through divine grace. Spiritual progress is inseparable from the education and purification of the heart.[4]

The heart is also the seat of passionate love for the beloved—whether this is understood as the spiritual master or God. The master cultivates love in his students through a variety of mechanisms to propel them onward in their quest for divine union.[5] But the importance of love and the range of other impulses that stroke or assail the heart should not diminish the emphasis on understanding. As Louis Gardet has argued, the Sufi conception of the heart should not be taken as requiring an "emotionalization of religious values" but as a formulation that presumes the possibility that the heart will, through training and purification, attain a superior capacity to perceive exterior and interior reality.[6]

Arezu Khanum's account of the role of her heart in her spiritual quest had obvious parallels with this Sufi tradition. She described her heart as the seat of intuitions that guided her on the journey and protected her from error. She said that she prayed to God to illuminate her heart so that her path would become clear. She further described her soul as gaining strength through ascetic exercise and the foregoing of carnal pleasures, a key element of the Sufi science of the heart. Despite these similarities, however, Arezu Khanum's understanding of the heart contained a subjectivist remainder. She noted that Eckankar's hierarchy of gods did not please her heart, and that she did not feel it to be her path, although she did not deny the possibility that it could be a path for others. Furthermore, in her disagreement with her teacher in the Cosmic Mysticism seminar over the nature of the angelic figures she had encountered, Arezu Khanum granted the possibility that Mr. Sheyda's perspective too may have been true insofar as it was based on his personal experience.

Arezu Khanum's estimation of spiritual data in terms of their ability to please her heart has affinities with a more recent trend in religious thought that has concerned itself primarily with the category of religious experience. As a theoretical concept, "religious experience" (*tajrobeh-ye dini*) began to circulate widely in Iranian intellectual circles around 1990 with growing interest among reformist religious intellectuals (*rowshanfekran-e dini*) in rethinking the role of Islam in public and private life. While it would be difficult to draw a straight line between this movement and the kinds of metaphysical experimentalism I have explored in this book, religious intellectuals did help shape the discursive environment that nurtured interest in alternative spiritualities. Moreover, some opponents of alternative spiritualities have singled out religious intellectuals as responsible for contributing to the former's upsurge.[7]

For the reformist intellectuals, religious experience is a privileged avenue to truth valued over—and at times against—the commandments of jurisprudence and the pronouncements of speculative theology. As such, it functions to carve out an interiorized space of religiosity independent from the disciplinary and coercive oversight of the Islamic Republic.[8] Over the years, their debates have drawn on the works of a range of Western thinkers, from William James to Karl Popper, Friedrich Schleiermacher to Rudolf Otto, Paul Tillich to Martin Buber, and many others.[9]

The central figure of this type of religious intellectualism has usually been identified as Abdol-Karim Soroush (b. 1945), a philosopher who came to be recognized as an ideologue of the reform movement and a theorist of religious pluralism and religious democracy.[10] Other important contributors to this trend include Mohammad Mojtahed Shabestari (b. 1936) and Mostafa Malekiyan (b. 1956). I cannot attempt a comprehensive review of religious intellectualism here.[11] Instead, I will focus briefly on two related discussions that have a bearing on the development of the discourse of religious experience.

One of the key normative distinctions upheld by Abdol-Karim Soroush has been that between a form of religiosity that is concerned with "expedience" (*maslahat-andishi*) and one that is oriented toward gnosis (*ma'refat-andishi*) or experience (*tajrobat-andishi*).[12] Expedient religiosity is governed by law and preoccupied with the regulation of outward behavior as a means to worldly or otherworldly ends, especially the securing of social and political order. But this is inferior, Soroush argues, to the mode of religiosity that has gnosis or experience as its goal. These latter are the paths of prophets and friends of God, and they are available for ordinary Muslims to follow. As Kathleen Foody puts it,

Increasingly central in Soroush's later works is a kind of leveling—a collapse, albeit incomplete, of the uniqueness of prophets, saints, and divinely guided leaders in light of universal access to interior mystical states. He reimagines works from the Islamic tradition to prioritize the religious experience of the individual and to void any external authority over that individual—particularly understandings of Islamic *legal* authority that figure the Islamic Republic's claim to power. Soroush denies the utility of the Islamic Republic to govern Muslim practice by positioning Islamic law as secondary and the experience of the individual as primary.[13]

To make the path of prophets open to the ordinary believer, Soroush redefined prophecy as a form of historically specific individual experience constrained by the prophet's limited personality. One who follows the prophet Muhammad, in this view, shares in the joy of his mystical experiences, rather than merely following his commands and prohibitions. This is a formulation that depends to a large extent on reimaginings of key premodern Sufi texts, but Soroush departs from this tradition by granting authority to individual experience and stripping religiosity of institutional and political entanglements in a way that would be alien to earlier forms of Sufism.[14]

This brings us to the philosopher Mostafa Malekiyan, whose most interesting contribution for my purposes has been to rethink the value of religious experience in emotional and psychologistic terms.[15] For Malekiyan, "traditional" institutional religion (by which he obviously has orthodox Shiʿi Islam in mind) is no longer viable for moderns, who should instead strive to fashion themselves into "spiritual" beings so as to ensure that they are leading authentic, autonomous lives.[16] He sees spirituality (*maʿnaviyyat*) as an ahistorical core of contingent and historically differentiated forms of religiosity (*tadayyon*). Religions have primarily functioned to alleviate suffering or to at least make it possible for believers to cope by enshrouding suffering in meaning. But in the modern era, individuals can no longer remain religious in the "traditional" way if they are to maintain logical coherence. The primary reason for this, according to Malekiyan, is that rationality is central to modernity, whereas traditional religiosity is based on unquestioning faith and acceptance of others' authority. Hence, moderns must either forego religion altogether (thus losing the benefits that come with it), or rework their understandings of traditional religion into something that would be compatible with modernity. This reworked religiosity is spirituality: it is rational, skeptical of the historical narratives of major religious traditions, stripped of religion's heavy mythological "burden," oriented toward the here and now (which aligns spirituality with secularity), empiricist, egalitarian, opposed to the sacralization of authoritative figures, and shorn of any parochial elements (spirituality thus aspires to universality).

For Malekiyan, the mission of spirituality is to define and provide solutions for the fundamental problems that human beings face. Ultimately, it should aim to answer the human need for inner contentment (*rezayat-e baten*) by providing means to peace and tranquillity (*aramesh*), joy (*shadi*), and hope (*omid*). Malekiyan acknowledges his understanding of spirituality to be functionalist and psychologistic. Further, when he argues that spirituality should be empiricist, he means that its effects on emotional well-being should be individually testable through experience in the here and now, rather than being anchored in unverifiable rewards and punishments in a deferred afterlife.

Malekiyan places the historical moment of spirituality's emergence as a self-conscious movement in nineteenth-century Europe and North America. This spirituality, he argues, is not the same as any of the new religious movements in the world, although it has something in common with all of them. Although Malekiyan never makes this explicit, it is clear that he is attracted to some of the possibilities encapsulated in what are typically rendered as New Age forms of spirituality, particularly those that—like Cosmic Mysticism—posit multiple levels of consciousness and a unified cosmic mind or energy.[17] It should come as no surprise, then, that he has emerged as the foremost intellectual exponent of ideas that have found their most explicit expression in the myriad forms of alternative spirituality gathering followers among ordinary Iranians. When Arezu Khanum said that Eckankar did not please her heart, she was—probably unknowingly—agreeing with the functionalist and psychologistic approach articulated by Malekiyan, according to which beliefs and practices should not be accepted necessarily because they have superior theological underpinnings, but because they succeed at securing inner contentment. Lili Bayati, who told me that her attachment to Cosmic Mysticism finally had to do with its success in bringing her tranquillity, would concur.

The empiricism of Malekiyan's theory of spirituality—the notion that spiritual systems should succeed at bringing tranquillity, joy, and hope in ways that their practitioners can verify—is in tension with the kinds of appeal to scientific authority in validating religious truth that I have explored so far. To the best of my knowledge, neither Malekiyan nor any other religious intellectuals make this connection, but its significance is clear. When scientific arguments are suspected to have failed in demonstrating the empirical truth of metaphysical statements like those propounded by the Cosmic Mystics, a psychologistic spiritual doctrine like what Malekiyan offers provides an escape: a rational pathway for circumventing any disorientations that may result from the realization that scientific justifications of metaphysical experimentation may end in failure.

EXPERIMENTS IN SYNTHESIS

The seductions of modern science have proved irresistible for the Iranian religious imagination. Believers have drawn on scientific epistemology to legitimize their doctrines and practices, constructed flexible models to grant plausibility to intangible phenomena and metaphysical conceptions, and borrowed from the virtues of organized scientific activity to fashion their subjectivities as moral reformers.

Avant-garde as each of these deployments have been in their own time, they are hemmed in by a range of hazards. Rhetorical appeals to science's authority are vulnerable to skepticism and debunking. Attempts to borrow from its professional virtues run the risk of equating theological reason with (and perhaps subordinating it to) scientific rationality. In responding to the former threat, some religious practitioners have developed a future-orientation that characterizes contemporary science as constrained by a kind of underdevelopment or dogmatism to be overcome. To dissolve the latter difficulty, theologians have scrupulously maintained a separation between their own inquiries and those of professional scientists, even while drawing inspiration from their theoretical, methodological, and moral offerings.

Since the 1990s, metaphysical experimentation has received a boost from a reformist discourse that valorizes personal experience at the expense of theological and legal orthodoxy. The same discourse of experience has also provided refuge from science-minded criticism. When a practitioner argues that what matters most in a given spiritual doctrine is neither its theological coherence nor its fidelity to scientific method, but rather its success in furnishing subjectively evaluated tranquillity and joy, there is little left for the skeptic to argue against.

The empirical sensibilities nurtured by the discourses of scientism and religious experience have propelled a range of metaphysical experiments that have in turn invited orthodox polemics and coercive state action aimed at protecting society's spiritual hygiene. But as the Shiʻi ulama's engagements with Spiritism have taught us, similar sensibilities have found their way to professional theological practice, making it difficult to draw any neat one-to-one connections between doctrine and epistemology, or simple oppositions between the orthodox and heterodox.

The ulama's experiments with Spiritism, both speculative (as with Khomeini) and empirical (as with Makarem), have also shown us that theological epistemology may contort and expand in the process of accommodating new and unusual forms of evidence. These were instances of unreflective, unarticulated shifts that remained constrained to the very specific contexts of public theological polemics about the permanence of the soul beyond death. The potential for a new articulation of theological epistemology was never seized, although it may yet be taken up at some point in the future.

The failure of these experiments to make a lasting impact on the professional practice of theology should not obscure a more important point: transformations in traditions of intellectual and moral inquiry do not always occur self-consciously, as through deliberate argumentation or planned legal and institutional change. The possibility always exists that practices will produce unintended consequences, whether these have to do with epistemic structures, as in the case of Spiritism's reception, or in effecting shifts in the affective patterns through which dominant discourses are apprehended or inhabited, such as with the flexible and playful deployment of physics-inspired models for grasping the metaphysical.

The forms of rationalization I have examined thus far in this book have been oriented toward ensuring that metaphysical knowledge and practice is in harmony with reason. Rational coherence, however, has never been purely an end in itself. There has always been a larger social goal on the horizon: guaranteeing the virtue, health, loyalty, or happiness of the public, usually with an eye toward promoting national progress. These social objectives have also been subject to historical processes of rationalization, not only in terms of intellectualization but also in the sense of systematization, instrumentalization, and bureaucratization. Since the establishment of the Islamic Republic in 1979, some of these efforts have come under the aegis of state projects of "cultural engineering" (*mohandesi-ye farhangi*), with the promotion of piety and elimination of vice articulated as central goals.

We have already caught glimpses of these projects in the efforts to demarcate and combat superstition, in the polemics against Cosmic Mysticism and other forms of alternative spirituality, and in the coercive state action against their leaders. In part 3, I turn my attention to a different arena that is no less attached to the realm of the metaphysical: the promotion of hagiographies of "friends of God," men whose heroic acts of piety and ascetic discipline have won them spectacular divine favors. More than any other metaphysical engagement I have described, the stories of God's friends have become entangled with the Islamic state's mission to cultivate a pious citizenry. As we will see, these entanglements are extremely complicated and have engendered their own share of disorientations and unintended consequences, not least of which is the instrumentalization of the friend of God and his metaphysical powers. I turn to a close examination of the hagiographies and to Iranians' encounters with God's friends next.

PART 3   **FRIEND OF GOD**

A PROTECTOR LOST

Pedram owned and managed an Internet café on the third floor of a commercial building in Ariyashahr. In 2009 he was thirty-two years old and had recently welcomed his first child, a son. I came to know Pedram through a web forum on Islamic mysticism and occult sciences that I will call Asrar. He had been a regular contributor to the forum for about a year and moderated a section dedicated to debunking "deviant schools" (*makateb-e enherafi*), by which was meant the kinds of heterodox spiritual systems I examined in part 2.

I met with Pedram at his Internet café to discuss his interests in the occult. We spoke for three hours, interrupted less than a handful of times by customers asking to surf the Internet or print out a document. Business was slow, and as Pedram explained, that day was no exception. A few months later Pedram grudgingly shut down his company and found employment as a network security specialist at a telecommunications firm. At the time of our meeting he was visibly distressed by his business difficulties and the vexed social conditions that he considered to lie at their root.

Pedram's earliest exposure to the occult had been mediated by two very different friendships in the early years of his youth, each of which was marked by particular forms of intimacy, power, and inequality. The first of these friends was a young man with extraordinary metaphysical powers (*qodrat-ha-ye mavara'i*) who introduced Pedram to animal magnetism when he was sixteen:

> He encouraged me to read various books, like *Manyetizm-e Shakhsi* (Personal Magnetism).[1] And I started doing some of the exercises, even trying it out on other people, which was not a good thing to do. It wastes your energies. You're not supposed to try these things out on other people. The consequences return to you. That's how I became acquainted with these books. And I would spend time with people who had many of these powers.

The magnetist friend had tremendous influence, not only on Pedram but on a few of his friends as well:

> If he told you that he thought it would be a good idea for you to throw yourself out the window, you would do it. If he told you to stop talking to your parents,

you would. He had the kind of mental control over people around him that enabled him to command them to do anything.

Pedram cut off his relations with this friend when he saw how his power had corrupted him. The magnetist became very arrogant, claiming to have reached a station of inerrancy. Even so, Pedram's decision to abandon him cost him his friendship with several others who were still in his awe. He was vindicated two years later when he learned that the magnetist had fallen into a path of "transgression" (*khalaf*), having sex with seventeen- and eighteen-year-old boys who did his bidding. "His power got him into trouble," Pedram said. "He lost the people around him and was humiliated." Pedram was so disgusted that he stopped practicing or even reading about magnetism and other metaphysical arts, throwing out the books he owned and returning those he had borrowed.

Friendship with the magnetist taught Pedram about one way in which metaphysical power, personal character, and social influence came together. It was a damning picture of arrogance, lust, danger, and, finally, humiliation. This was not the only possible outcome, however, and he came to know a very different assemblage of power and character in another friend, the late Ayatollah Mirza 'Abd al-Karim Haq Shenas.

Ayatollah Haq Shenas (1919–2007) was the prayer leader of the Amin al-Dowleh mosque near the Tehran Bazaar until his death. Trained as a jurist with close ties to the howzeh establishment in Qom and to Ayatollah Khomeini, he was better known for his lectures on ethics (*akhlaq*) and mysticism (*'erfan*). Many of these lectures were recorded, but they were not disseminated in his lifetime, as the ayatollah preferred to avoid undue public attention. After he died, some of his devotees transcribed and published his lectures, making them available both in print and as free downloads online.

Pedram began to attend the elderly ayatollah's lectures when he was eighteen, and he quickly secured his affections. In the course of several interactions, he realized that the ayatollah could peer into his soul and read his mind:

> Several times I went and sat near him. I was very shy. Whenever I had a question I would go sit near him and he would give me the answer [without my asking it]. This happened to me a lot. Whenever I sat near him he knew I had a question, and he would automatically give me the answer. Or if he felt that the answer would offend me, he would turn to someone else and say, "If you do this thing, this kind of calamity (*bala*) will befall you. Don't do it." I knew he was saying it to me. But back then I didn't really appreciate it. There were many young people whom he took by the hand and led to higher spiritual stations. I did not appreciate him as I should have. It was with him that I finally realized what the metaphysical was (*mavara ro tazeh fahmidam chiyeh*). What kind of power is this? I haven't even asked him a question and he answers it.

If the magnetist had used his knowledge of the metaphysical to satisfy his own lusts, Ayatollah Haq Shenas deployed it for the spiritual care of his followers, molding their character and guiding them toward higher stations. Pedram felt that he had not taken advantage of the ayatollah's guidance as he should have, but at least he had "gotten a whiff of his fragrance" (*rayehash behemun khord*), and he understood that people like him, rare though he was in his asceticism and spiritual power, truly did exist.

When Ayatollah Haq Shenas died, Pedram realized that he missed more than the opportunity to benefit from his spiritual guidance. He also lost a powerful protector. By this he meant that he could no longer count on his late teacher's moral supervision and social patronage, but above all, that he felt exposed to metaphysical danger in a way he had never experienced as long as the ayatollah was alive. As Pedram understood it, this danger was the symptom of a diseased social condition marked by widespread jealousy and materialist ambition.

Pedram had heard reports of sorcery here and there before, but he had never paid much attention until cases emerged too close to him to ignore. A highly educated woman in his family could not find a suitable job until she consulted a rammal who told her that she had been bewitched by a suitor. A businessman among his friends noticed one day that the sidewalk outside his shop was wet and he subsequently went bankrupt for the next two months, because whoever spilled the water had recited prayers over it with the intention to ruin him. Clearly, Pedram realized, there were dangerous metaphysical forces and people willing to exploit them to obstruct the progress of others. These events prompted Pedram to educate himself in the occult sciences by reading Persian-language grimoires and joining the Asrar web forum. He wanted to be able to protect himself and his family should such forces threaten, and he intended likewise to offer assistance to others among his acquaintances who were struggling with similar problems.

Later Pedram found disturbing signs that he himself had been bewitched. One day he opened his Qur'an, a copy that only he used in his house, and found several pieces of string, each with a number of knots. His wife had no knowledge of the strings' origin. Pedram's friend Salman, the founder of Asrar, asked him to count the knots on each string and tell him their order. Salman considered the numbers and the order in which they had appeared, finally ruling that the strings were a talisman placed in the Qur'an by a sorcerer's jinn agent or movakkel. He instructed Pedram to untie the knots, recite some prayers over the strings, and cast them into flowing water to neutralize them.

This apparent case of sorcery had its correlate in material misfortunes. The most distressing was a dispute that lay at the heart of Pedram's business problems in his Internet café. Until a few months prior to our meeting, Pedram rented the space one floor below his current address. He had a thriving business there, but then his landlord asked him to vacate the premises so that he could start his own Internet café. The landlord thus stole Pedram's customers, who were used to the old location. When Pedram rented the space upstairs, the ex-landlord and now competitor even prevented him from placing a sign in the shared hallway indicating the move. Most customers saw an Internet café on the second floor and did not think to walk up a few additional steps to Pedram's address.

Pedram struggled for months to regain his lost business, pleading with the ex-landlord to desist, threatening him with legal action, and trying various tactics to attract customers. In despair, he turned to the occult sciences. He made protective amulets for himself and wrote prayers for warding off the evil of his enemies, all to no avail. At one point he found instructions for a potent curse (*nefrin*) and decided to give it a try. Pedram did not give me any details about the curse other than that it was deadly and that the instructions required that it be recited seven thousand times. I knew that Pedram often relied on a grimoire attributed to the seventeenth-century Safavid philosopher Mir Damad. I had acquired a lithograph print of the grimoire in the Tehran Bazaar and an electronic copy on a CD. Pedram's description of his curse resembled the twenty-eighth of forty so-called Idrisi names of God near the end of the book:[2]

> The twenty-eighth name—*Ya qahir ya dha-l-batsh al-shadid anta-l-ladhi la yutaqu intiqamuh* [O vanquisher, O possessor of the terrible grip, you are the one whose vengeance cannot be endured]
>
> …
>
> There are many qualities for this name, from friendship and enmity and binding sleep and binding tongues and attracting hearts and so on… Know that this name is extremely great in stature. The heavens and earth and sun and moon and whatever God exalted has created, he created by the power and greatness of this name. And it is said that this name is written on the forehead of 'Izra'il [the angel of death] and that 'Izra'il seizes souls by the power of this name. One of its qualities is that if two armies face one another in battle and [one] recites [the name] seventy-one times and at that moment the wind blows toward the enemy, tremors will fall into that army and all will be destroyed. If someone has a strong enemy and wants to destroy him, he should recite this name seven thousand and one times every day, and first make the enemy's face yellow and after three days imagine his face as red such that it becomes absent from imagination. In the first three days that he has imagined [his enemy as] yellow, he will be killed or he will die. There is much more to be explained, the rest will become clear through experience.

Pedram did not make it beyond the first day of the curse's execution. After reciting the name two thousand times, he felt his head grow heavy and he fell into a momentary slumber. "I saw a terrible scene that I can't describe," he told me, "but something happened such that when I woke up I closed the book and left it." Pedram decided he would never again attempt such a curse on anyone, no matter how severe or unfair their enmity. "I asked myself, 'Why are you doing this?'" he said. "I left the punishment to God. Even if someone has done something so terrible to me, I have no right to curse them like this."

I asked Pedram if he thought incidents of sorcery like those he had experienced were on the rise. He responded that this was certainly the case, as people were now more preoccupied with difficulties (*gereftar*) and they resorted to metaphysical means to alleviate their problems and crush their enemies. "But did people not have more difficulties during the war?" I asked. I was referring to the 1980–88 war with Iraq, the massive death and destruction it brought about, and the austerity and hardship that accompanied it. "No," he answered. "Let me put it a different way. In the past there was peace of mind but no comfort [*aramesh bud vali asayesh nabud*]. Now there is comfort but no peace of mind." He thought for a moment and continued:

> I feel that people have grown greedier and each person wants more for himself. People are not content with their own share. How can you obtain what you want? [The metaphysical] is one way: to interfere into the unseen, into what is your divinely designated allotment [*taqdir*]. There is nothing wrong with wanting to change certain things. We have prayers for improving business and sustenance [*ruzi*], for example. But many people are interfering with the allotment of others. And when you do that, you have to expect the consequences too.

Pedram blamed the increasingly selfish appeals to the occult on social changes that emerged after the end of the war. "During the war," Pedram told me, "people's views were celestial [*asemani*]. They would say that Imam Khomeini has carried out a revolution and we may be martyred but we will stand together." But with the end of the war, social solidarity evaporated, leaving only greed and competition:

> Now the war is over and people are asking, "What will be our share of the world?" People started demanding their share. Like, "What kind of car do I have?" There was a time when the source of their pride was that "my son has been martyred" or "I am helping others." My own grandfather would go around and take fuel to poor people at the time of the revolution. This same person was fighting all of us, his own family, over wealth and possessions to the day he died a few years ago. We have all changed. People say, "We've fallen behind the rest of the world." "We have fallen behind in terms of leisure." "We want to find comfort." And they have sped up. If you look at the acceleration that exists in society, it's bothersome. Why has this happened to us? They used to say that people's glances were celestial. People would say, "We will not plan for our tomorrow because there may not be a tomorrow. We may be martyrs." But today

they will say, "Okay, I'm going to take my six million apartment loan and invest it to turn it into nine million. I will register to buy a car and in a year I need to make two hundred thousand in profits. The property I buy has to grow this much." It doesn't grow, property remains stagnant, and people's hollers reach the sky. Cars get expensive or get cheap, and people protest. Society falls into turmoil. Why has this happened? It's because we are sitting and planning. Planning is excellent. But worldly thought will not leave us alone.

After his botched attempt to curse his ex-landlord, Pedram decided never again to employ the occult sciences for his own benefit. He did continue to educate himself in the occult, however, so that he could protect himself and his family should dangers arise, and to provide advice to friends and relatives in need. His decision to forego proactive appeals to the occult had to do not only with his realization that there were dangers that could backfire on him, but also that he did not have the moral-spiritual capacity—what he called *janbeh*—to handle occult powers. "If you don't have the janbeh to handle something," he told me, "God will not give it to you. This is why I sometimes thank God for not granting me certain powers. If I had these powers, I would use them when I got into a quarrel with someone and shred them to pieces. Then on Judgment Day I would have to pay for having wronged another person."

It was clear that for Pedram, no man he ever knew possessed the janbeh to handle occult powers like Ayatollah Haq Shenas. He was a man who had lived a "godly life," a kind of life that Pedram could never imagine living himself. "Not that I don't want to," he insisted, "but we are not men of this arena [*marde in meydun nistim*]"—or, in other words, he lacked the will and the strength. If the ayatollah had still been alive, Pedram knew that he would not have allowed him to experiment with the occult the way he had. "In fact, if he were still alive," he said, "I may not have pursued these sciences at all. He would say that as long as I am alive, no calamity will befall this people. It is only since he has died that all these things have happened." Pedram sighed as if to emphasize the absolute uncertainty of his situation. "I did not often go see him, but I always felt that he was there. There is a human being who protects me from afar. When he died I lost my support [*poshtam khali shod*]. And I thought to myself, 'Such men will never appear again.' "

WHIPS FOR THE WAYFARERS

Men like Ayatollah Haq Shenas, revered for their ascetic piety and held in awe for their marvelous powers, are known in Islamic tradition as "friends of God" or *awliya' allah*.[1] Readers of the Qur'an recognize them in those verses that praise the righteous (*abrar* or *salihin*) and the sincere lovers of truth (*siddiqin*) whom God places in the company of prophets and promises that they have nothing to fear or grieve.[2] Among the Shi'a, they are those who have attained the highest stations available to humankind short of the sinless prophets and imams, although a few may exceed even some prophets in stature.

In the course of my research, I heard the names of a small number of living men repeatedly mentioned as friends of God, although not everyone agreed about who deserved such reverence. My interlocutors were familiar with many more such men through hagiographies composed after their deaths, as we shall see below. There was a consensus that friends of God were rare and that they were not typically known widely in their lifetimes. Those who were known, moreover, were difficult to approach and they did not easily accept students. As a result, talk about contemporary friends of God was often heavy with longing and regret—longing to benefit from the presence of such blessed beings and regret that opportunities for nearness to them were few and fleeting.

The extraordinary piety and spectacular marvels of God's friends has long provided material for moral instruction and self-discipline.[3] Much of this instruction is imparted orally in face-to-face settings like mosques and Islamic study circles. But with mass literacy and the widespread availability of inexpensive books, periodicals, and Internet access, written hagiographies increasingly afford individuals the possibility to read and reflect on the lives and marvels of friends in private. Although a few of my interlocutors—like Pedram—had enjoyed the living presence of such friends, their knowledge about most of them came from printed hagiographies. As I will show in this chapter and the ones that follow, hagiographies of God's friends are complexly interwoven with processes for instrumentalizing the metaphysical: not only as technologies of pious self-discipline but also as tools of cultural engineering in the hands of the state, and as means for individuals to come to grips with the radical spiritual uncertainties engendered by the bureaucratization of piety.

For Iranians, the most widely available hagiographies are those detailing the lives, sayings, and deeds of the prophet Muhammad, his daughter Fatima, his cousin and son-in-law ʿAli, and the eleven imams from their progeny. Then there are the stories of famous Sufi masters of old: Hallaj, Bayazid Bistami, Rumi, Hafiz, and so on. Some are included in hagiographic compilations that are known and loved, not just for their accounts of saintly lives but for their literary genius. Such is Farid al-Din ʿAttar's *Tadhkirat al-Awliyaʾ* (Remembrance of God's Friends) from the early thirteenth century CE, some of whose stories are still enacted in theatrical plays and included in school textbooks. Much less common (though not entirely absent) are hagiographies of contemporary Sufi poles; that is, the heads of prominent Sufi orders. The scarcity of such hagiographies is a partial index of the embattled condition of Sufi orders as minority communities frequently accused of heresy or deviance, particularly after the 1979 revolution, which reinvigorated—though not always consistently or systematically—a long history of persecution against Sufis.[4]

Shortly after the 1979 revolution and especially during the 1980–88 war with Iraq, hagiographic fragments emerged in printed memoirs, testaments, biographies, and commemorative collections dedicated to the martyrs of the revolution and war. In the years following the end of the war, these fragments gradually coalesced into full-fledged book-length hagiographies. Forming parts of a state-promoted mystical discourse, the new hagiographies aided the production of exemplars on the model of the friends of God of old, but in the mold of modern, pious, revolutionary activism.[5] The state promoted Ayatollah Khomeini himself as a mystic and friend of God shortly after his death, and somewhere along the way he even gained the sobriquet *emam al-ʿarefin* (imam of the mystics). This was hastened by the discovery and publication of a number of philosophical-mystical treatises and mystical poetry that Khomeini had composed at various points during his lifetime.[6]

Beginning in the early 1990s, a different crop of hagiographies gained widespread public attention, and within a few years they were dominating the genre.[7] These books focused on previously little-known Shiʿi mystics of the twentieth century—jurists, preachers, philosophers, and laymen who were known as moral teachers and mystic masters only to limited circles of students and devotees.[8] With rare exceptions their lives were a far cry from the revolutionary leaders and martyrs of the previous two decades. They largely led obscure lives of asceticism, spiritual teaching, and scholarship, away from the hubbub of politics, revolution, and war. They became exemplars not as socially engaged revolutionaries and fighters but as pious scholars and laymen who had gained mastery over themselves through arduous spiritual exercise.

In promoting the new friends of God, the authors and distributors of their hagiographies seemed to have sensed that the models of piety that had been propagated earlier, particularly those emphasizing radical politics, self-sacrifice, and martyrdom, were unsuited to a youthful postwar society characterized by growing institutional stability, entrepreneurship, and consumption. This anxiety has existed at least since the end of the war with Iraq, with religious authorities expressing growing concern about the decline of pious virtues, "flight from religion" (din-gorizi), and "spiritual deviance" (enheraf-e ma'navi), particularly among the youth. A cursory glance at publications over the past two decades reveals a plethora of material debating the prevalence and sociological, moral, and political roots of youthful straying from Shi'i orthodoxy, analyzing the implications of the phenomenon and recommending solutions.[9] What critics deem a decline of virtue is a consequence of dramatic shifts in the values organizing social life largely through direct state planning. I described these shifts in chapter 15: economic liberalization and the promotion of a culture of competition and individuality, a growing interest in professional psychiatry and pop psychology, the rise of a prosperity-oriented self-help industry, and the proliferation of therapeutic spiritualities addressing urban desires for tranquillity, concentration, and peace of mind.

Concerns about irreligion arising from the spread of "deviant" forms of spirituality have powerfully impacted state policies for more than a decade. In February 2005, the office of the Supreme Leader, Ayatollah Sayyed 'Ali Khamenei, ordered state institutions to address the emergence of "deviant individuals, groups, and associations [operating] under the cover of mystical and spiritual issues [and aiming] to attract the country's youth."[10] The order was consistent with Khamenei's long-held worries about "cultural onslaught" (tahajom-e farhangi) against Islamic revolutionary values, and his view that a central mission of the Islamic Republic was "cultural engineering" (mohandesi-ye farhangi), a systematic attempt to understand the cultural problems plaguing Iranian society and devise and implement solutions with reference to an overarching framework of "Shi'i rationality."[11] His directive was taken up by the Supreme Council on the Cultural Revolution (SCCR; Shura-ye 'Ali-ye Enqelab-e Farhangi), an influential state institution that was established shortly after the 1979 revolution to cleanse universities of liberals, Marxists, and other "counterrevolutionaries," but whose mission later expanded to stewardship over all cultural matters deemed nationally significant. Shortly thereafter, the issue was assigned to a committee of the SCCR called the Public Culture Council of Iran, whose chair is the Minister of Culture and Islamic Guidance, and whose other members include representatives from the Islamic Republic of Iran Broadcasting organization (state radio, television, and other media), the howzeh, the Science Ministry, the Education Ministry, the Intelligence Ministry, the Interior Ministry, the police, the Ministry of Sports and Youth, the Vice President's Office for Women and Families, and the Islamic Development Organization (Sazman-e Tablighat-e Eslami), among other institutions. The council held eleven meetings over about ten months to discuss the matter and produced a list of general and specific recommendations. These were subsequently approved by the SCCR and disseminated, with some revisions, to the relevant state bodies between February 2007 and March 2010, with the instruction that they report back regularly on their progress.[12]

The list of recommendations is long and complex, so I will confine myself to only a few of the most important points, namely, those that emphasize the production of expert knowledge, coercive mechanisms for combating alternative spiritualities, and measures for instrumentalizing the friends of God. First, the SCCR called on state institutions to conduct studies within each of their specific domains of responsibility to ascertain the extent to which deviant forms of mysticism and spirituality had proliferated, what had caused their spread, and what negative consequences they had brought about. Second, these institutions were asked to prevent the production and dissemination of any material that propagated deviant spiritual ideas, and to engage in "intelligent and precise criticism." Athletic groups that promoted tranquillity and concentration—such as yoga—were singled out as requiring special attention to ensure that they were not spreading deviant teachings. Third, these institutions were called to produce "attractive" materials (books, articles, films, online programming, and so on) disseminating and bolstering "authentic Islamic mysticism" and the "correct path to spiritual wayfaring," using the words of major recognized personalities of Islamic "shariʿa-oriented" mysticism ("personalities" here encompassing those who are considered to be God's friends), with an emphasis on the lives of Ayatollah Khomeini, Ayatollah Khamenei, and the martyrs of the revolution and war.[13]

The full range of state attempts to combat deviant spirituality is beyond the scope of this book. What concerns me are the ways in which these governmental projects have become entangled with nongovernmental attempts to promote Shiʿi mysticism through the production and dissemination of hagiographies of God's friends. As I mentioned above, hagiographies of contemporary friends gained prominence from the early 1990s, more than a decade before state officials grew worried about the deviance of alternative spiritualities. Their authors were concerned about youthful straying from the Shiʿi path of piety already from this earlier time, even if this anxiety was directed primarily toward materialism and irreligion rather than heterodoxy. Worries about alternative spiritualities did eventually shape some nongovernmental projects too, but this had to wait until the late 2000s; that is, after the state initiated the cultural engineering initiatives whose outlines are reflected in the SCCR recommendations above.

The authors of the hagiographies of God's friends frequently cited worries about irreligion among the youth as a motivation for composing their texts. They blamed the decline of pious observance on the prevalence of materialism and worldly desire without singling out the liberalizing state policies that encouraged material ambition as a condition for economic growth. For example, ʿAli Meqdadi Esfahani expressed precisely this kind of concern in his introduction to *Neshan az Bineshan-ha* (Trace of the Traceless), a popular hagiography he published in 1992 to document the life and marvels of his father Shaykh Hasan 'Ali Esfahani Nokhodaki (1863–1942). My interlocutors often cited *Trace of the Traceless* as the one book that set off the wave of interest in contemporary Shi'i friends of God. Esfahani wrote in his introduction:

> It is clear to the conscience of the people of insight and the wayfarers of the path of truth that after the divine speech [the Qur'an] and the words of the revered prophets of truth and the guided imams, peace be upon them, which are healers of sick hearts and illumination for the hearts of the pious and the God-fearing, there is no word loftier than the speech of practicing scholars (*'olama-ye 'amelin*) and godly mystics (*'orafa-ye mote'allehin*) and the description of their states [e.g., their spiritual biographies] which cleanses souls from the darkness of the material world and encourages and affirms the wayfarers on the path of gnosis… And the exalted have said: The words of the friends of God are whips for the wayfarers.
>
> Thus it is mandatory for the people of righteousness… to recite the verses of the noble Qur'an every morning and read closely the traditions of the most noble Prophet and narratives from the pure imams… and review and reflect on a few pages from the book of life and description of the spiritual states and marvels and words of the great men of religion so that it may free them from the snare of satanic whispers and guide them to the straight path… *In this time, when the multiplicity of the material world and attention to corporeal forms has made many members of humanity ignorant of the truth, and as some have been so absorbed in lusts that they have forgotten God and deny many of the bases of religious rulings and the worlds beyond the human senses, it is mandatory and necessary for every Muslim individual as much as possible to remind the ignorant and teach the unaware and encourage those who practice* [my emphasis].[14]

According to Esfahani, the words, deeds, and marvels of the friends of God are powerful instruments for pious self-care under normal circumstances but gain special urgency in a time when corporeality, materialism, lust, and forgetfulness of God and his commands have become widespread.

Other authors singled out the youth as those most in need of spiritual instruction through the telling of accounts of the lives of God's friends. Mohammad Reyshahri, the first intelligence minister in the Islamic Republic, was one such author. In 1997 he published *Tandis-e Ekhlas* (Icon of Sincerity) about Shaykh Rajab 'Ali Neku-Guyan, a humble tailor and purported giant of mysticism. Reyshahri substantially revised his book in 1999 and retitled it *Kimiya-ye Mohabbat* (Alchemy of Love), and the book has been reprinted numerous times since. As he explained in the preface to his book and in a subsequent interview, Reyshahri wanted to introduce the tailor to Iranian society as a "superior example."[15] "The youth," he said, "are in dire need of the tailor's words"; words that can be used to spread profound secrets about spiritual wayfaring and self-construction.[16] In his preface to the revised edition of the hagiography, he wrote that the book was not meant as mere "commemoration" or "prescription" but actual "medicine for the heart," which worked as an "impetus for self-improvement, guiding the spiritual seeker toward the station of the righteous and the truth-seeker by means of the Holy Qur'an and traditions of the infallible imams."[17]

In some justifications of contemporary hagiographies, the themes of moral decline and the special needs of the youth are brought together. One example is the private cultural institute Shams al-Shomus (Sun of Suns), an organization founded in 2000 by a group of male university students in Tehran and devoted to propagating information about the lives and spiritual states of contemporary and near-contemporary friends of God. The institute has published about a dozen books and several DVDs and hosted annual and biannual seminars in Tehran to celebrate friends' lives from 2002 to 2010. On their official website, the founders note that they had initially come together to aid families of material need in their neighborhoods but soon realized that "solely distributing bread will not cure society's pains. We are afflicted by cultural poverty [*faqr-e farhangi*] in addition to material poverty." They then define their mission as follows:

> Familiarizing human beings with their God and reconciling them with religion, by:
>
> • Propagating religion in a new language
> • Explicating the Islamic model of life—the good life [*hayat-e tayyebeh*]
> • Attempting to make society more ethical (reducing any kind of darkness and corruption)[18]

Elsewhere on the website the group states its objectives as follows:

> • Familiarizing society, especially the youth, with the beauties of religious spirituality
> • Introducing contemporary spiritual models
> • Explicating authentic spiritual values against inauthentic values
> • Providing criteria for distinguishing the people of spirituality (*ahl-e ma'ni*) from [false] claimants [this item was added after 2010]
> • Introducing some of the prevalent pathologies (*asib*) and explaining solutions and ways to avoid them [this also was added after 2010][19]

By the mid-2000s, the authors of the new hagiographies found themselves fighting on two fronts to shore up the virtues they had seen deteriorate. On the one hand, they had to reorient Shi'i spirituality in keeping with the social changes that came with stability and growing prosperity. On the other hand, they had to compete with the alternative spiritual models that were fast gaining ground. They waged both as conservative battles. For the former, they sought recourse in the virtues associated with ascetic piety in the madrasa and marketplace: renunciation of material desires, business honesty, chastity, seclusion, and passionate attachment to God, the Prophet, and imams, expressed through sustained and intense acts of devotion. Utterly missing were any references to the kinds of virtues propagated earlier as necessary for creating and upholding a modern revolutionary Islamic state. Judging by the hagiographies, the new friends of God would not have been out of place if they had been transported to an early modern Shi'i shrine city.[20]

To compete with the emerging models of alternative spirituality, the authors of the new hagiographies emphasized the authenticity of their friends' paths, their rootedness in the Islamic tradition, and their total fidelity to the teachings of the imams. This they counterpoised to the flimsy, materialistic, and fraudulent paths of what my friend Ahmad—a former member of Shams al-Shomus—called "heroin spiritualities," by which he meant the kinds of therapeutic spirituality I examined in part 2. His associates had the same thing in mind when they stated on their website that their accounts of the friends of God should be distinguished from those of inauthentic, pathology-infested spiritual "claimants," among whom they would surely have included Mr. Taheri, Mr. Sheyda, and other masters of Cosmic Mysticism.

The new hagiographies proved popular and lucrative, spawning multiple reprints, elaborations, and competing editions, and encouraging more authors to enter the fray and write about God's friends. For example, from 1997 to the time of this writing in 2015, at least eight different books were published about Shaykh Ja'far Mojtahedi, seventeen about Shaykh Rajab 'Ali the tailor, and more than thirty about Ayatollah Mohammad Taqi Bahjat, many of which have been renewed in multiple editions. Numerous television programs, web pages, and CDs were dedicated to the lives and deeds of these and other friends. Between 2002 and 2010, the events held by Shams al-Shomus at a large auditorium in the Interior Ministry building near Fatemi Circle were consistently filled to capacity, attracting hundreds of participants each time. The hagiographies also inspired new practices of grave visitation. Some of my interlocutors mentioned specifically visiting the graves of Shaykh Rajab 'Ali in Rey and Shaykh Ja'far Mojtahedi in the shrine complex of Imam Reza in Mashhad whenever the opportunity presented itself. Moreover, large popular commemorations have been held for several years at Shaykh Rajab 'Ali's tomb on the anniversary of his death, sometimes with state television coverage and invited lectures by state officials.

The new hagiographies captured the imaginations of a multitude of pious young urban Iranians who came of age after the war. They instilled in them a sense of awe in the spiritual heroism of fallible men who inhabited roughly the same time and space as themselves. They inspired them to try to be better people, more God-fearing, more meticulously concerned with their ritual conduct, and more anxious about avoiding sin. They made them fall in love with God and his chosen friends. And they helped them imagine what it might look like to enjoy the certainty of faith in a time of pervasive moral ambiguity and anxiety. The new friends of God did not do all of this on the strength of their asceticism and moral uprightness alone. A fundamental aspect of the hagiographies—for many, the single most important reason for their appeal—was the thrilling accounts of the friends' marvelous powers, signs of their closeness to the divine realm of the unseen.

One of the first people who introduced me to the attractions of the marvels of God's friends was Sa'id, a taxi driver in his early forties. "I am not very educated," he told me one day, "and I don't read many books." But some twenty years earlier, one book had absolutely captivated him. It was the early 1990s. Sa'id was a member of the Basij militia and worked in a state-owned consumer cooperative. One day he heard his friends raving about *Trace of the Traceless*, the book that recounted the life, words, and marvels of Shaykh Esfahani (Nokhodaki). He decided he needed to get his hands on a copy. Eventually, as he told me, he bought the book for three times its cover price. "The book was not so widely available back then," he explained, but he was willing to pay whatever it took to acquire it. "I read sixty or seventy pages in an hour or two, even though I'm not much of a reader," he said. "What did you like about the book?" I asked him. In response, Sa'id mentioned some of the extraordinary stories narrated about Esfahani, particularly his marvels or *karamat*. The book was brimming with such anecdotes—tales of extraordinary healing, foreknowledge, clairvoyance, teleportation, and the ability to communicate with the souls of prophets and imams. The passage below recounts one story that Sa'id specifically mentioned as having fascinated him:

> Sayyed Abol Qasem Hendi recounts that one day, Haj Shaykh [Esfahani] ordered me to travel to the city of Torbat and stay overnight in the mountain of Bijak Salat. Before sunrise, I was to pick a certain quantity of an herb he had described to me and bring it back to him [in other stories we learn that the herbs Shaykh Esfahani collected may have been used for alchemy]. As per his orders, I went to Torbat. The residents warned me against staying in the mountain overnight. They said that there are spirits [*arvah*] that dwell in the mountain and they will harm anyone who sleeps there. But I did not listen to them and went to the mountain anyway. When the sun set I heard a great clamor. I saw that my horse was restless and looked as though it wanted to run away. So I shouted, "I have been sent by Shaykh Hasan 'Ali. If you harm me I will complain to him about you." With those words the clamor subsided and I was not harmed. I spent the night in the mountain. Before dawn I picked the herbs as instructed, but as I was doing this it occurred to me that I should pick some for myself too. No doubt it will be of use to me one day. As I attempted to pick some of the herbs for myself, I suddenly noticed that some enormous boulders were sliding down the mountain. My horse tore its harness to escape. I grabbed it and refastened it. I thought perhaps the movement of the boulders had been a natural

occurrence. I wanted to try to pick the herbs once more, when again I saw the boulders begin to slide. This time I realized that it was not a natural event. So I decided to forego picking the extra herbs and returned to Mashhad and to Haj Shaykh. When he saw me, Haj Shaykh said, "What of you and this nosiness? Why did you want to pick more of that herb than I had ordered?" It was at that point that I realized that that great man had been observing and protecting me [*moraqeb-e hal o kar-e man budeh ast*] throughout my mission.[21]

Around the same time, Sa'id had become interested in soul travel and the power of teleportation (*tayy al-arz*), which he had heard attributed to the friends of God, including Shaykh Esfahani. One of his coworkers practiced "soul flight" (*parvaz-e ruh*) or astral projection, and he gave Sa'id a translated book on the topic so that he could also learn.[22] Sa'id told me that because he is not very educated, he could not understand much of the text, and even though he had tried some of the exercises enumerated in the book, he had not accomplished much. Sa'id's friend told him that soul flight required a lot of mental concentration. Souls can travel through walls and other obstacles, Sa'id said, in the same way that the friends of God are said to have moved in the blink of an eye between two cities. Accounts of several such instances of rapid travel are included in the book about Shaykh Esfahani. Here is one:

> The late Sayyed Abol Qasem Hendi recounts that he had accompanied Shaykh Hasan 'Ali to the Ma'juni hills outside of Mashhad. There, a brigand by the name of Mohammad Ghush Abadi who had caused insecurity in that region appeared next to the hill and warned us, "If you move, you will be killed." Haj Shaykh turned to me and asked, "Have you made ablutions?" I said yes. He took my hand and said, "Close your eyes." A few seconds passed. We had taken no more than two or three steps when he told me, "Open your eyes." I opened my eyes and saw that we were near the gates of the city.[23]

In hagiographies, marvels like clairvoyance and teleportation work as signs of the elevated spiritual status of God's friends by demonstrating their connection to a realm beyond and superior to the mundane world—more lofty, more solid, more certain, if also less likely to be revealed to the perception of ordinary human beings. Accounts of marvels are ubiquitous in Islamic textual hagiography as well as in oral narratives through which anecdotes about friends of God circulate.[24] In narrating such marvels through the remembrance of eyewitnesses—usually intimate associates and devotees of the friend—the new hagiographies highlight the ways in which a small number of people of exceptional spirit penetrate into another realm and bring its fruits to their everyday existence. These extraordinary fruits are heartwarming signs to the friend of God as well as to his devotees, who are seeking an anchor of stability beyond the infirmities of the mundane.

Although widely acclaimed among the pious, the hagiographies of God's friends are subject to various forms of contestation that trouble their instrumental deployments. There are disagreements over the manner in which friends are to be represented, what should and should not be said about them, and most important of all, who can legitimately be considered a friend and what qualifies him to be counted as such. These differences have subtle bearings on the manner in which values are produced around the figure of the friend and the individuals and institutions to whom these values accrue. They thus have complex repercussions for the frictions that exist between nongovernmental projects for promoting piety and those initiatives that are explicitly aligned with the interests of the state. Chapters 21 and 22 focus on some of these disputes.

DISCRETION AND PUBLICITY

Disputes concerning God's friends can be broadly divided into those over the manner in which these men are to be represented and those over what qualifies a man as God's friend. The problem of representation can itself be broken down into questions about the ethics of writing about friends and the place of the marvel in these texts. The hagiographer's legitimacy may also be at stake in these questions: Just who can rightfully represent the friend? Disputes over the qualifications of the friend, on the other hand, are rooted in disagreements about appropriate paths for spiritual wayfaring, the relationship of official learning to spiritual status, and contrasting attitudes toward political involvement and loyalty to the leaders and ideals of the 1979 revolution. This chapter is about the problem of representation, and I turn to the qualifications of God's friends in the next. I will pay specific attention to the hagiographies of two men, Shaykh Ja'far Mojtahedi (1925–96) and Shaykh Rajab 'Ali the tailor (1883–1961). Both have been immensely popular, but they have also incited a range of criticisms.

An important dimension of the ethics of hagiographic writing has to do with discretion; that is, ensuring the continued concealment of those details of the friends' character, words, and experience that are thought to be inappropriate or dangerous for the uninitiated.[1] Hagiographers face the delicate task of providing enough provocation to attract pious readerly interest while guarding against the uninhibited mass-propagation of secrets.[2] Some secrets are considered more appropriate for public transmission than others. There are obscure facts about the lives of friends that the hagiographers treat as precious gems to be discovered through devoted inquiry, subsequently to be revealed to the public. Then there are matters to which they make fleeting references without elaboration, with the suggestion that they may only reveal these secrets to trusted confidants (*mahram-e asrar*). Sometimes the only secret revealed about a particular piece of knowledge is that it is a secret. Such is, for example, the mystery of the *esm-e a'zam*, or God's greatest name, which can work wonders in the world in the hands of whoever consciously deploys it but is unknown except to the most intimate of God's friends.

Hagiographers do not always agree over which secrets deserve to be protected, and their disputes sometimes make their way to the pages of their published work. A revealing example can be glimpsed in the books honoring

Shaykh Jaʿfar Mojtahedi, especially the earliest two, which have also been the most popular. They are notable for their dialogic link: the first text depends in part on oral anecdotes recounted by the author of the second book, and the latter is largely construed as a direct response to the deficiencies of the first.

Hamid Sefidabiyan, an author and independent researcher based in Isfahan, published *Laleh-i az Malakut* (A Tulip from the World of Divine Sovereignty) in 2001, and his book has been reprinted multiple times since. In his research, Sefidabiyan relied primarily on interviews with the late Shaykh Jaʿfar's friends and devotees. One of these was the Qom-based author and poet Mohammad ʿAli Mojahedi, who is known for his praise poetry for the family of the prophet Muhammad. Mojahedi was so dissatisfied with the product of Sefidabiyan's effort that he decided to compose his own hagiography titled *Dar Mahzar-e Lahutiyan* (*In the Presence of the Divines*), which was published first in 2003 with a second volume added in 2005.

Sefidabiyan comments on the problem of secrecy and other difficulties in writing about a friend of God in his introduction:

> This valuable collection includes small portions and significant points about the life of this great mystic [Shaykh Jaʿfar], the knowledge of which, one can say with certainty, has been possible for elite individuals and people of the sanctuary... The author has, to the extent possible, met with every one of these individuals, and if... certain topics within the pages of this book have been discussed in a very circumscribed and synoptic manner, or if certain events have not been described at all, it has been only because the author has wanted the book to respect all the various dimensions [of the matter]... But in spite of all this, I admit that I have not been able to properly carry out the extremely serious responsibility I have undertaken... and I admit that the character and grandeur of the eminent Shaykh is much greater than what could be constrained to the very few and limited pages of this book by the feeble pen of this slight author.[3]

Several issues bear comment in this passage. First, Sefidabiyan recognizes that prior to the publication of his book, intimate knowledge of Shaykh Jaʿfar's life and spiritual path was only available to "people of the sanctuary" (*ahl-e haram*), by which he means people who are themselves spiritually advanced enough that they are admitted into elite circles where secret spiritual knowledge is communicated. Nowhere does Sefidabiyan claim that he is a member of any such sanctuary: he is only a researcher who has done his best to inform the public about a great man. And yet, and this is the second point, Sefidabiyan does claim to know more than his readers. There are topics that, so he claims, he has avoided mentioning in his book, and others that he has described only "synoptically." Third, he tells us that his circumspection is meant to ensure that "the various dimensions" of the matter are respected. By this cryptic phrasing, what we as readers are to understand is that the author possesses the appropriate discretion not to reveal secrets that are unsuitable for the uninitiated. He may also mean that not every report he has gathered is reliable, and it is best not to repeat those that cannot be verified. Fourth, with all of his avowed caution and care, Sefidabiyan still admits that he has failed to represent the life and grandeur of God's friend as is his due. This is a gesture of humility that has the status of a topos in hagiographic writing. By confessing failure in adequately appreciating and successfully representing the life of a friend of God, the author adopts the only possible ethical relationship toward him, one by which he confirms his status as a devotee and perhaps even a disciple. Together with his subtle assertion of superior knowledge and the proper ethical comportment for handling that knowledge, this humility rhetorically positions the author as precisely a man of the "sanctuary" to which, as we saw, he makes no explicit claim.

The contours of the life that Sefidabiyan sketches in his hagiography are by and large the same as those of competing texts. He tells us that Shaykh Ja'far Mojtahedi was born into a wealthy family in Tabriz. His father possessed substantial holdings in land and business interests. But in what may be read as auguring his son's future loving attachment to the imams, he spent a considerable portion of his life leading caravans of pilgrims to the Iraqi shrine cities of Karbala and Najaf. Beginning at a very young age, Ja'far received visions and blessings from the infallible members of the prophet Muhammad's household. During his youth, he became obsessed with occult sciences, like alchemy and the control of jinn. He devoted significant time, ascetic discipline, and inherited wealth on these pursuits until he heard a voice from the heavens revealing to him that "real alchemy" was the love of the imams. Violently shaken, Ja'far abandoned his life of comfort in Tabriz and embarked on a fateful journey to Iraq. He suffered various hardships that included arrest and imprisonment but finally managed to attach himself to Imam 'Ali's shrine in Najaf and found employment as a shoemaker's apprentice. A few years later, he resettled in Karbala after receiving a vision from Imam 'Ali permitting him to visit the shrine of Imam Husayn. In 1958, at the age of thirty-three, Ja'far returned to Iran just as conditions for Iranian residents and pilgrims in Iraq took a turn for the worse after 'Abd al-Karim Qasim seized power in a coup d'état. Details of his whereabouts and activities in Iran in the following decades are murky. What emerges from Sefidabiyan's hagiography is that he traveled between various cities and seldom remained in any particular location for long. This ostensibly had to do with the specific missions that God assigned him, demanding that he be constantly on the move, mostly on foot, but sometimes by teleportation. Some of these missions involved working marvels, like curing illnesses, fixing factory machines, and delivering messages from the imams. He died in 1996 after a period of illness and was buried in the shrine complex of the eighth imam, 'Ali ibn Musa al-Rida (Persian: Imam Reza) in Mashhad.

By most accounts I heard from readers of Sefidabiyan's hagiography, the book's distinctive feature is its recounting of a significant number of spectacular marvels. We learn that two lions escorted the caravans that Shaykh Ja'far's father led on pilgrimage to Iraq. As a young man Shaykh Ja'far could summon jinn at will and threatened to burn them when they refused his commands. In his old age, he continued to call forth the jinn for a variety of services, including a tension-relieving massage. When working as a shoemaker's apprentice in Najaf, he helped Iraqi schoolchildren achieve perfect scores on their exams by foretelling the questions they would receive. He could summon deceased persons flanked by angels by reciting the opening chapter of the Qur'an over their graves. In his travels in Iran, he was known to have conversed with strange and intimidating creatures in the forest, as well as exchanging secrets with companions of the occluded Imam Mahdi. And in several instances, he delivered painful long-distance punishments to world leaders oppressing Islam: he slapped Nikita Khrushchev in the face, cursed Colonel Gaddafi so that his wife and son died in an American bombing, and encouraged John F. Kennedy's assassin to calm his nerves and pull the trigger.

While Sefidabiyan's hagiography proved immensely popular, it also generated a fair share of animosity. The most virulent attacks on his book came from one of his erstwhile informants, the author Mohammad 'Ali Mojahedi. In his two-volume *In the Presence of the Divines*, Mojahedi sets out to correct Sefidabiyan's "errors" and "exaggerations," and by extension to seize authority over claiming and defining the legacy of Shaykh Ja'far. In his introduction, Mojahedi explains that he was an intimate student and devotee of Shaykh Ja'far for thirty-two years. He proceeds to provide a three-page apology for having authored his hagiography. During Shaykh Ja'far's lifetime, he writes, he was so absorbed in the mystic's "existential attractions" that he could not extricate himself to write about his experience.[4] After his teacher's death, he was repeatedly pressured to write a book about him, but he refused because Shaykh Ja'far's legacy was being abused by certain "pretenders," and he believed that publishing a hagiography "would only pour water in [the pretenders'] mill."[5] Later, Mojahedi was approached by Hamid Sefidabiyan, who said he wanted to record some of the former's recollections for a book he was writing about Shaykh Ja'far. Sefidabiyan promised Mojahedi that he would show him the text of the recollections so that he could vet them for accuracy. But then, claims Mojahedi, he "forgot his commitment" and went on to publish a nice-looking but error-laden book that "brought immense profits for its authors and publishers."[6] At this point, Mojahedi decided that writing a hagiography was a matter of religious responsibility and refusing to write a corrective would be tantamount to "ignoring the great responsibility that I owed Shaykh Ja'far."[7]

In attacking Sefidabiyan and discrediting his hagiography, Mojahedi thus asserted his authority over the representation of Shaykh Ja'far's life and marvels. He thereby also staked an implicit claim to the latter's discipleship, something that brought him substantial attention. As he acknowledged in the fifty-seven-page introduction to the second volume of his book, Mojahedi was repeatedly invited to conferences to speak about Shaykh Ja'far. He expressed dismay that the conference hall at a particular event could not accommodate all of the many participants, so that some of those in attendance were forced to view the event through closed-circuit television. On several websites and forums where his books are introduced or reviewed, I noticed occasional comments by readers requesting Mojahedi's contact information so that they could consult him about their problems or ask about some specific aspect of Shaykh Ja'far's spiritual guidance. To these readers, Mojahedi was not merely a reporter of Shaykh Ja'far's life but a man who had inherited his teacher's spiritual authority and perhaps some of his marvelous abilities as well.

In the introduction to his second volume, Mojahedi all but gloats over the numerous reprints of his book, something for which he had castigated Sefidabiyan:

> The enthusiasm of lovers of Shi'i literature and mysticism for the [first volume of] *In the Presence of the Divines* has been so much that in the two years since its first publication, it has been reprinted nine times, and more than forty-three thousand copies have been given to those seeking this work; and now that I am revising the last print of the second volume of this book, some friends have recommended that it be translated into Arabic and English so that the requests of Shi'as in other Islamic countries will also be taken into account.[8]

Why did Mojahedi take issue with Sefidabiyan's hagiography? He never details the latter's errors and exaggerations, so we need to attend to the differences between the two books to find out. The principal distinction apparent between them is that Mojahedi takes a far more cautious approach than Sefidabiyan in reporting marvels. There are no accounts of lion escorts, encounters with jinn, summoning the dead, alchemical feats, or meetings with the companions of Imam Mahdi. This is not to say that Mojahedi eschews marvel anecdotes altogether. For example, he cites a story about Shaykh Ja'far's "supratechnical" power (*niru-ye balatar az teknik*) in making an industrial machine resume its operations after the German technicians working on the equipment lost all hope. He also mentions that Shaykh Ja'far once teleported to Germany to save the life of a young terminally ill boy whose mother had appealed to the Virgin Mary. The Virgin told this woman that the affair was out of her hands, but that she should try appealing to the prophet Muhammad's daughter Fatima and her sons instead. In a separate incident, Shaykh Ja'far teleported to the Austrian Alps to save three young men trapped in an avalanche while skiing.

What distinguishes these marvels from those that Mojahedi refuses to include? He claims that his marvel reports are more reliable, more attentive to the necessities of discretion, and more consistent with Shaykh Ja'far's path of

spiritual wayfaring. Furthermore, these stories serve some pedagogical purpose, rather than merely generating astonishment.[9] Mojahedi writes:

> I admit that some of the things I remember about this great man, with the as-
> tonishment that they create in people's minds, may be doubted by those who
> are not acquainted with such extraordinary events and existential marvels of
> the men of God. Therefore, I will refrain from mentioning these stories as much
> as possible except in cases where their pedagogical value is so great that I will
> have no choice but to recount them.[10]

As far as Mojahedi is concerned, then, some of the marvel anecdotes described in Sefidabiyan's book are at best unreliable and at worst false. Others
may be true, but they serve no pedagogical purpose, instead serving only to
astonish some readers and stir doubts in others. Both kinds of reports should
be avoided.

Mojahedi's ambivalent attitude to marvels is symptomatic of broader concerns about hagiographies. Partly these have to do with worries that fantastic
marvel reports may turn away otherwise sympathetic but skeptically minded
readers. Others are concerned that readers will look for marvels as proof of
spiritual stature at the expense of more important criteria, with the result that
they may be duped by any charlatan feigning wonderwork. At issue in this
latter concern is a historical tension between adherence to the shariʿa as interpreted by the jurists and commitment to a mystical path embodied in the
person of a charismatic Sufi shaykh. Ata Anzali aptly describes this tension
in the premodern world:

> The immanent and easily accessible God whom the Sufi shaykh of the khanaqah
> and the syncretistic wandering dervish claimed to mediate through their cha-
> risma was a formidable threat to the authority of the jurists claimed as interpret-
> ers of God's will, commandments, and preferences. The promise of an ever-
> present, immanent God whose presence could be experienced in fresh and
> tangible ways was perhaps the most powerful aspect of the Sufi message—one
> that made Sufism popular with lay masses who found little solace in the philoso-
> pher's dry notion of God or the jurist's obsession with obedience to a remote
> and often demanding God. Saintly Sufi figures offered what neither the philoso-
> pher nor the jurist could. They promised a direct connection to the supernatural
> and the possibility of tapping into the infinitely abundant resources of the un-
> seen realm to meet worldly and otherworldly needs. They brought heaven and
> earth and the mundane and sublime together in the present moment—here, now,
> embodied.[11]

For the contemporary hagiographer writing within a milieu dominated by
Shiʿi juristic and philosophical rationalism, marvel anecdotes thus need to be
subordinated to the rule of the shariʿa in order to pass muster and avoid the
taint of Sufi heterodoxy (I examine this theme in more depth in chapter 22).

We can see this orientation clearly articulated in the mission statement of the now defunct website Salehin (The Righteous), a large online collection of hagiographies in the Persian language:

> The wayfarer must know that the true mystic and master is one who moves solely on the path of Islam's shari'a and who never commits any violation, otherwise his fall is certain, even if, in appearance, he has marvels, visions, and dreams. These things can be inspired by Satan and his armies and delusions and satanic fantasies as well....
>
> Given that visions and marvels have an apparent (*zaher*) and a concealed (*baten*) aspect, and we hear only of the appearance and have no information about the concealed aspect, we cannot rely on them as principles or references. Our intention in reporting these matters on this website is only a reminder that we should know and believe that there are truths and a concealed aspect to this world and if people are to act in accordance with the holy shari'a of Islam, they can attain a place where they see nothing but God, and extraordinary feats may issue from them, or they might have visions. However, these states are only meant to encourage the wayfarer and they are not the main principle. The objective is to grow close to God the compassionate by way of serving him.

Other critics go still further to argue that marvels are distractions not only for the readers of hagiographies but even for the friends of God who possess them. I heard this position most starkly articulated by a young howzeh-trained scholar who held regular sessions on ethics and mysticism for a group of young men in Tehran. He told me that marvels were the "menstruation of mystics" (*heyz-e 'orafa*). What he meant by this was that acquiring marvels distracts friends of God from their spiritual struggle, in the same way that menstruation prevents women from performing regular daily prayers, fasting, and certain other ritual obligations. In other words, the acquisition of marvels is less an end in itself than a challenge to be overcome in the path of unity with God.

A final point bears comment in Mojahedi's criticism of Sefidabiyan's hagiography. Remember that Mojahedi avoided mentioning any accounts of Shaykh Ja'far's encounters with jinn, summoning the souls of the dead, or engaging in alchemy. This was because, for Mojahedi, Shaykh Ja'far's interests in the occult sciences were no more than youthful obsessions that he overcame on his path of spiritual development when he discovered the transformative power of love for the household of the Prophet. To claim that even in his years of spiritual maturity he engaged with jinn or deployed the occult sciences for predicting the future and other practical ends would be to tarnish his spiritual accomplishments. Sefidabiyan recounted stories of Shaykh Ja'far's meetings with jinn and summoning the dead in his mature years as though they were marvels. But Mojahedi likely believed—or worried that his readers would believe—that these powers could scarcely be differentiated from sorcery. This is probably what he had in mind when he argued that some of the marvels re-ported by Sefidabiyan were inconsistent with Shaykh Ja'far's path of spiritual wayfaring.[12]

It is here that we can transition to the second type of question haunting modern Shi'i hagiographies: What qualifies a person as a friend of God or, better, what disqualifies him from achieving such a station? It is to a discussion of these problems and their political implications that I now turn.

THE POLITICS OF VENERATION

We saw in part 1 of this book that the occult sciences occupy an ambivalent position in Shi'i thinking. They are almost universally considered to be dangerous, but they are also recognized to have lofty origins in the teachings of prophets and angels, and to have been learned and passed down for millennia in the lines of the great prophets, imams, and friends of God. Accordingly, not everyone sees a contradiction in valorizing a friend of God like Shaykh Ja'far, holding that he possessed marvels *and* recognizing that he was a master practitioner of the occult sciences to the day he died. To some, including Sayyed Yazdi, the rammal we met in chapter 6, Shaykh Ja'far's occult prowess and spiritual stature were inextricably connected.

If occult practices are cause for unease, there are other accusations leveled at some ostensible friends of God that incite full-throated vehemence. Chief among these is the charge of Sufism. The hagiographers of contemporary Shi'i friends of God are participants in a social milieu molded in part by centuries of orthodox disparagement of Sufism as deviant, heretical, and—in its organized forms—marked by superstition, corruption, and despotism. As Ata Anzali has shown, the rise of the Safavid dynasty (1501–1736) empowered a group of Shi'i ulama who launched a successful anti-Sufi campaign that, over time, shifted attitudes toward influential Sufi groups and their leaders.[1] At the same time, a new tradition of elitist mysticism—known as 'erfan—developed in scholarly Shi'i circles, assimilating central aspects of Sufism while eschewing others, especially the institutional framework of the master-disciple relationship and communal practices like vocal zekr recitations and the ritual *sama'* dance. Shunning Sufism's most visible features, however, did not save the proponents of 'erfan from having to consistently fend off the suspicions of the less mystically minded ulama. In a prominent example close to our own time, Ayatollah Ruhollah Khomeini faced stiff opposition among high-ranking Shi'i ulama in the 1950s against teaching mystical philosophy in the howzeh in Qom. Even after the 1979 revolution, which, as we have seen, helped elevate Shi'i mysticism to the level of state planning and discourse, the anti-Sufi ulama did not grant Khomeini a free pass to promulgate his mystical teachings.[2]

Whenever governmental or nongovernmental actors draw on mysticism to promote Islamic piety, they are forced to reckon in some fashion with this long-sedimented anti-Sufi dispensation. When haunted by accusations of

Sufism, the usual response by the proponents of ʿerfan is to intensify their own anti-Sufi discourse and to highlight the distinctions between ʿerfan and Sufism.[3] The hagiographies of contemporary friends of God are no exception, although some distinguish the ways of their friends more subtly than others. For example, Sefidabiyan mentions repeatedly that Shaykh Jaʿfar's method of spiritual wayfaring consisted exclusively of love for the imams. By this we are to understand that he was not a member of any organized Sufi lineage, but that he did not participate in the elitist scholarly ʿerfan found in the seminaries either. Mojahedi, on the other hand, goes much further and explicitly condemns the proponents of institutional Sufism as "non-men" and "ghouls" who "conceal their ugly faces behind the mask of *khanaqah*-style wayfaring."[4] Unsatisfied with mere ideological refutation, he also recounts several anecdotes about Shaykh Jaʿfar's confrontations with pretenders. In one case, Shaykh Jaʿfar denounces an unnamed Sufi pole (*qotb*) in Mashhad as a demagogue and charlatan after hearing about his claims, and the same evening the hapless Sufi falls into a latrine and dies.[5]

Such anti-Sufi rhetoric has been crucial in enabling the emergence of a public space in which mysticism is openly discussed and promulgated. But it has not completely satisfied the less mystically minded or the stauncher opponents of Sufism. Suspicions of Sufism thus continue to hound some of God's friends, often with material results. For example, organizers for a well-attended conference at an Interior Ministry auditorium honoring Shakyh Jaʿfar in 2007 publicly complained that Tehran municipal officials had refused to allow billboards announcing the event, while "banners featuring Iranian and foreign film actors and advertising western commodities covered the city's walls and doors."[6] A member of the Shams al-Shomus institute that planned the event later confirmed to me privately that some city officials were displeased with their program because they viewed Shaykh Jaʿfar's method of spiritual wayfaring as strikingly similar to that of the Sufis.

These officials were not alone. A similar suspicion is reflected in an answer to a question posted on porseman.org, the official Q&A website of the Office Representing the Supreme Leader in Universities.[7] The questioner asks for an explanation regarding "the character of Shaykh Jaʿfar Mojtahedi," and about "his ʿerfan and spiritual wayfaring." A lengthy answer is provided by an anonymous respondent. First, it offers a brief biography of Shaykh Jaʿfar, including a few accounts of his marvels as published in his hagiographies. The respondent then casts doubt on these accounts. He begins with this revealing phrase: "We have two kinds of mystics [ʿaref], Sufi mystics, and mystic jurists whose ʿerfan is taken from the Qur'an and the path of the Prophet's family (peace be upon them)… Only the experts of true ʿerfan [that is, the mystic jurists] can verify the righteousness of Sufi mystics and assess their claims, especially those that run counter to the shariʿa and the teachings of the family of the Prophet." The respondent goes on to say that a "precise and final judgment about the character of Mr. [Jaʿfar] Mojtahedi and the books that have been written about him" is extremely difficult, however, a few points can be made. The first and most important of these for our purposes is that "Mr. Mojtahedi's 'erfan and the path upon which he embarked have the color and scent of Sufis more than the 'erfan of the jurist mystics. Therefore his claims and behavior need to be treated with caution." The respondent also advises care in evaluating the accounts of Shaykh Ja'far's marvels, whose abundance—when contrasted with the rare marvels attributed to the jurist mystics—makes them "a little bit difficult to prove."

As this respondent's words show, Shaykh Ja'far is an uncertain, even polarizing, friend of God. However, those who revere him and those who suspect him of deviance cannot be neatly divided on the basis of easy oppositions like "progovernment" and "antigovernment," or even "pro-'erfan" and "anti-'erfan." The Interior Ministry granted a discount to organizers who wanted to honor him, while the municipality refused them permits to advertise their event. A respondent for the Supreme Leader's office in universities cautioned that he gave off a "Sufi scent," while Mojahedi, the poet widely considered to have written the authoritative hagiography about him, is typically seen as close to the Supreme Leader. We can interpret this ambivalence as a symptom of the broader uncertainty that plagues the project of Shi'i mysticism, its modernization, and its adoption by the postrevolutionary state.[8] I will return to an explicitly political dimension of this uncertainty as it concerns the revolutionary allegiances (or lack thereof) of God's friends at the end of this chapter.

Public disparagement of Shaykh Ja'far has been rather tentative. By contrast, Shaykh Rajab 'Ali (1883–1961) has been at the receiving end of open and scathing criticism in spite of his mass popularity and explicit support from state institutions and government-allied scholars. Before I focus on some of this criticism, I will briefly elaborate on some points I made in chapter 20. The first and most influential hagiography about Shaykh Rajab 'Ali was published in 1997 by Mohammad Reyshahri, a dyed-in-the-wool revolutionary, career jurist, and onetime presidential candidate who has served variously as judge in the Islamic Revolutionary Courts, prosecutor general, prosecutor for the Special Court for Clergy, a founder of the Intelligence Ministry, and—in the turbulent years of 1984–89—the first official to hold the powerful ministry's portfolio. Reyshahri was not a lone advocate for Shaykh Rajab 'Ali. His book received glowing coverage in state-funded newspapers and periodicals. It inspired others to publish books about the friend of God, with more than a dozen different hagiographies printed until the time of this writing, many with reprints. Annual commemoration ceremonies on the day of the tailor's death have drawn thousands of devotees to his tomb in Rey. In some years the ceremony has received state television coverage and prime-time advertising, and has featured lectures by prominent state officials, including cabinet ministers.

Shaykh Rajab 'Ali's most vociferous detractors have been howzeh-trained jurists. One of these is Mansur Kiyani, a critic of Sufism who has published a few books attacking the Dhahabi order. His best-known and most controversial book, however, is *'Aref-sazi va Ma'refat-suzi: Naqdi bar Edde'a-ha-ye Naql-shodeh az Marhum Rajab 'Ali Khayyat* (Manufacturing Mystics, Burning Knowledge: A Critique of the Claims Quoted from the Late Rajab 'Ali the Tailor) first printed in 2007.[9] Kiyani's book is an antihagiography, a caustic assault on almost every aspect of the texts about the tailor, with special scorn reserved for Reyshahri's text. Moreover, it is clear that he meant his polemic to target more than Shaykh Rajab 'Ali and to encompass a number of other ostensible friends of God without formal howzeh learning to whom fantastic marvels have been attributed. Although he does not mention Shaykh Ja'far by name, the latter could easily fit the same profile.

The crux of Kiyani's problem with Shaykh Rajab 'Ali is that he was allegedly a Sufi with heretical teachings and exaggerated claims. He breaks this down into four major points elaborated in the course of sixteen critiques. First, he says, Islamic 'erfan is reduced in Rajab 'Ali's stories to "rammali and fortune-telling." To substantiate this charge, Kiyani seizes on accounts of the tailor's clairvoyance and his superior insights into the interior reality of other people to argue that he is a better fit for the label of sorcerer than friend of God. Second, he argues that the hagiographies about Rajab 'Ali participate in a "profanation of the sacred." "The only thing that has any sacredness in this [Reyshahri's] book," Kiyani writes, "is Mr. Tailor, and every other sacred thing is filthy and devoid of value." He bases this claim on the way in which sacred sites like the Ka'ba and sacred figures like Imam 'Ali become objects of everyday experience for the tailor, his family, and his devotees. Third, Kiyani objects that the stories about the tailor silently demean and undermine the clergy. They do this, he argues, through accounts that render howzeh students or learned scholars subservient to the "illiterate" tailor—for example, by claiming that howzeh students would leave their studies in Qom to listen to the tailor's teachings, with some even working as his cooks or servants. "Worse," he adds, are the accounts of "scholarly and mystical leaders among the clergy who are singled out by name and humiliated by Rajab 'Ali the tailor on the slightest pretext." Fourth, and finally, Kiyani takes umbrage with the fact that the hagiographies about Rajab 'Ali valorize his lack of education. "Islam possesses thousands of mystical exemplars," he writes, "who are all famous for efforts and struggles in the path of knowledge, expanding monotheism and morality in religious society." In the stories in Reyshahri's book, however, "not only is there no pride about knowledge, there is boasting about illiteracy and the absence of knowledge."[10]

Viewed from the standpoint of a proponent of 'erfan, the elitist scholarly form of mysticism rooted firmly in the howzeh and hemmed in by the shari'a as interpreted by jurists, Shaykh Rajab 'Ali and Shaykh Ja'far are dangerous because they provide means for engaging in spiritual wayfaring, accessing mystical insights and marvelous powers, and achieving superior ethical stations while bypassing the mediation of the ulama and their expert knowledge and oversight. Even if the paths offered by the two friends of God are not Sufi in institutional affiliation, they appear to the jurists to be "Sufi-like" in their provision of parallel and perhaps competing means for ethical cultivation and salvation.

There are subtler, more intellectually refined critiques of Shaykh Rajab ʿAli that are all the more powerful because they directly criticize the man himself rather than the hagiographies about him. The most damaging of these is quoted from Sayyed ʿAli Qazi Tabatabai (1869–1947), a Najaf-based jurist and mystic revered as a friend of God, who acted as a spiritual teacher for a small group of mystically inclined scholars who went on to gain prominence as jurists, Qurʾan exegetes, philosophers, and mystics in Iran—the most influential of whom was Allameh Mohammad Hoseyn Tabatabai.[11] The criticism of Shaykh Rajab ʿAli was published in a hagiography of Sayyed ʿAli Qazi authored by his son Sayyed Mohammad Hasan Qazi. The section in which it appears is titled *The Difference between the Path of Fortifying the Self and [that of] Knowledge of the Self (Tafavot-e Tariq-e Taqviyat-e Nafs ba Maʿrefat-e Nafs).* It is introduced with the phrase, "a clear example of attachment to the desires of the self rather than overcoming them," and is followed by an anecdote from Ayatollah Haj Shaykh ʿAbbas Quchani:

> One of the famous masters of visions resident in Tehran named Haj Rajab ʿAli the tailor came to the house of the late Qazi and said, "I had [achieved] a state where all the plants would tell me their qualities and effects. It is some time that a veil has appeared and [the plants] no longer speak to me. I ask you to look into it so that this state will return to me." The late Qazi told him, "My hands are empty." [Rajab ʿAli] left to perform pilgrimage to Karbala, Kazimayn, and Samarra, and returned to Najaf. One day when all of the late Qazi's students had gathered at his home, he came and poked his head through the door and said, "What I asked you and you did not give me, I obtained from his eminence [the hidden Imam Mahdi], and his eminence said, 'Tell Qazi to come to me, I have something to tell him!' " The late Qazi lifted his head toward him and said, "Tell him Qazi won't come!"[12]

The younger Qazi makes several comments on this passage. First, he says the story illuminates the difference between a path of spiritual wayfaring based on monotheism and knowledge of self, which is the disciplinary method of the mystics from among the first rank of Shiʿi ulama, and a path of fortifying the self, which is the method of those engaged in ascetic exercises for obtaining visions and marvels. For the former, he says, marvels and visions are distractions to be overcome, while for the latter, they are ends in themselves. The seeker of marvels experiences a pleasure that is "hundreds and thousands of times greater than apparent sensual pleasures," such that he fails to overcome them and instead finds ways to justify their pursuit by telling himself that he uses these marvels to assist people in despair.[13] But in pursuing such

marvels, the wayfarer misses the ultimate point of ʿerfan, which is to "anni-
hilate all effects and impurities of the self, from their lowest degrees to the
highest stages that are even accompanied by intense luminosity."[14] Second,
the author draws attention to Qazi's cold response that "his hands are empty."
He interprets this to mean not that Qazi is incapable but that his hands, heart,
soul, and innermost being are fully free of any impurity, desire, and power
attributed to the "I" of the self. This is to be contrasted with Rajab ʿAli, who
claims to have possessed the power of hearing plants and other marvels.[15]
Third, the younger Qazi says that his father's scornful response during the
tailor's second visit, where the latter delivered a supposed message from the
hidden Imam Mahdi rebuking Qazi, undercut the flimsy "delusions and assertions of numerous claimants to meeting the Imam of the Age . . . This response
means that your claim is nothing but an imaginary, delusional, carnal thing
that is fabricated by your self or Satan."[16]

Although the substance of these criticisms of the tailor are doctrinal and
focus on the ethical nuances of mystical wayfaring, their greater significance
overlaps with other critiques we have encountered that aim to shore up the
elite spiritual authority of howzeh-trained jurists. As we have seen, marvel
anecdotes are an important reason for the allure of contemporary hagiographies. Even Sayyed ʿAli Qazi has not been immune from marvel-centric depictions, as most of the hagiographies that detail his life and teachings are replete
with spectacular marvel stories. On one level, then, the younger Qazi's criticism as channeled through anecdotes about his father may be seen as an attempt to preserve the elite nature of ʿerfan from the corrosion of folksy admiration and wonder-seeking. There may also be a specifically partisan motive
at work to buttress one particular lineage of mystical wayfaring within scholarly Shiʿi circles against those favored by a dominant faction within the state—
especially Ayatollah Khomeini and his teachers and students, but also "lay"
friends like Shaykh Rajab ʿAli, whose popularity, as we have seen, is in part
indebted to state largesse.[17]

This brings us to a final topic of contention over the friends of God: their
political allegiances. As we have seen, a distinctive feature of the hagiographies that gained popularity after the late 1980s was that none of the friends
they valorized (with the notable exception of Ayatollah Khomeini) were
known as revolutionaries or even as spiritual leaders with commitments to
social reform or political criticism. In this way, the propagation and defense
of Islamic values was disaggregated from allegiance to the Islamic Republic,
at least on the level of overt discourse. This detachment has been an important
factor in the popularity of the friends for many readers. But it has not gone
uncontested. The matter of political allegiance has been reintroduced in two
diverging ways: On the one hand, there have been attempts to attribute political views to some of God's friends that would make them into protorevolu-
tionaries. On the other hand, absence of allegiance to revolutionary values has

been used as a pretext for attacking some friends. Finally, some admirers of contemporary friends have pushed back against the attribution of pro–Islamic Republic loyalty to their favored mystics, and sometimes of any kind of political involvement at all. This resistance is guided by the view that such political engagement would be spiritually contaminating.

None of the earlier, more influential hagiographies of Shaykh Jaʿfar Mojtahedi mention any political activity on his part, and they are silent on his political views as well. In informal conversations, I sometimes heard that he was not on the best of terms with Ayatollah Khomeini and his circle of revolutionary jurists. Sayyed Yazdi, the rammal in chapter 6 who claimed to have received years of spiritual guidance from Shaykh Jaʿfar, explicitly positioned the mystic as a righteous friend against "corrupt charlatans" associated with the Islamic Republic. It came as a surprise to me then when I encountered the following blog post from June 7, 2012, by Hoseyn Maddahi, a young preacher in eastern Tehran:

> I don't remember exactly, but I think the first time I read *A Tulip from the World of Divine Sovereignty* was in the year 2005. A biography of the late mystic Shaykh Jaʿfar Mojtahedi, may God be content with him. I encountered some astonishing points around his character which I had neither read in the biographies of [other] friends of God, nor heard told anywhere. They have trained us in the howzeh in such a way that we don't easily accept any word except the word of God, the infallibles, and God's righteous friends. When I read the biography of this mystic I repeatedly looked at this friend of God with skepticism, and I imagined [that he might have had] associations with Sufism. I began conducting research about his character, and thank God I reached some good conclusions.
>
> A little bit later I realized that [Shaykh Jaʿfar] had had some interactions with his eminence Imam [Sayyed ʿAli] Khamenei, may God protect him. The current location of his tomb in the shrine of Imam Reza, peace be upon him [in Mashhad], was designated by our leader. I found him to be one of the friends of God, and I had to be thankful to God for having discovered his eminence.
>
> Some time later I gained plentiful spiritual contact with his eminence, and some marvels of his also encompassed me, even years after he had passed away.
>
> But my intention in writing this post is a profound point that [Shaykh Jaʿfar] had uttered about Imam [Ruhollah] Khomeini, God's mercy upon him. He had said: "Imam Khomeini has reached a point in monotheism that not a single one of the friends of God has attained."[18]

I want to draw attention to a circle of authentication in this passage. At first, the author experienced doubt when reading Shaykh Jaʿfar's hagiography, even suspecting him of Sufism. He attributes this skepticism to his howzeh training, which would not allow him to believe everything he read. But we may also interpret this to mean that the author was familiar with the elite 'erfan of the howzeh and based his judgment of mystical assertions on this knowledge, such that he could distinguish the authentic mysticism of 'erfan from the deviant mysticism of Sufism. To dissolve his skepticism, the author conducted research about Shaykh Ja'far, which led him to eventually accept that he was indeed a friend of God. In part, this acceptance came with the discovery that the current Supreme Leader of the Islamic Republic, Ayatollah Khamenei, had confirmed Shaykh Ja'far. Howzeh learning and allegiances, then, helped the author confirm an uncertain case. Subsequently, this uncertainty was transformed so thoroughly into certainty that the author began to experience the salutary effects of Shaykh Ja'far's marvels from beyond the grave. The circle was completed when the author encountered Shaykh Ja'far's attestation to Ayatollah Khomeini's spiritual grandeur: a man of marvels trained outside of the howzeh provided confirmation of a mystic schooled in the howzeh's elite discipline of 'erfan. The significance of this last confirmation is illuminated clearly in the post's concluding section (not quoted above) where the author expresses dismay that pilgrims pay their respects at the tomb of Shaykh Ja'far but neglect to visit Imam Khomeini. The point of his post, then, was not so much to confirm the legitimacy of Shaykh Ja'far as to confirm the legitimacy of Khomeini through Shaykh Ja'far.

Maddahi's blog post attracted numerous comments, initially supportive, but with increasing numbers of detractors as time went on. As these responses show, a significant contingent of readers saw the essay as a barely concealed attempt to instrumentalize Shaykh Ja'far and his marvels for political ends. On August 5, an anonymous commenter retorted:

> With my respects, the late leader of the revolution had [achieved] great spiritual stations but he was certainly not perfect, and Mr. Mojtahedi's words in this respect are not proof because he himself had not attained [perfect] monotheism either. None of the contemporary mystics considered him [that is, Shaykh Ja'far] to be perfect.

On December 12 of the same year, a commenter named Hamed rejected the author's post in stronger terms:

> I have heartfelt devotion for Shaykh Ja'far Mojtahedi, but the author of this blog has gone a bit too far with the sentence "Imam Khomeini has reached a point in monotheism that not a single one of the friends of God has attained." Shaykh Ja'far never said this. The meaning of this sentence is that Khomeini is higher than the twelve infallible imams, because these infallibles were God's friends. What it means is that these righteous imams whose seal is the Imam of the Age—peace be upon him—did not reach that [perfect] point in monotheism, but Khomeini did attain it. Be careful not to wrong the late Shaykh Ja'far with such lies.

Note that this commenter refers to the founder of the Islamic Republic simply as "Khomeini" without any honorifics, whereas he refers to Mojtahedi with the more respectful "the late Shaykh Jaʿfar," thereby clarifying his own allegiance in a much more explicit fashion than the previous post. A still more vehement response was posted by "alone" on April 3, 2013:

> I once complained about the lie that you wrote here about Mr. Mojtahedi, and said that this was a complete lie, and not only did it have nothing to do with the manners of Mr. Mojtahedi, but it also has nothing to do with this anti-Christ of a clerical revolution [*enqelab-e akhundi-ye dajjaliyyeh*] that is far from God... Now that you insist on lying, I ask God, God, whoever attributed a lie to you, make your hell manifest to him, and make his lot in life a distance from righteousness. May your life be ruined.

Two months later, another anonymous commenter named "truth seeker" wrote: "Politics and ʿerfan cannot be combined except by the infallible imams." Various other critical comments have been posted over the intervening years, accusing the author of lying or demanding that he provide proof of his assertion.

What we see in operation in these disputes is a contestation over the role of God's friends in authorizing a certain form of politics. To the author of the blog post, and to others who have similarly circulated the quote about Ayatollah Khomeini's monotheism, Shaykh Jaʿfar's status as a popular friend of God can be usefully appropriated in the service of shoring up the legitimacy of the Islamic Republic and its projects (including those directed toward cultural engineering). To the more vigorous of the blogger's critics, Shaykh Jaʿfar's status as a friend of God is irreconcilable with support for the current political system, or perhaps any regime at all. It is not unlikely that these commenters' devotion for Shaykh Jaʿfar partly hinges on their very perception that he was an opponent of Ayatollah Khomeini and his circle.

Political allegiance plays a positive role in the dispute over Shaykh Jaʿfar to the extent that the argument concerns the beneficiaries of the friend's spiritual blessings. The opposite is at work in some criticisms of our other example, Shaykh Rajab ʿAli. As we saw, the latter's popularity has in large part been indebted to the sponsorship of state institutions and state-allied individuals. Criticism of the tailor has accordingly taken aim at his alleged collusion with the Pahlavi regime to show that state support for him is misguided. This position has been most clearly formulated by Mansur Kiyani, the author whose work I discussed earlier in this chapter. The sixteenth and final critique in his book is titled "Companionship with Tyrants and the Pahlavi Regime." Kiyani builds an argument through a close reading of Reyshahri's *Alchemy of Love*, in which the latter claims that Rajab ʿAli was "not in the realm of politics, but he was intensely opposed to the hated Pahlavi regime and its ruling politicians."[19] Kiyani counters that the tailor's hagiographer has whitewashed him, and that attention even to his own text shows that the mystic was intimately associated with high-ranking officials in the Shah's regime. These included the head of the National Bank (*bank-e melli*), which was "the tip of the economic pyramid of the Shah's regime," colonels in the Pahlavi military, and officers in the secret police or SAVAK, who are reported to have attended the tailor's spiritual gatherings as devotees and consulted him for help.[20] Kiyani ends by calling on Rajab ʿAli's devotees not to "justify companionship with the entourage of the filthiest agent of combating religion [i.e., the Shah]."[21]

It is too early to assess the ways in which efforts to demolish Shaykh Rajab ʿAli's image or appropriate Shaykh Jaʿfar Mojtahedi into an ideologically coherent pantheon of friends loyal to the Islamic Republic may have impacted the popularity of these friends. What is certain, however, is that in the larger scheme of things, hagiographers attempting to promote virtue and spiritual refinement by instrumentalizing the stories of God's friends are forced to contend with a number of lines of attack, chief among them suspicions of Sufism and dubious political loyalties. As ostensibly wholesome alternatives to what my friend Ahmad called "heroin spiritualities," the exemplary models on offer through the stories of God's friends have themselves touched off disagreements that have further multiplied the spiritual options available in an increasingly diversified field.

I have examined the ways in which governmental and nongovernmental actors have attempted to instrumentalize God's friends to promote piety and combat both "flight from religion" and "deviant spirituality." In chapters 23 and 24, I turn to a final mode of metaphysical instrumentalization, this time among pious aspirants who find themselves caught up in anxious uncertainty about distinctions between truth and falsity, piety and charlatanry in post-revolution Iranian society. As we will see, these anxieties have their roots in the bureaucratization of piety and its assimilation into a state-centered instrumental reason of which the "cultural engineering" projects I have briefly examined are only one, albeit crucial, manifestation.

METAPHYSICS OF VISION

Among ordinary readers of hagiographies with no affiliation to the howzeh, or any stakes in competitions among different factions within or outside the state, disputes like those I have detailed in the previous chapters may never pose any problems. It is not at all strange for an admirer of God's friends to express simultaneous enthusiasm and devotion for Sayyed ʿAli Qazi, Shaykh Rajab ʿAli the tailor, Shaykh Jaʿfar Mojtahedi, and Ayatollah Khomeini. These readers concern themselves less with the intricacies of doctrinal differences and more with the narrative and ethical content of specific texts, and the ways in which they might bear on their own lives. Even so, these disputes are significant to the extent that they shape the milieu within which hagiographies are published and receive permission to circulate. As so much of the popularity of the hagiographies depends on state support, encouragement, or at the very least, lenience and accommodation, the fate of any particular text promoting a specific mystic's life and marvels hangs in the balance when the arguments I have examined flare up into the public scene.

There is another, subtler way in which the hagiographies of the mystics become entangled with governmental policies for cultivating a pious citizenry. This has to do with the criteria and practices through which pious individuals assess their own and others' status in the eyes of God. With the bureaucratization of piety and the instrumentalization of procedures for assessing Islamic commitment since the 1979 revolution, some pious Iranians have faced the disorienting realization that they lack any reliable yardsticks by which to ascertain their spiritual progress (or lack thereof). The hagiographies of the mystics hold forth a possible remedy for this unhomeliness of the conscience, the worry that the very faculty by which a pious aspirant discerns true from false may fall victim to satanic corruption. The mystic, as represented in his hagiographies, has managed to purify his conscience through arduous spiritual exercise, and this unpolluted conscience becomes an imaginative resource for ordinary believers to employ as instrument and technique in clarifying their own relationship to God. To explain how this happens, how the bureaucratization of piety enters the picture, and what consequences this process brings about for contemporary spirituality, I first need to take a chapter-long detour through Shiʿi mystical theology. In doing so, my aim is to explicate how some key concepts, including insight (*basirat*), extrasensory vision, and the imaginal manifestations of sin and virtue, have become available for ordinary, pious Iranians struggling to live virtuously in uncertain times.

As technologies of ethical self-fashioning, hagiographies invite their pious readers to embark on lives of spiritual cultivation, with an eye toward the minute possibility that they might receive a marvelous gift somewhere in the process.[1] The narratives model the virtuous endeavors of God's friends as struggles that culminate in marvels, which in turn stamp those struggles with a divine seal of approval. Few marvels do so as dramatically as clairvoyance, the extraordinary vision with which the friend of God perceives truths to which he had previously been blind, and receives confirmation of his trajectory as a spiritual wayfarer. As we will see, this same power of clairvoyance may be taken up in the anxious operations by which pious aspirants relate to their own conscience.

Shaykh Rajab ʿAli is one of the best-known contemporary exemplars of clairvoyance. In a number of his hagiographies, we read that at the age of twenty-three, he once found himself cornered by a beautiful girl from among his relatives who had been pursuing him for some time. Face-to-face with the seductress in a quiet house, with all the conditions for sin ready before him, the tailor tells himself, "Rajab ʿAli! God can test you all your life, why don't you test him for once? Forego this available and pleasurable sin for God." He then addresses himself directly to his Lord: "O God! I forsake this sin for you," he says, "so you, cultivate me for yourself!" Much like the prophet Joseph whom he adopts as his model, Rajab ʿAli makes a daring escape from his trap of sin.[2] His pious feat, his refusal to submit to fornication with the young woman, wins him insight (*basirat*) and vision (*binaʾi*). He begins to see what is invisible to others around him. One day, while walking along the northern fringe of the bazaar, the tailor sees every passerby in animal form, each taking on the shape of their most prominent sin. Only one man appears to him with a human face.

The popularity of clairvoyance as a marvel is based in part on its corroboration by ordinary people who claim to have experienced its terrifying disciplinary force. A few of my interlocutors narrated such experiences on the part of acquaintances who had met Ayatollah Mohammad Taqi Bahjat. An elderly marjaʿ living in Qom, Ayatollah Bahjat was the one living man I heard mentioned most frequently as an exemplary mystic and friend of God before he died in 2009 at the age of ninety-two. Young people snatched up videos of his moving communal prayers and shared them on CDs and online. Some kept his framed photographs in their homes. Many tried to see his illuminated visage (*chehreh-ye nurani*) at least once, if only from a distance, in his favored mosque in Qom. Mr. Hamidi, a middle-aged merchant in the Tajrish bazaar, had this to tell me about him:

Ayatollah Bahjat is from Fuman [a small town in the northern province of Gilan]. He does not interfere at all in politics. A person I know had a lot of problems, and he went to see him. Ayatollah Bahjat wouldn't look at him. He doesn't look at you because he has wide-open eyes of insight. When you visit him, you'll stand there and cover yourself [Mr. Hamidi stood in front of me covering his crotch] and say *ya sattar al-ʿuyub* [O Concealer of faults] so that God will protect you from being exposed. Ayatollah Bahjat told the man I know, "Go pray for forgiveness," in order for your problems to be solved.

I heard this supplication—"O Concealer of faults"—invoked very frequently in relation to a friend of God's ability to see people in their true form. The prayer is uttered by people who encounter those of God's friends thought to possess clairvoyant vision, and it is also reportedly uttered by the friends themselves in order that God will conceal the hideous forms of other people from them. The short blog post below by a howzeh student in Qom refers wistfully to both kinds of supplication. It is titled "Concealer of Faults":

> As a new student in the howzeh of Qom, the first location that comes to my mind as a place to pray the morning prayer communally is the Fatemiyyeh mosque where Mr. Bahjat prays.
>
> I wait for Mr. Bahjat [at the entrance] so that I might see him.
>
> And since I've heard that Mr. Bahjat possesses eyes of insight, I continually repeat the zekr "O Concealer of faults."
>
> From afar, I see the old man approaching, walking-stick in hand. When he reaches me, he smiles at me and says, "O Concealer of faults."[3]

As with Shaykh Rajab ʿAli, the "eye of insight" (*chashm-e basirat*) or "isthmus eye" (*chashm-e barzakhi*) was the marvel that defined Ayatollah Bahjat for many of my interlocutors. Kamran, a master's student in mechanical engineering in Tehran who was critical of this widespread tendency to define Bahjat by his marvels, told me the following story:

> Once Mr. Bahjat had gone to the shrine [of Fatima Maʿsuma in Qom]. All of a sudden, he turned around at the entrance and went back. Rumors immediately spread that he had seen an ugly scene [with his eyes of insight] or that Imam Mahdi had forbidden him from going, and that sort of thing. The rumor was circulating with intensity. Then at night, [Mr. Bahjat's] bodyguard went to the mosque and said, "What is this nonsense? The man had to pee. He returned to go to the bathroom and he decided against worshipping at the shrine!"

If the dominant quality by which a friend of God like Ayatollah Bahjat is recognized is his eye of insight, then for many people, the principle mode of being that governs their encounters with him (imagined, anticipated, or real) is to worry about his penetrating gaze, and to entreat God to conceal their hideous internal states from him. This has disciplinary significance: if I am worried that the sins I commit will be revealed in the presence of the friend of God, I might take care not to commit those sins.[4] Precisely this kind of anxiety is evident in an interview in *Keyhan-e Farhangi* magazine with Dr. Hamid Farzam, a prominent professor of literature and former devotee of Shaykh Rajab ʿAli:

> Keyhan: Mr. Farzam! When you would go visit his eminence the Shaykh, given what you said about his ability to see individuals' interiors [*baten-e afrad*], were you not upset that he would know your affairs and realize your weaknesses and sins?
>
> Dr. Farzam: Yes, we knew this, and for this reason we more or less restrained ourselves [*khoddari mikardim*]. But he would still know and sometimes he would tell a friend: "You have to close your eyes again." Or "don't look at just anybody." Or "don't look at the *na-mahram* [unrelated women]." One of his eminence the Shaykh's devotees used to say, "One day I was going to visit him. On my way a sinful thought occurred to me. When I came face-to-face with the Shaykh, he told me, 'What do I see in your face?' I realized what his eminence the Shaykh was saying, so I said in my heart, 'O Concealer of faults!' God willed it and focused the Shaykh's mind on something else. The Shaykh laughed and looked at me again and said, 'What did you do? I was seeing something just now and it disappeared.' You know that God is *sattar al-ʿuyub* (the Concealer of faults). If you take refuge in him, he will give you refuge. Yes, his eminence the Shaykh really saw things."[5]

In contexts like this, the gaze of God's friend can function as a tool of pious reflexivity outside of the subject while the friend himself functions as exemplar.[6] But within the master-disciple relationship, there is also a limit to the friend's disciplinary power, as marked by the utterance "O Concealer of faults." The utterance indexically constitutes three gazes ordered in a hierarchical series: the first is that of the pious aspirant who notices that the mystic can peer into his soul and see his faults.[7] The second belongs to the mystic, from whom the faults need to be concealed. The third, superior gaze is that of the Concealer, God, whose vision is all-encompassing and all-penetrating, and who uniquely has the power to deny the vision of that which he sees to anyone he chooses, including the mystic whom he himself has granted extrasensory vision. The sinning supplicant recognizes that he has faults to be concealed, and that his sin is potentially available for visual perception to the friend of God in the form of a hideous animal—a pig, wolf, monkey, scorpion, or whatever. But by appealing to a higher gaze, that of God the Concealer, the sinner can momentarily obstruct the friend's vision, cordoning himself off to account for his sin alone, under the ultimate, unidirectional, inescapable gaze of his Creator.

By uttering "O Concealer of faults," does one then render the friend's gaze irrelevant? No. Because it is in the encounter—imagined, anticipated, or real—with the friend's gaze that God's superior vision is invoked. To that extent, God's vision has something of the friend's gaze in it: he already sees his sinning creatures in the form of pigs, wolves, monkeys, scorpions, and so on, though he may choose to close off that vision to his friends. It is in simultaneously recognizing and averting the friend's gaze, then, that the imagination of a God's-eye-view image of myself-as-animal becomes possible.

The eye of insight, the sense that allows friends of God to see things as they truly are, not as they appear to the material eye, has been a staple of Sufi tradition.[8] In Persian, this sense is known as *basirat* (insight), *chashm-e basirat* (the eye of insight), or *chashm-e del* (the heart's eye).[9] In everyday usage, none of these terms need be limited in sense to the actual formation of images of some external being in one's mind. They often have to do with an acute ability to perceive, decode, comprehend, or understand the nuances and complexities of things beyond that which meets the eye. Iranians like to quote the Sufi poet Nizami Ganjavi (1141–1209), who, speaking through the mad lover Majnun, wrote, "You see the hair, I see the hair's curls. You see the eyebrow, I see the eyebrow's gestures."[10] A female taxi driver once quoted this verse to me in Tehran while explaining that she understood the economic situation better than me, and hence was right to raise her cab fare even if I, judging by mere appearances, thought she was wrong. *Basirat* might also refer to enlightened wisdom and a perceptiveness born of age and experience. In the past decade the term has been used by right-wing politicians and commentators to refer to political insight—which they accuse opposition leaders of lacking. Since 1998, ideological training programs required for all members of the Basij paramilitary forces have included a series dubbed "insight."[11] And after the controversial presidential election of 2009, Ayatollah Khamenei, the Supreme Leader of the Islamic Revolution, repeatedly emphasized the importance of insight for navigating the treacherous political waters and distinguishing truth from falsehood. Furthermore, he accused opposition elites of "lacking insight" for alleging that the elections had been fraudulent.[12]

There is, however, a more restricted sense to these terms, having to do with the visual perception of things unseen to the physical organ of sight. The eye of insight or the heart's eye is that inner sight with which the Virgin Mary and the prophet Muhammad both saw the angel Gabriel in human form. It is the same sight that allows God's friends to literally peer into secrets laid bare before them. To understand this more restricted sense of the eye of insight, we need to know something of Islamic philosophy in the illuminationist (*ishraqi*) tradition of Shahab al-Din Suhrawardi (1151–91) and the transcendent wisdom (*al-hikma al-muta'aliyya*) of Mulla Sadra (1571–1641)—the two philosopher-mystics who have towered over Iranian-Islamic philosophy for centuries. The concept of extrasensory vision, as developed through these philosophical traditions, circulates through philosophical journals, the sermons of preachers, newspapers, books, websites, and radio and television programs. Simplified versions circulate through many of the same media alongside the subtler philosophical formulations, and together they inform people's conceptions of the subject.

According to the traditions of Suhrawardi and Mulla Sadra, the world of being is multiple and consists of three layers.[13] The lowest is the sensible, corporeal world of nature with which we are most familiar. The highest is the world of intellects and immaterial souls, which we might in the simplest terms call the abode of angels—what Suhrawardi called the "dominant lights" (al-anwar al-qahira).[14] The intermediary layer—the most important for our present purposes—is the world of *mithal*, the imaginal realm or, as Suhrawardi called it, the world of "separate imagination" (al-khayal al-munfasil). This is the world of "suspended images," of dreams, miracles, and occult wonders.[15] The imaginal realm is not completely opposed to either the natural world or the world of the immaterial intellects. On the one hand, the beings in this world have forms and are therefore similar to beings of the natural world. On the other hand, to the extent that they are immaterial, they are similar to the beings of the world of intellects. They have shape and quantity but not matter or duration.[16] It is due to this dual nature of the imaginal realm, its partaking in worlds both material and immaterial, that it is also known as *barzakh*, or isthmus.[17]

In the imaginal realm it is possible for immaterial intellects or souls—such as angels or the divine attributes—to take on perceptible forms, just as it is possible for material things to become soul-like and travel from the world of nature to the imaginal realm.[18] Images from this realm can also become material—through the miraculous acts of a prophet or the occult techniques of a sorcerer, for example.

One way in which beings from the material world may wind up in the imaginal realm is through what is called the "embodiment of works" (tajassom-e a'mal), a controversial concept developed by Mulla Sadra.[19] According to this formulation, every action, intention, and thought that humans produce, whether good or evil, has specific visual manifestations. With repetition these "accidents" ('arad; pl., a'rad) gradually sediment into enduring dispositions (malaka) in the soul. They may then exist in the image world as independent forms or they may become the principle of the visual form of the actor's soul him- or herself, so that they transform the actor's imaginal form for good or evil. Good deeds beautify the soul and shower it in light or may appear as paradisiacal gardens, streams, and so on. Bad deeds appear as hellfire and other chastisements, or transmogrify the soul into animal shapes. Morteza Aqa Tehrani, a jurist and philosopher once renowned as the ethics teacher (ostad-e akhlaq) of Mahmoud Ahmadinejad's cabinet, has enumerated a number of these animal forms and their associated sins.[20] People who constantly deceive others, he writes, appear as monkeys. Hypocrites have two tongues, one of which emerges from the back of their heads. The arrogant are ants: they are smaller than everyone else and scurry about under others' feet in the hereafter. Lechers are swine. The verbally abusive are scorpions. The usurpers of orphans' wealth eat fire, and those whose sustenance is haram devour filth.

The notion of a descent into animality through sin rests on a cosmic hierarchy already present in the Qur'an, which places nonhuman animals at the bottom, humans above them, and God at the summit.[21] Following Aristotle, Muslim philosophers assimilated this hierarchy to a "great chain of being" that started with inanimate matter at the bottom and moved upward through plants, animals, humans, angels, and, finally, God.[22] In Islamic philosophical psychology, the soul has often been divided into powers according to a scheme that corresponds to this same cosmic hierarchy: the lowest power is the "nutritive" or "vegetative" soul that furnishes basic life functions. It is followed by the "sensitive" or "animal" soul that produces sense perceptions and emotions. Finally, there is the "rational" or "intellective" soul responsible for thought and speech.[23] All living bodies possess the vegetative soul. Animals and humans have the additional sensitive soul. But humans alone possess the rational soul.

A different set of Qur'anic concepts deployed primarily in the ethical and mystical literature distinguishes the soul that is *ammara bi-l-su'* (commanding to evil) from the soul that is *lawwama* (upbraiding, blaming), and finally, the soul that is *mutma'inna* (tranquil). In the mystical path of purification, the wayfarer struggles against the base soul that commands to evil, so as to attain the condition of the tranquil soul.[24] The Sufis have compared the base soul to an arrogant pharaoh or a disobedient seductress. But they have also likened this soul to various animals: a black dog searching for food, a fox, a rat, a restive horse or mule, an unruly camel, a pig, or a snake.[25] These comparisons do not emphasize particular vices as much as a more general characteristic of the lower soul as disobedient and prone to excess. To the extent that human beings are able to rein in their lower soul, they ascend toward the angelic abode and God. Those who persist in satisfying their lower soul descend into animality.

In the tradition of *firasa*, the Islamic physiognomic sciences, Muslim scholars frequently established connections between the characters of humans and animals on the basis of physical resemblances.[26] The Caireen scholar Muhammad al-Munawi (d. 1621), for example, wrote:

> If the heart is characterized by cunning, treachery and immorality and totally suffused with that, its owner takes on the outward appearance of the animal of his description: the monkey, the pig, etc. As that characterization continues to grow in him, it will covertly appear in the external features of his face, then strengthen and increase until it becomes clearly manifest. So anyone who has *firāsa* [knowledge of physiognomy] will perceive in the forms of people a meta-

morphosis of the forms of the animals whose characters the people have internally taken on. Consequently you won't see a deceitful, cunning, deceiving
person who doesn't have on his face the metamorphosed shape of a monkey,
nor a greedy, gluttonous person without that of a dog in his face.[27]

Some authors drew links between physiognomic judgments based on outward appearance and the discernment of mystics who were awarded the gift
of extrasensory insight. The great Andalusian philosopher-mystic Ibn ʿArabi
(1165–1240), for example, provided a list of outward physical signs by which
to judge human character, but then argued that inner vision was superior:

> We think that we see with our eyes. The information, the influences of percep-
> tion, are due to our senses—while the real influence, the meaning of things, the
> power behind what sees and what is seen, can be reached neither by the senses,
> nor by deduction and analysis, comparisons, contrasts, and associations made
> through intellectual theories. The invisible world can only be penetrated by the
> eye and the mind of the heart. Indeed, the reality of this visible world also can
> only be seen by the eye and the mind of the heart.[28]

For the friend of God equipped with the proper power of sight—that is, the
heart's eye or eye of insight—forms in the imaginal realm may be perceptible
both in dream states and in wakeful life. The way this works is much like
ordinary sight, except that the sense organ involved is not the physical eye.
There are, as Hoseynzadeh puts it, isthmus versions of the five senses with
which imaginal forms may be seen, heard, smelled, tasted, or touched.[29] The
forms that are ultimately perceived, however, are much like the forms of
sensible things in the material world. The cogitative faculty with which perception of sensible and imaginal forms occurs is also the same, whether one
is to place this faculty within the brain, the heart, or the soul—as has been
done by various thinkers from the Greeks through the Muslim philosophers.
Only the sense organ is different. This is why for the friend of God, an image
from the isthmus realm is as real, if not more so, as anything he sees with his
physical eyes.

Sinful images of animality appear in hagiographies like those of Shaykh
Rajab ʿAli in the context of stories of spiritual progress and the marvelous
gifts that God bestows on his friends. Among the hagiographies' readers, such
images sometimes become focal points for anxiety about moral uncertainty
and the pious subject's uncanny otherness to itself. In contemporary Iran,
these anxieties are heightened by disorientations linked to the bureaucratization and instrumentalization of piety since the 1979 revolution. I turn to this
topic next.

TECHNOSPIRITUAL
REFLEXIVITY

Late May 2009: I arrived at around 7:00 p.m. at Park-e Goftogu ("Dialogue" or "Conversation" Park) for a meeting. Only three days earlier, Salman Rezai, a twenty-six-year-old industrial engineer and founder of the online discussion forum Asrar had e-mailed the more than two thousand registered members of his community to announce a face-to-face gathering.[1] When I arrived at our rendezvous point, Salman was there with three other young men and two women. Most of our meeting time was spent away with idle conversation. Then, a new member joined our group and the mood took an immediate turn for the serious. Mr. Makeri, a tall forty-something businessman with a thin moustache and a wry smile, told us that he had long been searching for the answer to one question, and this was why he had joined us this evening. He added moreover that he had taken his question to every Shi'i mystic and philosopher he could find, including Ayatollah Hasanzadeh Amoli, Ayatollah Javadi Amoli, and Ayatollah Bahjat, who had died only a week earlier. None had provided a solution.

The question was this: "Is there an instrument (*abzar*) that one can employ to determine whether one is a good servant of God? Is it possible, in the same way that one checks a car's oil by inspecting a dipstick [*geyj* from English "gauge"], for a believing Shi'i Muslim to assess his status before God?" He continued: "There are various traditions that indicate that Satan is stronger than mankind. He is able to cast a beautiful appearance over the errant paths that lead to him so that we might believe we are on the path of serving God [*rah-e bandegi*] when we are actually serving Satan."

I was taken aback by this question, and Salman and the others appeared to be perplexed as well. We offered a few standard off-the-cuff responses. One person rejected the notion that Satan is stronger than man.[2] "How can man be the noblest of God's creation then?" he quipped. Salman cited a tradition from Imam Sadeq saying that the criteria for being good servants of God were simply good speech (*husn al-hadith*) and trustworthiness (*husn al-amana*). But Mr. Makeri was unimpressed. "You have misunderstood my question," he said. "I want to know if there is some tool, like a dipstick, with which one can self-determine the status of one's servanthood with God. Can I pull out such a dipstick from my thoughts and, with the power of discernment (*tashkhis*) that God has given me thus far, determine if I've been a good servant?"

I offered that the instrument Mr. Makeri was looking for was our conscience (*vojdan*): "Doesn't Imam 'Ali say," I asked, "that before going to bed every night we should call ourselves to account, to consider our words and actions during the day and ask whether they were right or wrong?" But Mr. Makeri waved this solution away, suggesting it was too simple. "I've been asking about for an answer for two years," he said. "Nobody has provided a satisfying response. I am sure that Ayatollah Bahjat, Ayatollah Hasanzadeh, and Ayatollah Javadi Amoli know. Maybe when they looked at me they didn't see in my face the capacity to properly employ such a gauge. Isn't it true that they have divine sight [*chashm-e ladonni*]? When I repeatedly pleaded with Ayatollah Hasanzadeh and pressured some of his students to seek an answer, he wrote a one-line response saying that 'The discernment of this path is only possible after at least fifty years of worship.'"

Finally, in a wistful tone, Mr. Makeri said, "I insist that there is a solution to this. Maybe we will reach a point when we'll know that if we recite, say, the Al-Hashr chapter of the Qur'an along with a certain supplication—let's say the 'Adila prayer—or if we repeat the Al-Tawhid chapter of the Qur'an five hundred times, that in one moment, we will attain a point where we can evaluate all of our actions up to that instant—in my case, a life of forty-some years."

In the course of my research, I encountered other people with a pious interest in some technical means by which to discover the truth of their inner being. Where did this interest—in some cases an anxiety—come from? Why would anyone think it possible to know exactly what was inside their soul? And why should this imagined possibility take the form of a technical or even technological fantasy? The explanation, I suggest, lies partially in the imaginative possibilities occasioned by the mass production and circulation of the new hagiographies of the friends of God. As we have seen, these hagiographies often impute a marvelous ability to God's friends to perceive people around them in their true form, which often means seeing hideous animals that represent their most salient sins. In the imaginations of some readers, the eye of insight has become a detachable object or an explicitly definable and isolable power that can be known, desired, and obtained through purposive struggle.

The hagiographies invite their readers to embark on paths of ethical self-care. But readers' ethical practices are sometimes modulated by anxieties about the sincerity of others' visible piety and uncertainties over the lines that distinguish virtue from vice. These uncertainties fuel a longing for assurance untainted by ordinary human intervention and mischief. In some imaginative formulations, such desires find their object in a fusion of the transcendental truth of divine knowledge with the mechanical objectivity of science—the eye of God as an oil gauge. The extraordinary vision of the friend of God turns into an instrument to be acquired, both to ensure a reliable diagnosis of the sinful self and to facilitate virtuous self-cultivation. In its mass circulating incarnation through hagiographic texts and other media, the appearance-penetrating gaze of the friend aids imaginings of society as a collection of human-looking animals whose inner truths are available for discovery by superior technical-spiritual means.

Those of my interlocutors who were avid readers of hagiographies frequently complained of the murkiness of moral standards, the blurring of boundaries between right and wrong, the spread of hypocrisy, and the difficulty in distinguishing true friends of God from impostors. When Mr. Makeri spoke of the unreliability of individual conscience, its susceptibility to satanic insinuation, he was giving voice to this concern. This sense of the ambiguity of morals and the difficulty of distinguishing the virtuous from the wicked was one that I found to be widespread. It was a complaint that I heard expressed repeatedly in taxicab conversations, in gatherings of friends around the dinner table, and among participants in online discussion forums. The theme even found its way into multiple television serials and movies. Amir, an electrical engineer I have known since college, captured the feeling in very simple terms when he asked me rhetorically, "How can you distinguish a good person from a bad person these days? Everything is mixed up. Hypocrisy has really filled every space."

On the one hand, this is an uncertainty that plagues everyday decision making among the pious: decisions about how to conduct themselves in their relationships with others, how to engage in business, how to regulate their desires and passions, and so on. On the other hand, it reflects a distrust of external signs of piety, a frustrating inability to judge moral character on the basis of appearances and observable behavior. As far as everyday decision making is concerned, some people resolve their uncertainties by seeking the advice of jurists in the form of fatwas.[3] But for many others, the moral legitimacy of the fatwa-givers has itself become a matter of uncertainty. In part, this has to do with disillusionment with the political and economic power wielded by jurists under the Islamic Republic. But it also has to do with a perceived disjuncture between the demands and values of a postwar liberalizing economy marked by competition and wealth accumulation, and ethical sensibilities that remain rooted in the social structure of the traditional marketplace.

The gap between values and extant socioeconomic reality is compounded by the particular relationship that has been established since the 1979 revolution between Islamic law and state-legitimated practices, and the contradictions that arise from attempts to provide Islamic sanction to apparently un-Islamic behavior. Usury, for example, is a matter of universal prohibition. And yet state banks engage in high-interest lending. While some jurists condemn the practice as forbidden, others make allowance for it in the service of expedience (*maslahat*) or protecting the interests of the Islamic state. Still others engage in jurisprudential acrobatics of various sorts to find justification for lending with interest within the Islamic ethicolegal tradition. For the ordinary pious individual, this provides a confusing array of options when facing an everyday decision like whether or not to invest in a particular bank, or whether or not to engage the services of a moneylender outside state-sanctioned financial institutions. The boundary between legitimate practice and religious sleight-of-hand (what is known as *kolah-e shar'i*) has become progressively more blurry.

While some pious Iranians find it increasingly challenging to live their lives ethically, there is also a common complaint that trustworthy people are hard to come by, and that visible signs of piety can mislead rather than indicating inner virtue. Hypocrites, I was told, often adopt the markers of piety in order to deceive others and get ahead. This sense of social mistrust is by no means new.[4] But since the 1979 revolution, the state has positively valued pious appearances and conduct, so that adroit individuals need to adapt to these codes in certain contexts of interaction in order to succeed. Moreover, preexisting modes of communal regulation and surveillance based on face-to-face relationships and cooperative hierarchies are in decline, increasingly giving way to impersonal, coercive mechanisms centered in state institutions.[5]

The Islamic Republic has standardized and bureaucratized pious signs, even as it has attempted to inculcate authentic Islamic subjectivities among the populace. Modest dress for men and women, beards and long-sleeve shirts for men, chadors and the avoidance of makeup have either been legislated as dress code or promoted as ideals. Nowhere has this bureaucratization been more salient than in the interview process for government jobs, known as *gozinesh* (selection). Jokes abound about the superficial piety for which one is tested in a gozinesh interview. The common wisdom is that even the least pious men and women would feign piety to secure government positions. Candidates are asked about all aspects of their religious beliefs and even political convictions, and simple tactics like adopting chadors and sporting beards may improve one's chances of success. Often interviewers inquire about the candidates with references in their former workplace, school, or neighborhood. The need for maintaining outward appearances of piety, then, sometimes extends beyond the interview time and space and into those more intimate places where such discrepancies between inside and outside can incite suspicion and ridicule. These apparent duplicities can also extend to other matters, like winning business contracts and currying official favors.

Those pious individuals who decry the hypocrisy of charlatans sporting beards or donning chadors usually complain that outward signs of piety can no longer be relied upon as indicators of sincere religiosity.[6] In the past, communal mechanisms existed for ascertaining the trustworthiness of the sign as well as the patterns of its variation based on context, particularly through assigning reputations and histories to individuals in the marketplace. Small face-to-face communities and tightly woven commercial networks provided plenty of such means through connections of kin, friendship, longtime business relationships, recognition as co-congregants in the same mosque, and so on. But such communities have grown increasingly fragmented, some communal hierarchies having been replaced by coercive ones and local reputations supplanted in part by the semipermanent and semisecret dossiers of government files, so that face-to-face connections are felt to be less reliable than they have ever been.

For many of my interlocutors who participated in the Asrar discussion board, the problem of moral uncertainty and the unreliability of pious signs threatened to lay waste to the fabric of religion and leave them stranded in a world of duplicity. In March 2010, the founder and administrator of the forum invited participants to comment on a poignant phrase he had heard someone utter: "Religion," went the phrase, "was a harsh prank that my environment played on me. I was religious for many years but had no god." He proceeded to say the following:

> In my humble opinion, this phrase is a good description of our present condition. Our religion has become a matter of peripheral issues. Our god has become money, power, and those who sit at desks [bureaucrats and politicians]. Our *ahl-e beyt* [family of the Prophet] has been reduced to worthless ceremonies, replete with hypocrisy. Our belief has become appearance and beards and imitation rather than action... Our work and business have become deceit, theft, and shar'i fraud [that is, fraudulent practice clothed in the legitimizing language of shari'a].

Many other users contributed responses, with hypocrisy remaining the central topic. One participant wrote:

> Everything has become a plaything. Grow a beard and your work will go through anywhere you want... Unfortunately, in our times if you grow a beard and wear two agate rings and hold a rosary in your hand, you're set.

Another participant blamed the widespread hunger for power and wealth:

> Perhaps the biggest damage that Islam and the ummah have suffered has come from those who are consumed by power and wealth... These people hide their power-hungry faces behind facades of apparent virtue and keep their inner truth [*baten*] concealed with duplicity.

As the conversation continued, one brief post by another user caught my attention:

> In this world that is full of human-looking creatures [*mowjudat-e ensan-nama*], O dear God, do not let go of my hand for one moment, and do not leave me to myself, as you have innumerable servants, but I have only one God.

It is into this context of uncertainty and distrust, this fear of "human-looking animals," that the hagiography of the contemporary friend of God enters as a technology of the self. The friend is a paragon of moral perfection and certainty. He lives among the sinful of the earth and yet his eyes are raised toward the abode of the angels. He is able to traverse this chasm through the rigorous practice of virtue, and the readers of his hagiography are invited to do the same. His outward appearance and internal truth are in perfect symmetry. He exudes light from his face, his eyes, and his forehead—light that shines forth from a pure heart. He thus embodies the Qur'anic description of the companions of the Prophet:

> You will see them bow and prostrate themselves in prayer, seeking grace from God and his good pleasure. On their faces are their marks, the traces of their prostration [48:29].

The hagiographies of God's friends represent the relationship between ethical practice and marvelous gift as mutually reinforcing, where one follows from and confirms the other. Through pious self-cultivation, the friend of God brings about an equivalence between his interior state and his exterior conduct. For achieving this sincerity, he is gifted with the marvel of true insight with which he is able to peer through the dissimulations of others. This same interpretation is taken up by many readers. It is what we might call an orthodox reading of the friend's hagiography, articulated as such by the authors and confirmed by many readers. But as complex narratives, these texts also make possible other readings that, while usually becoming harnessed to projects of pious self-fashioning, do not always do so in ways endorsed or anticipated by their authors. For example, for some readers, extraordinary vision becomes an instrument for overcoming religious doubts and performing moral duties with certainty. For others it becomes a tool by which to discover the truth of their own inner being.

These nonorthodox readings depend on an objectification of the friend of God's extraordinary vision as a capability or instrument that is detachable from the person of the friend himself. Objectification takes place by way of collapsing the intimate master-disciple relationship represented in hagiographies. Most of the readers with whom I spoke desired to enter into a relationship with a spiritual teacher. But very few of them succeeded in locating such teachers or securing their agreement to accept them as students. Instead they read hagiography after hagiography, sharing notes among friends and contributing to discussions online, perhaps as a way of living the devotee life vicariously through the recounted experiences of actual devotees of deceased friends of God. But in addition—and this is where the imaginative readings emerge—they sometimes refigured the narrative elements of the texts in ways that suited their own desires and anxieties.

In the first of these alternative readings, doubt about the unseen plays a much more prominent role than what we saw with the orthodox interpretation. If extraordinary vision can confirm the truth of a realm beyond material existence, perhaps one can attempt to obtain this vision in order to alleviate one's doubts and embark on the pious path with assurance. Here the causal relationship between pious practice and extraordinary vision is inverted: piety is no longer seen as a prerequisite for obtaining vision. Rather, vision calms one's uncertainties so that one may confidently reform oneself. This reading was expressed by a contributor to the Asrar forum in May 2009 in a discussion thread about the eye of insight:

> The smallest effect of the opening of the eye of insight is that it delivers man to certainty in distancing himself from sin and performing his [religious] duties. For example, if people pour colored poison into someone's water vessel, he will refrain from drinking it. But if it is colorless, he will drink it and be killed. Moreover, [the eye of insight] will be a decisive response to the whispers of Satan about the futility of worship. It will give the person a high level of immunity in the face of sins whose consequences he has seen with his own eyes. This way, he will have objective proof [hojjat-e 'eyni] for all of his religious actions to the end of his life.

If successful avoidance of sin can hinge on the kind of certainty provided by the eye of insight, how might the eye itself be obtained? Among some enthusiasts of the new hagiographies, the solution may take on a decidedly technical dimension in the form of repeatable zekrs or practices of meditation.[7] For example, some authors instruct supplicants that they can open their eye of insight by reciting a prayer known as the Zekr-e Yunosiyyeh (Jonah's Zekr), an excerpt from verse eighty-seven of the twenty-first chapter of the Qur'an (There is no god but thou: glory to thee: I was indeed wrong!) four hundred times a night in a state of prostration, preferably in darkness, for a total of one year. Others look to sources outside the Islamic tradition for additional techniques, with the result that they sometimes equate the eye of insight with the "third eye" or "ajna" chakra of Hinduism, with which they have become familiar through New Age formulations. This view surfaced frequently on Asrar. In a thread discussing the eye of insight in April 2009, one of the forum administrators wrote the following:

> The eye of insight, or "ajna" or "third eye" in the language of the science of metaphysics, is a condition that is given to the sincere. God endows some people with this gift after they have purified their souls for years and cleansed it of wicked attributes and gained spiritual strength. However, there have also been individuals who have attained this condition in one night, like Rajab 'Ali the tailor, whose tale is lengthy.

Other threads go into great detail about the chakras (of which the third eye or ajna chakra is only one), meditation techniques for activating them, and information about the auras and other forms perceived by the third eye.

The eye of insight acquired through technical means may have uses beyond that of overcoming religious uncertainty and strengthening moral resolve. It could, for example, aid in ascertaining the inner truth of other human beings, particularly those whom one suspects of hypocrisy and malice. The friend of God, with his power to see sinners in their true animal forms, is uniquely capable of penetrating the surface of illusory human appearances and distinguishing honest people from hypocrites. To become like the friend, therefore, would be to become similarly discerning.

Few of my interlocutors admitted to me that they were interested in the eye of insight for this particular purpose. But that the eye afforded such a possibility was considered obvious. Nafiseh, the metaphysical enthusiast we met in chapter 1, told me that the eye can give you insight into the "real me" as opposed to the "fake me" on the surface. If you see the "real me," she said, you may refuse to appear anywhere within a hundred meters of me. The friend's extraordinary vision, therefore, may function as a kind of X-ray device providing insights into the inner states of others without relying on social aptitudes for discernment, which are imperfect and vulnerable to deception.

We can see a similar imagination at work in a television serial broadcast during the month of Ramadan in 2006. *The Final Sin* (*Akharin Gonah*) depicted the adventures of Farhad, a young orthopedist who unexpectedly gains the eye of insight. One of Farhad's medical school instructors was an ophthalmologist known among his students as a friend of God. Shortly before his death, the friend writes in his will that his cornea should be gifted to one of his patients, an old man with a serious eye condition that he had failed to cure. But Farhad, who also suffers from an eye disease and is in need of a cornea transplant, becomes the unwitting recipient of his teacher's organ through the complicated schemes of the latter's daughter, who also happens to be Farhad's fiancée. The cornea gives Farhad the ability to see people in their true forms— as hideous animals or enshrouded in dazzling light depending on their actions. The drama follows his exploits as he tries desperately to come to grips with his newfound marvelous ability and the moral dilemma of having acquired a cornea that belongs rightfully to someone else. Gradually, he descends into vengeful madness as the images of others' sins prove too much for him to bear and he contemplates murdering some of the more shameless sinners he encounters.

In *The Final Sin*, Farhad's extraordinary cornea implant gives him much more than the ability to perceive sinners in animal form and the virtuous in a brilliant glow. His new biospiritual prosthesis functions also as an invisible-vision monocle, a lie detector, and a mystical X-ray. It allows him to see the souls of the dead and communicate with them, most notably, his teacher, the ophthalmologist mystic. When his fiancée lies to him, a menacing black smoke appears behind her figure. And in one scene, after he breaks into the warehouse of a corrupt businessman who is smuggling illegal or expired medicine, he fixes his gaze upon an innocuous-looking box of pills, only to realize that it contains abortifacient drugs after receiving a terrifying vision of a barren field littered by screaming, dying fetuses.

The extrasensory vision monocle, lie detector, and mystical X-ray are not incredible science fiction fantasies. Urban Iranians already encounter similar instruments in their everyday lives or are familiar with them from the news and the realist genres of documentary television, popular science magazines, books, and so on. X-ray devices are some of the most commonplace tools of extrasensory vision, available in any hospital or airport security checkpoint. Polygraphs are by now mundane. And although goggles for viewing the spirit world are not in wide use, some of my interlocutors were familiar with Kirlian cameras for displaying the colored auras that surround the body and had read about spirit photography or referred to it as a matter of course.[8]

In her book *Time Travels*, Elizabeth Grosz discusses a kind of human relationship to the material world that involves the incorporation of "prosthetic objects."[9] "Living bodies," she writes, "tend toward prostheses: they acquire and utilize supplementary objects through a kind of incorporation that enables them to function as if they were bodily organs."[10] In this she includes any "external, inert objects, prosthetic extensions, organs artificially or culturally acquired rather than organically evolved."[11] For my purposes here, it is helpful to think of familiar technologies of detection and objective visualization—X-rays, polygraphs, and Kirlian cameras but also home video intercom systems, digital cameras, and camcorders—as prosthetic devices that have been adopted to meet specific needs or deficiencies of the body, but that when employed lead to "unexpected and unplanned-for emergence of new properties and abilities."[12] In the case of my interlocutors, this meant combining technologies of visualization with the extrasensory eye of insight to imagine a tool with which one may be able to visualize the spiritual invisible.

If the eye of insight can provide reliable knowledge of the interior states of others, what if one were to turn its gaze upon oneself? In the intimate relationship between spiritual master and disciple, the eye of insight can function as a disciplinary instrument of pious reflexivity. If I am worried that the sins I commit will be revealed in the presence of God's friend, I might take care not to commit those sins. But in the absence of such a master, might it be possible to appropriate his vision for a similar purpose? The duplicitous deployment of pious signs and behavior has heightened anxieties that one's own self may be concealing sinful intentions, impossible to detect in the everyday flow of seemingly moral behavior. God clearly knows the truth. He knows that which I reveal and that which I conceal, even from myself. But the friend of God, if I should come within the range of his gaze, also knows. He can see me as the true animal that I have become by committing sins of which even I am not fully cognizant. If only I were able to see what he sees, to obtain the accurate diagnosis produced by his vision, perhaps I could set myself back onto the straight path.

By itself, and separated from the person of the friend and his eye, the yearning for a snapshot of the soul is a desire for the certainty of spiritual self-constitution. Kamran told me the following regarding his anxieties about his spiritual condition when he was a student of no more than nineteen years:

> I never pursued occult sciences and I was never after instructions for opening my eye of insight. But the mystical atmosphere is such that it pulls you by itself. You read a book about Mr. Bahjat, which says he possesses twenty marvels including the ability to see from the back of his head, or you go visit [Ayatollah] Hasanzadeh and fear envelops you that he might see you in the form of a pig. This feeling of need had automatically been created in me. I didn't care about seeing others [with the eye]. It was important for me that I see myself. I once saw myself in the form of a disgusting white rat. Really disgusting. It was a series of dreams, either in the month of Ramadan or Muharram. After I saw myself as the rat, I worked on myself for a while and tried to reform myself. In the next dream, my soul detached itself from my body. I traveled to [the shrines in] Najaf and Samarra. But I wasn't allowed into Karbala because I was told that I wasn't worthy. The next time, after I had worked on myself some more, I was allowed to enter Karbala.
>
> When my soul left my body, a green halo enveloped me from my waist all the way up to my shoulders. And then it carried me with speed to Karbala. In the next dream, I saw Imam Mahdi, who gave me tidings of his return. And in the final dream I was one of his soldiers.
>
> At the time, I took these dreams seriously. Why? Because Mr. Bahjat also dreamed. Because so-and-so described others' dreams to me from the preacher's pulpit.

Kamran had been granted the eye of insight in his dreams. He saw his grotesque inner reality and thereafter resolved to reform himself. With each subsequent dream he was able to gauge his progress, both through shifts in his inner appearance and through proximity to holy Shiʿi shrines. At length he was transformed from a dirty rat to a soldier of the Imam Mahdi; from a reject of the saintly shrines to a pilgrim welcome in their sanctuary.[13]

A similar anxiety about a hideous interior can be glimpsed in the following selection from a blog post by a young pious Basij activist in Tehran on November 1, 2008. It is titled "O Concealer of faults, O Concealer of faults, O Concealer of faults":

A friend of mine was extremely sharp-tongued until recently. Even though he was aware of his own ugly quality and intended to reform himself, he had gotten used to it. Then we realized that his conduct had all of a sudden changed. I was close to him and insisted that he tell me what had led to this transformation. Finally he told me this story:

"I had become so harsh and aggressive that I felt like I'd become like a wild dog. On Thursday night last week, around two or three past midnight, I suddenly woke up. I thought to myself, 'Thursday night is the time for praying and keeping the night alive.' I went to the bathroom to perform ablutions, but when I looked in the mirror to wash my face, I froze. I saw my face in the form of a dog with a huge, foaming snout. I ran out of the bathroom feeling as though I was about to have a heart attack. But the dog was still with me. I recalled my own actions and remembered that a foul-mouthed person is like a savage animal. I raised my hand to touch my face, but before I could reach my face, my hand hit a snout and a set of sharp canines. It was as though the dog, which was me myself, wanted to tear me to shreds too. I called God's name until it calmed down.

"I began to beg God for forgiveness, saying 'O Forgiver of sins, and O Concealer of faults, and O Concealer of faults,' begging God to help me straighten up [adam besham—lit., "that I may become human"], until I fell asleep. When I woke up for the morning prayer, there were no more signs of that savage animal. But I am still afraid of myself, my own nature, even my own face."

I tried to console my friend by telling him that I had never heard or read anywhere that a sinner may be able to see his own isthmus form. People who have the isthmus eye are always pure, sinless individuals. [I said,] "Maybe you had watched a werewolf movie beforehand. It was dark and you were alone. Maybe a shadow had been cast in the mirror and you were frightened and the rest was produced by your creative mind." It was a good thing that happened nonetheless, and it effected a good change.[14]

Through the stories that circulate about the lives and marvels of God's friends, the reader knows that true knowledge of the sinner's inner state is possible. Through everyday interactions with sinful others and through the kind of pious self-examination that is an elementary step on the path of ethical self-formation, the reader also knows that he himself is a sinner. And yet, perhaps in the same way that he suspects seemingly virtuous others to be concealing hideous interiors, he is concerned that behind his practices of apparent virtue lies a sinister reality of which even he is unaware. He desires true knowledge of this inner reality because he wants to be able to reform himself. But no friend of the caliber promoted in hagiographic lore is willing to adopt him as a student, to train and cultivate him through the discipline of his gaze. And hence his desire may be directed toward the gaze itself as an instrument of self-knowledge to be acquired through pious practice or technical procedure.

Friends of God gaze into the universe of God's creation, into their own souls, and into the souls of others. What they see is truth in images; images that have their own separate existence in an imaginal isthmus realm. But if the images have a being independent of the mystics' gaze, what actualizes them as image can only be the higher gaze of God. These images are imagined as something akin to the objective images of reality available to the scientist. The latter also peers into the universe of creation, into the bodies and psyches of others, and perhaps into himself. His gaze is a technoscientific one and the images it produces have an independent existence. They are imagined to be impartial representations of reality actualized not by the mind of the scientist but by the laws of nature and the workings of technology.

We can finally return to Mr. Makeri's search for a dipstick with which to gauge his soul's status in the eyes of God. That evening in the park, he told me and the other members of Asrar that he thought Ayatollah Bahjat and other friends of God knew what such a gauge might be. "But maybe," he said, "when they looked at me they didn't see in my face the capacity to properly employ such a gauge. Isn't it true that they have divine sight?" But the friend of God's divine sight is already the gauge. If Mr. Makeri was a sinner, which he knew he was (and thus he may have beseeched God to conceal his faults), then Ayatollah Bahjat could assess the precise nature of his sin with his gaze/gauge. Mr. Makeri sought possession of that gaze/gauge so that he too could look into his soul and uncover just what it was that he concealed. For Mr. Makeri, then, the mystic's gaze was no longer the medium of an intimate disciplinary relationship between spiritual master and pious aspirant but an external instrument imagined on the model of modern technologies of visualization.

Objectified in this way, the friend of God's inner eye is the product of multiple converging instrumentalizations: the mass production of mystical hagiography for protecting the public from deviance, the deployment of alternative spiritualities for achieving concentration and peace of mind (and of older occult techniques for a range of ends), the use of imaging technologies in various contexts, and the bureaucratization of piety in the service of state interests. The extrasensory vision that has thus emerged is a true marvel of synthetic imagination, one in which technologically mediated solutions command attention, and distrust of the socially mediated conscience runs amok.

HAGIOGRAPHIES UNBOUND

The hagiographies of God's friends enable manifold readings. They allow pious aspirants to envision the attractions of exemplary mystical achievement, encouraging them to embark on paths of virtuous discipline and avoid the temptations of materialist desire and spiritual deviance. They also help readers imagine extraordinary means with which to overcome the pangs of religious doubt, achieve spiritual self-certainty, and protect themselves against the machinations of human-looking animals in a social world marked by envy and greed.

The view that the marvels of God's friends may be acquired through something other than pious discipline both depends on the Islamic mystical tradition and exceeds it. On the one hand, it relies on prescriptions in that tradition for formulaic repetitions of prayers or zekrs to achieve specific ends, which often overlap with or have structural similarities to the procedures of Islamic occult science. On the other hand, it excises these prescriptions from the context of structured, hierarchical master-disciple relationships with their very particular ethical determinants, and places them in conceptual proximity to metaphysical or parapsychological arts with which Iranians have become acquainted through translation from European languages. Teleportation is likened to astral projection ("soul flight"), the eye of insight becomes the ajna chakra, and both are rendered accessible through technical mastery.

Hagiographic readings thus enable different forms of attachment to Islamic discourses of ethical self-care and spiritual wayfaring. At one end of a continuum, these readings fully inhabit a mystically inclined Shiʿi tradition that has powerful proponents as well as influential detractors. At the other end, reading becomes an exercise in a kind of unspoken eclecticism that brings Islamic mysticism under the sign of a universal spirituality through the mediation of the imported sciences of metaphysics. The latter orientation has remained invisible to the guardians of Shiʿi orthodoxy. But this is not least because it is so fragmented and inarticulate that it may never emerge into anything coherent beyond a sensibility among readers who share simultaneous interests in Shiʿi hagiographies and new forms of translated spirituality.

Viewed in a larger frame, the search for technical formulas for securing pious self-certainty shares a set of features with other forms of metaphysical experimentation that I examined in part 2, namely, those that emphasize personal experience, empiricist methods, and scientific models. But the instrumentalist logic that impels some readers of mystical hagiographies also allows us to expand our understanding of metaphysical rationalization beyond considerations of scientific fidelity or avoidance of superstition. Whether as "dipsticks" (Mr. Makeri), "medicine for the heart" (Reyshahri), "whips for the wayfarers" (Esfahani), or tools of "cultural engineering" (Ayatollah Khamenei and his allied cultural managers), the friends of God teach us that their lives of pious heroism have uses that far exceed their own immediate contexts of spiritual struggle, self-purification, and communal instruction. Some of these uses are as old as Islamic hagiography as an oral and textual genre. Others are inextricably linked with modern technoscientific rationality, the bureaucratic logics of the nation-state, and the mass-mediated publics who are subject to its operations.

CONCLUSION

One evening in late April 2009, I was invited to listen to a blacksmith describe his encounter with death. Abolfazl Gorji claimed he had died several years earlier and journeyed through hell and heaven before returning to his earthly body a transformed man. He now went around recounting his adventures and proclaiming a series of aphorisms—insights he gained in the otherworld, like "Everything is math, math is speed, and speed is time." Our host was Ziba, a novelist and travel writer with an interest in folklore. Besides me, her guests included a journalist, a photographer, an aspiring pop singer, two engineers, two housewives, and a makeup artist.

Reactions to Mr. Gorji's story ranged from bemusement to aesthetic delight, from dismissive ridicule to spiritual affirmation. When the blacksmith left our gathering, the journalist expressed admiration for his simplicity and marveled at the profundity of his spiritual insights. The photographer sneered that he was on drugs. The makeup artist remarked that his experience reminded her of visions she had received through Reiki practice. The pop singer pointed out parallels in his account with Dante's *Divine Comedy* and the Zoroastrian *Arda Viraf Nameh.* An engineer asked if his pronouncements on speed and time had anything to do with relativity theory. Ziba wondered if we might understand his narrative through the lens of Márquezian magical realism.

I found it remarkable that a brief meeting like ours could accommodate discussion of such radically diverging views about a man and his spiritual adventures. What made mutual understanding possible was in part the fact that we all (with the notable exception of the blacksmith) spoke the rationalized language of metaphysics. Not only did the participants frequently invoke the concept of *metafizik,* their comments drew on a constellation of approaches and sensibilities that I have identified in this book as integral to the emergence of modern metaphysical experimentation. These included the deployment of scientific concepts and methods in approaching the unseen, as well as the universalization of spirituality and the concomitant notion that mystical experiences across different traditions were comparable. Some of their remarks further personalized and psychologized mysticism, or framed metaphysics as an object of entertainment and literary delight.

I have argued in this book that metaphysical exploration, far from being a marginal activity, has comprised a crucial dimension of contemporary religious thought and practice in Iran. Like the men and women who had gathered for the meeting with the risen blacksmith, metaphysical explorers are model subjects of the state's attempts to create rational citizens. They understand themselves in ways that overlap and intertwine with some of the most influential discourses shaping the religious and intellectual landscape.

Beginning with the Islamic tradition of occult sciences, we saw that for the highest-ranking Shi'i ulama, the occult could not be easily dismissed as either sinful or fraudulent. The danger of charlatanry and vice did, however, prompt these leaders to recommend virtuous caution. While meant as a deterrent, this recommendation also provided an avenue for the pious to accommodate even such a figure of suspicion and scorn as the rammal. Some of the most prominent secularist thinkers of the twentieth century were no less ambivalent about the status and worth of occult knowledge-practice. And even for those who insisted on dismissing rammals as swindlers and drug addicts, the occult could still become an object of literary pleasure, aesthetic delight, or excitement at the mysterious and inexplicable.

Modern disdain for the rammal in part depends on sensibilities shaped by the prevalence and prestige of the empirical sciences. But the same sensibilities have encouraged Iranians (like their contemporaries elsewhere in the world) to look to science as a resource for coming to grips with metaphysics. Thinkers grappling with the religious and moral valences of metaphysical phenomena have variously drawn on empirical methods, scientific models, and the virtues associated with professional scientific practice. Such inquiries have engaged the minds of some of rationalism's most ardent advocates, including proponents of a positivist religion like Spiritism, rationalist jurists like Ayatollahs Khomeini and Makarem, and science-minded liberal Islamists like Mehdi Bazargan. Their various legacies continue to reverberate in the present, not least through the emergence of scientifically oriented therapeutic spiritualities, of which Cosmic Mysticism is a prominent example.

The motivation for rationalizing the metaphysical has been partly rooted in commitments to wide-scale moral reform. Some such commitments have found expression in Islamic projects like those of the Shi'i revolutionary leaders of the 1960s and '70s, and the intellectuals and statesmen who succeeded them. Others, like Spiritism and Cosmic Mysticism, have been conceived at a distance from Islam. Since the establishment of the Islamic Republic, Islamic moral reform has turned into an explicit object of state planning, with visions of "Shi'i rationality" and "cultural engineering" shaping the frameworks within which metaphysics may be deployed in cultivating a pious citizenry and steering them clear of deviance and irreligion. As we have seen, the friends of God and their marvels play a complex role in these schemes as attractive pious exemplars whose credibility is subject to heated disagreement.

While metaphysical inquiries have been integral to modern Iranian thought, the consequences of such experiments have sometimes evaded the gaze of intellectuals and religious leaders. The Shi'i ulama's inquiries into Spiritism and psychical research, for example, effected unnoticed epistemic shifts in theological argumentation. More importantly, in drawing on the virtues of scientific practice to articulate their qualifications as reformers, scholars like Ayatollah Makarem connected theological and scientific rationality without pondering the implications of making the two commensurable. In another instance of commensuration, the bureaucratization of pious signs and the universalization of spirituality motivated attempts to make sense of the marvels of God's friends in terms of technically attainable mental powers, like the third eye of Hinduism. While the rationalization process was clearly at work in all of these instances, their outcomes exceeded the rationalizers' hopes of bringing metaphysical knowledge and practice into conformity with some specific conception of reason.

This book has also been about the failure of rationalization. We saw that attempts to suppress the rammal can occasion the uncanny return of a repressed "irrationality" when metaphysical explorers come to grips with empirical evidence that the rammal may not, after all, lack remarkable powers. Scientific rationalizations of the metaphysical, on the other hand, invite rebuttals that produce the disorienting feeling that science is not cut out to provide the anticipated high road to the validation of metaphysics. Finally, the bureaucratization of piety and instrumentalization of the spectacular marvels of God's friends have rendered the pious conscience of some individuals alien to itself, with the result that nothing less than a technological deus ex machina can save it from the wilderness of absolute moral uncertainty.

In none of these cases has the failure of rationalization been absolute. More often than not, the obstacles that have emerged have functioned as invitations to conceive new pathways for bringing metaphysical exploration into harmony with rational commitment. On a larger discursive scale, then, "failure" is better understood in terms of dynamism and edginess—the continual production of new modes of sociality that take the metaphysical as object. The thrill of occult experimentation, for example, partook in trends toward appreciating the metaphysical as a vehicle for entertainment and aesthetic pleasure. Twentieth-century séances with the souls of the dead introduced an empiricist epistemology and scientific virtues into Islamic theology just as moral reformers were looking to the modern sciences for inspiration. The clairvoyant marvels of Shi'i mystics, meanwhile, allowed the readers of their hagiographies to assert an ambivalent power of spiritual self-constitution in a time of troubling moral uncertainty. The individuating tendencies in these readings further overlapped with a broader contemporary valorization of "experience" as the authentic ground of religious truth, which found expression in influential reformist philosophical formulations, as well as newly emerging spiritual and therapeutic practices.

The story that this book has told about rationality has been one of both harmony and disunity. On the one hand, all three aspects of rationalization I identified—demarcating and excluding superstition, engaging with science as a resource, and instrumentalizing the metaphysical in the service of moral reform—have been present in most forms of metaphysical inquiry I have examined. On the other hand, rationalization has produced widely diverging possibilities for orienting oneself toward the metaphysical. It would be impossible to speak of a singular rationality or a uniform reason emerging from these processes. Metafizik is a concept that circulates far and wide, but it serves diverse projects that rely on competing conceptions of reason.

These divergences notwithstanding, it is worth dwelling on one pervasive form of reason with which this book has been concerned—that of the Shi'i Islamic tradition. We have seen Shi'i reason exercised in a number of places: in the ulama's attitudes toward the occult sciences and their counsel of virtuous caution, in the theological deployment of empirical evidence to argue for the existence of the soul, in the polemics against Spiritism and Cosmic Mysticism and the articulation of scholarly virtues, in the propagation of stories of God's friends in defense of public piety, and in the governmental logics of bureaucratized religiosity and cultural engineering.[1] What grants unity to these practices is both a shared anchor in Shi'i Islamic sources of authority with their associated epistemic structures, notions of evidence, and styles of reasoning, and a common commitment to cultivating the virtues necessary for achieving closeness to God. While this shared discursive space makes it possible for people to aspire toward coherence, it also allows for plenty of disagreement as well as change.[2] I discussed some instances of disputes in chapter 22 on the politics of venerating God's friends, but the examples can easily be multiplied.

What can my examination of metaphysical inquiries teach us about Shi'i reason? For one, it helps us see that Shi'i reason does not completely overlap with the *reasoning of Shi'as*. While many Iranians aspire to organize their lives in accordance with Shi'i reason, other rationalities also structure their thought and practice. This is not an argument about a gap between an idealized Islamic model and imperfect (or failed or ambivalent or flexible) Muslim approximations of that model. A number of anthropologists of Islam have pursued this latter line of inquiry, in large part in response to studies of pious self-discipline inspired by the work of Talal Asad.[3] My aim, instead, is to reflect on the ways in which different possibilities for reasoning become available to people. When scholars or laypeople draw on Shi'i Islamic styles of argumentation in their metaphysical inquiries, they extend the tradition from which these arguments have been drawn, even if this extension involves a transformation. To the extent that such inquiries leave traces for public appreciation and circulation, they make it possible for others also to take them up and extend them in their own ways. But these same scholars and laypeople may engage in other kinds of argument, helping to extend and entrench styles of reasoning that do not necessarily become assimilated into the repository of Shi'i reason. In doing so, they make it possible for other rationalities to flourish.

These are not mutually exclusive alternatives. When Ayatollah Makarem claimed on the basis of empirical evidence that Iranian Spiritism was baseless but that European psychical research was sound (chapter 13), he was both extending Shiʿi reasoning in novel ways *and* helping entrench an empiricist mode of argumentation that exceeded the Shiʿi tradition and was at times turned against it. I suspect that whether or not a new style of reasoning becomes assimilated into a tradition like the Shiʿi Islamic one depends on already established pathways—the "weight" of tradition as it were—but also on the accidents of history and the agencies of individual actors. It is something we can only understand in retrospect.

As we see in Ayatollah Makarem's example and others I have discussed in this book, metaphysical inquiries have often provided avant-garde possibilities for inhabiting the Shiʿi tradition. That is, such inquiries have at times become occasions for experimental extensions of the tradition in ways that both strengthen orthodoxy and open pathways for undermining it. This historical feature of modern metaphysical inquiries allows us to take a fresh look at Islamic practices as activities that may produce unintended consequences. In some of the most sophisticated scholarship in the anthropology of Islam, pious practices are understood as goal-oriented activities through which Muslims attempt to secure specific virtues—they are technologies of the self, to use Michel Foucault's phrase.[4] If pious Muslims' self-conscious goal is in part to inhabit an Islamic tradition of moral self-fashioning, we can also think of their practices as producing the unintended effect of reinforcing the very discourse that guides their behavior. But if we agree that practices have the power to reinforce a discourse by inhabiting it, then they can also undermine or reshape it by effecting small-scale and temporary shifts in its epistemic or affective structures. These shifts may go unnoticed and perhaps continue a subterranean life as immanent to practice. Alternatively, they may become targets of orthodox sanction or appropriation, or they may find future articulation in some other more-or-less coherent discursive form.

Analyzed in this way, edgy practices like metaphysical inquiries give us a view of the processes through which traditions—including Islamic ones—undergo expansion, contraction, and contortion. By focusing on the ways in which practices are rendered uncomfortable or avant-garde, we can develop an understanding of the ways in which a tradition may change, whether this occurs through jettisoning, resignifying, or incorporating various sorts of inquiry and practice, or through epistemic and affective transformations.

These processes also apply to the rationalities that flourish within (or at the intersections of) different traditions. I began this book by describing rationality as a malleable historical object that both gives shape to people's self-conscious practices and is in turn reshaped by those very practices. One of the central aims of this book has been to demonstrate how this happens by attending closely to the metaphysical experiments of people with widely diverging theological commitments, ethical concerns, and access to expert discourses. At issue, finally, is not *whether* metaphysical experimentation is rational but the specific ways in which it draws on, inhabits, recasts, and displaces those modes of reason that have been central to the constitution of Iranian modernity.

NOTE ON THE COVER IMAGE

The unsigned painting here and on the paperback edition's cover has been attributed to the great Iranian painter of the nineteenth to twentieth century Mohammad Ghaffari (Kamal al-Molk) or someone in his circle. It depicts a rammal summoning his jinn to discover the sorcery afflicting his clients—most likely one of the women seated on the right. As a number of my interlocutors recounted to me, rammals claimed that they sent their jinn out into the world to bring back any objects (talismans, amulets, etc.) used to bewitch their clients. Once the jinn discovered these objects, they would cast them into a pot of water or at the clients' feet. The rammal could then neutralize the objects and cancel the sorcery.

The women in the painting are accompanied by a cleric who is aiding the rammal by reciting something—most likely prayers or verses from the Qur'an. The cleric is probably husband to the older woman sitting on the left and father to the younger girl. The painter has effected a separation between the space of ritual performance (the men) and that of observation (the women) by positioning the wooden chest (on top of which sits a pair of geomantic dice used for divination) between cleric and wife. But in doing so, the painter has also given expression to an early twentieth-century modernist imaginary in which the ulama were ostensibly accomplices of rammals, and women their collective victims. It is also possible, however, to interpret the cleric's relationship with the rammal in a different vein and in keeping with an alternative social imaginary: far from participating in the sorcery himself, the cleric draws on his rational, scriptural knowledge (the book) to rein in, subdue, and render harmless the chaotic, undisciplined powers (the jinn) with which the rammal traffics.

That the image expresses a modernist intention may find further confirmation in the depiction of the jinn dancing and playing around the rammal. Maryam Ekhtiar has argued that this is a fantastical depiction—a novel addition to the iconographic repertoire of the time—and that it is likely meant in the spirit of mockery of popular superstition.[1] But again, it is possible to interpret the image against a modernist grain by asking whether we can, in fact, so easily make a distinction between realist and fantastical representations when dealing with such figures as jinn. What would a realist depiction of jinn look like, if not fantastical?

Finally, the women. The young girl gazes intently at the rammal, perhaps feeling some of the thrill and terror of the fantastic that several of my interlocutors reported to me. Her mother is the only person in the painting who is not engrossed in the rammal's ritual. She stares into a space beyond the frame, pondering something. What is it that she ponders? Her daughter's fate? The nature of the activity in which her family is participating? Or perhaps questions about the truth or falsity of the apparently metaphysical phenomena unfolding in her presence? Among all the figures in this painting, the mother's reflective gaze brings her closest to the disposition of a metaphysical experimenter.

---

[1] Maryam Ekhtiar, "Exorcist and Clients," in *Royal Persian Paintings: The Qajar Epoch, 1785–1925*, ed. Layla Diba (New York: I. B. Taurus), 274–75.

NOTES

INTRODUCTION

1. I have changed all names except those of public figures and published authors.

2. See Rahnema (2011).

3. My understanding of rationalization as a process that is continuous with the premodern past and inherits many of its legacies sets it apart from what Dale Eickelman and James Piscatori have called the "objectification" of Islam. For Eickelman and Piscatori, objectification is "the process by which basic questions come to the fore in the consciousness of large numbers of believers" (1996, 38). These are "modern queries" (ibid.) that depend on the systematization of doctrine and the transformation of beliefs into a "conscious system" (ibid., 41–42). While I share a concern with the authors in the changes wrought by widespread education, mass media, and the rise of the modern state, I do not think these transformations by themselves justify the claim that there is something radically new and discontinuous about how Muslims relate to Islam. Nor do I share the authors' conception of Islamic "tradition" as invented (see Hobsbawm 1983), a perspective that blinds us to historical continuities and posits Muslims as self-interested obfuscators of their own history rather than as subjects whose modes of reasoning, ethical conduct, and political action are dynamically shaped by a historically constituted tradition (see also Agrama 2012, 10–17).

4. Amir-Moezzi (1994); Boer & Rahman (2012); Mottahedeh (1985); Nusseibeh (2017); Walbridge (2011).

5. For the rise of modern science in the first half of the twentieth century, see Schayegh (2009). For educational reform in the Qajar and Pahlavi periods, see Ringer (2001) and Koyagi (2009). Arjomand (1997) discusses some aspects of the early reception of modern astronomy. Najmabadi (2014) offers insights into the rise and influence of modern biomedicine, psychology, psychiatry, and psycho-sexology, including their impact on Shiʿi legal epistemology. Lotfalian (2004b) examines critiques of technoscience after the Islamic Revolution.

6. The assumption that new forms of knowledge and technology were always introduced by modernizers needs to be reexamined. On this issue, see Daniel Stolz's (2015) discussion of precision mechanical timekeeping among the ulama in eighteenth- and nineteenth-century Egypt.

7. See Adelkhah (2000); Chehabi (2007); Hoodfar & Assadpour (2000); Mireshghi (2016); and Najmabadi (2014).

8. See Qur'an 2:2–3 and the discussion in chapter 4.

9. In ordinary parlance *gharib* is often paired with *'ajib*—strange, astonishing, or wondrous. I discuss wonder and astonishment in part 1 of this book, but also see the section on "uncanny reason" below.

10. Druart (2005).

11. Albanese (2007). See also Bender (2010).

12. For an insightful set of anthropological ruminations on these topics written at the height of the reform movement, see Adelkhah (2000).

13. On the religious intellectuals, see Foody (2015a, 2015b, 2016); Ghamari-Tabrizi (2008); Jahanbakhsh (2001); Sadeghi-Boroujerdi (2017); and Sadri (2001).

14. For examples of this approach, which relies on a strong dichotomy between oppressive state and resisting populace, see Khosravi (2008); Mahdavi (2009); and Varzi (2006). For a critique, see Olszewska (2013).

15. E. E. Evans-Pritchard's landmark *Witchcraft, Oracles, and Magic among the Azande* (1937) is usually cited as the text that set off these questions.

16. Sperber (1982).

17. For critical overviews of these debates, see Kapferer (2002); Luhrmann (1989, 345–56); Stoller (1998); and Tambiah (1990).

18. Kapferer (2002).

19. Ibid. See also Taussig (1987).

20. Crapanzano (1985); Mittermaier (2011); Pandolfo (1997).

21. Luhrmann (1989).

22. Ibid., 353.

23. See, for example, Hammer (2001).

24. The OT literature is now quite rich and varied. My account is based on Goslinga (2012); Henare, Holbraad & Wastell (2007); and Viveiros de Castro (2015). The OT standpoint on radical alterity has resonances with some earlier phenomenological approaches too. See, for instance, Stoller (1998).

25. Kapferer (2002, 24).

26. It suffices to mention here the rich and varied literature in the history and philosophy of science. The works that have been most influential in shaping my own thinking include Chandler, Davidson & Harootunian (1994); Daston (1995); Daston & Galison (1992); Daston & Park (1998); Dear (1995); Foucault (1994); Hacking (1983, 2002, 2006); Jardine (2000); Shapin (1994); and Shapin & Schaeffer (1989).

27. See, for example, Darnton (1968), Kaiser (2011), Morrisson (2007), and Owen (2004).

28. See also Graeber (2015).

29. On the concept of tradition, see MacIntyre (2012); Asad (1986, 2015); Agrama (2010); and Grewal (2013). On the embeddedness of rationality within traditions of inquiry, see MacIntyre (1988). My study of epistemic structures and styles of reasoning draws on Foucault (1994); Hacking (1985, 2002); and Jardine (2000).

30. My analysis of rationalization has affinities with a framework established long ago by Max Weber, with a number of caveats. According to Weber, modern Western culture was fundamentally shaped by several intertwined rationalizing processes. These ranged from the intellectualization of Protestant theology and the systematization of this-worldly ascetic activity to the growth of capitalist discipline, the matura-

tion of empirical science, and the emergence of modern bureaucratic statecraft (Weber 1946a, 1946b, 1992). See also Gane (2002) for a summary of Weber's theses. As is clear even from this abbreviated treatment, Weber's concept of rationalization was meant to capture several meanings—intellectualization, systematization, increased calculability, instrumental efficacy, and so on (Eisen 1978; Kalberg 1980). For my purposes, what matters most is the Weberian understanding of rationality as plural and contingent, and his insight that theological, scientific, and governmental modes of rationalization can become entangled with one another. I am interested in probing these entanglements and their consequences without adhering to Weber's historical developmentalist schema (Roth 2006) or his specific conclusions. For other uses of Weberian rationalization in anthropology, see Keyes (2002). For a recent study in the anthropology of Islam that emphasizes instrumental efficacy and calculability, see Rudnyckyj (2010).

31. See Eickelman (1985); Fischer (2003), Grewal (2013); Lambek (1993); Messick (1993); Nakissa (2014); Salomon (2013); and Starrett (1998). Although not an anthropological monograph, Roy Mottahedeh's *Mantle of the Prophet* (1985) remains the most nuanced account of continuities and transformations in Shi'i traditions of scholarship. On argument and virtue, see Asad (1986, 1993b); Bowen (1993); Deeb (2006); Hirschkind (2006); Khan (2012); Li (2012); and Mahmood (2005). On the ethicolegal tradition and its transformations under modern bureaucracies, see Agrama (2012); Asad (2003); Hallaq (2012); Hussin (2016); and Messick (1993). On the impact of mass media on Islamic styles of reasoning, see Eickelman & Anderson (1997, 1999); Hirschkind (2006, 2012); Larkin (2008); Moll (2010); and Spadola (2013). Recently, anthropologists have begun to examine the ways in which Islamic theological and ethicolegal reason has become intertwined with modern scientific rationality, although much work remains to be done. See Doostdar (2016); Hamdy (2012); Mireshghi (2016); Moumtaz (2012); Najmabadi (2014); Rudnyckyj (2010); Telliel (2015); and Vinea (2015).

32. Boddy (1989); Clarke (2014); Crapanzano (1973, 1985); Ewing (1997); Gilsenan (1990); Khan (2006); Mittermaier (2011); Pandolfo (1997); Taneja (2013). The treatment of the occult as counterhegemonic finds echoes in a much older tradition of research on the Islamic intellectual tradition, for which the occult has consistently occupied a position marginal to the more supposedly respectable pursuits of jurisprudence, theology, medicine, and so on (recent scholarship is beginning to reverse this trend). I owe this insight to Ana Maria Vinea.

33. Boddy (1989).

34. Khan (2006, 252).

35. Mittermaier (2011).

36. See Vinea (2015) for an exception. Emilio Spadola's (2013) analysis of Salafi exorcisms as practices aimed at expunging superstitions from Muslim society can also be read in this vein, as can Mittermaier's examination of the epistemic interplay between the Islamic tradition of dream interpretation and Freudian psychoanalysis (2011, chapter 6).

37. Brower (2010); Darnton (1968); Denzler (2001); Galvan (2010); Hanegraaff (1996); Kaiser (2011); Kripal (2011a, 2011b); Lachapelle (2011); Monroe (2008); Morrisson (2007); Owen (1990, 2004); Van der Veer (2001).

38. Comaroff & Comaroff (1999, 2002); Geschiere (1997); Kendall (1996); Meyer &

Pels (2003); Moore & Sanders (2001); Morris (2002); Smith (2008); Taussig (1980, 1992); West (2005); West & Sanders (2003).

39. Harry West (2007) argues persuasively that such metaphorical significations belong to the anthropologists, not their interlocutors. West thinks such interpretations no less compelling for this reason, but I am inclined to agree with Talal Asad who—in a different context—has criticized approaches to ritual as symbolic texts to be read (Asad 1993c).

40. Boroujerdi (2006); Chehabi (1990); Dabashi (1993); Ghamari-Tabrizi (2008); Jahanbegloo (2004); Sadeghi-Boroujerdi (2017); Tavakoli-Targhi (2001); Vahdat (2002).

41. Withy (2015, 12–29). The texts she discusses are Freud (2001) and Jentsch (1996).

42. Withy (2015, 17).

43. Ibid., 17–18.

44. Ibid., 21.

45. Ibid., 23.

46. Ibid., 22–29.

47. Berlekamp (2011); Daston & Park (1998); Mottahedeh (1997); Zadeh (2010).

48. Rubenstein (2008).

49. Berlekamp (2011).

50. Brower (2010); Certeau (2000); Monroe (2008); Stephens (2003); Taves (1999).

51. See especially Claude Lévi-Strauss's *The Sorcerer and His Magic* (1963) and James Siegel's masterful discussion of this essay (2006). Also relevant is the intellectualist school running from the Victorian anthropologist E. B. Tylor (1874) through Robin Horton and the "neo-Tylorians" whose central argument is that "primitive" animistic beliefs should be understood as theories to explain reality comparable to those that characterize science. See Horton (1967a, 1967b, 1968).

52. Favret-Saada (1980); Geschiere (2013).

53. For comparison, see McIntosh (2004) and Taussig (2006). In McIntosh's analysis, her interlocutor's inquiry into spirit possession eventually shaded into disenchantment. For Taussig, skeptical inquiry is constitutive of magic's power. To the extent that I emphasize the open-endedness of metaphysical inquiries, my study remains open to both possibilities.

54. Also see Ewing (1994) and McIntosh (2004).

55. Doostdar (2013).

56. Ewing (1994).

CHAPTER 1: CROSSING THE LINE

1. Goat's bile is sometimes cited as a sympathetic magical remedy for enhancing love and sexual potency. The remedy rests on a view of the male goat as an animal of exceptional virility. Some traditional healers rub goat's bile on a man's penis to increase love and affection with his sexual partner. It is possible that the dervish thought the sorcery on Nafiseh had rendered her sexually impotent or bound her sexually and therefore constrained her affection. It is also possible that he really did intend to have his way with her and the bile was a convenient excuse.

2. The ihram dress is a simple costume worn by Muslim men during the hajj pilgrimage to Mecca. It consists of two white pieces of cloth, one fastened around the

waist and the other thrown over the shoulders to cover the torso (with some variation between Sunni and Shiʿi prescriptions for covering the shoulders).

CHAPTER 2: POPULAR NONSENSE

1. In this sense, the figure of the rammal performs some of the same conceptual and ethical work that the amorphous notion of "magic" has done in securing the categories of "religion" and "science" in the Western academy. See Styers (2004).

2. Mehr News Agency (2011); *Arman-e Emruz* (2014). These numbers have been repeated numerous times in the press, but they are misleading. Based on an oral report from an incomplete national study of mental health care drawing on a sample of eight thousand psychiatric patients between the ages of fifteen to sixty-four, the figure of 10 percent represents the portion of the Iranian population who sought mental health care from individuals other than mental health professionals. This included not only rammals but also practitioners of traditional medicine, whose work may not have anything to do with the occult. Conversely, not everyone who visits a rammal seeks what might fit the description of mental health care, however expansively the latter is conceived. Finally, it is not clear from the journalistic accounts how the researchers extrapolated from their eight thousand mental health patients to the entirety of the Iranian population, rather than just the population of mental health patients.

3. The report in *Arman-e Emruz* (2014) asserts that three-quarters of rammals' customers are educated. See note 2 above for some caveats about these numbers.

4. In the course of my research, I was asked on at least two occasions by male friends and acquaintances to recommend a good occult specialist to them. In one of those cases, a friend wanted to consult a rammal about his love troubles—he was worried that the reason his attempts at marriage consistently failed might have to do with sorcery. In my visits to rammals for observations or interviews, I saw as many if not more male customers as female. Even so, the trope of the "gullible woman" was pervasive. As the antisuperstition discourse has shifted to account for the involvement of educated women, however, there is less emphasis on women's hardwired psychology as on their precarious social status. Critics also increasingly provide explanations in terms of large-scale failures in cultural, educational, religious, judicial, and police administration. This shift has occurred just as more psychologists and sociologists have been called to weigh in on the problem of superstition. See, for example, Alef (2012) and *Arman-e Emruz* (2014).

5. Michael Gilsenan writes of a similar anxiety about encounters between Sufi shaykhs and their (often female) customers in terms of tropes of penetration and submission (Gilsenan 2000, 610). See also Dole (2006) and Ewing (1997), especially the latter's discussion of the *qalandar* (ibid., 201–29).

6. Jaʿfarian (2013). He specifically cites the prose writer and theologian al-Jahiz (d. 868/869 CE), the historian al-Mutahhar al-Maqdisi (fl. 966), and the Jewish theologian and physician Maimonides (d. 1204) for singling out women or men who were "womanlike" in their immaturity.

7. As Kathryn Babayan has argued, Khʷansari's satire was written near the apex of a process of sedentarization, centralization, and rationalization of the empire, when

Imami Shi'i Islamic law and social norms provided a powerful foundation for Safavid rule (Babayan 1998, 351).

8. "The bigger the turban, the more *namahram* its owner," writes Kh^wansari (1970, 28). *Namahram* (nonintimate) is a member of the other sex in relation to whom the highest degree of separation and modesty should be observed.

9. Kh^wansari (1970, 28).

10. On these debunkers, see Bosworth (1976). On physicians' views of charlatans and quack doctors, see Pormann (2005).

11. Wild (1972).

12. Amin (2002, 67–71); Najmabadi (1993; 2005, 147–48); Schayegh (2009, 35).

13. Amin (2002, 16–18).

14. Schayegh (2009, 35–36).

15. Najmabadi (1993).

16. These modernists included female critics. See ibid.

17. Daryush Rahmaniyan and Zahra Hatami (2012) have argued that before the emergence of Qajar-era modernists, critics thought that women were drawn to super-stition due to their essence as women and not just due to their social position. Their suggestion is that premodern critics of superstition saw women as intellectually infe-rior to men by nature. But matters are more complicated. To be sure, the view that women were inferior to men for social reasons rather than essential intellectual ones was not uncommon. See, for example, Belo (2009) and Fadel (1997). On early Shi'i views, see Dakake (2007, 223–30).

18. Kia (1998).

19. Kasravi (1943, 3). See also Fischer (2003, 130–33). *Pakdini* was the name Kasravi gave to an "unadulterated," "rational," and ultimately—as Lloyd Ridgeon argues—deistic religion that he envisaged would eventually supplant Islam (Ridgeon 2006, 47–48).

20. The modernist denigration of the superstitions of women could also be viewed in relation to a secular nationalist project of defining a modern masculinity. See, for example, Minoo Moallem's discussion of Sadeq Hedayat's *Haji Agha* (Moallem 2005, 71–72), as well as her broader analysis of the modernist project of reconstituting gender norms in the Pahlavi period.

21. Keddie (1968, 169–70).

22. Ibid.

23. For example, see Elshakry (2013, 161–218) and Mittermaier (2011, 41–47).

24. Richard (1988).

25. Ibid.

26. Most studies of *Kashf-e Asrar* have focused on its arguments about govern-ment, taxation, and the social and political role of the ulama. See, for example, Martin (1993). On Kasravi's attacks on Shi'ism, see Chad Kia (2014). On Sangalaji, see Richard (1988).

27. Khomeini (n.d., 98). In chapter 5 we will see that Shi'i jurisprudential views on occult professions are more complicated than what Khomeini presents here.

28. Ibid.

29. Ibid., 103–4.

30. Ibid., 122.

31. Kasravi (1943, 37). On dream visions in Islam, see Mittermaier (2011).

32. Hedayat (1967, 364).

33. Tabari (1969, 40–41). He was likely favorably inclined toward such research in the Soviet Union, on which see Velminski (2017).

CHAPTER 3: LEGAL CENSURE

1. See Farhad & Bağci (2009); Saliba (1992); Savage-Smith (2004); and Wild (1978). Scholars have frequently remarked on the prevalence of astrology and other esoteric interests in the Qajar court in the nineteenth century. See, for example, Amanat (1997).

2. A fourteenth-century *hisba* text by the Egyptian Ibn al-Ukhuwwa (d. 1329), for example, instructed *muhtasibs* (those who inspected behavior in markets and other public spaces to enforce conformity with shariʿa) to ensure that astrologers practiced in the streets and not in back alleys or inside shops. This, he explained, was because women were the primary customers of astrologers and young men would congregate around them to eavesdrop on their horoscopes and use this to approach them later. Presumably such unseemly behavior would be easier to regulate if it occurred out in the open (Mottahedeh & Stilt 2003, 743–44); Saliba (1992, 61–62). Kristen Stilt (2006, 70) offers a glimpse of a more uncompromising view in an early Mamluk appointment document for muhtasibs in Cairo and Fustat: "As for the street sellers/performers... astrologers... and anyone who takes people's money with ruses and dupes them with sweet talking, and each bad person of this type—and actually he is a devil, not a person—forbid them completely, break them like glass so they cannot recover, and impose upon them an exemplary punishment... Otherwise, there is no use in punishing them at the level of disciplining... and a slap. Terminate all of these evil elements and cut out these worn-out tricks that seduce/harm weak people."

3. Ettehadiyyeh (1998, 109–17).

4. Ibid., 121–52.

5. Kiyanfar (1999, 92).

6. See Shah Rezai & Azari (1998, 88). According to Ettehadiyyeh, when disputes were not resolved by police, they would be referred to shariʿa judges or, in the case of religious minorities and foreigners, to the Foreign Ministry (Ettehadiyyeh 1998, 127). There are no indications in this report that the fortune-teller's Jewishness was a factor in his treatment by the chief butler and his eunuch. Muslims have, however, historically associated Jews and other religious others (especially Hindus) with the occult. For a brief treatment of early Islamic views, see Zadeh (2014). In my own research, I was frequently told by Iranians that I should look to India or the Jews for real occult knowledge and power. Conversely, a Jewish antique seller in the Tehran bazaar told me that the most powerful fortune-teller his family knew was a Muslim.

7. The cataclysmic events of the Constitutional Revolution ushered in an era of modernist reform that eventually led to the demise of the Qajar monarchy and accelerated efforts at state centralization. See Chehabi & Martin (2010); Enayat (2013); and Martin (2013).

8. On legal change, see Enayat (2013). The scholarly literature on shifting views of public order in late nineteenth- and early twentieth-century Iran is unfortunately sparse. In particular, I am not aware of any research on the early history of the institution of the municipality and of municipal policies (Tavakoli-Targhi [2012] provides some preliminary remarks). On hygiene, see Schayegh (2009). On Reza Shah's imposition of a dress code, see Amin (2002) and Chehabi (1993, 2003).

9. Enayat (2013, 109).

10. The Fourth Book of the 1810 Code Pénal prescribes a fine of eleven to fifteen francs or up to five days imprisonment for "persons who exercise the profession of divining, or prognosticating, or of explaining dreams" (*Les gens qui font le métier de deviner et pronostiquer, ou d'expliquer les songes*). See text at http://web.archive.org /web/20070216122522/http://ledroitcriminel.free.fr/la_legislation_criminelle/anciens _textes/code_penal_1810/code_penal_1810_4.htm.

11. Peter Geschiere (1997) presents a fascinating account of witchcraft in Cameroon where the judiciary did accept the reality of witchcraft and prosecuted occult offenses accordingly. In Saudi Arabia, too, fortune-tellers, astrologers, and others have been accused of witchcraft and at times handed the death penalty. There are journalistic accounts and human rights reports of witch prosecutions in Saudi Arabia but not, as far as I am aware, any academic work on the topic. See Human Rights Watch (2015).

CHAPTER 4: DO JINN EXIST?

1. On the *barzakh* and its significance, see Pandolfo (1997); Mittermaier (2011); and part 3 of this book.

2. Tabatabai (1953, 43–44). See Iranpur (2007) for a more detailed treatment of the notion of *ghayb* in the exegesis of Tabatabai. For a biography of Tabatabai, see Algar (2006).

3. Tabatabai (1953, 43).

4. "One who is of sound creation cannot but attest to his poverty and neediness toward something that is outside himself, and similarly of the need of all other things that can be perceived, imagined or intellected for something outside themselves that stands above the chain of needs. So [the person of sound creation] attests and has firm belief in the existence of a being that is absent from his sense perception from whom everything originates and to whom everything ends and returns" (Tabatabai 1953, 42).

5. Bar-Asher (2016). Also see MacDonald & Gardet (2012) for a discussion of al-ghayb as "the mystery."

6. Chabbi (2011). See Pouillon (1982) for a discussion of different valences of the verb "to believe," especially the slippage between "believing that" and "believing in."

7. Chabbi (2011).

8. I will return to the question of defining sorcery in chapter 5.

9. Ramezan Nargesi (2000).

10. Ibid., 69.

11. See, for example, Kennedy-Day (2003, 119–20 and 150–52) on Avicenna. Also see Tahanawi (1966, 261–62).

12. Muhammad Husayn al-Dhahabi has detailed some Muʿtazili theologians' skepticism toward these matters and their attempts to reinterpret Qurʾanic verses that deal with them. See Dhahabi (1976, 272–73; 281–82; 320; 324–25). Also see Zadeh (2014). For a broader treatment of Muʿtazili theology, see Frank (2007).

13. Tusi (1966, 485).

14. On dissociation and spirit possession, see Seligman & Kirmayer (2008).

15. Khorramshahi (1995, 95).

16. Ibid.

17. Haq Panah (2000, 175–76).

CHAPTER 5: VIRTUOUS CAUTION

1. Ibn ʿAbd al-Barr (1993, 240–44). See Brown's comments on the weakness of this hadith (2009, 279).

2. Ibn ʿAbd al-Barr (1993); Zadeh (2014).

3. Ramezan Nargesi (2000).

4. Ibid., 67–71.

5. Ibid., 71.

6. See Nasr (1976, 207); Fahd (2012c).

7. Savage-Smith & Smith (1980, 1).

8. Melvin-Koushki (2016, 2017). Jafr is a divinatory science premised on a complex relationship between letters and numbers. See Fahd (2012a, 2012b). On Awfaq or "magic squares," see Cammann (1969a, 1969b).

9. O'Connor (2016); Perho (1995); Ragab (2009); Savage-Smith et al. (2012); Spadola (2009); Vinea (2015); Zadeh (2009).

10. Agrama (2010).

11. On ihtiyat in Shiʿi legal theory, see Gleave (2000, 87–145).

12. I am grateful to Robert Gleave for helping me clarify this point.

CHAPTER 6: A SCHOLAR-RAMMAL

1. Sulayman Hayyim's *New Persian-English Dictionary* defines vasvas as scrupulousness, indecision, doubt, temptation, and evil thought. In the Qurʾan, waswas is a pernicious whisper murmured by a jinn-like schemer to plant an evil thought in the hearer's breast (Chabbi 2014). In everyday usage, a person characterized by vasvas is known to be overly scrupulous or even obsessive, usually in matters having to do with cleanliness and ritual purity. In his study of howzeh education in Qom, Michael M. J. Fischer described waswas as "doubt" or the disease of "extreme concern with ritual precision" (2003, 64–65). In psychiatric discourse, obsessive compulsive disorder is sometimes translated as vasvas.

2. On temporary marriage, see Haeri (2014).

CHAPTER 8: METAPHYSICAL PLEASURES

1. Pellat et al. (2012).

2. See the discussions in Bonebakker (1992); Drory (1994); and Zadeh (2010).

3. Drory (1994).

4. MacDonald (1924). See also Beaumont (1998, 126).

5. This was consistent with a view inherited from the Greeks of wonder as the starting point of philosophy. See Rubenstein (2008).

6. Mottahedeh (1997, 30).

7. Berlekamp (2011); Mottahedeh (1997); Zadeh (2010).

8. Berlekamp (2011).

9. Hunsberger (2014); Abrahamov (2014).

10. Berlekamp (2011); Zadeh (2010). See also Von Hees (2005). These texts had European counterparts as well (Daston & Park 1998).

11. Berlekamp (2011).

12. Zadeh (2010).

13. Ibid.

14. Mottahedeh (1997, 35–36).

15. Ibid., 32.

16. Bosworth (1976).

17. Wild (1978).

18. Kashefi (n.d., 4).

19. Lory (2003, 532).

20. Kashefi (n.d., 4).

21. Lory (2003, 535).

22. Jawbari (2006, 143–46).

23. Haddawy (1990, 111–37).

24. On Spiritist séances, see part 2 of this book.

25. See my forthcoming article, "Hollywood Cosmopolitanisms and the Occult Resonance of Cinema," in *Comparative Islamic Studies*. For comparison, see Meyer (2015) on occult films in Ghana; Nelson (2009) on horror movies in Guatemala; and Steedly (2013) on Indonesian horror films.

26. On *ma'nagara* cinema, see Pak-Shiraz (2011 and 2015).

27. Balaghi (2012, 25); Diba (2013, 57).

28. Hazard (2014).

29. Tanavoli (2006, 8).

30. Ibid., 9.

31. Ibid., 99.

32. Ibid., 12.

33. Ibid., 99.

34. I am grateful to Hoda Katebi for bringing a number of these items to my attention.

35. See Sindawi (2012) on the Shiʿi custom of wearing rings on the right hand and its connection to the Islamic textual tradition. Unfortunately, Sindawi too quickly dismisses the ornamental quality of such rings, arguing that "[these] rings are not worn for decoration, but rather in connection with the Shīʿite creed" (2012, 296). But this is to completely ignore the care with which Shiʿi men and women shop for rings, the attention they pay to workmanship, their connoisseurship about the types, origins, qualities, and hues of stones, and the ways in which they compliment one another on their rings' beauty.

CHAPTER 9: THE FANTASTIC

1. The salavat is a short supplication uttered on many occasions during Muslim devotional practice and in everyday situations. It is *Allahumma salli ʿala muhammad wa al-i muhammad*—"O God, bless Muhammad and Muhammad's family."

2. A movakkel is a jinn controlled by a human being, usually employed for very specific tasks.

3. This is the first half of verse sixty-two of the Al-Naml (The Ants) chapter of the Qur'an: *Am man yujibu-l-mudtarra idha da'ahu wa yakshifu-s-su'*—"Or, Who listens to the distressed when he calls on Him, and Who relieves his suffering?" It is frequently recited in groups to entreat God to heal the sick.

4. Nematollah Fazeli (2007) argues that the popularity of fortune-telling among Iranians should be understood in terms of the rise of postmodern forms of leisure, and that fortune-telling can be thought of as a kind of "cultural opiate." He has made these arguments by way of criticizing psychologistic and otherwise pathologizing analyses of fortune-telling. While he does not extend this analysis to encounters with more questionable occult specialists like rammals, his critique of the more pathologically oriented studies of fortune-telling is consonant with my own findings.

5. I am drawing here on Simon During's helpful argument that in post-Enlightenment Europe and America, declarations of belief or disbelief in magic do not so much express some internal state grounded in feelings or sensations, as "position [the person] in relation to the discursive web of rationality, civility, and enlightenment, and in a context where it is difficult to be a fully rational citizen and to declare a serious belief in magic" (2002, 49). See also Stacy Pigg (1996) who argues that denigrating superstition can be a way of demonstrating a cosmopolitan identity opposed to village life, hence, a form of spatial distancing as well as a social one. Stewart (1989) articulates similar arguments in terms of habitus and hegemony.

6. My argument here is also consonant with Michael Taussig's (2006) claim that the interplay of skepticism and faith is central to the power of magic.

7. Todorov (1975, 25).

8. Ibid., 168.

9. Note that I am not suggesting that the dichotomy between the real and the imaginary is the same as a distinction between the physical and the metaphysical. Many of my interlocutors believed in divine interventions in the form of *barakat* and answering prayers, as well as in the notion of the evil eye, even while they hesitated when faced with an apparent case of sorcery. Also see Clarke (2014) for some thoughtful reflections on the ordinariness of the extraordinary.

10. This attitude of hesitation is different both from that of "suspending disbelief," as among spectators of modern magic shows investigated by During (2002, 49–50), and the "cognitive dissonance" experienced by English ritual magicians who choose to bracket off their magical experience from everyday life through ritual-spatial separation on the one hand and post hoc rationalization on the other (Luhrmann 1989). All three attitudes might enable rich, "imaginative involvement," but the role of hesitation and doubt in relation to that involvement is not the same.

CHAPTER 11: QUANTUM UNDERSTANDING

1. Grand Ayatollah Naser Makarem Shirazi (b. 1924) is a prominent *marja'-e taqlid* or model of emulation. Prior to the 1979 revolution, he was a founder and regular contributor to *Dars-ha-yi az Maktab-e Eslam*, an Islamic journal published by the howzeh in Qom that played an important role in introducing educated Iranians to an activist, rationalist, science-friendly, socially responsible Shi'i Islam. He remains influential at the time of this writing. We will read about some of his interventions in chapter 13.

2. These are invocations of Shi'i holy figures, Imam 'Ali and his son Abu al-Fazl, sometimes uttered in moments of fear or apprehension.

3. Spalding (1935, 134–35).

CHAPTER 12: EMPIRICAL SPIRITS

1. Koyagi (2009); Ringer (2001); Schayegh (2009).

2. Schayegh (2009).

3. Ibid.; Tavakoli-Targhi (2008).

4. On the influence of engineering discourse on state reformist projects, see Tavakoli-Targhi (2012).

5. Chehabi (1990); Deeb (2006); Elshakry (2009); Fuchs (2014); Rudnyckyj (2010); Stolz (2012).

6. Two of the better-known figures are Ahmad Kasravi and Hoseyn Kazemzadeh Iranshahr. On Kasravi, who is usually described as a "deist," see Ridgeon (2006) and Vahdat (2002, 85–90). On Iranshahr, a Theosophist, see Boroujerdi (2006) and Vahdat (2002, 83–85).

7. See Bayat (2009) on Freemasonry; Warburg et al. (2005) on Baha'i globalism; and Van den Bos (2002) on modern Sufi reformulations. For the broader context of global Masonic, Occultist, and Spiritist/Spiritualist circulation, see Bogdan & Djurdjevic (2013); Green (2015); Van der Veer (2001); and Zarcone (2013). For the influence of Kardecist Spiritism beyond Europe, see Hess (1991) on Brazil; Palmié (2002) on Cuba; and Hoskins (2015) on Vietnam.

8. Saqafi (1943, 207).

9. Monroe (2008); Sharp (2006).

10. Brower (2010).

11. My account of the development of psychology in Iran and Siyasi's influence is indebted to Najmabadi (2014) and Schayegh (2009). In France, too, the early experimental psychologists struggled to distance their newborn field from introspective philosophical psychology. See Brower (2010).

12. On the concepts of *ruh* and *nafs* in Islam, see Calverley (2012).

13. On Luys, see Parent (2002); Parent & Parent (2011); and Monroe (2008, 238–39, 249). Khalil Khan was already familiar with neurology from his years at the Dar al-Fonun. In fact, he helped translate a chapter on neurological diseases from Augustin Grisolle's *Traité élémentaire et pratique de pathologie interne* (Schayegh 2009, 244n16).

14. Parent & Parent (2011, 133–34).

15. Modarresi Chahardehi (2008, 60); Saqafi E'zaz (1972, 105).

16. Saqafi E'zaz (1972, 101). Mohammad Nakhjavan Amir Movassaq, the son of Mohammad Baqer Khan, served as army chief of staff, war minister, senator, and governor of Khuzestan between 1927 and 1952. Haji 'Ali Razmara, the son of Mohammad Khan Razmara, served as army chief of staff several times between 1943 and 1948. He was appointed prime minister in June 1950 but was assassinated only nine months later.

17. Hadi (1972); Mazhari (1977); Saqafi E'zaz (1972).

18. Saqafi (1929, 288–309).

19. Ibid., 303–9.

20. Saqafi & Bahrami (1936, 52–53).

21. Lachapelle (2011, 5). On the uneasy relationship between French Spiritists and

the custodians of normal science on the one hand, and Catholic orthodoxy on the other, see Brower (2010); Monroe (2008); Lachapelle (2011); and Sharp (2006).

22. Monroe (2008, 110).

23. Saqafi (1943, 252–53).

24. Modarresi Chahardehi (2010, 271–73).

25. Van den Bos (2002, 80–81); Modarresi Chahardehi (2010, 315).

26. Bidokhti Gonabadi (2006).

27. Tabandeh Gonabadi (2006, 98).

28. On Wajdi, see Jansen (2012). On Wajdi's attacks on materialism and his debts to Spiritualism and psychical research, see Elshakry (2013, 281–83).

29. Wajdi was not a faithful reporter of European scientists' views on spirit phenomena. For example, he conflated Spiritists with psychical researchers and had them all attest unequivocally to the truth of the "spirit hypothesis" when many had openly opposed this hypothesis and others had been agnostic. For my purposes, the fact that Wajdi was not a reliable transmitter is irrelevant. His Shi'i readers treated him as if he was, and I discuss their understanding of European Spiritism (which should be understood as Spiritism and psychical research together) as filtered through Wajdi, rather than as presented by European sources.

30. I described some of Khomeini's arguments in chapter 2.

31. Kasravi (2011).

32. Khomeini (n.d., 30–31).

33. Ibid., 53.

34. Ibid., 55. Wajdi's account appears in Wajdi (1913, 369–70).

35. In its outlines, the relevance of recurring scientific testimony to the persuasiveness of psychical research is hardly unique to the Egyptian and Iranian contexts. European psychical researchers and Spiritists made similar arguments. See, for example, Monroe's account of Xavier Dariex, a doctor who directed the journal *Annales des Sciences Psychique* from 1891 and who believed that "the eminence of the 'men of science'" who had observed the séances of gifted mediums like Eusapia Paladino was "more than enough proof for any rational observer" (Monroe 2008, 209).

36. On Avicenna's epistemology, see Gutas (2012) and Black (2013).

37. For an excellent discussion of the concept of tawatur, particularly in the thought of Ghazali, see Weiss (1985).

38. In the Islamic legal tradition, recurring testimonies are a category of reports about the prophet Muhammad (his words and deeds) that have been narrated through so many different chains of transmission that they carry *hujjiyya* or probative force (Gleave 2002).

39. Calverley (2012).

40. Wajdi (1913, 381).

41. The jinn are widely considered by Muslim scholars to be invisible to the senses, but they do have a subtle material substance and may sometimes take on visible forms. See MacDonald et al. (2012).

42. I will examine this extrasensory vision more closely in part 3.

43. My thanks to Nir Shafir for pointing out to me that saints' graves were sometimes identified through tawatur.

44. On tajriba and the mujarrabat in Avicenna's thought, see Gutas (2012); Janssens (2004); and McGinnis (2003).

45. Peter Dear's (2008) study of science in sixteenth- and seventeenth-century

Europe provides an interesting comparative perspective. As he shows, testimony, authority, and trust became important in European mathematical sciences like optics and astronomy just as private experiments began to displace the Aristotelian emphasis on empirical observations that were public and commonsensical (for example, the sun rises in the east and fire burns cotton).

46. Kasravi (1943, 40–45). See also Fischer (2003, 130–33).

47. Ibid., 40.

48. Ibid., 43.

49. Ibid.

50. Ibid., 44.

51. Ibid.

CHAPTER 13: SCIENTIFIC VIRTUES

1. My understanding of tradition and virtue is derived chiefly from MacIntyre (2012) and Asad (1986, 1993a, and 2015).

2. Kia (2015a).

3. On modernists' diagnoses of the ills that plagued Iran and their prescriptions for reform, see Kashani-Sabet (2000); Kia (2015a); Schayegh (2009); and Tavakoli-Targhi (2008).

4. Kia (2015a).

5. Ibid.

6. Ibid., 148.

7. Schayegh (2009, 157–93). He does come close to recognizing the relevance of the virtues; for example, in his discussion of "the moralistic assumptions inherent in supposedly objective scientific statements" (ibid., 91).

8. Kia (2015b). See also the anthropological literature on ethical discipline in Islam, especially Asad (1986, 1993); Agrama (2010); Hirschkind (2006); and Mahmood (2005).

9. Karabela (2010, 167).

10. Masud (2015). Also see Agrama (2010) for an anthropological account of the practice of ethical self-care between mufti and fatwa-seeker in Egypt.

11. Daston (1995); Daston & Galison (1992); Schaeffer (1994); Shapin (1994); Shapin & Schaeffer (1989).

12. Daston (1995).

13. Shapin (1994).

14. Stanley (2007, 11).

15. For example, Hammer (2001) and Monroe (2008). Cecire (2015) takes up the question of "epistemic virtues" in literary experimentalism.

16. For example, Klassen (2011).

17. Saqafi (1935, 55).

18. Saqafi (1907); Vahid Sa'd (1929).

19. Schayegh (2009).

20. Monroe (2008, 106).

21. Kia (2015b).

22. Saqafi (1891–92, 1).

23. Ibid., 1–2.

24. On the use of hekayat in Persian moral advice literature, see M. Kia (2014). On

Iranian modernist translations of morally edifying European literature, including La Fontaine's fables (of which Khalil Khan was particularly fond), see Karimi-Hakkak (1995).

25. Saqafi (1943, 229).

26. Ibid., 232.

27. Ibid.

28. Ibid., 253. This emphasis on hard work and discipline as requirements for progress was very much a feature of modernist thought at the time. See Schayegh (2009).

29. Saqafi & Bahrami (1936, 43–45).

30. On Kardec's theory of inferior souls and the *esprit faux savant* or poseur spirit, see Monroe (2008, 130–35). Monroe views Kardec's distinctions between superior and inferior, genuine and poseur spirits as part of the latter's attempt to construct a Spiritist orthodoxy and bring unruly mediums in-line. Here I am taking a different approach, viewing Khalil Khan's writings on the management of séances as attempts to stabilize an "evidential context" in the sense examined by Simon Schaeffer (1994). For a séance to be able to yield positive moral facts unmediated by the whims of séance participants, the leader needed to exercise his authority and ensure proper conduct among both the living and the dead.

31. Makarem would go on to participate in the revolution in 1979. At the time of this writing he remains an influential marja'-e taqlid or model of emulation.

32. The role of *Lessons from the School of Islam* has been neglected in scholarship on the 1979 revolution. For studies of the intellectual backdrop to the revolution, see Abrahamian (1982, 1992); Adib-Moghaddam (2014); Behrooz (2000); Chehabi (1990); Dabashi (1993); Mottahedeh (1985); and Rahnema (2014).

33. Makarem Shirazi (1969a, 70).

34. Makarem Shirazi (1969c, 17).

35. Makarem Shirazi (1969b, 1969c, 1970b).

36. A *hamd va sureh* consists of the first chapter of the Qur'an (Al-Fatiha) followed by another short chapter, usually Al-Ikhlas (chapter 112). The combination is often recited silently as a prayer for the dead.

37. Ayatollah Hoseyn Tabatabai Borujerdi (1875–1961) was the powerful director of the Qom howzeh for seventeen years and the only marja'-e taqlid of the Shi'a world for the last fifteen years of his life (Algar 1989). Borujerdi practiced a policy of accommodation with the Pahlavi regime and his influence kept political activism among the Shi'i ulama in check. It was only after his death that a younger and more politically uncompromising generation of ulama rose to prominence, with Ayatollah Khomeini in their lead.

38. Makarem Shirazi (1969d).

39. Ibid., 9.

40. Makarem Shirazi (1970a).

41. Makarem Shirazi (1970b, 60).

42. Makarem Shirazi (1969a, 70).

43. The conflict between camps that emphasize scientific skepticism against credulity and those that stress scientific open-mindedness against establishment dogmatism has been a recurring feature in the development of modern fringe sciences from mesmerism through psychical research, parapsychology, and ufology. See Brower (2010); Denzler (2001); Kaiser (2011); and Monroe (2008).

44. See his book of advice (Saqafi 1907), especially numbers 33, 39, and 50.

45. Makarem Shirazi (1969d).

46. Tavakoli-Targhi has made similar arguments in his study of Muslim attempts to reconcile Islamic notions of purity with "post-Pasteurian" conceptions of hygiene (2008), as well as the discourse of cultural engineering in the Islamic Republic, which, he argues, has reduced Islamic rationality to a form of instrumental, bureaucratic reason (2012). While this is certainly an important part of the picture, as I also show in this book, I disagree that bureaucratic instrumentalism is all that is left of Islamic reason under the Islamic Republic.

47. Makarem Shirazi (1970c).

48. Makarem Shirazi (1969b).

49. This possibility is ignored by scholars who argue that the religious adoption of scientific concepts and models is aimed at justifying preexisting doctrines, and is therefore merely "rhetorical" or "strategic." See, for example, Dallal (2010) and Hammer (2001).

CHAPTER 14: WINGS OF IMAGINATION

1. My characterization of this epistemic dimension of scientific imaginaries somewhat resembles Sean Miller's (2013) exploration of the popularizations and literary appropriations of string theory. However, I do not adopt Miller's framework in its specificity. I am particularly unsure that the analytic distinction he makes between the abstraction of mathematical formalism and the concreteness of narrative or visual exposition is helpful in exploring the kinds of diffusion I am trying to understand.

2. This aspect of scientific imaginaries is closer to the usual way in which anthropologists deploy the concept. See, for example, DelVecchio Good (2001); Marcus (1993); and Sharp (2013).

3. On modern social imaginaries, see Appadurai (1990); Castoriadis (1987); and Taylor (2002). Benedict Anderson's 1991 *Imagined Communities* is also a seminal text in the literature on social imaginaries, even though Anderson did not use the term himself.

4. Chehabi (1990, 30).

5. See Lotfalian (2004a, 31–54) for an alternative discussion of Bazargan's deployment of thermodynamic models and their place within his peculiar "technoscientific identity."

6. Bazargan (1998, 249).

7. Ibid.

8. Ibid., 269.

9. Ibid., 389.

10. Ibid., 389n4.

11. Ibid., 393.

12. Lévi-Strauss (1966).

CHAPTER 15: COSMIC MYSTICS

1. Kashi (2009, 72). The book was published with approval from the Ministry of Culture and Islamic Guidance, with an introduction by Esmaʿil Mansuri Larijani, a well-known scholar of Islamic mysticism. Later on when Cosmic Mysticism came

under attack, Mansuri Larijani recanted and claimed that he was always aware of Taheri's deviations from Islamic orthodoxy but wrote the introduction to his book as a way of inviting him to the right path. The fact that the book was granted a permit in the first place alerts us to the vicissitudes of censorship practices. At the time of the book's publication, "deviant mysticisms" had just emerged as a problem in the eyes of state officials and religious leaders. Their concern did not immediately translate into official policy.

2. There were, no doubt, many more representatives scattered around Iran who preferred not to list their contact information for fear of state harassment or other reasons. For example, the master with whom I trained was not listed.

3. See the full report at http://irb-cisr.gc.ca/Eng/ResRec/RirRdi/Pages/index .aspx?doc=454879&pls=1.

4. See Behdad & Nomani (2009) for an analysis of state economic policy and its effects on social classes in Iran since the revolution.

5. Adelkhah (2000, 139–74). Her analysis is most persuasive when read as an account of social, cultural, and political change against the backdrop of the first decade of the revolution. However, many of the elements of commercialization, rationalization, and individualization that she writes about can be traced to the modernization programs of the Pahlavi era.

6. Behrouzan (2015).

7. The years 2002 and 2005 seem to have been peak years for publications of alternative spirituality. According to an informal count I made in 2009 using the website of the National Library and Archives of the Islamic Republic of Iran (which is required by law to hold a copy of every book published in Iran), there were, in 2002, at least 31 titles on Eastern spirituality (yoga, Buddhism, Hinduism, and so on), 22 on Eckankar, 20 by Osho, 17 by Gibran Khalil Gibran, 13 by Paulo Coelho, 3 by Krishnamurti, 1 by Carlos Castaneda, and 7 others that I would call New Age. In 2005, these figures were 35 titles for Eastern spirituality, 2 for Eckankar, 2 for Osho, 75 for Gibran Khalil Gibran, 22 for Paulo Coelho, 8 for Krishnamurti, 6 for Carlos Castaneda, and 28 other New Age. These figures include same-year reprints as well as printing by different publishers of the same texts (sometimes translated by different people). After Mahmoud Ahmadinejad became president in 2005 and a conservative culture minister was installed, texts on "deviant" mysticism were curbed somewhat, although not completely. For example, books by Paulo Coelho, Gibran Khalil Gibran, and Krishnamurti were still in print at the time of this writing. Texts by Carlos Castaneda or those promoting Eckankar were no longer published, but a few Iranian authors have published critical (sometimes polemical) texts on these topics. Yoga, pop-psychology, and self-help, as well as plenty of New Age titles that do not overtly promote religious alternatives to Islam, are still published en masse. For example, in 2010 alone, there were at least 46 translated titles by Wayne Dyer.

8. Other such capacities included enhancing memory, "reading" faces to understand others' personalities and motives (see chapter 24), recognizing body language, and "creative visualization" aimed at obtaining one's desires (on the latter, see my discussion of Mersedeh's sorcery in chapter 10).

9. Iranian experiments with alternative spiritual-therapeutic systems bring to mind the "seeker" of alternative religions examined by sociologists of Western societies a long time ago. John Lofland and Rodney Stark described seekers as "floundering

among religious alternatives, [with] an openness to a variety of religious views, frequently esoteric, combined with failure to embrace the specific ideology and fellowship of some set of believers" (1965, 870). Colin Campbell (2002) argued that "seekership" was characterized by openness, syncretism, ecumenicism, and tolerance. Scholars have also highlighted the individualistic character of seekership and its embeddedness within a spiritual marketplace where personal choice reigns supreme (for an overview and critique, see Bender [2010, 21–55]). Finally, some scholars have emphasized the importance of "self-spirituality" as a force uniting the disparate systems that are typically referred to as New Age (Heelas 1996; Hanegraaf 1996).

10. My treatment of Cosmic Mysticism's cosmology here will, by necessity, be brief. For a more detailed study, see Fezzeh Kashi's MA thesis in sociology at the University of Tehran (Kashi 2009).

11. This understanding of the relationship between consciousness and material reality has clear resonances in much of New Age thought. See Hammer (2001).

12. As Mr. Sheyda, the master with whom I studied (and who was himself a student of Mr. Taheri), explained to me, "The world of being is a sea of intelligence, where the details of the greatest structures—the macrocosm—exist in the smallest of elements—the microcosm."

13. Taheri (2007, 222–23).

14. Taheri (2010, 8).

15. Ibid., 9.

16. Taheri (2011a, 4).

17. Ibid., 7.

18. The term "inorganic beings" was coined by Carlos Castaneda. It first appeared in his 1984 book *The Fire from Within*, which was translated into Persian in 1986 and was reprinted multiple times in the following two decades. According to Castaneda, inorganic beings were creatures that possessed "the emanations of awareness in them and characteristics of life other than reproduction and metabolism," such as "emotional dependency, sadness, joy, wrath, and … love." Seers can employ these beings as "allies," with which they can attain marvelous power and work wonders. In Iran, the term "inorganic beings" has been adopted by a wide range of practitioners of alternative spirituality and enthusiasts of the occult, with varying degrees of faithfulness to Castaneda's original usage. Usually, the term overlaps with the Islamic notion of jinn and is employed as a technical or scientific rendition of the latter concept. In some systems, including Cosmic Mysticism, inorganic beings include jinn but are not limited to them.

19. Taheri (2011a, 10).

20. Taheri (2011b).

21. Ibid., 50–51.

CHAPTER 16: SPECTERS OF DOUBT

1. Taheri (2011a, 4).

2. Dallal (2010, 149–76); Elshakry (2009); Telliel (2015).

3. Zarcone (1991). These comparisons were made possible by the modernization and universalization of Sufism in the twentieth century. A detailed account of these transformations is beyond the scope of this book (but see Anzali [2017]; and Van den Bos [2002]). Suffice it to say that as European-style reforms gained favor among modernist intellectuals in the nineteenth and twentieth century, some erstwhile Sufis and

others sympathetic to the mystical tendencies within Islam argued for abandoning Sufism's institutional trappings and foregoing particularistic squabbling among various sects, so that people could instead strive toward a universal religion shared among all of humanity (Anzali 2017). The arguments of these thinkers have provided discursive grounds for Iranians to appropriate certain aspects of Sufi thought within a universalistic framework while being prepared to jettison overt commitments to Sufism and even Islam if necessary.

4. Hammer (2001).

5. Iranshahr (1974, 11–14).

6. Parvin Gonabadi (1956).

7. Farshad (2001). See Hammer (2001, 271–303) for a discussion of Capra's influence on New Age authors.

8. This special issue presents somewhat of an enigma. On the inside cover, *Danesh-e Pezeshki* is introduced as a journal belonging to the Medical Council of the Islamic Republic of Iran (MCIRI), a large and prestigious NGO that oversees private medical practice. However, I have not been able to find a single recent issue of *Danesh-e Pezeshki* other than the one on psymentology and a few others on metatherapy published in the same year. Moreover, my repeated calls to MCIRI to ask about the journal were fruitless; no one seemed to know anything about it. I also asked three veteran doctors among my acquaintances (a urologist, a psychiatrist, and an orthopedist), but none of them knew about the journal.

9. For a list of articles, see http://www.interuniversalism.org/#!science—research /cx19.

10. Taheri (2011a, 10).

11. Naseri Rad (2011, 111).

12. Ibid., 111–12.

13. Ibid., 208–11.

14. Gomaneh (2014).

CHAPTER 17: BECOMING WITNESS

1. Luhrman (2005); Seligman & Kirmayer (2008).

2. Moerman (2002).

3. Ibid.

CHAPTER 18: AUTHORITY IN EXPERIENCE

1. On Erfahrung and Erlebnis, see Jay (2005).

2. Sharifian (2008).

3. Gardet & Vadet (2012).

4. Ibid.

5. See Bashir (2013, chapter 4).

6. Gardet & Vadet (2012).

7. See, for example, Hamidiyyeh (2005).

8. Foody (2015b, 617).

9. William James has been known in Iran since at least the 1930s. *The Varieties of Religious Experience* was translated first by Mehdi Qa'eni in 1964 as *Din va Ravan: Mazhab az Dideh-ye Ravanshenasi* (*Religion and Psyche: Religion in the Eyes of Psychol-*

ogy). It has been republished multiple times, most recently in a new translation by Hoseyn Kiyani in 2006 and 2014. The first mention of Friedrich Schleiermacher that I have found in a Persian publication is from 1989. While Schleiermacher's work has been analyzed and critiqued numerous times since, I don't know of any Persian translations of his work. Rudolf Otto has been known to Persian speakers since around 1990. His *Das Heilige: Über das Irrationale in der Idee des Göttlichen und sein Verhältnis zum Rationalen* was translated by Homayun Hemmati in 2001. Paul Tillich's *The Courage to Be* was first translated by Morad Farhadpur in 1987. Other translations of his work include *Dynamics of Faith* in 1996, *Theology of Culture* in 1997, a collection of essays titled *The Future of Religions* in 1999, and *Systematic Theology* in 2002. Martin Buber's philosophical work has been known in Persian since the mid-1990s. His *Ich und Du* was first translated from an English edition by Khosrow Rigi in 1999. An English collection of lectures, *On Judaism*, and a collection of essays, *Eclipse of God*, have also been translated. These and other European thinkers (among them Kant, Hegel, Heidegger, Gadamer, Derrida, and Ricoeur) are frequently invoked in lectures, articles, and books on hermeneutics, religion and modernity, mysticism, and religious experience. Sometimes their work is placed in conversation with those of Muslim scholars, from Suhrawardi and Mulla Sadra to Tabatabai and Khomeini.

10. Ghamari-Tabrizi (2008); Jahanbakhsh (2001, 140–71); Sadri (2001).

11. For an overview of this movement with an emphasis on "political theology," see Sadeghi-Boroujerdi (2017). Also see Foody (2015a, 2015b, 2016).

12. Foody (2015b, 603).

13. Ibid., 603–4.

14. Foody (2015b). See also Safi (2000).

15. For an overview of Malekiyan's career and a critical assessment of his thought, see Sadeghi-Boroujerdi (2014).

16. Malekiyan (2002a, 2002b, 2002c).

17. I am indebted to Ata Anzali for this point, and for the further elaboration that Malekiyan was fascinated with the work of Ken Wilber and Robert Forman.

CHAPTER 19: A PROTECTOR LOST

1. *Manyetizm-e Shakhsi* is a Persian translation of *Traité Méthodique de Magnétisme Personnel: Votre Influence Invisible, Comment Augmenter sa Puissance et la Diriger avec Précision*, authored by the French occultists Paul-Clément Jagot and Pierre Oudinot in 1951. It was first translated in 1977 by the prominent Jewish journalist, author, and translator Moshfeq Hamedani.

2. The Islamic prophet Idris is usually identified with Enoch and with Hermes Trismegistus, to whom a significant occult corpus is attributed. On Hermes in the Islamic tradition, see Van Bladel (2009).

CHAPTER 20: WHIPS FOR THE WAYFARERS

1. On friends of God, see Cornell (1998); Gilsenan (1990, chapters 4–6); Millie (2009); and Renard (2008).

2. For example, Qur'an 4:69: "All who obey God and the apostle are in the company of those on whom is the grace of God—of the prophets, the sincere, the witnesses,

and the righteous: What a beautiful fellowship!"—and 10:62: "Behold! Verily on the friends of God there is no fear, nor shall they grieve."

3. Renard (2008, 144–45).

4. Lewisohn (1999); Van den Bos (2002). Van den Bos and Lewisohn detail both Shiʻi "traditionalist" and secular modernist attacks on Sufism in twentieth-century Iran. For the views of Ahmad Kasravi, one of the most ardent enemies of Sufism who had equal scorn for Shiʻism, see Ridgeon (2006). For a longer historical view of Shiʻi attacks on Sufism since the Safavid period, see Anzali (2017).

5. On the mysticism promoted by the Islamic Republic, see Van den Bos (2002, 134–63). Van den Bos incorrectly places the beginnings of "state mysticism" after Ayatollah Khomeini's death in 1989. Although there was a marked increase in state mystical discourse in the '90s, all of its ingredients existed long beforehand. See, for example, Seyed-Gohrab (2011) and Varzi (2006, 76–105).

6. Knysh (1992); Mottahedeh (1985, 183–87 and 242–43); and Ridgeon (2014).

7. Some hagiographies of contemporary Shiʻi mystics were published earlier. The more popular ones were Sayyed Hasan Abtahi's *Parvaz-e Ruh* (Flight of the Soul), published first in 1979, and Sayyed Mohammad Hoseyn Hoseyni Tehrani's *Mehr-e Taban* (Shining Sun/Love), published in 1982. However, although well received, these books did not spur publications of similar titles. This had to wait until the 1990s.

8. I know of one woman who is revered alongside what is otherwise an entirely male assembly: Sayyedeh Nosrat Beygom Amin (1891–1983) was a jurist and hadith scholar.

9. See, for example, Bahrami (2004); Editorial (2001); Esfahani (2003); Rabbani Khorasgani & Qasemi (2002); and Shojaʻi Zand et al. (2006).

10. See the website of the Secretariat of the Public Culture Council of Iran at https://tinyurl.com/deviant-cults.

11. Tavakoli-Targhi (2012).

12. See the website of the Secretariat of the Public Culture Council of Iran at https://tinyurl.com/deviant-cults.

13. Ibid.

14. Meqdadi Esfahani (2001, 5–6).

15. Parvinzad (2004).

16. Ibid., 8.

17. From the online English translation of the book at http://www.al-islam.org /elixiroflove/1.htm, with slight modification.

18. *Darbareh-ye ma* (About Us), http://www.shsh.ir/index.php?option=com_content &view=article&id=1&Itemid=2.

19. *Selseleh Hamayesh-ha-ye ba Aflakiyan-e Khakneshin* (the seminar series "With the Earth-Dwelling Celestial Beings"), http://www.shsh.ir/index.php?option=com _content&view=category&layout=blog&id=9&Itemid=14.

20. The virtues of revolutionary activism were not entirely eliminated from the scene. The hagiographies of the martyrs of war, for example, also underwent transformations in order to appeal to a younger audience who took peacetime material comforts for granted. See Mazaheri (2015, 2016). The state has been keen to promote these martyrs and revolutionaries, as indicated in the SCCR recommendations I discussed above.

21. Meqdadi Esfahani (2001, 52–53).

22. The book was *Have an Out-of-Body Experience in 30 Days: The Free Flight Program* by Keith Harary and Pamela Weintraub, published first in 1989. It was translated into Persian by Reza Jamaliyan in 1992 with the title *Parvaz-e Ruh*.

23. Meqdadi Esfahani (2001, 51).

24. Renard (2008, 91); Gilsenan (1973, 20–35); Millie (2008).

CHAPTER 21: DISCRETION AND PUBLICITY

1. On secrecy in Sufism, see Schimmel (1987).

2. For comparison, see Noah Salomon's analysis of the epistemological and political disputes around the sharing of secret knowledge in Sudan's Islamic state (Salomon 2013, 2016).

3. Sefidabiyan (2001, 43–44).

4. Mojahedi (2003, 16).

5. Ibid., 17.

6. Ibid., 17–18.

7. Ibid., 18.

8. Mojahedi (2006, 65). An Arabic translation was published in Beirut in 2012.

9. We saw in chapter 8 that premodern Muslim thinkers considered astonishment to serve pedagogic purposes as well. Here these purposes are balanced against the problem of skepticism.

10. Ibid., 52.

11. Anzali (2017, 65).

12. Mojahedi (2003, 51).

CHAPTER 22: THE POLITICS OF VENERATION

1. Anzali (2017).

2. See Anzali's discussion of the reception of 'erfan among supporters and opponents of Khomeini and his circle (ibid).

3. Ibid.

4. Mojahedi (2003, 13). A khanaqah is a Sufi lodge.

5. Ibid., 226–28.

6. A report about the event and the organizers' remarks was published on the online news service Raja News, but the website's archive no longer includes reports from 2007. Copies of the report were also published on various blogs, including at the following address: https://tinyurl.com/mojtahedi-commemoration.

7. The question and answer can be found here: http://www.porseman.org/q/vservice.aspx?logo=images/right.jpg&id=132811. Neither the question nor the answer is dated, but internal clues suggest that they were posted in 2004.

8. See Anzali (2017) and Rizvi (2015).

9. My discussion of the book is based on its third edition; Kiyani (2014).

10. Ibid., 14–15.

11. On Allameh Tabatabai and his relationship with Qazi, see Rizvi (2015).

12. Qazi (2013, 98–99).

13. Ibid., 99.

14. Ibid., 99–100.

15. Ibid., 100.

16. Ibid.

17. Sajjad Rizvi (2015) makes a similar argument.

18. See https://tinyurl.com/mojtahedi-khomeini.

19. Reyshahri (2004, 67), quoted in Kiyani (2014, 124).

20. Kiyani (2014, 124–30).

21. Ibid., 131.

CHAPTER 23: METAPHYSICS OF VISION

1. I am drawing here on Michel Foucault's well-known theorization of "technologies of the self" (1988).

2. Such explicit comparisons between a saint's marvels and prophetic miracles are common in hagiographies. See Renard (2008, 95–98).

3. *Sattar al-'uyub* [Concealer of Faults], from *Adam-ha-ye Khub-e Shahr* [The Good People of the City]. See http://adamhaye-khoob.blogspot.com/2006/10/blog-post_18.html.

4. Michael Gilsenan describes precisely such a condition in a village in North Lebanon where he conducted fieldwork (1990, 118–19).

5. *Keyhan-e Farhangi* (2004, 20).

6. See Mahmood (2005, 151) for comparison.

7. I use the masculine pronoun in referring to pious aspirants here because in my interviews, this conception of the extrasensory gaze only came up in descriptions of encounters between male seekers and their male spiritual teachers. For an exception in the realm of television serials, see chapter 24.

8. On hagiographic accounts of the gift of clairvoyance among friends of God, see Renard (2008, 112–15). On theological debates about clairvoyance, visions, and dreams, see ibid., 275–77.

9. See also my discussion of the heart in chapter 18.

10. Majnun spoke these words in response to a naysayer who thought there were many women more beautiful than Layli, the one woman whose love had driven Majnun mad. But Majnun could see things that were invisible to others around him who could not understand his obsession.

11. Golkar (2010).

12. See, for example, Keyhan (2010).

13. Hoseynzadeh (2006, 77).

14. Ebrahimi Dinani (2006, 177).

15. Walbridge (2000, 26).

16. Ebrahimi Dinani (2006, 177).

17. A number of anthropologists have written about the concept of barzakh in relation to Sufism. See especially Crapanzano (1985); Mittermaier (2011); and Pandolfo (1997). However, these scholars go on to transform barzakh into an anthropological concept having to do with "in-betweenness" in a sense that goes beyond its theologico-mystical meaning. I do not pursue this analytic path here.

18. Hoseynzadeh (2006, 77).

19. Keshavarz (2004); Shokr (2007).

20. See http://www.aghatehrani.ir/Myapp/current?cid=1209.

21. Foltz (2006, 15–17).

22. Ibid., 49; Nasr (2006, 77).

23. Black (2005); Haque (2004).

24. Schimmel (1975, 112).

25. Ibid., 112–13.

26. Hoyland (2007). On the Greek background to Islamic physiognomy, see Boys-Stones (2007) and Swain (2007).

27. Cited in Hoyland (2007, 253).

28. Ibn ʿArabi (1997, 105). I am grateful to Angela Jaffray for bringing this text to my attention.

29. Hoseynzadeh (2006, 78).

CHAPTER 24: TECHNOSPIRITUAL REFLEXIVITY

1. As of October 18, 2010, the website had 2,296 members. It consisted of an active core of more than 160 users who had contributed at least ten posts each over the previous five years, with the most active members having posted hundreds or thousands of entries. The remaining registered users were either silent readers of others' contributions or they were inactive. Unregistered users could also browse the content but could not post their own.

2. In Persian, the word for "human" is *ensan*. This term is not overtly male in the same way as the English "man," and is regularly used to refer to both male and female members of the human race, as well as the race in its entirety.

3. On fatwas as instruments of ethical self-care, see Agrama (2010).

4. Much of the Western scholarship on Iranian society in the 1960s and '70s underscored uncertainty, insecurity, and mistrust as prevailing aspects of social life and interpersonal relations (see Beeman [1986, 22–34]). William Beeman long ago criticized the tendency in this scholarship to psychologize mistrust, instead arguing for an overarching Iranian pattern of communicative pragmatics that values obscurity and multiple meanings. Whereas Beeman's solution was to emphasize culture instead of psychology, my analysis here is historical.

5. See Keshavarzian (2007) for an examination of this shift in the specific context of the Tehran bazaar.

6. See Lara Deeb's discussion of the relationship between veiling and inner piety among Shiʿi Lebanese "pious moderns" (2006, 115). For the concept of *nifaq* or hypocrisy in the Qurʾan, see Izutsu (2002, 178–83).

7. Of course, repeatable zekrs have long served as a Sufi technique of spiritual self-purification. What is new about them is the equivalence that some people establish between these zekrs and metaphysical meditation practices, as well as their imagination of these practices on the model of modern technology.

8. See Gunning (1995).

9. Grosz (2005, 145–52).

10. Ibid., 146–47.

11. Ibid., 145.

12. Ibid., 148.

13. Few of my interlocutors candidly described to me their desire for seeing their own isthmus image like Kamran, partly because, I think, the desire can reveal one as

deeply vulnerable. Even Kamran provided the caveat that he no longer believed the way he did when he was a teenager (that is, about five years prior to my interview with him), and he now believes his dream was probably just the result of suggestion from the books he had read and sermons he had heard. As we saw in his quote about Ayatollah Bahjat's botched visit to the shrine in chapter 23, he was generally derisive of the popular interest in the marvels of God's friends.

14. See http://heyatonline.blogfa.com/8708.aspx.

CONCLUSION

1. I am distinguishing Shi'i reason here from "Shi'i rationality" (*'aqlaniyyat-e shi'eh*), a concept I have discussed several times in this book, which points to one particular strand of Shi'i reason explicitly governed by the interests and concerns of the post-1979 Islamic state. I am not arguing for a conceptual difference between "reason" and "rationality," however. The two terms merely allow me to make a convenient (and temporary) distinction between a more general and a more specific articulation of reason.

2. See MacIntyre (2012) and Asad (1986).

3. See Deeb & Harb (2013); Marsden (2005); Schielke (2009); and Simon (2009). Also see Fadil & Fernando (2015) for a critique of the notion of "everyday Muslims" in this scholarship, and the responses of Deeb and Schielke in the same issue of Hau.

4. Hirschkind (2006); Mahmood (2005). Naveeda Khan offers a different way of understanding pious practice as open-ended aspiration (2012).

REFERENCES

Abrahamian, Ervand. 1982. *Iran between Two Revolutions*. Princeton: Princeton University Press.

———. 1992. *The Iranian Mojahedin*. New Haven: Yale University Press.

Abrahamov, Binyamin. 2014. "Signs." In *Encyclopaedia of the Qur'ān*, edited by Jane Dammen McAuliffe. Brill Online. http://referenceworks.brillonline.com/entries/encyclopaedia-of-the-quran/signs-EQCOM_00182.

Adelkhah, Fariba. 2000. *Being Modern in Iran*. Translated by Jonathan Derrick. New York: Columbia University Press.

Adib-Moghaddam, Arshin, ed. 2014. *A Critical Introduction to Khomeini*. Cambridge: Cambridge University Press.

Agrama, Hussein Ali. 2010. "Ethics, Tradition, Authority: Toward an Anthropology of the Fatwa." *American Ethnologist* 37 (1): 2–18.

———. 2012. *Questioning Secularism: Islam, Sovereignty, and the Rule of Law in Modern Egypt*. Chicago: University of Chicago Press.

Albanese, Catherine L. 2007. *A Republic of Mind and Spirit: A Cultural History of American Metaphysical Religion*. New Haven: Yale University Press.

Alef. 2012. "'Aqayedi keh dar Sayeh-ye Khorafeh Gom Mishavand." http://alef.ir/vdc jaaeviuqemmz.fsfu.html?167675.

Algar, Hamid. 1989. "Borūjerdī, Ḥosayn Ṭabāṭabā'ī." *Encyclopaedia Iranica*. Online edition. http://www.iranica.com/articles/borujerdi-ayatollah-hajj-aqa-hosayn-tabatabai-1292-1380-1875-1961.

———. 2006. 'Allāma Sayyid Muḥammad Ḥusayn Ṭabāṭabā'ī: Philosopher, Exegete, and Gnostic. *Journal of Islamic Studies* 17 (3): 326–51.

Amanat, Abbas. 1997. *Pivot of the Universe: Nasir al-Din Shah Qajar and the Iranian Monarchy, 1831–1896*. Berkeley: University of California Press.

Amin, Camron M. 2002. *The Making of the Modern Iranian Woman: Gender, State Policy, and Popular Culture, 1865–1946*. Gainesville: University Press of Florida.

Amir-Moezzi, Mohammad Ali. 1994. *The Divine Guide in Early Shi'ism: The Sources of Esotericism in Islam*. Translated by David Streight. Albany: State University of New York Press.

Anderson, Benedict. 1991. *Imagined Communities: Reflections on the Origin and Spread of Nationalism*. New York: Verso.

Anzali, Ata. 2017. *"Mysticism" in Iran: The Safavid Roots of a Modern Concept*. Columbia: University of South Carolina Press.

Appadurai, Arjun. 1990. "Disjuncture and Difference in the Global Cultural Economy." *Public Culture* 2 (2): 1–24.

Arjomand, Kamran. 1997. "The Emergence of Scientific Modernity in Iran: Controversies Surrounding Astrology and Modern Astronomy in the Mid-Nineteenth Century." *Iranian Studies* 30 (1–2): 5–24.

Arman-e Emruz. 2014. "Zendegi ba Mizan-e Ostorlab." *Arman-e Emruz* 2623:5. http://armandaily.ir/1393/09/02/Files/PDF/13930902-2623-19-5.pdf.

Asad, Talal. 1986. *The Idea of an Anthropology of Islam.* Occasional Paper Series. Washington, DC: Georgetown University Center for Contemporary Arab Studies.

———. 1993a. *Genealogies of Religion: Discipline and Reasons of Power in Christianity and Islam.* Baltimore: Johns Hopkins University Press.

———. 1993b. "The Limits of Religious Criticism in the Middle East: Notes on Islamic Public Argument." In *Genealogies of Religion: Discipline and Reasons of Power in Christianity and Islam,* 200–36. Baltimore: Johns Hopkins University Press.

———. 1993c. "Toward a Genealogy of the Concept of Ritual." In *Genealogies of Religion: Discipline and Reasons of Power in Christianity and Islam,* 55–80. Baltimore: Johns Hopkins University Press.

———. 2003. "Reconfigurations of Law and Ethics in Colonial Egypt." In *Formations of the Secular,* 205–56. Stanford, CA: Stanford University Press.

———. 2015. "Thinking about Tradition, Religion, and Politics in Egypt Today." *Critical Inquiry.* http://criticalinquiry.uchicago.edu/thinking_about_tradition_religion_and_politics_in_egypt_today/.

Babayan, Kathryn. 1998. "The ''Aqā'id al-Nisā'': A Glimpse at Safavid Women in Local Isfahani Culture." In *Women in the Medieval Islamic World: Power, Patronage, and Piety,* edited by Gavin Hambly, 349–81. New York: St. Martin's Press.

Bahrami, Mohammad. 2004. "Din-gorizi, 'Avamel va Rah-e Hal-ha dar Partov-e Qor'an." *Pazhuhesh-ha-ye Qor'ani* 37–38:38–69.

Balaghi, Shiva. 2012. "Iranian Visual Arts in 'the Century of Machinery, Speed, and the Atom': Rethinking Modernity." In *Picturing Iran,* edited by Shiva Balaghi and Lynn Gumpert, 21–38. New York: I. B. Taurus.

Bar-Asher, Meir M. 2016. "Hidden and the Hidden." In *Encyclopaedia of the Qur'ān,* edited by Jane Dammen McAuliffe. Brill Online. http://referenceworks.brillonline.com/entries/encyclopaedia-of-the-quran/hidden-and-the-hidden-EQSIM_00190.

Bashir, Shahzad. 2013. *Sufi Bodies: Religion and Society in Medieval Islam.* New York: Columbia University Press.

Bayat, Mangol. 2009. "Freemasonry and the Constitutional Revolution in Iran: 1905–1911." In *Freemasonry and Fraternalism in the Middle East,* edited by Andreas Önnerfors and Dorothe Sommer, 109–50. Sheffield: University of Sheffield.

Bazargan, Mehdi. 1998. "'Eshq va Parastesh, ya Termodinamik-e Ensan." In *Mabahes-e Bonyadin: Majmu'eh-ye Asar.* Vol. 1, 247–447. Tehran: Pejman.

Beaumont, Daniel. 1998. "'Peut-on…': Intertextual Relations in *The Arabian Nights* and Genesis." *Comparative Literature* 50 (2): 120–35.

Beeman, William O. 1986. *Language, Status, and Power in Iran.* Bloomington: Indiana University Press.

Behdad, Sohrab, and Farhad Nomani. 2009. "What a Revolution! Thirty Years of Social Class Reshuffling in Iran." *Comparative Studies of South Asia, Africa, and the Middle East* 29 (1): 84–104.

Behrooz, Maziar. 2000. *Rebels with a Cause: The Failure of the Left in Iran.* 2nd ed. New York: I. B. Tauris.

Behrouzan, Orkideh. 2015. "Writing *Prozāk* Diaries in Tehran: Generational Anomie and Psychiatric Subjectivities." *Culture, Medicine, and Psychiatry* 39 (3): 399–426.

Belo, Catarina. 2009. "Some Considerations on Averroes' Views regarding Women and Their Role in Society." *Journal of Islamic Studies* 20 (1): 1–20.

Bender, Courtney. 2010. *The New Metaphysicals: Spirituality and the American Religious Imagination.* Chicago: University of Chicago Press.

Berlekamp, Persis. 2011. *Wonder, Image, and Cosmos in Medieval Islam.* New Haven: Yale University Press.

Bidokhti Gonabadi, Soltan Mohammad. 2006. *Tanbih al-Na'emin, beh Payvast-e Kh^wab-e Meghnatisi.* Tehran: Haqiqat.

Black, Deborah L. 2005. "Psychology: Soul and Intellect." In *The Cambridge Companion to Arabic Philosophy,* edited by Peter Adamson and Richard C. Taylor, 308–26. Cambridge: Cambridge University Press.

———. 2013. "Certitude, Justification, and the Principles of Knowledge in Avicenna's Epistemology." In *Interpreting Avicenna: Critical Essays,* edited by Peter Adamson, 120–42. Cambridge: Cambridge University Press.

Boddy, Janice. 1989. *Wombs and Alien Spirits: Women, Men, and the Zār Cult in Northern Sudan.* Madison: University of Wisconsin Press.

Boer, Tjitze J. de, and Fazlur Rahman. 2012. "'Aḳl." In *Encyclopaedia of Islam,* edited by P. Bearman et al. 2nd ed. Brill Online. http://referenceworks.brillonline.com/entries /encyclopaedia-of-islam-2/akl-COM_0038.

Bogdan, Henrik, and Gordan Djurdjevic, eds. 2013. *Occultism in a Global Perspective.* Durham, NC: Acumen.

Bonebakker, Seeger A. 1992. "Some Medieval Views on Fantastic Stories." *Quaderni di Studi Arabi* 10:21–43.

Boroujerdi, Mehrzad. 2006. "'The West' in the Eyes of the Iranian Intellectuals of the Interwar Years (1919–1939)." *Comparative Studies of South Asia, Africa, and the Middle East* 26 (3): 391–401.

Bosworth, Clifford E. 1976. *The Mediaeval Islamic Underworld: The Banū Sāsān in Arabic Society and Literature.* 2 vols. Leiden: Brill.

Bowen, John R. 1993. *Muslims through Discourse: Religion and Ritual in Gayo Society.* Princeton: Princeton University Press.

Boys-Stones, George. 2007. "Physiognomy and Ancient Psychological Theory." In *Seeing the Face, Seeing the Soul: Polemon's Physiognomy from Classical Antiquity to Medieval Islam,* edited by Simon Swain, 19–124. Oxford: Oxford University Press.

Brower, M. Brady. 2010. *Unruly Spirits: The Science of Psychic Phenomena in Modern France.* Urbana: University of Illinois Press.

Brown, Jonathan A. C. 2009. "Did the Prophet Say It or Not? The Literal, Historical, and Effective Truth of Ḥadīths in Early Sunnism." *Journal of the American Oriental Society* 129 (2): 259–85.

Calverley, Edwin E. 2012. "Nafs." In *Encyclopaedia of Islam,* edited by P. Bearman et al. 2nd ed. Brill Online. http://referenceworks.brillonline.com/entries/encyclopaedia -of-islam-2/nafs-COM_0833.

Cammann, Schuyler. 1969a. "Islamic and Indian Magic Squares, Part I." *History of Religions* 8 (3): 181–209.

———. 1969b. "Islamic and Indian Magic Squares, Part II." *History of Religions* 8 (4): 271–99.

Campbell, Colin. 2002. "The Cult, the Cultic Milieu, and Secularization." In *The Cultic Milieu: Oppositional Subcultures in an Age of Globalization*, edited by Jeffrey Kaplan and Heléne Lööw, 12–25. Walnut Creek, CA: Alta Mira Press.

Castaneda, Carlos. 1984. *The Fire from Within*. New York: Simon and Schuster.

Castoriadis, Cornelius. 1987. *The Imaginary Institution of Society*. Translated by Kathleen Blamey. Cambridge: MIT Press.

Cecire, Natalia. 2015. "Experimentalism by Contact." *diacritics* 43 (1): 6–35.

Certeau, Michel de. 2000. *The Possession at Loudun*. Translated by Michael B. Smith. Chicago: University of Chicago Press.

Chabbi, Jacqueline. 2011. "Jinn." In *Encyclopaedia of the Qurʾān*, edited by Jane Dammen McAuliffe. Brill Online. http://referenceworks.brillonline.com/entries/encyclopaedia -of-the-quran/jinn-EQSIM_00237.

———. 2014. "Whisper." In *Encyclopaedia of the Qurʾān*, edited by Jane Dammen McAuliffe. Brill Online. http://referenceworks.brillonline.com/entries/encyclopaedia-of -the-quran/whisper-EQSIM_00458.

Chandler, James, Arnold I. Davidson, and Harry Harootunian, eds. 1994. *Questions of Evidence: Proof, Practice, and Persuasion across the Disciplines*. Chicago: University of Chicago Press.

Chehabi, Houchang E. 1990. *Iranian Politics and Religious Modernism: The Liberation Movement of Iran under the Shah and Khomeini*. Ithaca: Cornell University Press.

———. 1993. "Staging the Emperor's New Clothes: Dress Codes and Nation-Building under Reza Shah." *Iranian Studies* 26 (3–4): 209–29.

———. 2003. "The Banning of the Veil and Its Consequences." In *The Making of Modern Iran: State and Society under Riza Shah, 1921–1941*, edited by Stephanie Cronin, 193–210. London: Curzon.

———. 2007. "How Caviar Turned Out to be *Halal*." *Gastronomica: The Journal of Critical Food Studies* 7 (2): 17–23.

Chehabi, Houchang E., and Vanessa Martin, eds. 2010. *Iran's Constitutional Revolution: Popular Politics, Cultural Transformations and Transnational Connections*. New York: I. B. Tauris.

Clarke, Morgan. 2014. "Cough Sweets and Angels: The Ordinary Ethics of the Extraordinary in Sufi Practice in Lebanon." *Journal of the Royal Anthropological Institute* 20 (3): 407–25.

Comaroff, Jean, and John L. Comaroff. 1999. "Occult Economies and the Violence of Abstraction: Notes from the South African Postcolony." *American Ethnologist* 26 (2): 279–303.

———. 2002. "Alien-Nation: Zombies, Immigrants, and Millennial Capitalism." *South Atlantic Quarterly* 101 (4): 779–805.

Cornell, Vincent J. 1998. *Realm of the Saint: Power and Authority in Moroccan Sufism*. Austin: University of Texas Press.

Crapanzano, Vincent. 1973. *The Ḥamadsha: A Study in Moroccan Ethnopsychiatry*. Berkeley: University of California Press.

———. 1985. *Tuhami: Portrait of a Moroccan*. Chicago: University of Chicago Press.

Dabashi, Hamid. 1993. *Theology of Discontent: The Ideological Foundations of the Islamic Revolution in Iran*. New York: New York University Press.

Dakake, Maria Massi. 2007. *The Charismatic Community: Shiʿite Identity in Early Islam*. Albany: State University of New York Press.

Dallal, Ahmad S. 2010. *Islam, Science, and the Challenge of History*. New Haven: Yale University Press.

Darnton, Robert. 1968. *Mesmerism and the End of the Enlightenment in France*. Cambridge: Harvard University Press.

Daston, Lorraine. 1995. "The Moral Economy of Science." *Osiris*, 2nd series. Vol. 10, "Constructing Knowledge in the History of Science," 2–24.

Daston, Lorraine, and Peter Galison. 1992. "The Image of Objectivity." *Representations* 40 (Special issue, "Seeing Science"): 81–128.

Daston, Lorraine, and Katharine Park. 1998. *Wonders and the Order of Nature, 1150–1750*. New York: Zone Books.

Dear, Peter. 1995. *Discipline and Experience: The Mathematical Way in the Scientific Revolution*. Chicago: University of Chicago Press.

———. 2008. "The Meanings of Experience." In *The Cambridge History of Science, Volume 3: Early Modern Science*, edited by Katharine Park and Lorraine Daston, 106–31. Cambridge: Cambridge University Press.

Deeb, Lara. 2006. *An Enchanted Modern: Gender and Public Piety in Shiʿi Lebanon*. Princeton: Princeton University Press.

Deeb, Lara, and Mona Harb. 2013. "Choosing Both Faith and Fun: Youth Negotiations of Moral Norms in South Beirut." *Ethnos* 78 (1): 1–22.

DelVecchio Good, Mary-Jo. 2001. "The Biotechnical Embrace." *Culture, Medicine, and Psychiatry* 25 (4): 395–410.

Denzler, Brenda. 2001. *The Lure of the Edge: Scientific Passions, Religious Beliefs, and the Pursuit of UFOs*. Berkeley: University of California Press.

Dhahabi, Muhammad Husayn al-. 1976. *Al-Tafsir wa-l-Mufassirun*. Vol. 1. Cairo: Maktaba Wahba.

Diba, Layla S. 2013. "The Formation of Modern Iranian Art: From Kamal-Al-Molk to Zenderoudi." In *Iran Modern*, edited by Layla S. Diba and Fereshteh Daftari, 45–66. New Haven: Yale University Press.

Dole, Christopher. 2006. "Mass Media and the Repulsive Allure of Religious Healing: The *Cinci Hoca* in Turkish Modernity." *International Journal of Middle East Studies* 38 (1): 31–54.

Doostdar, Alireza. 2013. "Portrait of an Iranian Witch." *New Inquiry* 21:36–43.

———. 2016. "Empirical Spirits: Islam, Spiritism, and the Virtues of Science in Iran." *Comparative Studies in Society and History* 58 (2): 322–49.

———. Forthcoming. "Hollywood Cosmopolitanisms and the Occult Resonance of Cinema." *Comparative Islamic Studies*.

Drory, Rina. 1994. "Three Attempts to Legitimize Fiction in Classical Arabic Literature." *Jerusalem Studies in Arabic and Islam* 18:146–64.

Druart, Thérèse-Anne. 2005. "Metaphysics." In *The Cambridge Companion to Arabic Philosophy*, edited by Peter Adamson and Richard C. Taylor, 327–48. Cambridge: Cambridge University Press.

During, Simon. 2002. *Modern Enchantments: The Cultural Power of Secular Magic*. Cambridge, MA: Harvard University Press.

Ebrahimi Dinani, Gholam-Hoseyn. 2006. "The World of Imagination." In *Islamic Philosophy and Occidental Phenomenology on the Perennial Issue of Microcosm and Macrocosm*, edited by Anna-Teresa Tymieniecka, 177–82. Dordrecht: Springer.

Editorial. 2001. "Arzyabi az Maquleh-ye Din-gorizi (Sar-maqaleh—Nasl-e Javan dar pey-e Hoviyyati Jadid)." *Chashm-andaz-e Iran* 7:2–10.

Eickelman, Dale F. 1985. *Knowledge and Power in Morocco: The Education of a Twentieth-Century Notable.* Princeton: Princeton University Press.

Eickelman, Dale F., and James Piscatori. 1996. *Muslim Politics.* Princeton: Princeton University Press.

Eickelman, Dale F., and Jon Anderson. 1997. "Print, Islam, and the Prospects for Civic Pluralism: New Religious Writings and their Audiences." *Journal of Islamic Studies* 8 (1): 43–62.

———, eds. 1999. *New Media in the Muslim World: The Emerging Public Sphere.* Bloomington: Indiana University Press.

Eisen, Arnold. 1978. "The Meanings and Confusions of Weberian 'Rationality.'" *British Journal of Sociology* 29 (1): 57–70.

Elshakry, Marwa. 2009. "The Exegesis of Science in Twentieth Century Arabic Interpretations of the Qur'an." In *Nature and Scripture,* edited by Jitse van der Meer, 491–524. Leiden: Brill.

———. 2013. *Reading Darwin in Arabic, 1860–1950.* Chicago: University of Chicago Press.

Enayat, Hadi. 2013. *Law, State, and Society in Modern Iran: Constitutionalism, Autocracy, and Legal Reform, 1906–1941.* New York: Palgrave Macmillan.

Esfahani, Ebrahim. 2003. "Negahi be 'Avamel-e Jame'eh-shenakhti va Ravan-shenakhti-ye Din-gorizi ba Takiyeh bar Yafteh-ha-yi az Sureh-ye Mobarakeh-ye Hud." *Ma'refat* 64:13–30.

Ettehadiyyeh, Mansureh. 1998. *Inja Tehran Ast.* Tehran: Nashr-e Tarikh-e Iran.

Evans-Pritchard, Edward E. 1937. *Witchcraft, Oracles and Magic among the Azande.* Oxford: Clarendon Press.

Ewing, Katherine. 1994. "Dreams from a Saint: Anthropological Atheism and the Temptation to Believe." *American Anthropologist* 96 (3): 571–83.

———. 1997. *Arguing Sainthood: Modernity, Psychoanalysis, and Islam.* Durham, NC: Duke University Press.

Fadel, Mohammad. 1997. "Two Women, One Man: Knowledge, Power, and Gender in Medieval Sunni Legal Thought." *International Journal of Middle Eastern Studies* 29 (2): 185–204.

Fadil, Nadia, and Mayanthi Fernando. 2015. "Rediscovering the 'Everyday' Muslim: Notes on an Anthropological Divide." *Hau: Journal of Ethnographic Theory* 5 (2): 59–88.

Fahd, Toufic. 2012a. "Djafr." In *Encyclopaedia of Islam,* edited by P. Bearman et al. 2nd ed. Brill Online. http://referenceworks.brillonline.com/entries/encyclopaedia-of-islam-2/djafr-SIM_1924.

———. 2012b. "Ḥurūf ('Ilm al-)." In *Encyclopaedia of Islam,* edited by P. Bearman et al. 2nd ed. Brill Online. http://referenceworks.brillonline.com/entries/encyclopaedia-of-islam-2/huruf-SIM_2971.

———. 2012c. "Khaṭṭ." In *Encyclopaedia of Islam,* edited by P. Bearman et al. 2nd ed. Brill Online. http://referenceworks.brillonline.com/entries/encyclopaedia-of-islam-2/khatt-SIM_4237.

Farhad, Massumeh, and Serpil Bağci, eds. 2009. *Falnama: The Book of Omens.* London: Thames & Hudson.

Farshad, Mohsen. 2001. *Andisheh-ha-ye Kwantomi-ye Mowlana: Peyvand-e 'Elm va 'Erfan.* Tehran: Jame'eh.

Favret-Saada, Jeanne. 1980. *Deadly Words: Witchcraft in the Bocage.* Translated by Catherine Cullen. Cambridge: Cambridge University Press.

Fazeli, Nematollah. 2007. "Fal, Farhang va Faraqat." *Roshd-e Amuzesh-e 'Ulum-e Ejtema'i* 35:12–23.

Fischer, Michael M. J. 2003. *Iran: From Religious Dispute to Revolution.* Madison: University of Wisconsin Press.

Foltz, Richard C. 2006. *Animals in Islamic Tradition and Muslim Cultures.* Oxford: Oneworld.

Foody, Kathleen. 2015a. "Considering Public Criticism: Secularity, Citizenship, and Religious Argument in Contemporary Iran." *Muslim World* 105 (3): 299–311.

———. 2015b. "Interiorizing Islam: Religious Experience and State Oversight in the Islamic Republic of Iran." *Journal of the American Academy of Religion* 83 (3): 599–623.

———. 2016. "The Limits of Religion: Liberalism and Anti-Liberalism in the Islamic Republic of Iran." *Culture and Religion* 17 (2): 183–99.

Foucault, Michel. 1988. "Technologies of the Self." In *Technologies of the Self: A Seminar with Michel Foucault,* edited and translated by Luther Martin, Huck Gutman, and Patrick Hutton, 16–49. Amherst: University of Massachusetts Press.

———. 1994. *The Order of Things: An Archaeology of the Human Sciences.* New York: Vintage Books.

Frank, Richard M. 2007. *Early Islamic Theology: The Mu'tazilites and Al-Ash'ari; Texts and Studies on the Development and History of Kalam.* Edited by Dimitri Gutas. Vol. 2. London: Routledge.

Freud, Sigmund. 2001. "The 'Uncanny.'" In *The Standard Edition of the Complete Psychological Works of Sigmund Freud,* edited and translated by James Strachey, 217–56. Vol. 17. London: Vintage Books.

Fuchs, Simon Wolfgang. 2014. "Failing Transnationally: Local Intersections of Science, Medicine, and Sectarianism in Modernist Shi'i Writings." *Modern Asian Studies* 48, Special Issue (2): 433–67.

Galvan, Jill Nicole. 2010. *The Sympathetic Medium: Feminine Channeling, the Occult, and Communication Technologies.* Ithaca: Cornell University Press.

Gane, Nicholas. 2002. *Max Weber and Postmodern Theory: Rationalization versus Re-enchantment.* New York: Palgrave.

Gardet, Louis, and Jean-Claude Vadet. 2012. "Ḳalb." In *The Encyclopaedia of Islam,* edited by P. Bearman et al. 2nd ed. Brill Online. http://referenceworks.brillonline.com/entries/encyclopaedia-of-islam-2/kalb-COM_0424.

Geschiere, Peter. 1997. *The Modernity of Witchcraft: Politics and the Occult in Postcolonial Africa.* Translated by Peter Geschiere and Janet Roitman. Charlottesville: University Press of Virginia.

———. 2013. *Witchcraft, Intimacy, and Trust: Africa in Comparison.* Chicago: University of Chicago Press.

Ghamari-Tabrizi, Behrooz. 2008. *Islam and Dissent in Postrevolutionary Iran: Abdolkarim Soroush, Religious Politics, and Democratic Reform.* New York: I. B. Tauris.

Gilsenan, Michael. 1973. *Saint and Sufi in Modern Egypt: An Essay in the Sociology of Religion.* Oxford: Clarendon Press.

Gilsenan, Michael. 1990. *Recognizing Islam: Religion and Society in the Modern Middle East.* New York: I. B. Tauris.

———. 2000. "Signs of Truth: Enchantment, Modernity and the Dreams of Peasant Women." *Journal of the Royal Anthropological Institute* 6 (4): 597–615.

Gleave, Robert. 2000. *Inevitable Doubt: Two Theories of Shī'ī Jurisprudence.* Leiden: Brill.

———. 2002. "Modern Šī'ī Discussions of 'Ḫabar al-Wāḥid': Ṣadr, Ḫumaynī and Ḫū'ī." *Oriente Moderno*, new series 21, 82, 1 ("Hadith in Modern Islam"): 179–94.

Golkar, Saeid. 2010. "The Ideological-Political Training of Iran's Basij." *Middle East Brief* 44: 1–10.

Gomaneh. 2014. "Barresi va Naqd-e Arzesh-e 'Elmi-ye Madarek-e Mohammad 'Ali Taheri Bonyangozar-e 'Erfan-e Halqeh." https://tinyurl.com/gomaneh-cosmic -mysticism.

Goslinga, Gillian. 2012. "Spirited Encounters: Notes on the Politics and Poetics of Representing the Uncanny in Anthropology." *Anthropological Theory* 12 (4): 386–406.

Graeber, David. 2015. "Radical Alterity is Just another Way of Saying 'Reality': A Reply to Eduardo Viveiros de Castro." *Hau: Journal of Ethnographic Theory* 5 (2): 1–41.

Green, Nile. 2015. "The Global Occult: An Introduction." *History of Religions* 54 (4): 383–93.

Grewal, Zareena. 2013. *Islam Is a Foreign Country: American Muslims and the Global Crisis of Authority.* New York: New York University Press.

Grosz, Elizabeth. 2005. *Time Travels: Feminism, Nature, Power.* Durham, NC: Duke University Press.

Gunning, Tom. 1995. "Phantom Images and Modern Manifestations: Spirit Photography, Magic Theater, Trick Films, and Photography's Uncanny." In *Fugitive Images: From Photography to Video*, edited by Patrice Petro, 42–71. Bloomington: Indiana University Press.

Gutas, Dimitri. 2012. "The Empiricism of Avicenna." *Oriens* 40:391–436.

Hacking, Ian. 1983. *Representing and Intervening: Introductory Topics in the Philosophy of Natural Science.* Cambridge: Cambridge University Press.

———. 1985. "Styles of Scientific Thinking." In *Post-Analytic Philosophy*, edited by John Rajchman and Cornel West, 145–65. New York: Columbia University Press.

———. 2002. *Historical Ontology.* Cambridge: Harvard University Press.

———. 2006. *The Emergence of Probability: A Philosophical Study of Early Ideas about Probability, Induction and Statistical Inference.* 2nd ed. Cambridge: Cambridge University Press.

Hadi, 'Abdollah. 1972. "Khatereh-i az Ehzar-e Arvah." *Khaterat-e Vahid* 8:42–46.

Haddawy, Hussein, trans. 1990. *The Arabian Nights.* New York: W. W. Norton.

Haeri, Shahla. 2014. *Law of Desire: Temporary Marriage in Shi'i Iran.* Revised ed. Syracuse, NY: Syracuse University Press.

Hallaq, Wael. 2012. *The Impossible State: Islam, Politics, and Modernity's Moral Predicament.* New York: Columbia University Press.

Hamdy, Sherine. 2012. *Our Bodies Belong to God: Organ Transplants, Islam, and the Struggle for Human Dignity in Egypt.* Berkeley: University of California Press.

Hamidiyyeh, Behzad. 2005. "Iran va Roshd-e Din-nama-ha-ye Jadid." *Ketab-e Naqd* 35:187–96.

Hammer, Olav. 2001. *Claiming Knowledge: Strategies of Epistemology from Theosophy to the New Age.* Leiden: Brill.

Hanegraaf, Wouter J. 1996. *New Age Religion and Western Culture: Esotericism in the Mirror of Secular Thought.* Leiden: E. J. Brill.

Haq Panah, Reza. 2000. "Zabeteh-ye Tafsir-e Sahih va Bardasht-ha-ye Roshanfekraneh az Qor'an-e Karim." *Andisheh-ye Howzeh* 25:158–80.

Haque, Amber. 2004. "Psychology from Islamic Perspective: Contributions of Early Muslim Scholars and Challenges to Contemporary Muslim Psychologists." *Journal of Religion and Health* 43 (4): 357–77.

Hazard, Anna. 2014. "Placing the Saqqakhaneh Movement in Context." Unpublished manuscript.

Hedayat, Sadegh. 1967. "Jadugari dar Iran." Translated by Khanbaba Tabataba'i Na'ini. *Armaghan* 36 (7): 354–64.

Heelas, Paul. 1996. *The New Age Movement: The Celebration of the Self and the Sacralization of Modernity.* Oxford: Blackwell.

Henare, Amiria, Martin Holbraad, and Sari Wastell. 2007. "Introduction: Thinking Through Things." In *Thinking Through Things: Theorising Artefacts Ethnographically,* edited by Amiria Henare, Martin Holbraad, and Sari Wastell. London: Routledge.

Hess, David J. 1991. *Spirits and Scientists: Ideology, Spiritism, and Brazilian Culture.* University Park: Pennsylvania State University Press.

Hirschkind, Charles. 2006. *The Ethical Soundscape: Cassette Sermons and Islamic Counterpublics.* New York: Columbia University Press.

———. 2012. "Experiments in Devotion Online: The Youtube *Khuṭba.*" *International Journal of Middle East Studies* 44 (1): 5–21.

Hobsbawm, Eric. 1983. "Introduction: Inventing Traditions." In *The Invention of Tradition,* edited by Eric Hobsbawm and Terence Ranger, 1–14. Cambridge: Cambridge University Press.

Hoodfar, Homa, and Samad Assadpour. 2000. "The Politics of Population Policy in the Islamic Republic of Iran." *Studies in Family Planning* 31 (1): 19–34.

Horton, Robin. 1967a. "African Traditional Thought and Western Science, I." *Africa* 37:50–71.

———. 1967b. "African Traditional Thought and Western Science, II." *Africa* 37:155–87

———. 1968. "Neo-Tylorianism: Sound Sense or Sinister Prejudice?" *Man,* New Series 3 (4): 625–34.

Hoseynzadeh, Mohammad. 2006. "Havass-e Bateni az Manzar-e Ma'refat-shenasi." *Ma'refat-e Falsafi* 12:65–108.

Hoskins, Janet A. 2015. *The Divine Eye and the Diaspora: Vietnamese Syncretism Becomes Transpacific Caodaism.* Honolulu: University of Hawaii Press.

Hoyland, Robert. 2007. "The Islamic Background to Polemon's Treatise." In *Seeing the Face, Seeing the Soul: Polemon's Physiognomy from Classical Antiquity to Medieval Islam,* edited by Simon Swain, 227–80. Oxford: Oxford University Press.

Human Rights Watch. 2015. *World Report 2015: Saudi Arabia.* https://www.hrw.org /world-report/2015/country-chapters/saudi-arabia.

Hunsberger, Alice C. 2014. "Marvels." In *Encyclopaedia of the Qur'ān,* edited by Jane Dammen McAuliffe. Brill Online. http://referenceworks.brillonline.com/entries/ encyclopaedia-of-the-quran/marvels-EQSIM_00274.

Hussin, Iza R. 2016. *The Politics of Islamic Law: Local Elites, Colonial Authority, and the Making of the Muslim State.* Chicago: University of Chicago Press.

Ibn 'Abd al-Barr, Yusuf ibn 'Abd Allah. 1993. *Al-Istidhkar li-Madhahib Fuqaha' al-Amsar wa-ʿUlama al-Aqtar fi ma Tadammanahu al-Muwatta' min Maʿani al-Ra'y wa al-Athar.* Vol. 25. Damascus, Beirut: Dar Qutayba li-l-Tibaʿa wa-l-Nashr / Aleppo, Cairo: Dar al-Waʿy.

Ibn ʿArabi. 1997. *Divine Governance of the Human Kingdom.* Translated by Shaykh Tosun Bayrak al-Jerrahi al-Halveti. Louisville, KY: Fons Vitae.

Iranpur, Parvin. 2007. "Gheyb va Shahadat az Nazar-e ʿAllameh Tabatabai." *Bayyenat* 55:118–37.

Iranshahr, Hoseyn Kazemzadeh. 1974. "Qovveh-ye Fekr." In *Chahar Asar-e Arzandeh az Taʾlifat-e Iranshahr.* Tehran: Eqbal.

Izutsu, Toshihiko. 2002. *Ethico-Religious Concepts in the Qurʾān.* Montreal: McGill-Queen's University Press.

Jaʿfarian, Rasul. 2013. *Tarikh-e Khorafeh dar Tamaddon-e Eslami.* Khabar online weblog. http://www.khabaronline.ir/detail/327803/weblog/jafarian.

Jahanbakhsh, Forough. 2001. *Islam, Democracy, and Religious Modernism in Iran (1953–2000).* Leiden: Brill.

Jahanbegloo, Ramin, ed. 2004. *Iran: Between Tradition and Modernity.* Lanham, MD: Lexington Books.

Jansen, J.J.G. 2012. "Muhammad Farid Wadjdi." In *Encyclopaedia of Islam,* edited by P. Bearman et al. 2nd ed. Brill Online. http://referenceworks.brillonline.com/entries/encyclopaedia-of-islam-2/muhammad-farid-wadjdi-SIM_5395.

Janssens, Jules L. 2004. "ʿExperience' (tajriba) in Classical Arabic Philosophy (al-Farabi—Avicenna)." *Quaestio* 4:45–62.

Jardine, Nicholas. 2000. *The Scenes of Inquiry: On the Reality of Questions in the Sciences.* 2nd ed. Oxford: Oxford University Press.

Jawbari, Jamal al-Din al-. 2006. "Kitab al-Mukhtar fi Kashf al-Asrar." In *Al-Gawbari und sein Kasf al-Asrar: Ein Sittenbild des Gauners im Arabisch-Islamischen Mittelalter (7./13. Jahrhundert),* edited by Manuela Höglmeier. Islamic Studies, vol. 267. Berlin: Klaus Schwarz Verlag.

Jay, Martin. 2005. *Songs of Experience: Modern American and European Variations on a Universal Theme.* Berkeley: University of California Press.

Jentsch, Ernst. 1996. "On the Psychology of the Uncanny." Translated by Roy Sellars *Angelaki: A New Journal in Philosophy, Literature and the Social Sciences* 2 (1): 7–16.

Kaiser, David. 2011. *How the Hippies Saved Physics: Science, Counterculture, and the Quantum Revival.* New York: W. W. Norton.

Kalberg, Stephen. 1980. "Max Weber's Types of Rationality: Cornerstones for the Analysis of Rationalization Processes in History." *American Journal of Sociology* 85 (5): 1145–79.

Kapferer, Bruce. 2002. "Introduction: Outside All Reason: Magic, Sorcery and Epistemology in Anthropology." In *Beyond Rationalism: Rethinking Magic, Witchcraft and Sorcery.* Special issue of *Social Analysis: The International Journal of Social and Cultural Practice* 46 (3): 1–30.

Karabela, Mehmet Kadri. 2010. "The Development of Dialectic and Argumentation Theory in Post-Classical Islamic Intellectual History." PhD diss., Institute of Islamic Studies, McGill University.

Karimi-Hakkak, Ahmad. 1995. "From Translation to Appropriation: Poetic Cross-Breeding in Early Twentieth-Century Iran." *Comparative Literature* 47 (1): 53–78.

Kashani-Sabet, Firoozeh. 2000. "Hallmarks of Humanism: Hygiene and Love of Home-land in Qajar Iran." *American Historical Review* 105 (4): 1171–203.

Kashefi, Hoseyn Vaʿez. N.d. *Ketab-e Asrar-e Qasemi dar ʿElm-e Kimiya va Simiya va Rimiya va Limiya va Himiya.* Lithograph edition of the Mohammad Hasan ʿAlami Press.

Kashi, Fezzeh. 2009. "Khod dar Maʿnaviyyat-ha-ye Jadid." MA thesis, Faculty of Social Science, University of Tehran.

Kasravi, Ahmad. 1943. *Pendar-ha.* Tehran: Peyman.

———. 2011. *Shiʿi-gari.* Los Angeles: Ketab Corp.

Keddie, Nikki R. 1968. *An Islamic Response to Imperialism.* Berkeley: University of California Press.

Kendall, Laurel. 1996. "Korean Shamans and the Spirits of Capitalism." *American Anthropologist* 83 (3): 512–27.

Kennedy-Day, Kiki. 2003. *Books of Definition in Islamic Philosophy: The Limits of Words.* London: Routledge Curzon.

Keshavarzian, Arang. 2007. *Bazaar and State in Iran: The Politics of the Tehran Marketplace.* Cambridge: Cambridge University Press.

Keshavarz, Reza. 2004. "Tajassom-e Aʿmal va Tabyin-e ʿAqlani-ye an dar Hekmat-e Motaʿaliyyeh." *Elahiyyat va Hoquq* 12:103–24.

Keyes, Charles F. 2002. "Weber and Anthropology." *Annual Review of Anthropology* 31:233–255.

Keyhan. 2010. "Tahlil-e Naqsh-e Biganegan dar Fetneh-ye 88 az su-ye Rahbar-e Moʿazzam-e Enqelab." *Keyhan.* http://www.kayhannews.ir/890309/8.htm.

Keyhan-e Farhangi. 2004. "Maqam-e ʿEshq va ʿErfan." *Keyhan-e Farhangi* 203:5–27.

Khan, Naveeda. 2006. "Of Children and Jinn: An Inquiry into an Unexpected Friendship during Uncertain Times." *Cultural Anthropology* 21 (2): 234–64.

———. 2012. *Muslim Becoming: Aspiration and Skepticism in Pakistan.* Durham, NC: Duke University Press.

Khomeini, Ruhollah. N.d. *Kashf-e Asrar.* Tehran: S.n.

Khorramshahi, Bahaʾoddin. 1995. "Baztab-e Farhang-e Zamaneh dar Qorʾan-e Karim." *Bayyenat* 5:90–97.

Khosravi, Shahram. 2008. *Young and Defiant in Tehran.* Philadelphia: University of Pennsylvania Press.

Khwansari, Jamal al-Din. 1970. "ʿAqaʾed al-Nesa va Merʾat al-Bolaha": Do Resaleh-ye Enteqadi dar Farhang-e Tudeh. Edited by Mahmud Katiraʾi. Tehran: Tahuri.

Kia, Chad. 2014. "The Scum of Tabriz: Ahmad Kasravi and the Impulse to Reform Islam." *British Journal of Middle Eastern Studies* 41 (4): 498–516.

Kia, Mana. 2014. "Adab as Ethics of Literary Form and Social Conduct: Reading the Gulistān in Late Mughal India." In *No Tapping around Philology: A Festschrift in Honor of Wheeler McIntosh Thackston Jr.'s 70th Birthday*, edited by Alireza Korangy and Daniel J. Sheffield, 281–308. Wiesbaden: Harrassowitz Verlag.

———. 2015a. "Moral Refinement and Manhood in Persian." In *Civilizing Emotions: Concepts in Asia and Europe, 1870–1920*, edited by Margrit Pernau et al., 146–65. Oxford: Oxford University Press.

———. 2015b. "Defining a Modern Persianate Self: The Indian Friend as Ethical Interlocutor in the late 19th-Century." Unpublished manuscript.

Kia, Mehrdad. 1998. "Women, Islam and Modernity in Akhundzade's Plays and Unpublished Writings." *Middle Eastern Studies* 34 (3): 1–33.

Kiyanfar, Jamshid. 1999. "Dastur al-'Amal-e Ehtesabiyyeh va Tanzifiyyeh-ye Kamran Mirza, Na'eb al-Saltaneh beh Mohammad Hasan Khan Sani' al-Dowleh. *Vaqf-e Miras-e Javidan* 28:87–92.

Kiyani, Mansur. 2014. *'Aref-sazi va Ma'refat-suzi: Naqdi bar Edde'a-ha-ye Naql-shodeh az Marhum Rajab 'Ali Khayyat.* Qom: Hasaneyn.

Klassen, Pamela E. 2011. *Spirits of Protestantism: Medicine, Healing, and Liberal Christianity.* Berkeley: University of California Press.

Knysh, Alexander. 1992. "'Irfan' Revisited: Khomeini and the Legacy of Islamic Mystical Philosophy." *Middle East Journal* 46 (4): 631–53.

Koyagi, Mikiya. 2009. "Modern Education in Iran during the Qajar and Pahlavi Periods." *History Compass* 7 (1): 107–18.

Kripal, Jeffrey J. 2011a. *Authors of the Impossible: The Paranormal and the Sacred.* Chicago: University of Chicago Press.

———. 2011b. *Mutants and Mystics: Science Fiction, Superhero Comics, and the Paranormal.* Chicago: University of Chicago Press.

Lachapelle, Sofie. 2011. *Investigating the Supernatural: From Spiritism and Occultism to Psychical Research and Metapsychics in France, 1853–1931.* Baltimore: Johns Hopkins University Press.

Lambek, Michael. 1993. *Knowledge and Practice in Mayotte: Local Discourses of Islam, Sorcery and Spirit Possession.* Toronto: University of Toronto Press.

Larkin, Brian. 2008. "Ahmed Deedat and the Form of Islamic Evangelism." *Social Text* 26, 3 (96): 101–21.

Lévi-Strauss, Claude. 1963. "The Sorcerer and His Magic." In *Structural Anthropology*, translated by Claire Jacobson and Brooke Grundfest Schoeph, 167–85. New York: Basic Books.

———. 1966. *The Savage Mind.* Chicago: University of Chicago Press.

Lewisohn, Leonard. 1999. "An Introduction to the History of Modern Persian Sufism, Part II: A Socio-Cultural Profile of Sufism, from the Dhahabi Revival to the Present Day." *Bulletin of the School of Oriental and African Studies, University of London* 62 (1): 36–59.

Li, Darryl. 2012. "Taking the Place of Martyrs: Afghans and Arabs under the Banner of Islam." *Arab Studies Journal* 20 (1): 12–39.

Lofland, John, and Rodney Stark. 1965. "Becoming a World-Saver: A Theory of Conversion to a Deviant Perspective." *American Sociological Review* 30 (6): 862–75.

Lory, Pierre. 2003. "Kashifi's Asrar-i Qasimi and Timurid Magic." *Iranian Studies* 36 (4): 531–41.

Lotfalian, Mazyar. 2004a. *Islam, Technoscientific Identities, and the Culture of Curiosity.* Lanham, MD: University Press of America.

———. 2004b. "Keywords in Islamic Critiques of Technoscience: Iranian Postrevolutionary Interpretations." In *Iran: Between Tradition and Modernity*, edited by Ramin Jahanbegloo, 15–24. Lanham, MD: Lexington Books.

Luhrmann, Tanya M. 1989. *Persuasions of the Witch's Craft: Ritual Magic and Witchcraft in Present-Day England.* Cambridge: Harvard University Press.

———. 2005. "The Art of Hearing God: Absorption, Dissociation and Contemporary American Spirituality." *Spiritus: A Journal of Christian Spirituality* 5 (2): 133–57.

MacDonald, Duncan B. 1924. "The Earlier History of the Arabian Nights." *Journal of the Royal Asiatic Society of Great Britain and Ireland* 3:353–97.

MacDonald, Duncan B., and Louis Gardet. 2012. "Al-Ghayb." In *The Encyclopaedia of Islam*, edited by P. Bearman et al. 2nd ed. Brill Online. http://referenceworks .brillonline.com/entries/encyclopaedia-of-islam-2/al-ghayb-COM_0231.

MacDonald, Duncan B., H. Massé, P. N. Boratav, K. A. Nizami, and P. Voorhoeve. 2012. "Djinn." In *The Encyclopaedia of Islam*, edited by P. Bearman et al. 2nd ed. Brill Online. http://referenceworks.brillonline.com/entries/encyclopaedia-of-islam-2/djinn -COM_0191.

MacIntyre, Alasdair. 1988. *Whose Justice? Which Rationality?* Notre Dame: University of Notre Dame Press.

———. 2012. *After Virtue: A Study in Moral Theory.* 3rd ed. Notre Dame: University of Notre Dame Press.

Mahdavi, Pardis. 2009. *Passionate Uprisings: Iran's Sexual Revolution.* Stanford, CA: Stanford University Press.

Mahmood, Saba. 2005. *Politics of Piety: The Islamic Revival and the Feminist Subject.* Princeton: Princeton University Press.

Makarem Shirazi, Naser. 1969a. "Ertebat ba Arvah: Sargarmi ya Bimari-ye 'Miz-e Gerd.'" *Dars-ha-yi az Maktab-e Eslam* 10 (7): 68–71.

———. 1969b. "Dar Jalaseh-ye Ertebat ba Arvah Cheh Didam." *Dars-ha-yi az Maktab-e Eslam* 10 (8): 7–10.

———. 1969c. "Aya Ertebat ba Arvah Emkan-pazir Ast? Moshahedat-e Man dar Jalaseh-ye Ertebat ba Arvah." *Dars-ha-yi az Maktab-e Eslam* 10 (9): 17–19, 24.

———. 1969d. "Aya Ertebat ba Arvah Emkan Darad? Amma 'Aqideh-ye Ma darbareh-ye Ertebat ba Arvah." *Dars-ha-yi az Maktab-e Eslam* 10 (11): 9–11.

———. 1970a. "'Elmi beh Nam-e Espiritism." *Dars-ha-yi az Maktab-e Eslam* 11 (1): 10–12.

———. 1970b. "Ertebat ba Arvah: Natijeh-ye Nahayi-e Bahs-e Ertebat ba Arvah." *Dars-ha-yi az Maktab-e Eslam* 11 (2): 58–60.

———. 1970c. "Baz ham darbareh-ye Tanasokh va 'Owd-e Arvah." *Dars-ha-yi az Maktab-e Eslam* 11 (10): 16, 67–72.

Malekiyan, Mostafa. 2002a. "Ma'naviyyat, Gowhar-e Adyan 1." In *Sonnat va Sekularism: Goftar-ha-yi az 'Abdol-Karim Sorush, Mohammad Mojtahed Shabestari, Mostafa Malekiyan, Mohsen Kadivar,* 267–306. Tehran: Mo'asseseh-ye Farhangi-ye Serat.

———. 2002b. "Ma'naviyyat, Gowhar-e Adyan 2." In *Sonnat va Sekularism: Goftar-ha-yi az 'Abdol-Karim Sorush, Mohammad Mojtahed Shabestari, Mostafa Malekiyan, Mohsen Kadivar,* 307–43. Tehran: Mo'asseseh-ye Farhangi-ye Serat.

———. 2002c. "Porsesh-ha-yi Piramun-e Ma'naviyyat." In *Sonnat va Sekularism: Goftar-ha-yi az 'Abdol-Karim Sorush, Mohammad Mojtahed Shabestari, Mostafa Malekiyan, Mohsen Kadivar,* 345–404. Tehran: Mo'asseseh-ye Farhangi-ye Serat.

Marcus, George E., ed. 1993. *Technoscientific Imaginaries: Conversations, Profiles, and Memoirs.* Chicago: University of Chicago Press.

Marsden, Magnus. 2005. *Living Islam: Muslim Religious Experience in Pakistan's North-West Frontier.* Cambridge: Cambridge University Press.

Martin, Vanessa. 1993. "Religion and State in Khumaini's 'Kashf al-asrār.'" *Bulletin of the School of Oriental and African Studies, University of London* 56 (1): 34–45.

Martin, Vanessa. 2013. *Iran between Islamic Nationalism and Secularism: The Constitutional Revolution of 1906.* New York: I. B. Tauris.

Masud, Muhammad Khalid. 2015. "Adab al-Muftī." In *Encyclopaedia of Islam,* edited by Kate Fleet et al. 3rd ed. Brill Online. http://referenceworks.brillonline.com/entries/encyclopaedia-of-islam-3/adab-al-mufti-COM_26301.

Mazaheri, Mohsen Hesam. 2015. *Shokhm dar Mazraʿeh: Naqd-ha-yi bar Ravayat-e Rasmi-ye Jang.* Isfahan: Arma.

———. 2016. *Ostureh-ye Hemmat: Neshanehshenasi-ye Shahid Hemmat.* Isfahan: Arma.

Mazhari, Mohammad. 1977. "Anjoman-e Maʿrefat al-Ruh-e Tajrobati-ye Iran." *Vahid* 210:41–44.

McGinnis, John. 2003. "Scientific Methodologies in Medieval Islam." *Journal of the History of Philosophy* 41:317–27.

McIntosh, Janet. 2004. "Maxwell's Demons: Disenchantment in the Field." *Anthropology and Humanism* 29 (1): 63–77.

Mehr News Agency. 2011. "Morajeʿeh-ye 10 Darsad-e Irani-ha beh Doʿanevis va Rammal/Shoyuʿ-e Ekhtelalat-e Ravanpezeshki." http://goo.gl/bYvh9E.

Melvin-Koushki, Matthew. 2016. "Astrology, Lettrism, Geomancy: The Occult-Scientific Methods of Post-Mongol Islamicate Imperialism." *Medieval History Journal* 19 (1): 142–50.

———. 2017. "Powers of One: The Mathematicalization of the Occult Sciences in the High Persianate Tradition." *Intellectual History of the Islamicate World* 5:127–99.

Meqdadi Esfahani, ʿAli. 2001. *Neshan az Bineshan-ha.* Vol. 1. Tehran: Jomhuri.

Messick, Brinkley M. 1993. *The Calligraphic State: Textual Domination and History in a Muslim Society.* Berkeley: University of California Press.

Meyer, Birgit. 2015. *Sensational Movies: Video, Vision, and Christianity in Ghana.* Berkeley: University of California Press.

Meyer, Birgit, and Peter Pels, eds. 2003. *Magic and Modernity: Interfaces of Revelation and Concealment.* Stanford, CA: Stanford University Press.

Miller, Sean. 2013. *Strung Together: The Cultural Currency of String Theory as a Scientific Imaginary.* Ann Arbor: University of Michigan Press.

Millie, Julian. 2008. "Khâriq Ul-ʿÂdah Anecdotes and the Representation of Karâmât: Written and Spoken Hagiography in Islam." *History of Religions* 48 (1): 43–65.

———. 2009. *Splashed by the Saint: Ritual Reading and Islamic Sanctity in West Java.* Leiden: KITLV Press.

Mireshghi, Elham. 2016. "Kidneys on Sale? An Ethnography of Policy, Exchange, and Uncertainty in Iran." PhD diss., Department of Anthropology, University of California, Irvine.

Mittermaier, Amira. 2011. *Dreams that Matter: Egyptian Landscapes of the Imagination.* Berkeley: University of California Press.

Moallem, Minoo. 2005. *Between Warrior Brother and Veiled Sister: Islamic Fundamentalism and the Politics of Patriarchy in Iran.* Berkeley: University of California Press.

Modarresi Chahardehi, Nur al-Din. 2008. *Espiritism: ʿElm-e Ertebat ba Arvah.* Tehran: Afarinesh.

———. 2010. *Seyri dar Tasavvof: Dar Sharh-e Hal-e Mashayekh va Aqtab.* Tehran: Entesharat-e Eshraqi.

Moerman, Daniel E. 2002. *Meaning, Medicine, and the "Placebo Effect."* Cambridge: Cambridge University Press.

Mojahedi, Mohammad ʿAli. 2003. *Dar Mahzar-e Lahutiyan*. Vol. 1. Tehran: Lahut.

———. 2006. *Dar Mahzar-e Lahutiyan*. Vol. 2. Tehran: Lahut.

Moll, Yasmin. 2010. "Islamic Televangelism: Religion, Media and Visuality in Contemporary Egypt." *Arab Media and Society* 10. http://www.arabmediasociety.com/peer _reviewed/index.php?article=732.

Monroe, John Warne. 2008. *Laboratories of Faith: Mesmerism, Spiritism, and Occultism in Modern France*. Ithaca: Cornell University Press.

Moore, Henrietta A., and Todd Sanders, eds. 2001. *Magical Interpretations, Material Realities: Modernity, Witchcraft and the Occult in Post-Colonial Africa*. London: Routledge.

Morris, Rosalind C. 2002. "A Room with a Voice: Mediation and Mediumship in Thailand's Information Age." In *Media Worlds: Anthropology on New Terrain*, edited by Faye D. Ginsburg, Lila Abu Lughod, and Brian Larkin, 383–98. Berkeley: University of California Press.

Morrisson, Mark S. 2007. *Modern Alchemy: Occultism and the Emergence of Atomic Theory*. New York: Oxford University Press.

Mottahedeh, Roy. 1985. *The Mantle of the Prophet: Religion and Politics in Iran*. New York: Simon and Schuster.

———. 1997. " ʿAjāʾib in *The Thousand and One Nights*." In *The Thousand and One Nights in Arabic Literature and Society*, edited by Richard G. Hovannisian and Georges S. Sabagh, 29–39. Cambridge: Cambridge University Press.

Mottahedeh, Roy, and Kristen Stilt. 2003. "Public and Private as Viewed through the Work of the ʿMuhtasib.ʾ " *Social Research* 70 (3): 735–48.

Moumtaz, Nada. 2012. "Modernizing Charity, Remaking Islamic Law." PhD diss., Graduate Center, City University of New York.

Najmabadi, Afsaneh. 1993. "Veiled Discourse-Unveiled Bodies." *Feminist Studies* 19 (3): 487–518.

———. 2005. *Women with Mustaches and Men without Beards: Gender and Sexual Anxieties of Iranian Modernity*. Berkeley: University of California Press.

———. 2011. "Verdicts of Science, Rulings of Faith: Transgender/Sexuality in Contemporary Iran." *Social Research* 78 (2): 533–56.

———. 2014. *Professing Selves: Transsexuality and Same-Sex Desire in Contemporary Iran*. Durham, NC: Duke University Press.

Nakissa, Aria. 2014. "An Epistemic Shift in Islamic Law: Educational Reform at al-Azhar and Dār al-ʿUlūm. *Islamic Law and Society* 21 (3): 209–51.

Naseri Rad, ʿAli. 2011. *Afsun-e Halqeh: Naqd va Barresi-ye ʿErfan-e Halqeh*. Tehran: Sayan.

Nasr, Seyyed Hossein. 1976. *Islamic Science: An Illustrated Study*. World of Islam Festival.

———. 2006. *Islamic Philosophy from Its Origin to the Present: Philosophy in the Land of Prophecy*. Albany: State University of New York Press.

Nelson, Diane M. 2009. *Reckoning: The Ends of War in Guatemala*. Durham, NC: Duke University Press.

Nusseibeh, Sari. 2017. *The Story of Reason in Islam*. Stanford, CA: Stanford University Press.

O'Connor, Kathleen M. 2016. "Popular and Talismanic Uses of the Qurʾan." In *Encyclopaedia of the Qurʾān*, edited by Jane Dammen McAuliffe. Brill Online. http://

referenceworks.brillonline.com/entries/encyclopaedia-of-the-quran/popular-and
-talismanic-uses-of-the-quran-EQCOM_00152.

Olszewska, Zuzanna. 2013. "Classy Kids and Down-at-Heel Intellectuals: Status Aspiration and Blind Spots in the Contemporary Ethnography of Iran." *Iranian Studies* 46
(6): 841–62.

Owen, Alex. 1990. *The Darkened Room: Women, Power, and Spiritualism in Late Victorian
England.* Philadelphia: University of Pennsylvania Press.

———. 2004. *The Place of Enchantment: British Occultism and the Culture of the Modern.*
Chicago: University of Chicago Press.

Pak-Shiraz, Nacim. 2011. *Shiʻi Islam in Iranian Cinema: Religion and Spirituality in Film.*
New York: I. B. Tauris.

———. 2015. "Shiʻism in Iranian Cinema." In *The Shiʻi World: Pathways in Tradition and
Modernity,* edited by Farhad Daftary, Amyn B. Sajoo, and Shainool Jiwa, 300–25.
New York: I. B. Tauris.

Palmié, Stephan. 2002. *Wizards and Scientists: Explorations in Afro-Cuban Modernity
and Tradition.* Durham, NC: Duke University Press.

Pandolfo, Stefania. 1997. *Impasse of the Angels: Scenes from a Moroccan Space of Memory.* Chicago: University of Chicago Press.

Parent, André. 2002. "Jules Bernard Luys (1828–1897)." *Journal of Neurology* 249:1480–
81.

Parent, Martin, and André Parent. 2011. "Jules Bernard Luys in Charcot's Penumbra."
In *Following Charcot: A Forgotten History of Neurology and Psychiatry,* edited by
Julien Bogousslavsky, 125–36. Basel, NY: Karger.

Parvin Gonabadi, Mohammad. 1956. "Roshanbini—Kashf va Karamat-e Qadim."
Yaghma 94:74–76.

Parvinzad, Mehdi. 2004. "Hadis-e Kar-amadi va Danesh-gostari." *Keyhan-e Farhangi*
212:5–21.

Pellat, Charles, A. Bausani, P. N. Boratav, Aziz Ahmad, and R. O. Winstedt. 2012. "Ḥi-
kāya." In *Encyclopaedia of Islam,* edited by P. Bearman et al. 2nd ed. http://reference
works.brillonline.com/entries/encyclopaedia-of-islam-2/hikaya-COM_0285.

Perho, Irmeli. 1995. *The Prophet's Medicine: A Creation of the Muslim Traditionalist
Scholars. Studia Orientalia* 74. Helsinki: Finnish Oriental Society.

Pigg, Stacy Leigh. 1996. "The Credible and the Credulous: The Question of 'Villagers'
Beliefs' in Nepal." *Cultural Anthropology* 11 (2): 160–201.

Pormann, Peter E. 2005. "The Physician and the Other: Images of the Charlatan in
Medieval Islam." *Bulletin of the History of Medicine* 79 (2): 189–227.

Pouillon, Jean. 1982. "Remarks on the Verb 'to Believe.'" In *Between Belief and Transgression: Structuralist Essays in Religion, History, and Myth,* edited by Michel Izard
and Pierre Smith, translated by John Leavitt, 1–8. Chicago: University of Chicago
Press.

Qazi, Sayyed Mohammad Hasan. 2013. *Ayat al-Haq.* Translated by Sayyed Mohammad
ʻAli Qaziniya. Vol. 1. Tehran: Hekmat.

Rabbani Khorasgani, ʻAli, and Vahid Qasemi. 2002. "Negaresh bar Tahlil-e Asib-e Din-
gorizi dar Jameʻeh." *Jameʻeh-shenasi-ye Iran* 15:148–65.

Ragab, Ahmed. 2009. "The Prophets of Medicine and the Medicine of the Prophet:
Debates on Medical Theory and Practice in the Medieval Middle East." Paper pre-

sented at Harvard University, Center for Middle Eastern Studies and Harvard Society of Arab Students, Cambridge, MA. https://dash.harvard.edu/handle/1/4726204.

Rahmaniyan, Daryush, and Zahra Hatami. 2012. "Sehr va Jadu, Telesm va Ta'viz va Donya-ye Zanan dar 'Asr-e Qajar." *Jostar-ha-ye Tarikhi, Pazhuheshgah-e 'Olum-e Ensani va Motale'at-e Farhangi* 3 (2): 27–44.

Rahnema, Ali. 2011. *Superstition as Ideology in Iranian Politics: From Majlesi to Ahmadinejad.* New York: Cambridge University Press.

———. 2014. *An Islamic Utopian: A Political Biography of Ali Shariati.* New edition. New York: I. B. Tauris.

Ramezan Nargesi, Reza. 2000. "Sehr va Jadu az Didgah-e 'Elm va Din." *Ma'refat* 34:65–71.

Renard, John. 2008. *Friends of God: Islamic Images of Piety, Commitment, and Servanthood.* Berkeley: University of California Press.

Reyshahri, Mohammad Mohammadi. 2004. *Kimiya-ye Mohabbat.* Qom: Dar al-Hadis.

Richard, Yann. 1988. "Shari'at Sangalaji: A Reformist Theologian of the Rida Shah Period." Translated by Kathryn Arjomand. In *Authority and Political Culture in Shi'ism,* edited by Said Amir Arjomand, 159–77. Albany: State University of New York Press.

Ridgeon, Lloyd. 2006. *Sufi Castigator: Ahmad Kasravi and the Iranian Mystical Tradition.* London: Routledge.

———. 2014. "Hidden Khomeini: Mysticism and Poetry." In *A Critical Introduction to Khomeini,* edited by Arshin Adib-Moghaddam, 193–210. Cambridge: Cambridge University Press.

Ringer, Monica. 2001. *Education, Religion, and the Discourse of Cultural Reform in Qajar Iran.* Costa Mesa, CA: Mazda.

Rizvi, Sajjad. 2015. "The Philosopher-Mystic and the *marja'iya:* The Case of 'Allāma Ṭabāṭabā'ī [d. 1981] Contesting Authority in the *Ḥawza.*" Paper presented at the Shi'i Studies Workshop, Chicago, April 3–4, 2015.

Roth, Guenther. 2006. "Rationalization in Max Weber's Developmental History." In *Max Weber, Rationality and Modernity,* edited by Sam Whimster and Scott Lash, 75–91. London: Routledge.

Rubenstein, Mary-Jane. 2008. *Strange Wonder: The Closure of Metaphysics and the Opening of Awe.* New York: Columbia University Press.

Rudnyckyj, Daromir. 2010. *Spiritual Economies: Islam, Globalization, and the Afterlife of Development.* Ithaca: Cornell University Press.

Sadeghi-Boroujerdi, Eskandar. 2014. "Mostafa Malekian: Spirituality, Siyasat-Zadegi and (A)political Self-Improvement." *Digest of Middle East Studies* 23 (2): 279–311.

———. 2017. *Political Theology in Post-Revolutionary Iran: Disenchantment, Reform and the Death of Utopia.* London: Routledge.

Sadri, Mahmoud. 2001. "Sacral Defense of Secularism: The Political Theologies of Soroush, Shabestari, and Kadivar." *International Journal of Politics, Culture, and Society* 15 (2): 257–70.

Safi, Omid. 2000. "Bargaining with *Baraka:* Persian Sufism, 'Mysticism,' and Pre-Modern Politics." *Muslim World* 90 (3–4): 259–88.

Saliba, George. 1992. "The Role of the Astrologer in Medieval Islamic Society." *Bulletin d'Études Orientales* 44:45–67.

Salomon, Noah. 2013. "Evidence, Secrets, Truth: Debating Islamic Knowledge in Contemporary Sudan." *Journal of the American Academy of Religion* 81 (3): 820–51.

———. 2016. *For Love of the Prophet: An Ethnography of Sudan's Islamic State.* Princeton: Princeton University Press.

Saqafi Eʿzaz, Hoseyn. 1972. "Towzihat dar Khosus-e Khatereh-ye Aqa-ye ʿEyn Hadi va Mabhas-e Ruh-shenasi va Ertebat ba Arvah." *Khaterat-e Vahid* 9–10:99–105.

Saqafi, Khalil. 1891–92. *Tarbiyat-nameh.* Tehran.

———. 1907. *Kelid-e Zendegi.* Tehran: Matbaʿeh-ye Parsiyan.

———. 1929. *Haftad va Yek Maqaleh-ye Maʿrefat al-Ruh.* Tehran: Jameʿeh-ye Maʿaref-e Iran.

———. 1935. *Sad va Panjah Maqaleh Yadegar-e ʿAsr-e Jadid.* Tehran: Majlis.

———. 1943. *Maqalat-e Gunagun: Maqalat-e Tarikhi, Siyasi, Adabi.* Tehran.

Saqafi, Khalil, and ʿAli-Reza Bahrami. 1936. *Kelid-e Shenasaʾi dar ʿAlam-e Gheyr-e Marʾi.* Tehran: Majlis.

Savage-Smith, Emilie. 2004. "Introduction." In *Magic and Divination in Early Islam,* edited by Emilie Savage-Smith, xiii–li. Burlington, VT: Ashgate.

Savage-Smith, Emilie, and Marion B. Smith. 1980. *Islamic Geomancy and a Thirteenth-Century Divinatory Device.* Malibu, CA: Undena.

Savage-Smith, Emilie, F. Klein-Franke, and Ming Zhu. 2012. "Ṭibb." In *Encyclopaedia of Islam,* edited by P. Bearman et al. 2nd ed. Brill Online. http://referenceworks .brillonline.com/entries/encyclopaedia-of-islam-2/tibb-COM_1216.

Schaeffer, Simon. 1994. "Self-Evidence." In *Questions of Evidence: Proof, Practice, and Persuasion across the Disciplines,* edited by James Chandler, Arnold I. Davidson, and Harry Harootunian, 56–91. Chicago: University of Chicago Press.

Schayegh, Cyrus. 2009. *Who Is Knowledgeable Is Strong: Science, Class, and the Formation of Modern Iranian Society, 1900–1950.* Berkeley: University of California Press.

Schielke, Samuli. 2009. "Being Good in Ramadan: Ambivalence, Fragmentation, and the Moral Self in the Lives of Young Egyptians." *Journal of the Royal Anthropological Institute* 15 (S1): S24–40.

Schimmel, Annemarie. 1975. *Mystical Dimensions of Islam.* Chapel Hill: University of North Carolina Press.

———. 1987. "Secrecy in Sufism." In *Secrecy in Religions,* edited by Kees W. Bolle, 81–102. Leiden: Brill.

Sefidabiyan, Hamid. 2001. *Laleh-i az Malakut.* Qom: Kamal al-Molk.

Seligman, Rebecca, and Laurence J. Kirmayer. 2008. "Dissociative Experience and Cultural Neuroscience: Narrative, Metaphor and Mechanism." *Culture, Medicine, and Psychiatry* 32 (1): 31–64.

Seyed-Gohrab, Asghar. 2011. "Martyrdom as Piety: Mysticism and National Identity in Iran-Iraq War Poetry." *Der Islam* 87 (1–2): 248–73.

Shah Rezai, Ensiyeh, and Shahla Azari. 1998. *Gozaresh-ha-ye Nazmiyyeh az Mahallat-e Tehran.* Vol. 1. Tehran: Sazman-e Asnad-e Melli-ye Iran.

Shapin, Steven. 1994. *A Social History of Truth: Civility and Science in Seventeenth-Century England.* Chicago: University of Chicago Press.

Shapin, Steven, and Simon Schaeffer. 1989. *Leviathan and the Air-Pump: Hobbes, Boyle, and the Experimental Life.* Princeton: Princeton University Press.

Sharifian, Farzad. 2008. "Conceptualizations of *Del* 'Heart-Stomach' in Persian." In *Culture, Body, and Language: Conceptualizations of Internal Body Organs across Cul-*

tures and Languages, edited by Farzad Sharifian, René Dirven, Ning Yu, and Susanne Niemeier, 247–65. Berlin: Mouton de Gruyter.

Sharp, Lesley A. 2013. *The Transplant Imaginary: Mechanical Hearts, Animal Parts, and Moral Thinking in Highly Experimental Science*. Berkeley: University of California Press.

Sharp, Lynn L. 2006. *Secular Spirituality: Reincarnation and Spiritism in Nineteenth-Century France*. Lanham, MD: Lexington Books.

Shojaʿi Zand, ʿAlireza, Sara Shariʿati Mazinani, and Ramin Habibzadeh Khotbehsara. 2006. "Barresi-ye Vazʿiyyat-e Dindari dar beyn-e Daneshjuyan." *Faslnameh-ye Motaleʿat-e Melli* 7 (2): 55–80.

Shokr, ʿAbdol ʿAli. 2007. "Tajassom-e Aʿmal dar Hekmat-e Moteʿaliyyeh." *Kherad-nameh-ye Sadra* 49:74–81.

Siegel, James T. 2006. *Naming the Witch*. Stanford, CA: Stanford University Press.

Simon, Gregory. 2009. "The Soul Freed of Cares? Islamic Prayer, Subjectivity, and the Contradictions of Moral Selfhood in Minangkabau, Indonesia." *American Anthropologist* 36 (2): 258–75.

Sindawi, Khalid. 2012. " 'Tell your Cousin to Place a Ring on his Right Hand and Set It with a Carnelian': Notes on Wearing the Ring on the Right Hand among Shīʿites." *Journal of Semitic Studies* 57 (2): 295–320.

Smith, James H. 2008. *Bewitching Development: Witchcraft and the Reinvention of Development in Neoliberal Kenya*. Chicago: University of Chicago Press.

Spadola, Emilio. 2009. "Writing Cures: Religious and Communicative Authority in Late Modern Morocco." *Journal of North African Studies* 14 (2): 155–68.

———. 2013. *The Calls of Islam: Sufis, Islamists, and Mass Mediation in Urban Morocco*. Bloomington: Indiana University Press.

Spalding, Baird T. 1935. *Life and Teaching of the Masters of the Far East*. Vol. 3. Santa Monica, CA: DeVorss.

Sperber, Dan. 1982. "Apparently Irrational Beliefs." In *Rationality and Relativism*, edited by Martin Hollis and Steven Lukes, 149–80. Oxford: Blackwell.

Stanley, Matthew. 2007. *Practical Mystic: Religion, Science, and A. S. Eddington*. Chicago: University of Chicago Press.

Starrett, Gregory. 1998. *Putting Islam to Work: Education, Politics, and Religious Transformation in Egypt*. Berkeley: University of California Press.

Steedly, Mary Margaret. 2013. "Transparency and Apparition: Media Ghosts of Post–New Order Indonesia." In *Images that Move*, edited by Patricia Spyer and Mary Margaret Steedly, 257–94. Santa Fe: SAR Press.

Stephens, Walter. 2003. *Demon Lovers: Witchcraft, Sex, and the Crisis of Belief*. Chicago: University of Chicago Press.

Stewart, Charles. 1989. "Hegemony or Rationality? The Position of the Supernatural in Modern Greece." *Journal of Modern Greek Studies* 7 (1): 77–104.

Stilt, Kristen. 2006. "Recognizing the Individual: The Muhtasibs of Early Mamluk Cairo and Fustat." *Harvard Middle Eastern and Islamic Review* 7:63–84.

Stoller, Paul. 1998. "Rationality." In *Key Terms for Religious Studies*, edited by Mark C. Taylor, 239–55. Chicago: University of Chicago Press.

Stolz, Daniel A. 2012. " 'By Virtue of Your Knowledge': Scientific Materialism and the *Fatwās* of Rashīd Riḍā." *Bulletin of SOAS* 75 (2): 223–47.

———. 2015. "Positioning the Watch Hand: ʿUlamaʾ and the Practice of Mechanical

Timekeeping in Cairo, 1737–1874." *International Journal of Middle East Studies* 47 (3): 489–510.

Styers, Randall. 2004. *Making Magic: Religion, Magic, and Science in the Modern World.* Oxford: Oxford University Press.

Swain, Simon. 2007. "Polemon's *Physiognomy.*" In *Seeing the Face, Seeing the Soul: Polemon's Physiognomy from Classical Antiquity to Medieval Islam,* edited by Simon Swain, 125–201. Oxford: Oxford University Press.

Tabandeh Gonabadi, Soltan Hoseyn. 2006. "Resaleh-ye Khʷab-e Meghnatisi." In *Tanbih al-Naʾemin, beh Payvast-e Khʷab-e Meghnatisi,* by Soltan Mohammad Bidokhti Gonabadi, 77–144. Tehran: Haqiqat.

Tabari, Ehsan. 1969. *Barresi-ha-yi darbareh-ye Barkhi az Jahanbini-ha va Jonbesh-ha-ye Ejtemaʿi dar Iran.* Strassfurt, Germany: Hezb-e Tudeh-ye Iran.

Tabatabai, Mohammad Hoseyn. 1953. *Al-Mizan fi Tafsir al-Qurʾan.* Vol. 1. Tehran: Dar al-Kutub al-Islamiyya.

Tahanawi, Muhammad Aʿla ibn ʿAli. 1966. *Mawsuʿa Istilahat al-ʿUlum al-Islamiyya, al-Maʿruf bi-Kishaf Istilahat al-Funun.* Vol. 2. Beirut: Khayyat.

Taheri, Mohammad ʿAli. 2007. *Ensan az Manzari Digar.* Tehran: Pezhvak-e Andisheh.

———. 2010. "Moqaddameh." *Danesh-e Pezeshki, Vizheh-nameh-ye Takhassosi-ye Faradarmani* 4 (1): 5–9.

———. 2011a. "Moqaddameh." *Danesh-e Pezeshki, Vizheh-nameh-ye Takhassosi-ye Saymentolozhy* 4 (1): 4–10.

———. 2011b. *Mowjudat-e Gheyr-e Organik.* Yerevan: Grigor Tatʾevatsi.

Tambiah, Stanley J. 1990. *Magic, Science, Religion, and the Scope of Rationality.* Cambridge: Cambridge University Press.

Tanavoli, Parviz. 2006. *Telesm: Gerafik-e Sonnati-ye Iran.* Tehran: Nashr-e Bongah.

Taneja, Anand Vivek. 2013. "Jinnealogy: Everyday Life and Islamic Theology in Post-Partition Delhi." *Hau: Journal of Ethnographic Theory* 3 (3): 139–65.

Taussig, Michael. 1980. *The Devil and Commodity Fetishism in South America.* Chapel Hill: University of North Carolina Press.

———. 1987. *Shamanism, Colonialism, and the Wild Man: A Study in Terror and Healing.* Chicago: University of Chicago Press.

———. 1992. "Maleficium: State Fetishism." In *The Nervous System,* 111–40. New York: Routledge.

———. 2006. "Viscerality, Faith, and Skepticism: Another Theory of Magic." In *Walter Benjamin's Grave,* 121–55. Chicago: University of Chicago Press.

Tavakoli-Targhi, Mohamad. 2001. *Refashioning Iran: Orientalism, Occidentalism, and Historiography.* New York: Palgrave.

———. 2008. "Tajaddod-e Ruzmarreh va ʿAmpul-e Tadayyon.'" *Iran Nameh* 24 (4): 421–58.

———. 2012. "Mohandesaneh-andishi va Velayat-madari-ye Mojtahendesaneh." *Iran Nameh* 27 (2–3): 4–37.

Taves, Ann. 1999. *Fits, Trances, and Visions: Experiencing Religion and Explaining Experience from Wesley to James.* Princeton: Princeton University Press.

Taylor, Charles. 2002. "Modern Social Imaginaries." *Public Culture* 14 (1): 91–124.

Telliel, Yunus Dogan. 2015. "Miraculous Evidence: Scientific Wonders and Religious Reasons." Unpublished manuscript.

Todorov, Tzvetan. 1975. *The Fantastic: A Structural Approach to a Literary Genre.* Translated by Richard Howard. Ithaca: Cornell University Press.

Tusi, Muhammad ibn Mahmud. 1966. *ʿAjayeb al-Makhluqat.* Edited by Manuchehr Sotudeh. Tehran: Nashr-e Ketab.

Tylor, Edward B. 1874. *Primitive Culture.* Vol. 1. New York: Henry Hold.

Vahdat, Farzin. 2002. *God and Juggernaut: Iran's Intellectual Encounter with Modernity.* Syracuse: Syracuse University Press.

Vahid Saʿd, Mahmud. 1929. "Tasfiyeh-ye Akhlaq beh Vasileh-ye Tahammol-e Masaʾeb va Anjam-e Vazaʾef." In *Haftad va Yek Maqaleh-ye Maʿrefat al-Ruh,* by Khalil Saqafi, 248–78. Tehran: Jameʿeh-ye Maʿaref-e Iran.

Van Bladel, Kevin T. 2009. *The Arabic Hermes: From Pagan Sage to Prophet of Science.* Oxford: Oxford University Press.

Van den Bos, Matthijs. 2002. *Mystic Regimes: Sufism and the State in Iran, from the Late Qajar Era to the Islamic Republic.* Leiden: Brill.

Van der Veer, Peter. 2001. *Imperial Encounters: Religion and Modernity in India and Britain.* Princeton: Princeton University Press.

Varzi, Roxanne. 2006. *Warring Souls: Youth, Media, and Martyrdom in Post-Revolution Iran.* Durham, NC: Duke University Press.

Velminski, Wladimir. 2017. *Homo Sovieticus: Brain Waves, Mind Control, and Telepathic Destiny.* Translated by Erik Butler. Cambridge, MA: MIT Press.

Vinea, Ana Maria. 2015. "'May God Cure You': Contemporary Egyptian Therapeutic Landscapes Between Qurʾanic Healing and Psychiatry." PhD diss., Graduate Center, City University of New York.

Viveiros de Castro, Eduardo. 2015. "Who Is Afraid of the Ontological Wolf? Some Comments on an Ongoing Anthropological Debate." *Cambridge Anthropology* 33 (1): 2–17.

Von Hees, Syrinx. 2005. "The Astonishing: A Critique and Re-Reading of ʿAǧāʾib Literature." *Middle Eastern Literatures* 8 (2): 101–20.

Wajdi, Muhammad Farid. 1913. *Daʾira maʿarif al-Qarn al-Rabiʿ ʿAshar, al-ʿIshrin.* Vol. 4. Cairo: Matbaʿa al-Qaʿiz.

Walbridge, John. 2000. *The Leaven of the Ancients: Suhrawardi and the Heritage of the Greeks.* Albany: State University of New York Press.

———. 2011. *God and Logic in Islam: The Caliphate of Reason.* New York: Cambridge University Press.

Warburg, Margit, Annika Hvithamar, and Morten Warmind, eds. 2005. *Bahaʾi and Globalization.* Aarhus: Aarhus University Press.

Weber, Max. 1946a. "Religious Rejections of the World and Their Directions." In *From Max Weber: Essays in Sociology,* edited and translated by Hans Heinrich Gerth and Charles Wright Mills, 323–59. New York: Oxford University Press.

———. 1946b. "Science as a Vocation." In *From Max Weber: Essays in Sociology,* edited and translated by Hans Heinrich Gerth and Charles Wright Mills, 129–56. New York: Oxford University Press.

———. 1992. *The Protestant Ethic and the Spirit of Capitalism.* London: Routledge.

Weiss, Bernard. 1985. "Knowledge of the Past: The Theory of 'Tawatur' according to Ghazali." *Studia Islamica* 61:81–105.

West, Harry G. 2005. *Kupilikula: Governance and the Invisible Realm in Mozambique.* Chicago: University of Chicago Press.

———. 2007. *Ethnographic Sorcery*. Chicago: University of Chicago Press.

West, Harry G., and Todd Sanders, eds. 2003. *Transparency and Conspiracy: Ethnographies of Suspicion in the New World Order*. Durham, NC: Duke University Press.

Wild, Stefan. 1972. "Jugglers and Fraudulent Sufis." *Proceedings of the Sixth Congress of Arabic and Islamic Studies*, Visby-Stockholm, 58–63.

———. 1978. "A Juggler's Programme in Mediaeval Islam." *La signification du bas moyen âge dans l'histoire et la culture du monde musulman: Actes du 8me congrès de l'union européenne des arabisants et islamisants* (Aix-en-Provence, du 9 au 14 septembre 1976): 353–60.

Withy, Katherine. 2015. *Heidegger on Being Uncanny*. Cambridge: Harvard University Press.

Zadeh, Travis. 2009. " 'Fire Cannot Harm It': Mediation, Temptation and the Charismatic Power of the Qur'an." *Journal of Qur'anic Studies* 10 (2): 50–72.

———. 2010. "The Wiles of Creation: Philosophy, Fiction, and the ʿAjāʾib Tradition." *Middle Eastern Literatures: Incorporating Edebiyat* 13 (1): 21–48.

———. 2014. "Commanding Demons and Jinn: The Sorcerer in Early Islamic Thought." In *No Tapping around Philology: A Festschrift in Honor of Wheeler McIntosh Thackston Jr.'s 70th Birthday*, edited by Alireza Korangy and Daniel J. Sheffield, 131–60. Wiesbaden: Harrassowitz Verlag.

Zarcone, Thierry. 1991. "Une récupération d'Einstein chez quelques auteurs mystiques du monde Turco-Iranien." *Turcica* 21–23 (Mélanges offerts à Irène Mélikoff par ses collègues, disciples et amis): 131–54.

———. 2013. "Occultism in an Islamic Context: the Case of Modern Turkey from the Nineteenth Century to the Present Time." In *Occultism in a Global Perspective*, edited by Henrik Bogdan and Gordan Djurdjevic, 151–76. Durham, UK: Acumen.

INDEX